Learning Informatica PowerCenter 9.x

Learn the art of extracting data from disparate systems, integrating it using the leading data integration platform, and creating intelligent data centers for your business

Rahul Malewar

PUBLISHING

professional expertise distilled

BIRMINGHAM - MUMBAI

Learning Informatica PowerCenter 9.x

First published: December 2014

Production reference: 1231214

Published by Packt Publishing Ltd.
Livery Place
35 Livery Street
Birmingham B3 2PB, UK.

ISBN 978-1-78217-648-0

www.packtpub.com

Credits

Author
Rahul Malewar

Reviewers
Vikas Agrawal
Ralf Becher
Umamaheswaran T.G

Commissioning Editor
Vinay Argekar

Acquisition Editor
Vinay Argekar

Content Development Editor
Rohit Kumar Singh

Technical Editors
Shiny Poojary
Sebastian Rodrigues

Copy Editors
Neha Karnani
Stuti Srivastava

Project Coordinator
Mary Alex

Proofreaders
Simran Bhogal
Maria Gould
Ameesha Green
Paul Hindle

Indexers
Priya Sane
Tejal Soni

Production Coordinator
Aparna Bhagat

Cover Work
Aparna Bhagat

About the Author

Rahul Malewar has been working with various data warehousing tools for the past 8 years, mainly with Informatica PowerCenter. He has worked on various versions of Informatica PowerCenter, starting from Version 8.1 to the latest 9.x. He has worked for various MNCs in India, such as UST Global, Cognizant Technology Solutions, and Principal Financial Group in Pune. He has worked on the implementation of a data warehouse involving Informatica for Fortune 500 MNCs, such as Wellpoint and Principal. He has experience of working on multiple real-time projects in a couple of MNCs and utilized these skills to write this book. He has been running his own training center named Learnwell Technocraft (www.dw-learnwell.com) since 2010, where they provide training on more than 25 data warehousing technologies over classroom, corporate, and online sessions. He has also written a blog on data warehousing concepts. At the time of writing, he has provided training to more than 1,200 candidates, ranging from freshers to professionals with 20 years of experience.

He is also the director of a software firm named Gut Lernen Technocraft Pvt. Ltd.; the company works on data warehousing and mobile-related projects. He provides free assistance on Informatica installation-related issues and other technical issues for which he can be contacted at info@dw-learnwell.com.

Acknowledgments

Without a second thought, I would like to dedicate this book to my mother for taking all the pain of my childhood and making me capable enough to write a book, which is something wonderful to happen in anybody's life. I would also like to thank my wife, Swati, for providing suggestions while writing the book. A large share of this book goes out to all my students who took Informatica training from me, which gave me the ability and motivation to write a book to help all those who I cannot reach out to personally. This also calls for a thank you note to all the reviewers of the book for pointing out the mistakes that I made while writing and providing valuable suggestions—as we say, no one is perfect.

Also, a special thanks to Packt Publishing for giving me the opportunity to write this book and for showing confidence in my writing. A big thanks to the readers of the book. I hope you will like it and make a bright career in Informatica.

I wish you all the luck for future. Keep smiling, make others smile, and make our mother earth a better place to live.

About the Reviewers

Vikas Agrawal is a business intelligence evangelist with over 15 years of experience working in multiple industries with clients that include Fortune 500 companies. He has deep expertise and knowledge in the areas of Enterprise and Cloud BI, Big Data and Hadoop architecture and technology, OBIEE, Informatica, Oracle Data Integrator, Enterprise Data Warehousing, and master data management.

He currently manages the BI practice for a prime Oracle partner and has led implementations that have won the industry award for deployment of BI applications. He is also responsible for the development of product offerings and for building BI and Big Data applications.

In his spare time, he enjoys learning about new technologies and the ever-changing social media and marketing use cases, writing new software that helps customers leverage the most out of their investments, and traveling and spending time with his family.

> I would like to thank Packt Publishing and the author for giving me the opportunity to review their fantastic book.

Ralf Becher has worked as an IT system architect and data management consultant for more than 15 years in the areas of banking, insurance, logistics, automotive, and retail. He founded TIQ Solutions in 2004 with partners.

The Leipzig company specializes in modern, quality-assured data management. Since 2004, it has been helping its customers process, evaluate, and maintain the quality of company data, helping them introduce, implement, and improve complex solutions in the fields of data architecture, data integration, data migration, master data management, metadata management, data warehousing, and business intelligence.

Ralf started working with PowerCenter in 2002 and has realized many projects with it in the data warehouse realm. He runs his data integration blog at http://tiqview.tumblr.com/.

Umamaheswaran T.G has more than 15 years of experience in information technology, working as a development lead at C1X, which is a fast growing start-up in the Bay area. Before joining C1X, he worked as a senior Java consultant with Yahoo, Wells Fargo USA, Citibank Japan, Bank of America, Fidelity Information Systems, and Kaiser Permanente. He has also reviewed *Drools Developer's Cookbook, Packt Publishing*.

I want to thank my wife, Chitra, and my two kids, Sivasweatha and Sivayogeith, for their cooperation and support.

www.PacktPub.com

Support files, eBooks, discount offers, and more

For support files and downloads related to your book, please visit www.PacktPub.com.

Did you know that Packt offers eBook versions of every book published, with PDF and ePub files available? You can upgrade to the eBook version at www.PacktPub.com and as a print book customer, you are entitled to a discount on the eBook copy. Get in touch with us at service@packtpub.com for more details.

At www.PacktPub.com, you can also read a collection of free technical articles, sign up for a range of free newsletters and receive exclusive discounts and offers on Packt books and eBooks.

https://www2.packtpub.com/books/subscription/packtlib

Do you need instant solutions to your IT questions? PacktLib is Packt's online digital book library. Here, you can search, access, and read Packt's entire library of books.

Why subscribe?

- Fully searchable across every book published by Packt
- Copy and paste, print, and bookmark content
- On demand and accessible via a web browser

Free access for Packt account holders

If you have an account with Packt at www.PacktPub.com, you can use this to access PacktLib today and view 9 entirely free books. Simply use your login credentials for immediate access.

Instant updates on new Packt books

Get notified! Find out when new books are published by following @PacktEnterprise on Twitter or the *Packt Enterprise* Facebook page.

Table of Contents

Preface

There has to be a motive behind everything, and there is one behind this book too: to present a technology to the readers in its simplest form. The simple thought behind writing this book is to put all the essential ingredients of Informatica, starting from basic things such as downloading, extraction, and installation to working on client tools and high-level aspects, such as scheduling, migration, and so on, in simple words. There are multiple blogs available across the Internet that talk about the Informatica tool but none present end-to-end answers. We have tried to put up all the steps and processes in a systematic manner to help you start learning easily. In this book, you will get a step-by-step procedure for every aspect of the Informatica PowerCenter tool.

Informatica Corporation (Informatica), which is a multi-million dollar company incorporated in February, 1993, is an independent provider of enterprise data integration and data quality software and services. The company enables a variety of complex enterprise data integration products, which include PowerCenter, PowerExchange, enterprise data integration, data quality, master data management, business-to-business (B2B) data exchange, application information life cycle management, complex event processing, ultra messaging, and cloud data integration.

In this book, we are going to learn about the PowerCenter tool from Informatica. PowerCenter is Informatica's most widely-used tool across the globe for various data integration processes. The Informatica PowerCenter tool helps with the integration of data from almost any business system in almost any format. This flexibility of PowerCenter to handle almost any data makes it the most widely used tool in the data integration world.

While writing this book, we have kept in mind the importance of live, practical exposure of the graphical interface of the tool to the audience and so you will notice a lot of screenshots illustrating the steps to help you understand and follow the process. We have arranged the chapters in such a way that we cover all the aspects of the Informatica PowerCenter tool, and we have also made sure they flow properly in order to achieve functionality.

What this book covers

Chapter 1, Starting the Development Phase – Using the Designer Screen Basics, talks about the basics of the Informatica PowerCenter Designer client tool. You will learn how to create/import files and tables as the source and target. You will also learn about the basic components of the client screen, such as the toolbar, navigator, workspace, output panel, and status bar. By the end of this chapter, you will have a clear idea of the look and feel of the PowerCenter tool.

Chapter 2, Using the Designer Screen – Advanced, talks about the advanced topics of the Designer screen. It is an extension of *Chapter 1, Starting the Development Phase – Using the Designer Screen Basics*. In this chapter, we will discuss debuggers, parameters and variables, target loan plan, reusable transformations, and mapplets.

Chapter 3, Implementing SCD – Using Designer Screen Wizards, covers a single but very important aspect of data warehousing, SCD. We will see the implementation of SCD1, SCD2, and SCD3 using wizards. You should be clear with data warehousing concepts to understand this implementation.

Chapter 4, Finishing the Development – Using the Workflow Manager Screen Basics, describes the basics of the Workflow Manager screen. We will get to learn the different options present on the Workflow Manager screen. We will learn how to create session tasks and workflows. We will also see various connections, such as relations, FTP, and so on, that can be created on the Workflow Manager screen.

Chapter 5, Using the Workflow Manager Screen – Advanced, teaches you the advanced concepts of the Workflow Manager screen. This chapter describes the various tasks present on the Workflow Manager screen. We will also see how to create reusable tasks and mapplets. We will learn some very important concepts, such as scheduling, partitioning and parameter files, file list, and incremental aggregation and workflow recovery options.

Chapter 6, Monitoring Your Code – Using the Workflow Monitor Screen, describes the Workflow Manager screen of PowerCenter. This screen allows you to monitor the process we execute in Workflow Manager. We will see different logfiles, statuses, and statistics on the Monitor screen.

Chapter 7, The Lifeline of Informatica – Transformations, is meant for the most important aspect of the Informatica PowerCenter tool, transformations. We will talk about the various types of transformations in this chapter. We will implement mapping using each transformation so that you get to understand each and every transformation in detail. We will end this chapter with the classifications of transformations.

Chapter 8, The Deployment Phase – Using Repository Manager, teaches you about the fourth client screen, Repository Manager. Repository Manager is basically used for migration (deployment) purposes. We will see the various options to migrate the code from one environment to other. We will also see how to create folders on the client screen.

Chapter 9, Optimization – Performance Tuning, has the contents for the optimization of the various components of the Informatica PowerCenter tool, such as sources, targets, mappings, sessions, and systems. Performance tuning at a high level involves two stages: finding issues called bottlenecks and resolving them.

Appendix, Installing Informatica and Using Informatica Administration Console, describes the detailed steps for the process of installation, starting from downloading the software, extracting the software, and installing the software, to configuring the software. We will also look at the administrator console of the PowerCenter tool and learn about the different services.

What you need for this book

Before you make your mind up about learning Informatica, it is always recommended that you have a basic understanding of SQL and Unix. Though these are not mandatory and you can easily use 90 percent of the Informatica PowerCenter tool without knowledge of these, the confidence to work in real-time SQL and Unix projects is a must-have in your kitty. People who know SQL will easily understand that ETL tools are nothing but a graphical representation of SQL. Unix is utilized in Informatica PowerCenter with the scripting aspect, which makes your life easy in some scenarios.

Who this book is for

Anybody who wishes to make a career in data warehousing or Informatica must go for this book. If you are a college graduate, an IT professional working in other technologies, or a university professor, this book is for you.

Conventions

In this book, you will find a number of styles of text that distinguish between different kinds of information. Here are some examples of these styles, and an explanation of their meaning.

Code words in text, database table names, folder names, filenames, file extensions, pathnames, dummy URLs, user input, and Twitter handles are shown as follows: "We are using HR as our user for making the connection."

A block of code is set as follows:

```
STEVE 1000 2000 3000 4000
JAMES 2000 2500 3000 3500
ANDY 4000 4000 4000 4000
```

Any command-line input or output is written as follows:

```
IIF( ISNULL (JOB_ID), NEXTVAL, JOB_ID)
```

New terms and **important words** are shown in bold. Words that you see on the screen, in menus or dialog boxes for example, appear in the text like this: "To open the PowerCenter Designer screen, navigate to **Start | All Programs | Informatica 9.5.1 | Client | Power Center Client | Designer**."

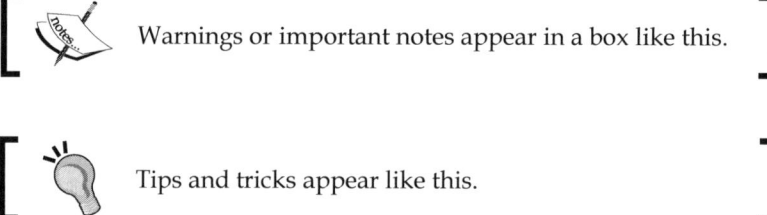

Warnings or important notes appear in a box like this.

Tips and tricks appear like this.

Reader feedback

Feedback from our readers is always welcome. Let us know what you think about this book—what you liked or may have disliked. Reader feedback is important for us to develop titles that you really get the most out of.

To send us general feedback, simply send an e-mail to feedback@packtpub.com, and mention the book title via the subject of your message.

If there is a topic that you have expertise in and you are interested in either writing or contributing to a book, see our author guide on www.packtpub.com/authors.

Customer support

Now that you are the proud owner of a Packt book, we have a number of things to help you to get the most from your purchase.

If the readers face any issues, they can contact the author at info@dw-learnwell.com.

Errata

Although we have taken every care to ensure the accuracy of our content, mistakes do happen. If you find a mistake in one of our books—maybe a mistake in the text or the code—we would be grateful if you would report this to us. By doing so, you can save other readers from frustration and help us improve subsequent versions of this book. If you find any errata, please report them by visiting http://www.packtpub.com/submit-errata, selecting your book, clicking on the **errata submission form** link, and entering the details of your errata. Once your errata are verified, your submission will be accepted and the errata will be uploaded on our website, or added to any list of existing errata, under the Errata section of that title. Any existing errata can be viewed by selecting your title from http://www.packtpub.com/support.

Piracy

Piracy of copyright material on the Internet is an ongoing problem across all media. At Packt, we take the protection of our copyright and licenses very seriously. If you come across any illegal copies of our works, in any form, on the Internet, please provide us with the location address or website name immediately so that we can pursue a remedy.

Please contact us at copyright@packtpub.com with a link to the suspected pirated material.

We appreciate your help in protecting our authors, and our ability to bring you valuable content.

Questions

You can contact us at questions@packtpub.com if you are having a problem with any aspect of the book, and we will do our best to address it.

1
Starting the Development Phase – Using the Designer Screen Basics

With the installation phase over, we are all set to have our first try on the PowerCenter Client tools. We have the following four client tools available in Informatica PowerCenter:

- PowerCenter Designer
- PowerCenter Workflow Manager
- PowerCenter Workflow Monitor
- PowerCenter Repository Manager

Informatica PowerCenter Designer

In this chapter, we are going to discuss the basics of the Informatica PowerCenter Designer screen. The designer screen lets you build and manage PowerCenter objects, such as sources, targets, transformations, and mappings.

To open the PowerCenter Designer screen, navigate to **Start** | **All Programs** | **Informatica 9.5.1** | **Client** | **Power Center Client** | **Designer**.

This will open the designer screen.

The Designer screen's components

The **designer** screen, as can be seen in the following screenshot, is divided into five sections. Each section has its own purpose. You need to understand each component properly as we will be referring to these components regularly in the next chapters. They are as follows:

- **Navigator**: This is used to connect to repositories and open folders. You can copy objects and create shortcuts within the navigator. Navigator allows you to reuse the existing components.

- **Workspace**: This is the space where you actually do the coding. Open different tools in this window to create and edit the repository objects, such as sources, targets, mapplets, transformations, and mappings. In the designer workspace, you can see different tabs, such as **Source Analyzer**, **Target Designer**, **Transformation Developer**, **Mapplet Designer**, and **Mapping Designer**.

- **Toolbar**: This shows the various components to be used in the designer screen and other shortcuts.

- **Output/control panel**: This lets you view details about tasks you perform, such as saving your work or validating a mapping. You can view whether your code is valid or invalid. If invalid, the output panel shows you the reason for the error.

- **Status bar**: This displays the status of the current operation. The status bar shows you the status of the operation that you are trying to perform.

The preceding screen components are shown in the following screenshot:

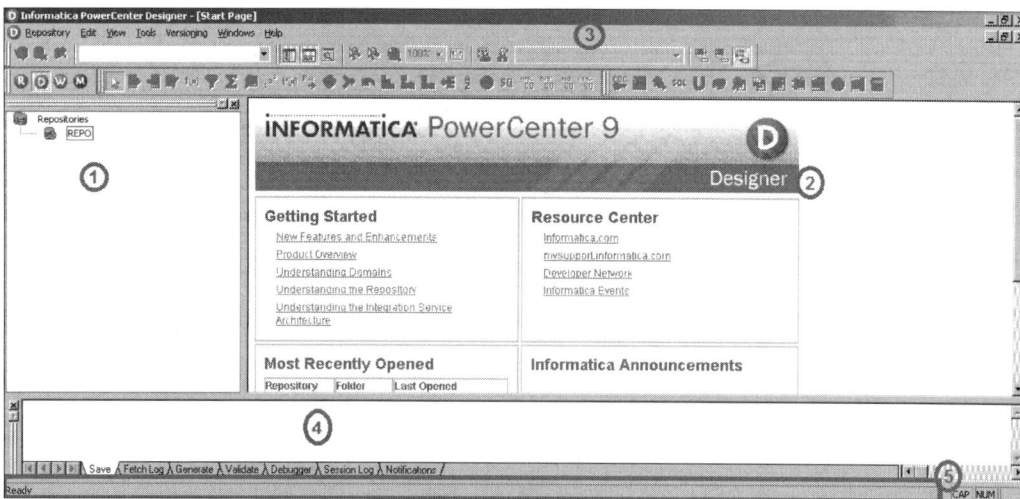

The components shown are as follows:

- Navigator (**1**)
- Workspace (**2**)
- Toolbar (**3**)
- Control panel (**4**)
- Status bar (**5**)

PowerCenter Designer has the following tools that allow us to work on different types of sources, different types of targets, and build mappings using different types of transformations:

- **Source Analyzer**: This allows you to import or create source definitions. You can work on various types of files (flat files, XML, .xls, and so on) and database tables. Source Analyzer lets you modify the existing source definitions.

- **Target Designer**: This allows you to import or create target definitions. You can work on various types of files (flat files, XML, .xls, and so on) and database tables. Target Designer lets you modify the existing target definitions.

- **Transformation Developer**: This allows you to create reusable transformations to use in mappings. Reusable components are important because they allow you to use the existing transformations.

- **Mapplet Designer**: This allows you to create a group of transformations to use in mappings. Mapplets are groups of reusable transformations that can be used in multiple mappings as reusable components.

- **Mapping Designer**: This allows you to create mappings that the Integration Service uses to extract, transform, and load data. Mappings contain sources, targets, and transformations linked to each other through links. You can add multiple sources, multiple targets, and multiple transformations in a mapping.

The following screenshot shows the **Source Analyzer** screen components:

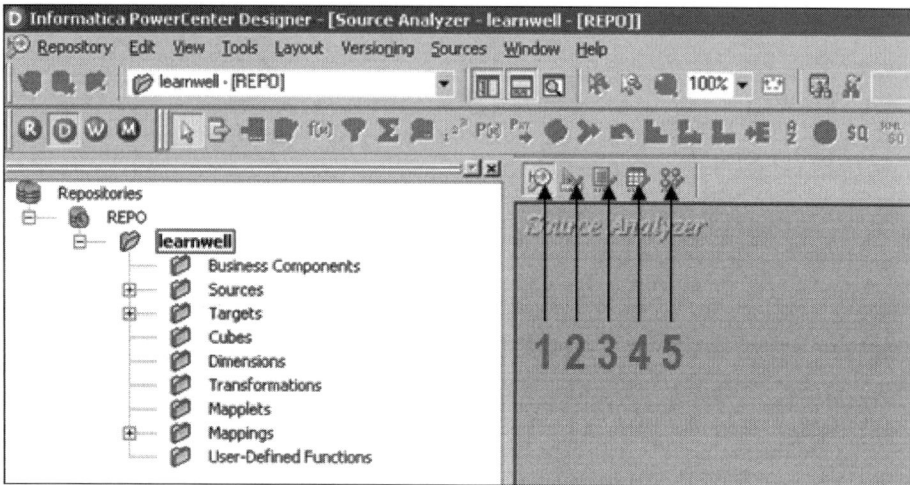

The components shown are as follows:

- Source Analyzer
- Target Designer
- Transformation Developer
- Mapplet Designer
- Mapping Designer

As a general rule, we should work first on the sources, then the targets, and at last the transformations, which completes the mappings.

Working with sources

Any file or table from where we can extract the data in PowerCenter is referred to as a source. You can import or create the source definition.

When you import the source definition in designer, we import only the metadata, that is, column names, data type, size, indexes, constraints, dependencies, and so on. Actual data never comes with the source structure in designer. The data flows through the mapping in a row-wise manner when we execute the workflow in Workflow Manager.

PowerCenter allows you to work on various types of sources, as listed below:

- **Relational database**: PowerCenter supports relational databases such as Oracle, Sybase, DB2, Microsoft SQL Server, SAP HANA, and Teradata

- **File**: Flat files (fixed width and delimited files), COBOL files, XML files, and Excel files

- **High-end applications**: PowerCenter also supports applications such as Hyperion, PeopleSoft, TIBCO, WebSphere MQ, and so on

- **Mainframe**: Additional features of Mainframe such as IBM DB2 OS/390, IBM DB2 OS/400, IDMS, IDMS-X, IMS, and VSAM can be purchased

- **Other**: PowerCenter also supports Microsoft Access and external web services

We have seen the components that PowerCenter supports. In the next section, we will learn to import the relational database tables. Before that, a database connection needs to be added to the designer screen as mentioned in the next section.

Adding a new ODBC data source

To add a new database data source connection to import tables, follow this procedure:

1. In the designer screen, navigate to **Tools | Source Analyzer** to open the Source Analyzer tool, as indicated earlier.

2. Navigate to **Sources | Import from Database**.

3. To add a new database connection, click on the tab shown in the following screenshot:

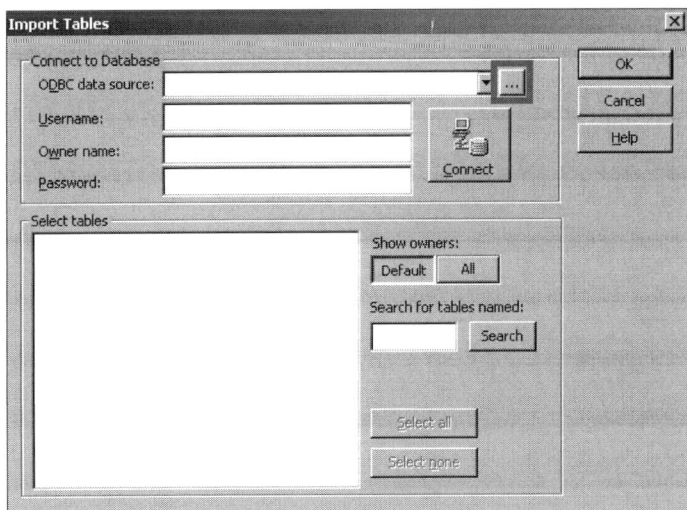

4. A pop up window to add a new connection will appear on the screen, as shown in the following screenshot:

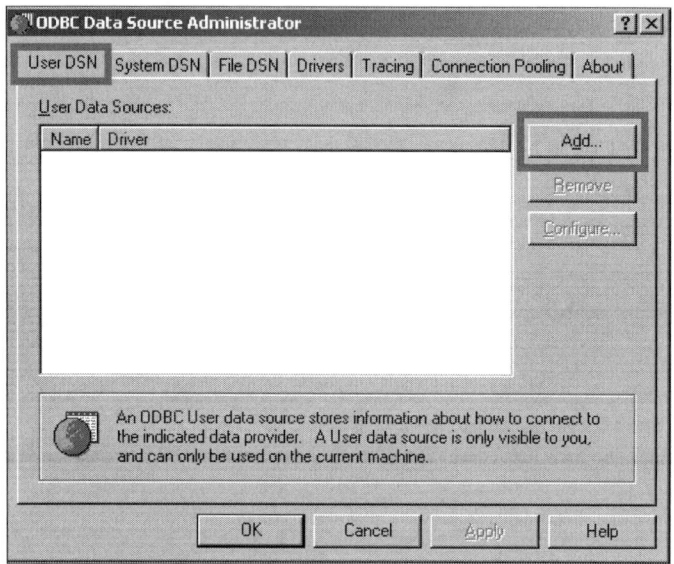

We need to add a new User DSN.

5. The next screen will allow you to select the desired database from the list of databases. For our reference, we are using Oracle Database in this book. If you are using another database, select the appropriate option from the list.

    Select the type of database driver you wish to add and click on **Finish**.

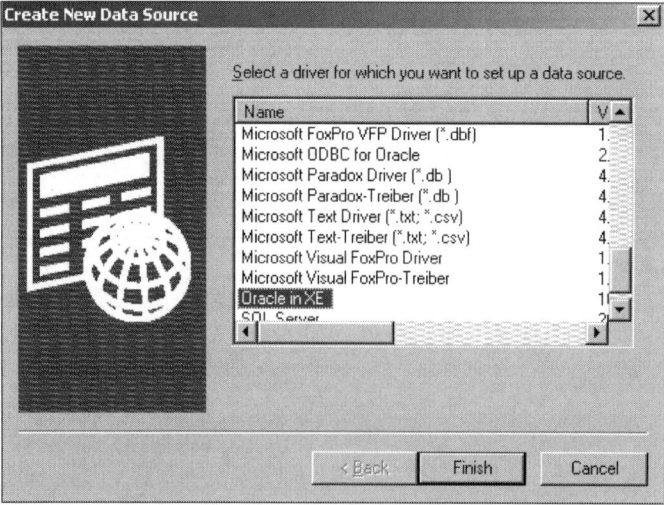

6. A new window will pop up on your screen. Mention the following details to add a new connection, as shown in the following screenshot.

    ◦ **Data Source Name**: Enter the name of the data source. This can be any name for your reference.

    ◦ **Description**: Please specify some description for the connection.

    ◦ **TNS Service Name**: Mention the service name for your connection. We are taking service name as XE; this is the default service name for Oracle 10g Database.

    ◦ **User ID**: Mention the user ID. We are using HR as our user to make the connection.

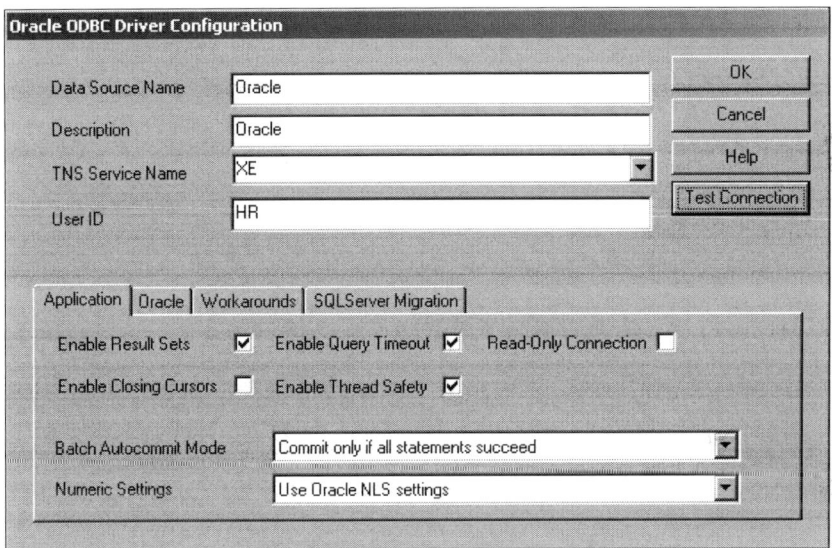

7. After providing all the details, click on **Test Connection**.

8. A new window will pop up as shown in the following screenshot:

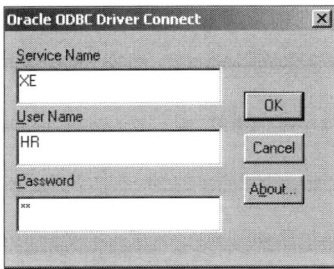

Specify the password for Oracle Database and click on **OK**.

9. If all the values mentioned by you are correct, the test connection will be successful.

With this, we have added a new database connection to our repository, and we can import the tables using the new connection.

You can add different type of databases to your repository. This is just a one-time process that you need to perform before you can start using the tables.

Working with relational database tables – the Import option

We will first start working on the relational tables. You can import or create the table structure in Source Analyzer. After you add these source definitions to the repository, you use them in a mapping.

Perform the following steps to import the table source definition:

1. In the **Designer** screen, navigate to **Tools | Source Analyzer** to open the Source Analyzer tool.

2. Navigate to **Sources | Import from Database**:

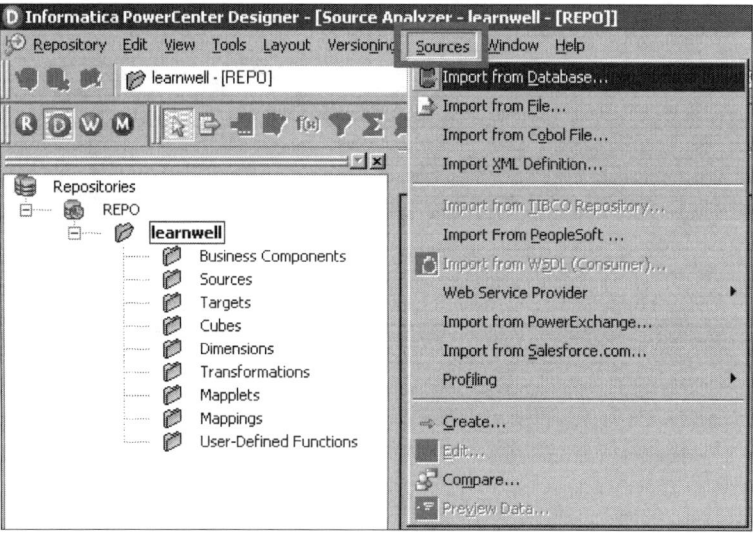

3. From the **ODBC data source** field, select the ODBC data source that you created to access source tables in the previous section.

4. Enter the username and password to connect to the database. Also, enter the name of the source table owner if necessary.

5. Click on **Connect**.

6. In the **Select tables** list, expand the database owner and the **TABLES** heading.

7. Select the tables you wish to import and click on **OK**.

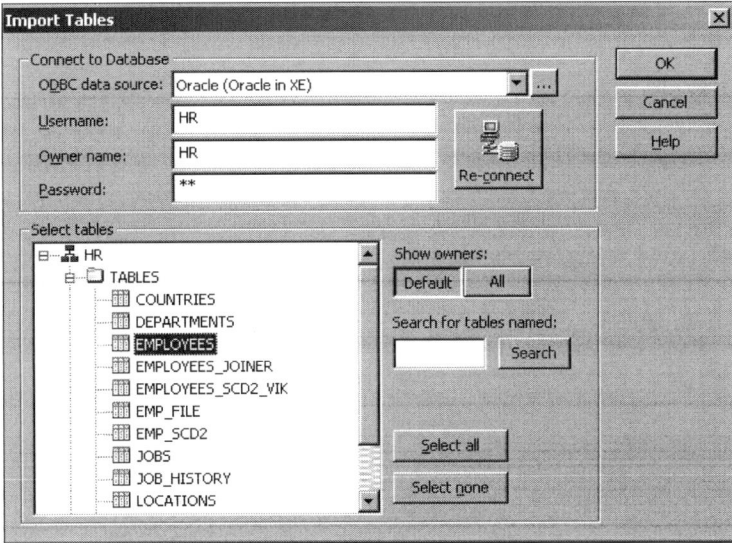

The structure of the selected tables will appear in the workspace as shown in the following screenshot:

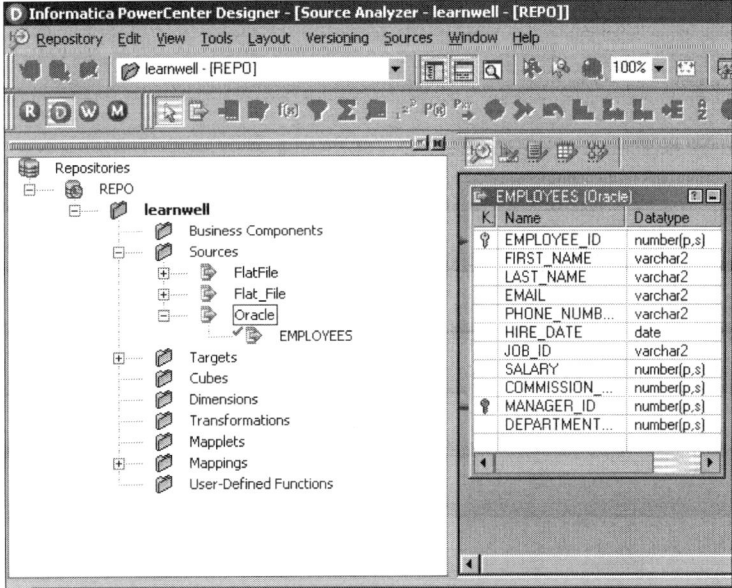

Working with flat files – the Import option

In the previous section, we discussed about importing the relational tables. Before we start working on importing the flat files, we will discuss some important aspects about flat files.

Flat files are of two types: delimited and fixed width. They are explained as follows:

- In delimited files, the values are separated from each other by a delimiter. Any character or number can be used as delimiter, but usually for better interpretation we use special characters as delimiters. In delimited files, the width of each field is not a mandatory option as each value gets separated from the other using a delimiter. Please see the following screenshot to understand a delimited file. The delimiter used in the file is a comma (,).

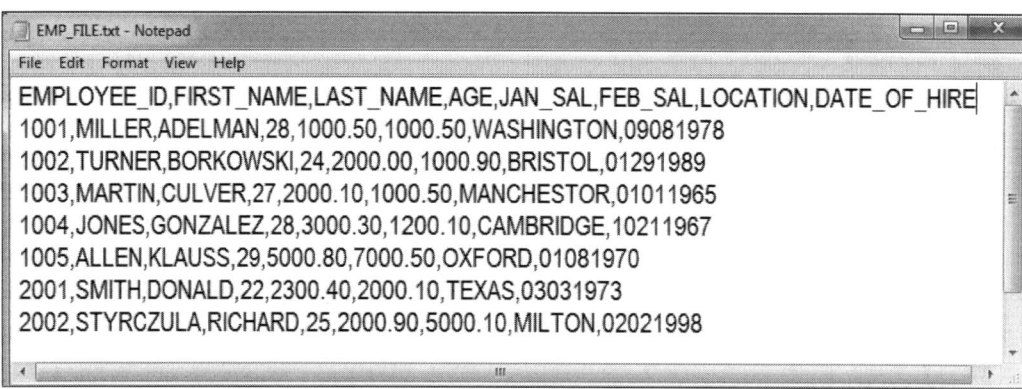

- In fixed-width files, the width of each field is fixed. The values are separated from each other by the fixed size of the column defined. There can be issues in reading the data if the size of each column is not maintained properly. Please see the following screenshot to understand a fixed-width file.

  The width of each field in the file is fixed. See the description of each field:

  - ○ EMPLOYEE_ID: 4 bytes
  - ○ FIRST_NAME: 10 bytes
  - ○ LAST_NAME: 10 bytes
  - ○ AGE: 2 bytes
  - ○ JAN_SAL: 10 bytes
  - ○ FEB_SAL: 10 bytes
  - ○ LOCATION: 10 bytes
  - ○ DATE_OF_HIRE: 8 bytes

If the size of a particular value is not equal to the size mentioned, we need to pad the value with spaces:

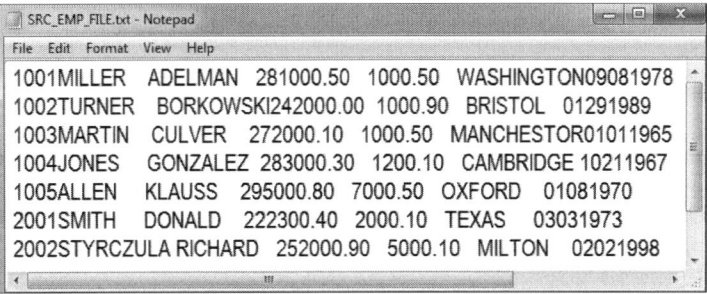

Working with delimited files

Perform the following steps to import the delimited files:

1. In the designer screen, navigate to **Tools | Source Analyzer** to open the Source Analyzer.

2. Navigate to **Sources | Import from File**.

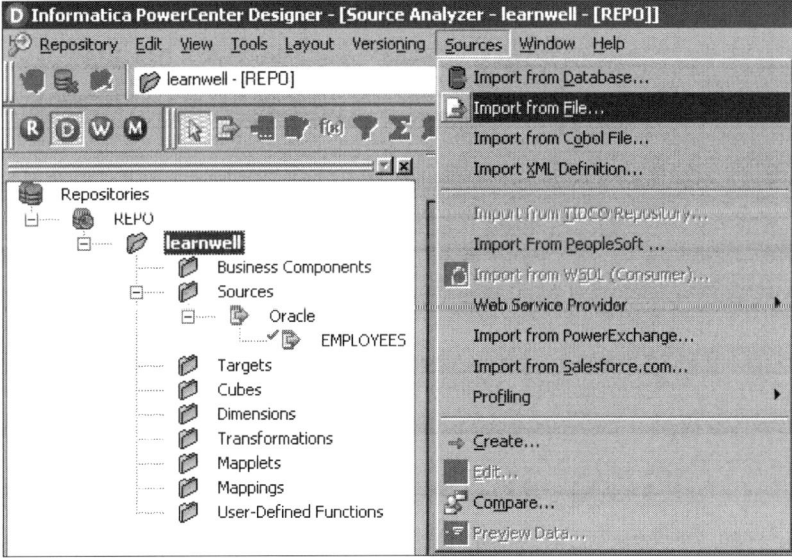

3. Browse the files you wish to import as source files.

4. The **Flat File Import Wizard** screen will pop up. The **Flat File Import Wizard** screen will help you specify the properties for importing the file in a proper format. Please complete the following steps in the wizard.

5. Select the file type as **Delimited** as shown in the following screenshot:

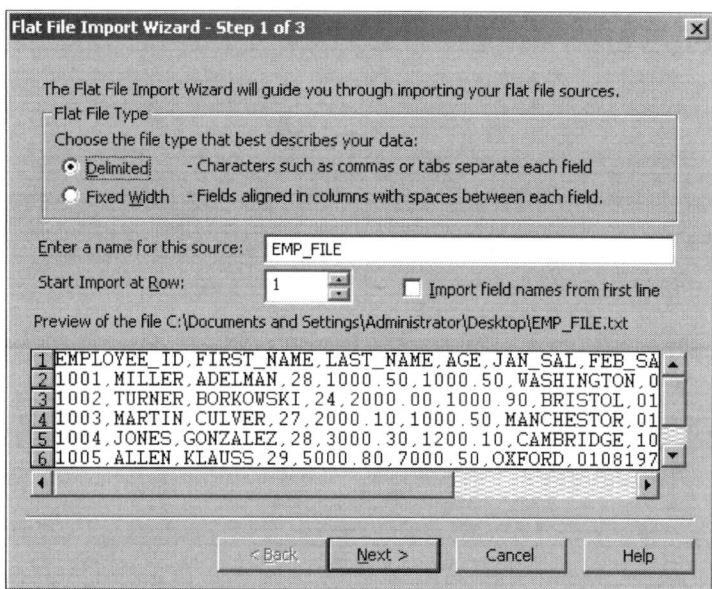

If the file contains headers as column names in the first line, then we will need to start the import at row **2**, as this option indicates from which row the actual data has to be imported. If the file doesn't contain the headers in first line, we will import the data from the first line only.

Files may contain the column names in the first line as headers. You need to verify the file properly before you start working on the file. The **Import field names from first line** option enables us to import the header names into the source definition. If you do not select this option, the header names will not be imported.

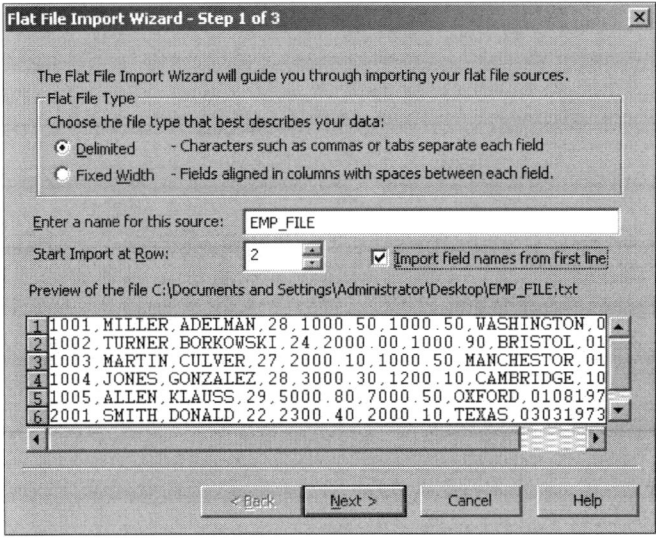

Click on **Next**.

6. Select the type **Delimiter** to be used in the file. In our case, we are using comma as a delimiter. You can select the delimiter as per the file you are using.

7. Also, check the quotes option: **No quotes, Single quotes**, and **Double quotes** — to work with the quotes in the text values. This option enables us to import the data with single or double quotes in text values. We are using **No quotes** as our option since the sample file we are using does not have any data with quotes.

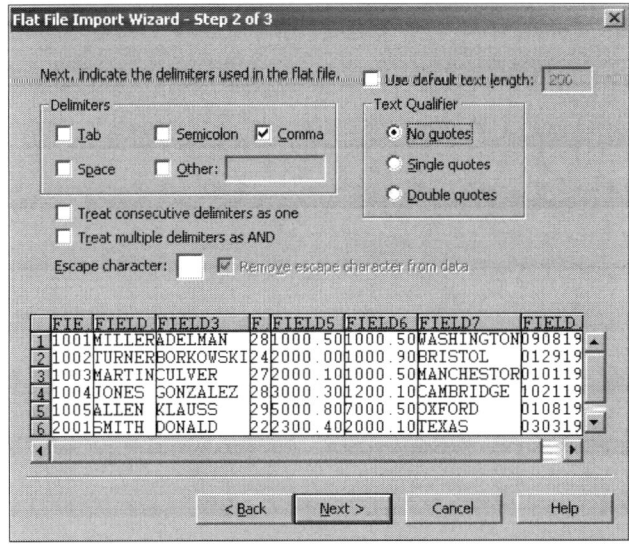

8. Click on **Next**.

9. Verify the column name, data type, and precision in the data view option. You can edit the column names and other details in this view. Generally, you do not need to do so. This is shown in the following screenshot:

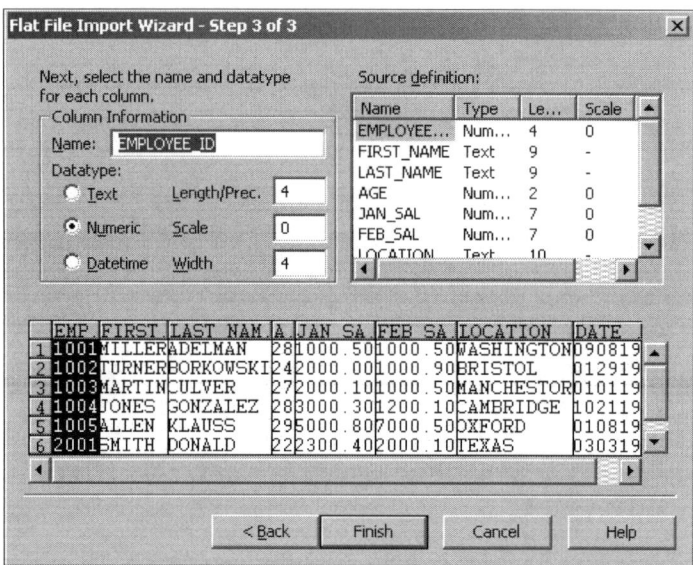

10. Click on **Finish** to get the source imported in the Source Analyzer, as shown in the following screenshot:

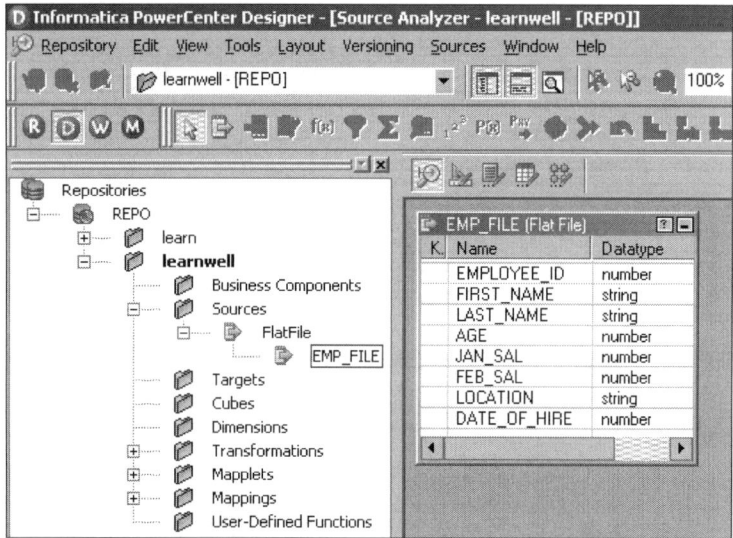

Working with fixed-width files

Perform the following steps to import the fixed-width files:

1. In the designer screen, navigate to **Tools** | **Source Analyzer** to open the Source Analyzer.

2. Navigate to **Sources** | **Import from File**.

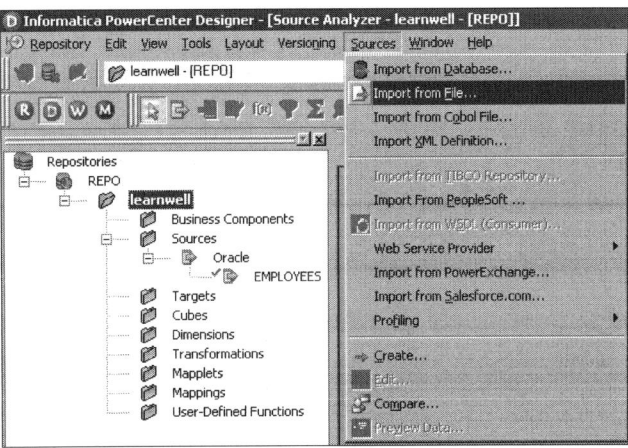

3. Browse the files you wish to use as source files. We are using `EMP_SRC_FILE` as a reference to import the fixed-width file.

4. The **Flat File Import Wizard** screen will pop up.

5. Select the file type **Fixed Width**.

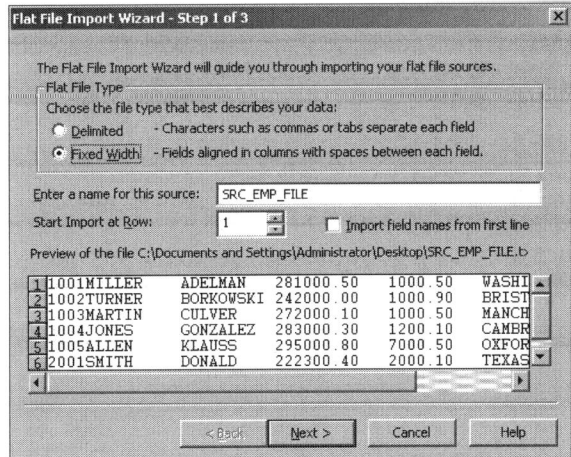

6. Click on **Next**.

7. As against the delimited files, we will now need to set the width of each column as per the requirement. This will help us divide the file in a proper column-wise manner, as shown in the following screenshot:

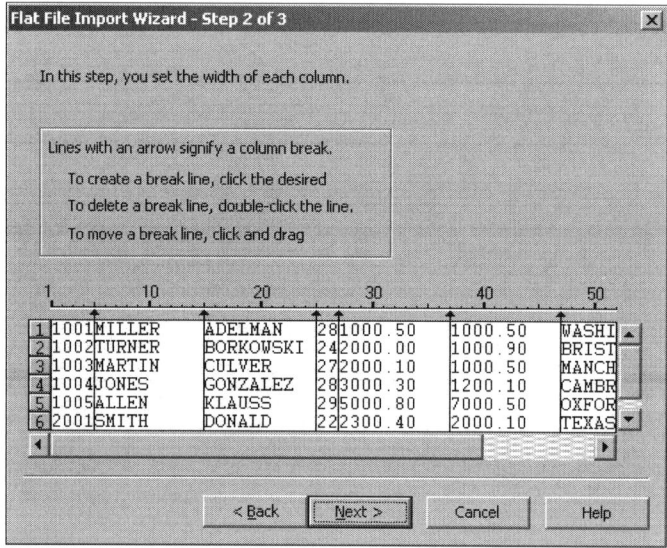

8. Click on **Next**.

9. Specify the column name, data type, and precision in the data view option. You can edit the column names and other details in this view:

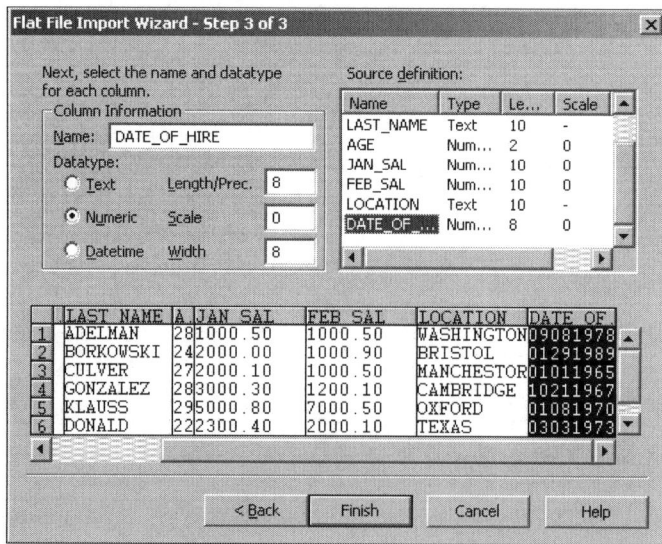

10. Click on **Finish** to get the source imported in the Source Analyzer, as shown in the following screenshot:

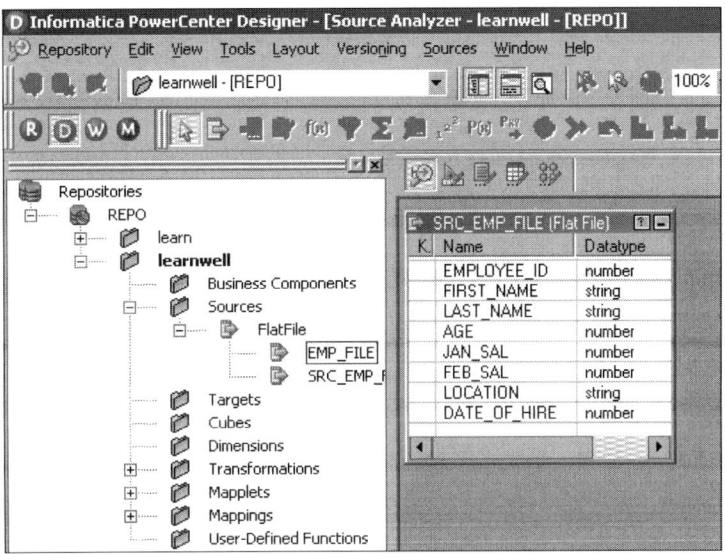

Working with sources – the Create option

Apart from importing the file or table structure, we can manually create the source definition. When the sample source file or the table structure is not available, we need to manually create the source structure. When we select the **Create** option, we need to define every detail related to the file or table manually, such as the name of the source, the type of the source, the column names, the column data type, the column data size, indexes, constraints, and so on. When you import the structure, the import wizard automatically imports all these details. We perform the following steps:

1. In the designer screen, navigate to **Tools | Source Analyzer** to open the Source Analyzer.

2. Navigate to **Sources | Create**.

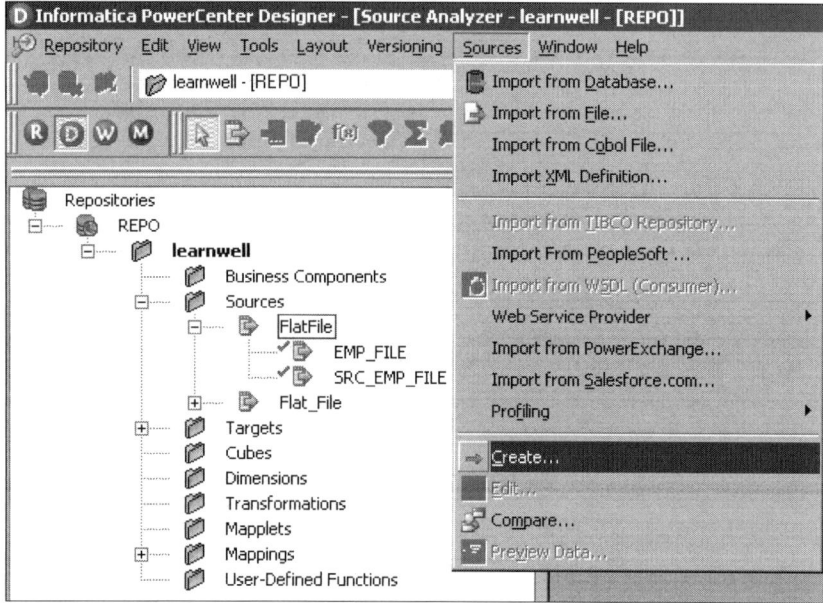

3. Mention the name of the source as per your requirements and select the type of source you wish to create from the drop-down list. For your reference, we are choosing **Flat File** as our source type and using SRC_STUDENT as the source filename. Also, select the database type for the new source to be created. This is shown in the following screenshot:

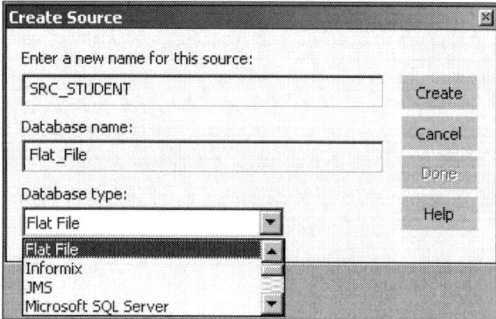

4. Click on **Create** and then click on **Done**.

5. An empty source structure with the name SRC_STUDENT will appear in the Source Analyzer as shown in the following screenshot:

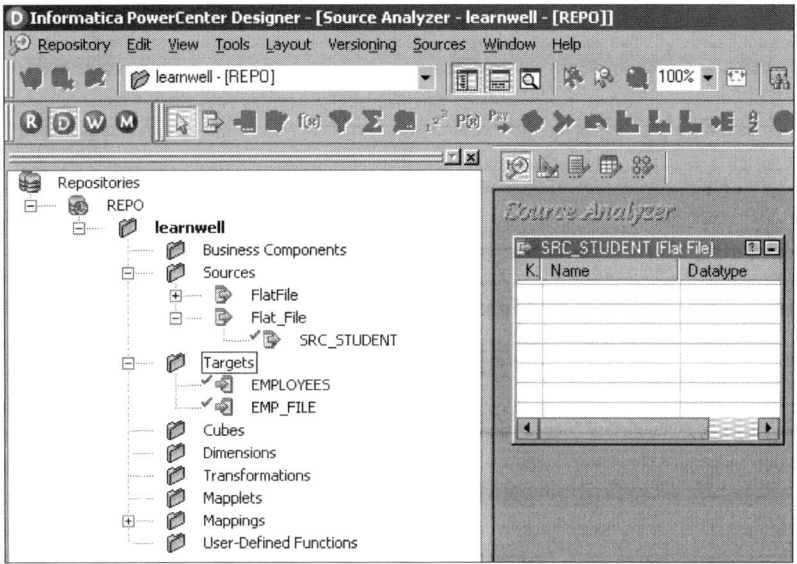

6. Since we are using the **Create** option, we need to manually specify all the details, such as the column names, data type, precision, and so on.

7. Double-click on the title bar of the **SRC_STUDENT** source structure to open the source definition. The **Edit Tables** dialog box appears and displays all the properties of this source definition. The **Table** tab shows the name of the table, the owner name, and the database type. You can add a comment in the **Description** section. The **Business name** field is empty.

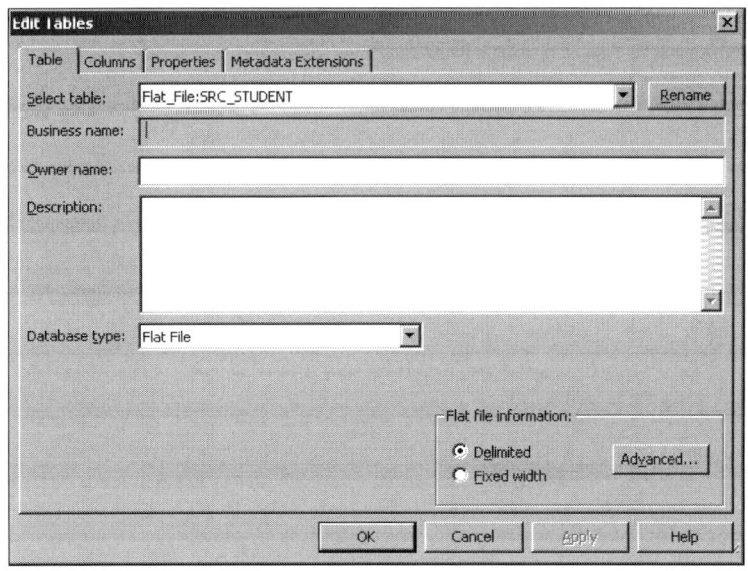

8. Click on the **Columns** tab. The **Columns** tab displays the column descriptions for the source. In the **Columns** tab, we have options to add a new column, delete an existing column, and so on.

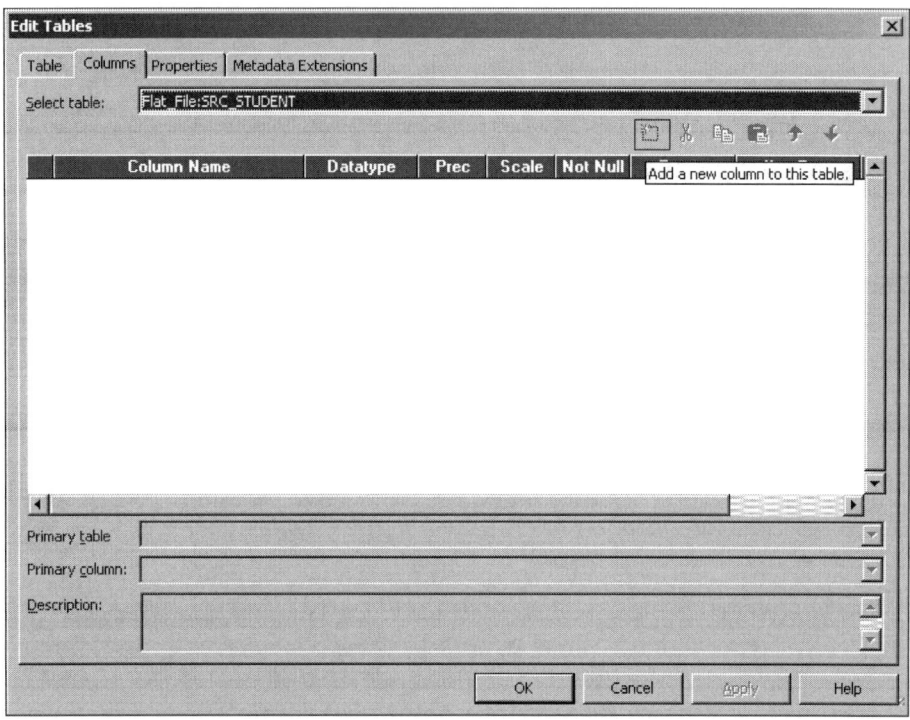

The options available in the **Columns** tab are explained as follows:

- **Add a new column**: You can click on this option to add a new column. You can add multiple columns as per your requirement. Once you add a new column, you need to specify other details such as data type, precision, and so on for the column you added.

- **Delete a column**: To delete a column, click on the column you wish to delete and press the **Delete** button.

- **Copy an existing column**: You can copy an existing column if you wish to make a column similar to that column.

- **Paste the copied column**: You can paste the copied column as per your requirement.

- **Move up or down the column**: You can move up or down the column to rearrange the columns inside the source definition.

We have added a few columns to the source, as shown in the following screenshot:

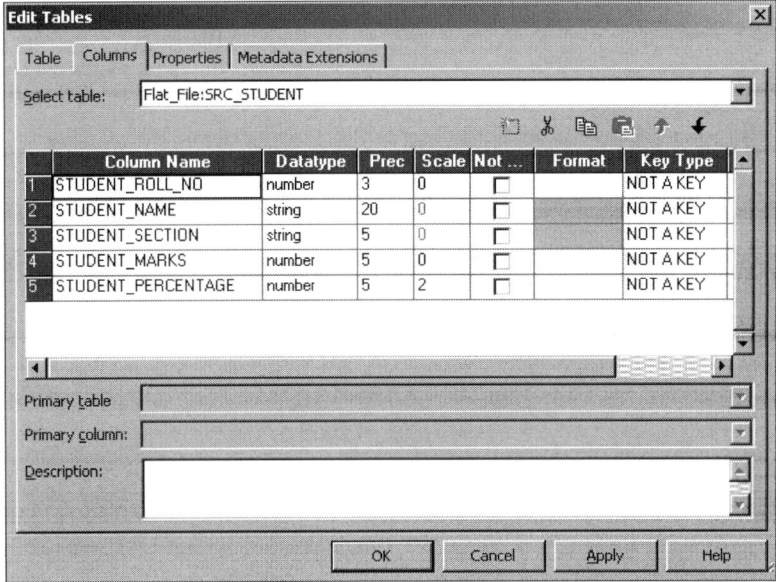

9. Click on the **Metadata Extensions** tab. Metadata extensions allow you to extend the metadata stored in the repository by associating information with individual repository objects. For example, you can store contact information, such as name or e-mail address with the sources you create. This is optional and is usually left empty.

10. Click on **Apply** and then click on **OK** to close the dialog box and get the source definition in the Source Analyzer as shown in the following screenshot:

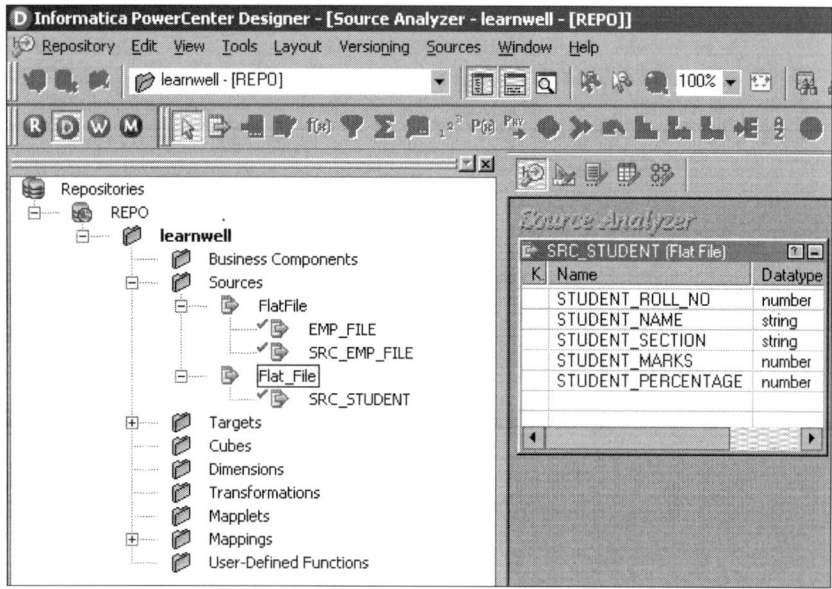

11. Navigate to **Repository** | **Save** or press *Ctrl + S* to save the changes to the repository.

Working with targets

We have seen in the earlier section that PowerCenter can use different types of sources. Similarly, PowerCenter is capable of working with different types of targets to load data. The targets are explained as follows:

- **Relational database**: PowerCenter supports all the relational databases such as Oracle, Sybase, DB2, Microsoft SQL Server, SAP HANA, and Teradata

- **Files**: PowerCenter supports flat files (fixed-width and delimited files), COBOL files, XML files, and Excel files

- **High-end applications**: PowerCenter also supports applications such as Hyperion, PeopleSoft, TIBCO, WebSphere MQ, and so on

- **Mainframe**: Additional features of Mainframe such as IBM DB2 OS/390, IBM DB2 OS/400, IDMS, IDMS-X, IMS, and VSAM can be purchased

- **Other**: PowerCenter also supports Microsoft Access and external web services

Working with target relational database tables – the Import option

As we discussed about importing and creating source files and source tables, the same way, we need to work on target definitions.

The process of importing the target table is exactly the same as importing the source table; the only difference is that you need to work in **Target Designer**.

You can import or create the table structure in **Target Designer**. After you add these target definitions to the repository, you can use them in a mapping.

Perform the following steps to import the table target definition:

1. In the designer screen, navigate to **Tools | Target Designer** to open the Target Designer screen.
2. Navigate to **Targets | Import from Database**.
3. From the ODBC data source button, select the ODBC data source that you created to access the source tables. We have already added the data source while working on the sources.
4. Enter the username and password to connect to the database.
5. Click on **Connect**.
6. In the **Select tables** list, expand the database owner and the **TABLE** heading.
7. Select the tables you wish to import and click on **OK**.

The structure of the selected tables will appear in the **Target Designer** screen in the workspace.

As mentioned, the process is exactly similar to importing the source in Source Analyzer. Please follow the preceding steps if you have any issues.

Working with target flat files – the Import option

The process of importing the target file is exactly the same as importing the source file; the only difference is that you need to work in Target Designer.

Working with delimited files

Perform the following steps to import the delimited files:

1. In the **Designer** screen, navigate to **Tools | Target Designer** to open the Target Designer.

2. Navigate to **Targets | Import from file**.

3. Browse the files you wish to import as source files.

4. The **Flat File Import Wizard** screen will pop up.

5. Select the file type: **Delimited**. Also select the appropriate option to import the data from the row and import file names from the first line, as we did in case of importing the source. Click on **Next**.

6. Select the type of delimiter used in the file. Also check the quotes option: **No quotes**, **Single quotes**, and **Double quotes** — to work with the quotes in the text values. Click on **Next**.

7. Verify the column name, data type, and precision in the data view option.

8. Click on **Finish** to get the target file imported in the Target Designer.

Working with fixed-width files

Perform the following steps to import the fixed width files:

1. In the **Designer** screen, navigate to **Tools | Target Designer** to open the Target Designer.

2. Navigate to **Targets | Import from file**.

3. Browse the files you wish to use as source files.

4. The **Flat File Import Wizard** screen will pop up.

5. Select the file type: **Fixed Width**. Click on **Next**.

6. Set the width of each column as required by adding a line break. Click on **Next**.

7. Specify the column name, data type, and precision in the data view option.

8. Click on **Finish** to get the target file imported in the Target Designer.

Working with the target – the Create option

Apart from importing the file or table structure, we can manually create the target definition. When the sample target file or the table structure is not available, we need to manually create the target structure. When we select the **Create** option, we need to define every detail related to the file or table manually, such as the name of the target, type of target, column names, column data type, column data size, indexes, constraints, and so on. When you import the structure, the import wizard automatically imports all these details. We perform the following steps:

1. In the designer screen, navigate to **Tools | Target Designer** to open the Target Designer.

2. Navigate to **Target | Create**.

3. Select the type of target you wish to create from the drop-down list.

4. An empty target structure will appear in the Target Designer.

5. Double-click on the title bar of the target definition for the **T_EMPLOYEES** table. This will open the **T_EMPLOYEES** target definition.

6. A pop-up window will display all the properties of this target definition. The **Table** tab will show the name of the table, the owner name, and the database type. You can add a comment in the **Description** section. Usually, we keep the **Business name** section empty.

7. Click on the **Columns** tab. This will display the column descriptions for the target. You can add, delete, or edit the columns.

8. Click on the **Metadata Extensions** tab; usually, you keep this tab blank. You can store some metadata related to the target you created. Some personal details and reference details can be saved. Click on **Apply** and then click on **OK**.

9. Navigate to **Repository | Save** to save the changes to the repository.

Working with the target – the Copy option

PowerCenter provides a very convenient way of reusing the existing components in the repository. It provides the **Drag-Drop** feature, which helps when reusing the existing components.

Using the **Drag-Drop** feature, you can copy the existing source definition, created earlier, into the Target Designer to create the target definition with the same structure.

Perform the following steps:

1. In the **Designer** screen, navigate to **Tools | Target Designer** to open the Target Designer.

2. Drag the **SRC_STUDENT** source definition from the navigator to the **Target Designer** workspace as shown in the following screenshot:

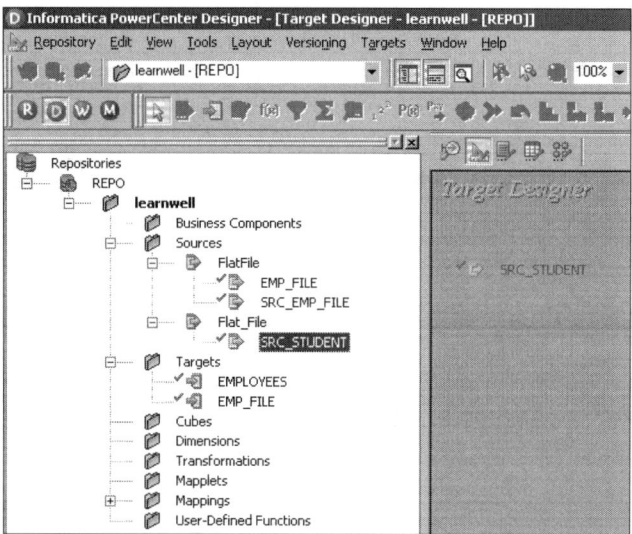

3. The designer screen creates a target definition, SRC_STUDENT, with the same column definitions as the SRC_STUDENT source definition, and the same database type.

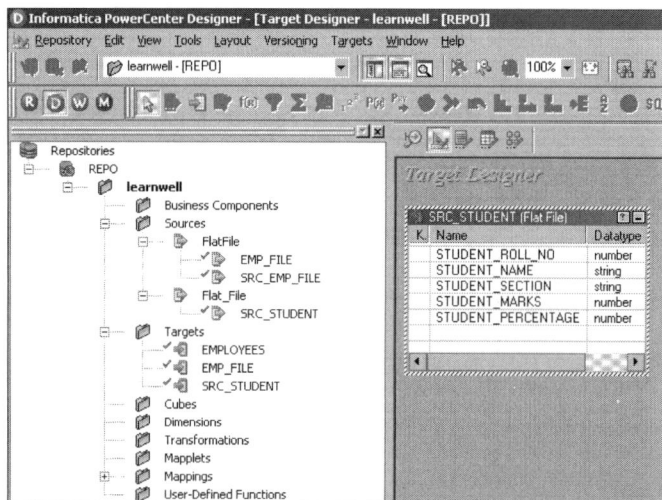

4. Double-click on the title bar of the **SRC_STUDENT** target definition to open it and edit its properties if you wish to change them.

5. Click on **Rename**.

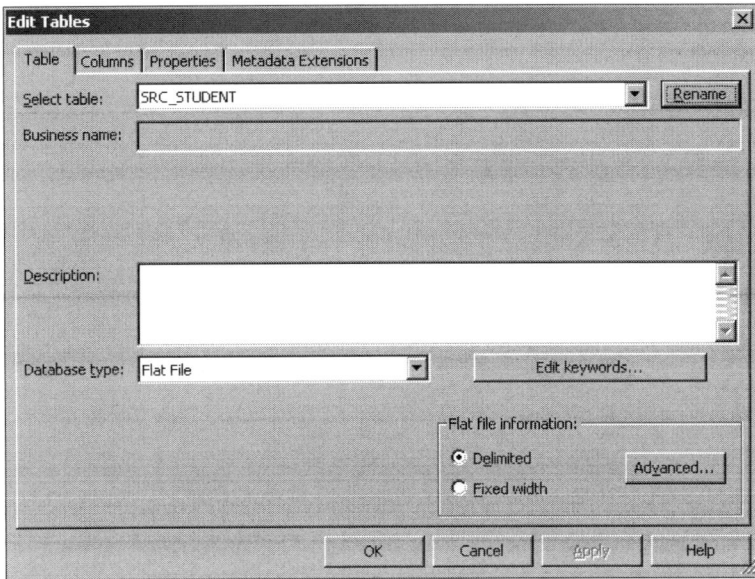

6. A new pop-up window will allow you to mention a new name. Change the target definition name to TGT_STUDENT as shown in the following screenshot:

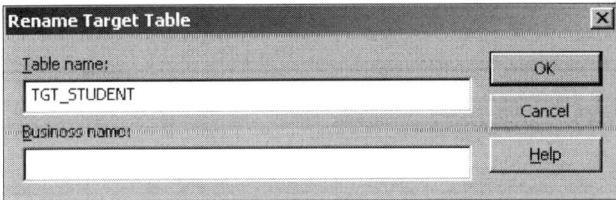

7. Click on **OK**.

8. Click on the **Columns** tab. The target column definitions are the same as the SRC_STUDENT source definition. You can add a new column, delete an existing column, or edit the columns as per your requirements.

9. Click on **OK** to save the changes and close the dialog box.

10. Navigate to **Repository | Save**.

A feel of the data inside the repository – a preview

Now that you have learned to use sources and targets in PowerCenter, we will start using these sources and targets in mappings. As mentioned earlier, in the PowerCenter Designer we only deal with the metadata of sources and targets; we do have an option to preview the data of the source and target, which we imported by providing the path/connection for files or tables. This gives us an option to understand the data clearly before we move ahead with the next step.

Previewing the source data – flat files

Perform the following steps to preview the data in the source:

1. Drag-and-drop the source from the navigator section to Source Analyzer. We are using EMP_FILE as our reference to preview data.

2. Right-click on the source definition and click on **Preview Data**.

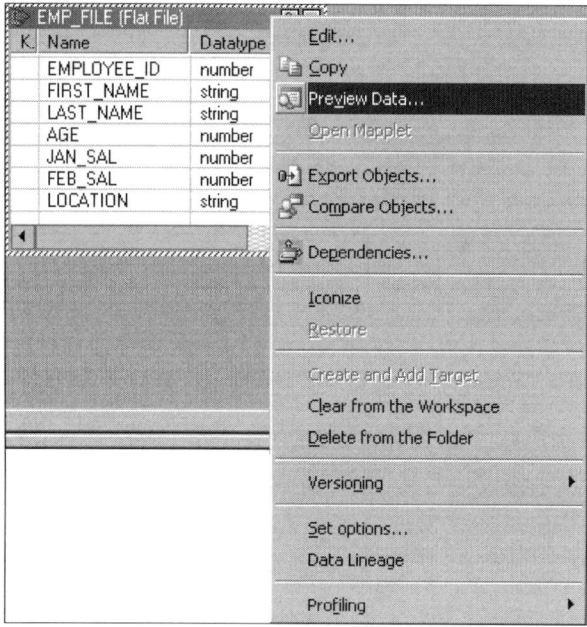

3. A new window will pop up that will ask you to provide the path where your file is stored. The following screenshot shows the pop-up window:

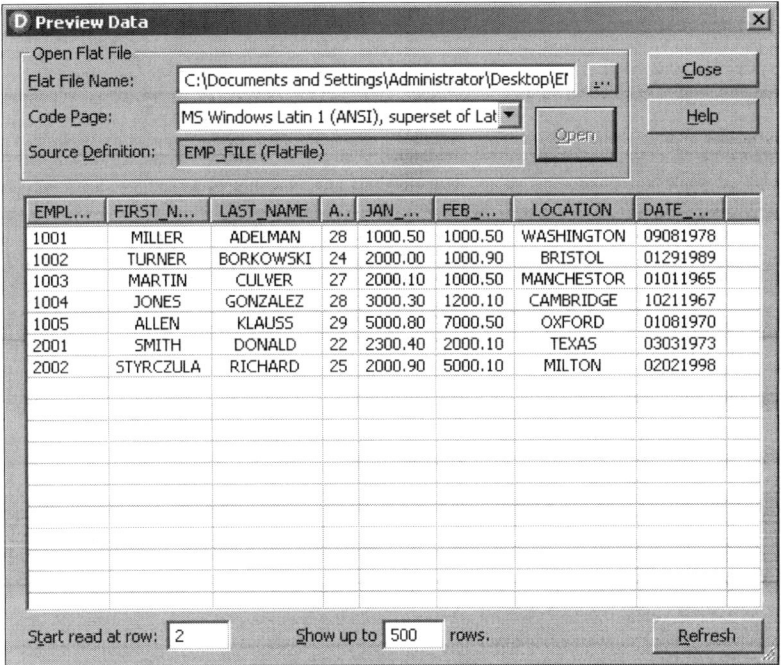

4. Click on **Open** to view the preview data.

5. Once you are done, click on **Close**.

Previewing the source data – a relational table

Perform the following steps to preview the data in the relational data source:

1. Drag-and-drop the source table from the navigator section to Source Analyzer. We are using the EMPLOYEES Oracle table as our reference to preview data.

2. Right-click on the **EMPLOYEES** source definition and click on **Preview Data**.

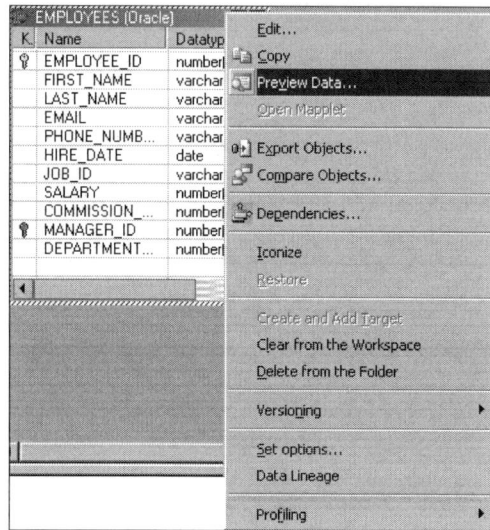

3. A new window will pop up, which will ask you to provide the database connection details. The following screenshot shows the database connection details:

4. Click on **Connect** to view the preview data.

5. Once you are done, click on **Close**.

Creating a database table

In the earlier section, you saw the steps to import the database table into Informatica.

Informatica PowerCenter tools allow you to create a database table from Informatica. If you have a table structure available in PowerCenter but the corresponding table is not available in the database, you will not be able to use the table for your mapping purpose as you will not be able to provide the required connections to load the data. PowerCenter provides a very efficient and faster way to generate a database table directly, so you need not write a CREATE SQL statement to generate a table in your database.

For your reference, we will create a table named TGT_EMPLOYEES in Oracle Database. We will perform the following steps:

1. In the designer screen, navigate to **Tools | Target Designer** to open the Target Designer.

2. In the workspace, select the **TGT_EMPLOYEES** target definition.

3. Navigate to **Targets | Generate/Execute SQL**.

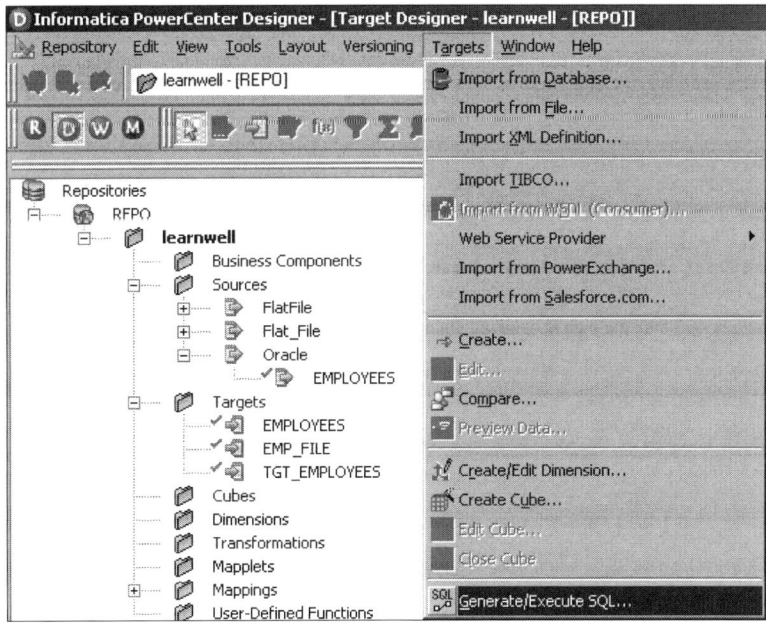

4. The **Database Object Generation** dialog box appears.

5. In the **Filename** field, enter the following text to generate a SQL script called `MKTABLES.SQL`: `C:\MKTABLES.SQL`. You can provide any path. Informatica PowerCenter will generate a SQL file at the specified location.

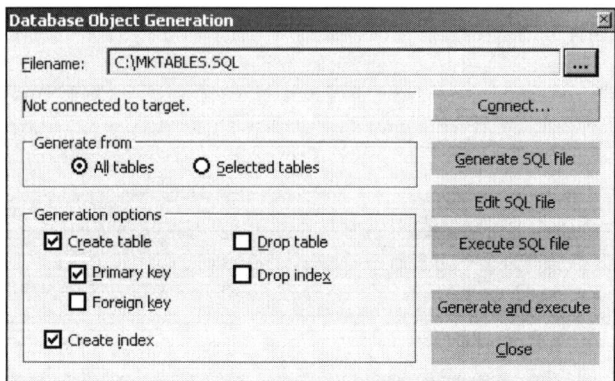

6. Select the ODBC data source to connect to the target database.

7. Enter the necessary username and password, and then click on **Connect**:

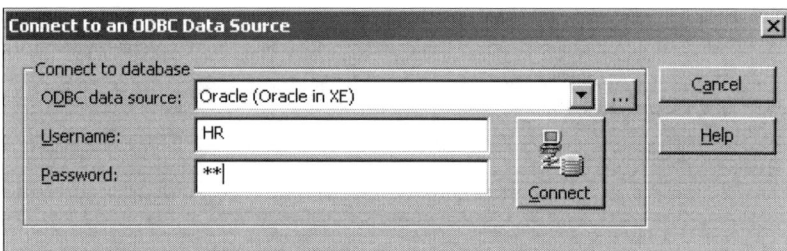

8. Select the appropriate option to generate the table.

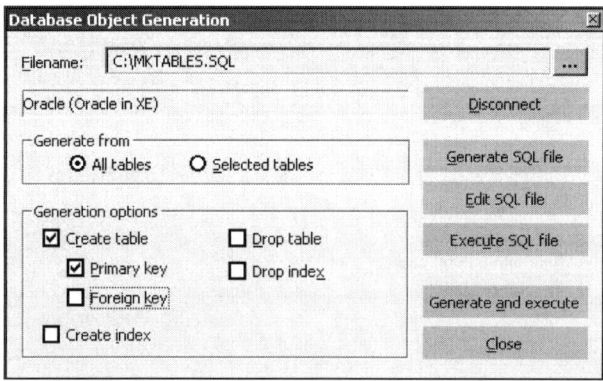

9. Click on **Generate and execute**.

10. Click on **Close** to exit the **Database Object Generation** dialog box.

With this, the TGT_EMPLOYEES table will be generated in the Oracle database.

The skeleton – a mapping

In the earlier section, you learned about all the prerequisites to create a mapping. Mapping is a structural flow of data from the source to target through transformations.

To understand the basic steps of creating a mapping, let's start by creating a pass-through mapping. A pass-through mapping inserts all the source rows into the target without any modifications.

We will use the EMPLOYEE Oracle table as source and the TGT_EMPLOYEE table as target to create a pass-through mapping.

By performing the following steps, you will create a mapping and link columns in the source EMPLOYEES table to a source qualifier transformation:

1. Navigate to **Tools | Mapping Designer** and then to **Mappings | Create** to create a new mapping.

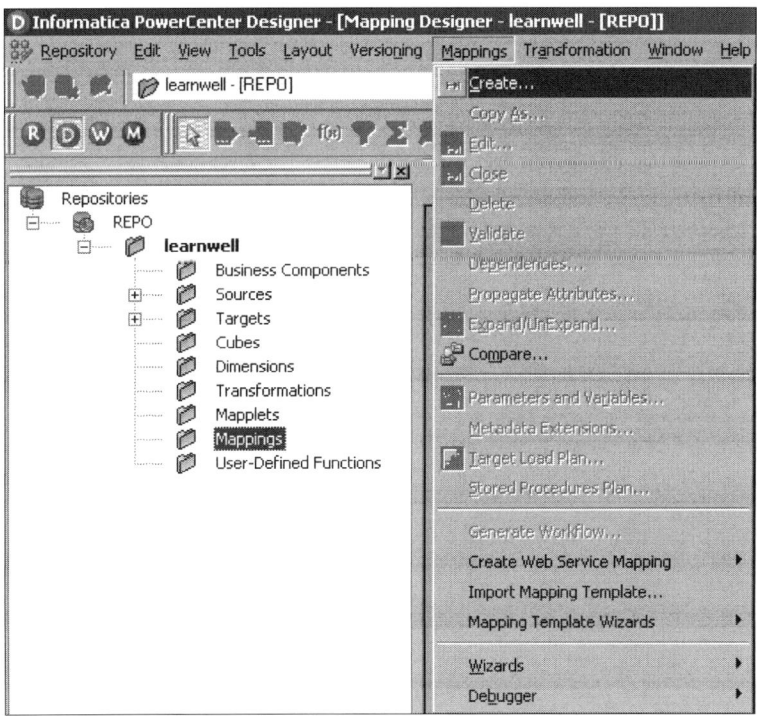

2. In the **Mapping Name** dialog box, enter m_PASS_THROUGH_EMPLOYEES and click on **OK**.

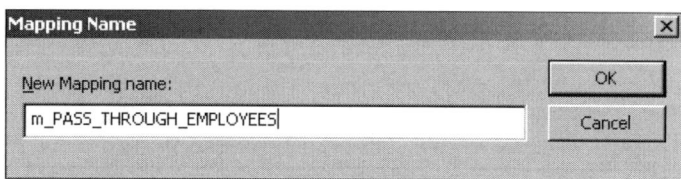

3. Drag the **EMPLOYEES** source definition into the **Mapping Designer** workspace.

4. The source definition appears in the workspace. The Designer tool creates a source qualifier transformation and connects it to the source definition. Source qualifier is a default transformation, which comes automatically with a source. We will see the use of source qualifier transformation in the next section.

5. Expand the **Targets** node in the navigator section to open the list of all target definitions. Drag the **TGT_EMPLOYEES** target definition into the workspace. The target definition appears in the **Mapping Designer** section.

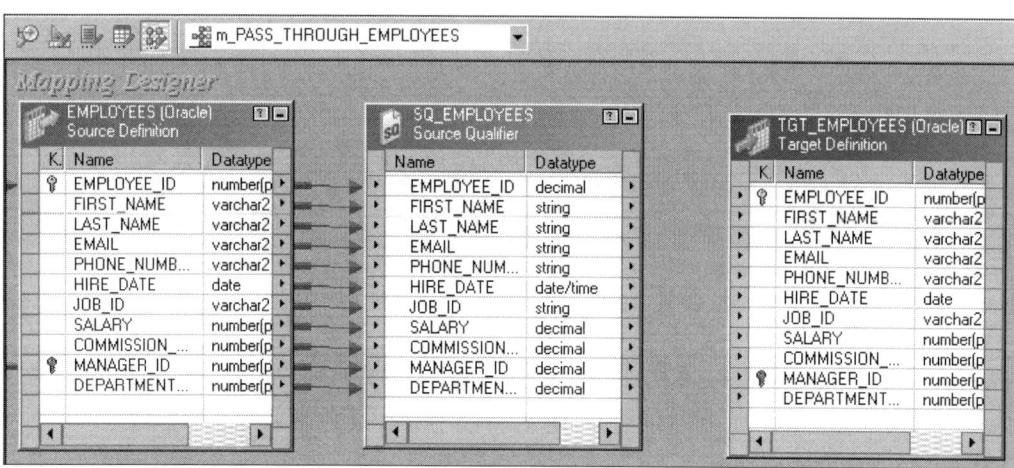

6. The final step is to connect the source qualifier transformation to the target definition.

7. Drag the columns from the source qualifier transformation to the target. Make sure you are linking the ports properly as any mismatch in linking the ports will make the data movement incorrect. This is shown in the following screenshot:

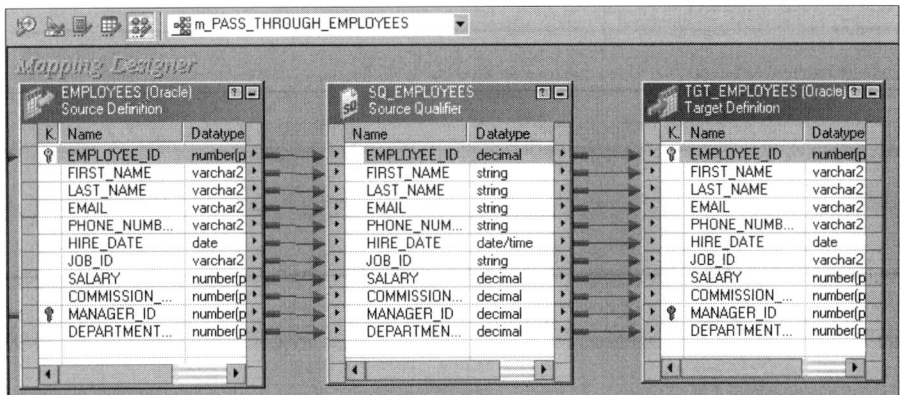

8. If you connect the links incorrectly by mistake, you can delete the links by clicking on the link and pressing the **Delete** button on your keyboard.

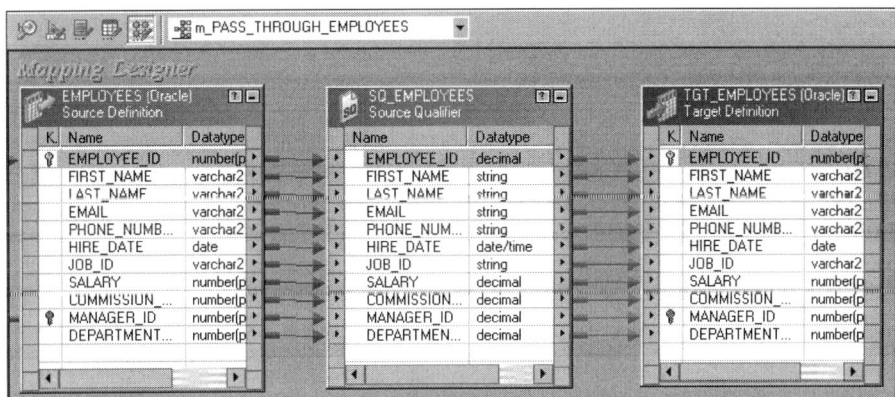

9. Navigate to **Repository | Save**.

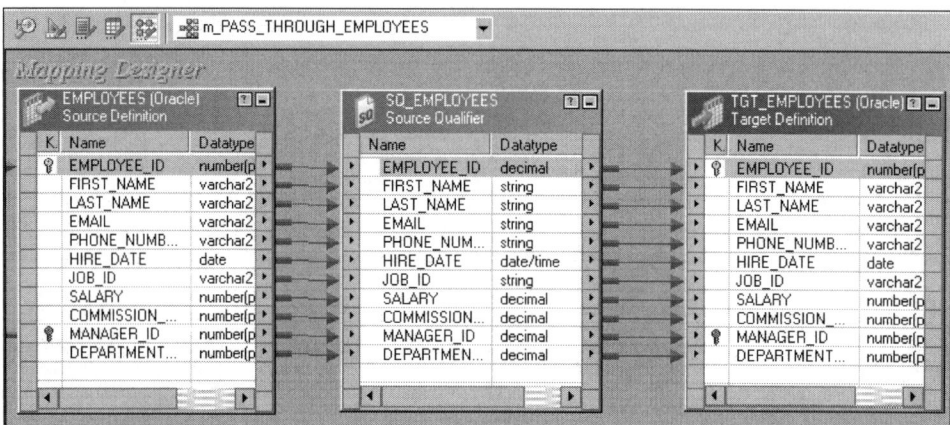

With this, the mapping is completed and saved in the repository. You can check the details in the **Output** panel.

Summary

We started the chapter with the basic components of the PowerCenter Designer screen, that is, Source Analyzer, Target Designer, Transformation Developer, Mapplet Designer, and Mapping Designer. You then learned to work on different types of sources, which included flat files (delimited files and fixed-width files) and relational databases. Similarly, we worked on different types of targets. We also worked on the import and create functionalities of sources and targets. Later in the chapter, you saw how to preview the data. The last and most important aspect that you learned in this chapter was how to create mappings using sources and targets.

The Informatica PowerCenter Designer screen, of course, cannot be that simple. Moving ahead, in the next chapter, we will see the advanced concepts of the designer screen. There are a lot of high-level functionalities that are added in the designer window to help better and faster processing.

In the next chapter, you will see how to process the data by managing the constraints in the database. You will also see the utility to debug the mapping, which will help in finding any errors, and will study the concept of the reusable functionality of transformations and mapping.

2
Using the Designer
Screen – Advanced

In our first chapter, we developed our skills in order to use the PowerCenter Designer screen; you also learned how to create mappings using sources, targets, and transformations.

Before you read this chapter, make sure that you have a complete understanding of the various components of the PowerCenter Designer screen that we discussed in *Chapter 1*, *Starting the Development Phase – Using the Designer Screen Basics*. You should be clear on how to use sources and targets and how to create mappings.

In this chapter, we will talk about the high-level aspects of the PowerCenter Designer screen. Once we are clear with the basics of the designer screen, we are all set to work on the advanced concepts of PowerCenter Designer.

Apart from the basic functionalities of creating mappings, the designer screen offers multiple utilities that assist you in smoother execution of the ETL processing. Some of these functionalities will be regularly used, and some will be rare for you. It is always good to have an understanding of these functionalities in order to have an upper hand while using the tool.

The topics that will be covered in this chapter are as follows:

- Debugger
- Reusable transformations
- Mapplets
- Target load plans
- Parameters and variables
- Comparing objects

Debug me please – the debugger

Informatica PowerCenter provides a utility called debugger that debugs the mapping so that you can easily find issues with the mapping that you created. Using the debugger, you can see the flow of every record across the transformations.

As you are aware, Informatica PowerCenter is not a data storage tool, it is a data manipulation tool that helps you manipulate the data. This point is important to the debugger, as once you finish the process, you only have either the source or the target to check the result and compare it in order to verify the data. Debugger jumps in with a functionality that provides you with the option to actually see the data flow from each and every transformation in your mapping.

When you execute the mapping through the session task, the data automatically starts flowing from the source to the target through transformations. You manually execute the same process using the debugger.

Take a look at the upcoming example to understand the debugger functionality.

You created a mapping with 100 transformations, and you have 1,000 records present in your source. You executed the mapping and got the results. When you started analyzing the output in your target table, you found that the data in few columns was incorrect. Now, the problem is that you are not sure where out of the 100 transformations the issue actually started — debugger is your solution. It will allow you to see the movement of each record from every transformation so that you can catch the origin of the error and rectify it accordingly.

To set up and execute the debugger, perform the following steps:

1. In the designer, navigate to **Tools | Mapping Designer | Mapping | Debugger | Start Debugger**, as shown in the following screenshot:

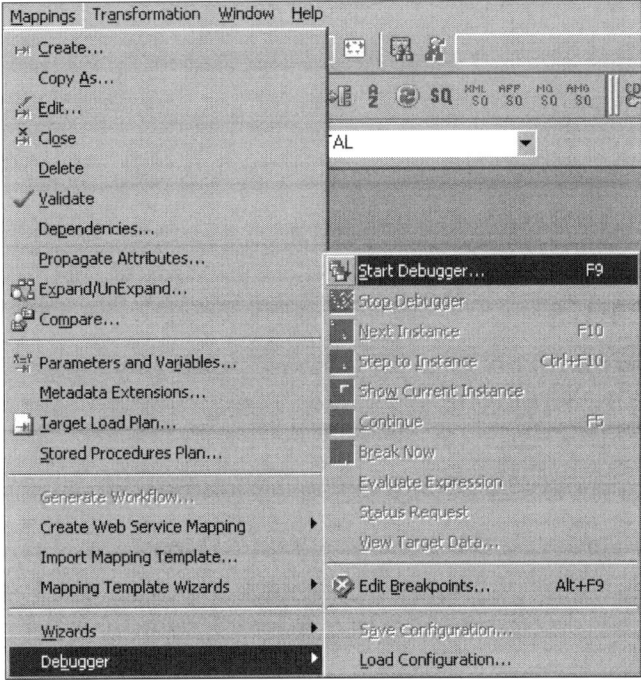

2. A new window will pop up mentioning the prechecks for the debugger as follows:

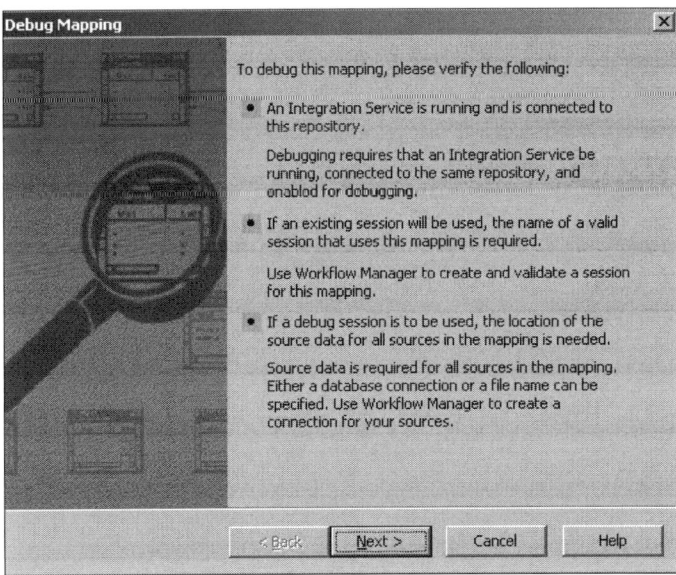

Read the points clearly before you proceed and click on **Next**.

3. The next screen will ask you to select the session task for the mapping you wish to debug. Select the session task you created in order to execute the mapping.

Even though running a debugger is a manual process, you still need a session task because Integration Service needs to get the path to extract and load the data that is provided in the session task.

Note that you can use an existing session or create a new debug session to run the debugger. If you use an existing session, the debugger will use the properties mentioned in the session. You need to mention all the details if you create a new debug session.

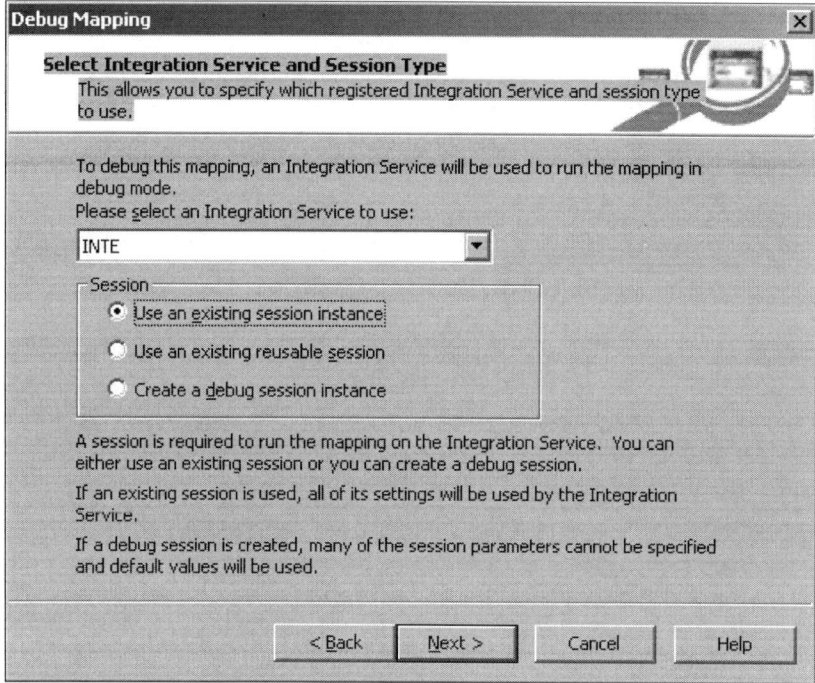

After selecting the session, click on **Next**.

4. Select the appropriate session in the next window and click on **Next**.

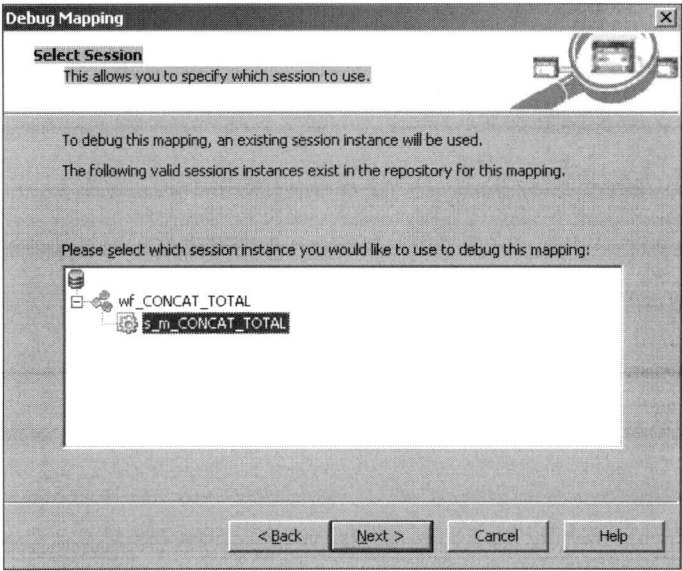

5. In the next screen, you will see the option to discard the target data. This option indicates what you wish to do with the data you loaded in the target using the debugger. As you run the debugger for testing purposes, you basically wish to discard the target data.

   Checking this option will discard the data in the target. Now, click on **Finish**.

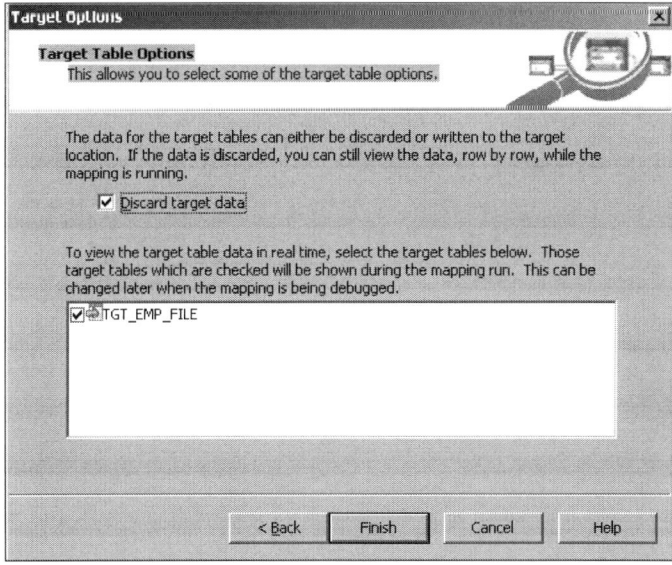

The output panel of your screen will get divided into three sections, as shown in the following screenshot:

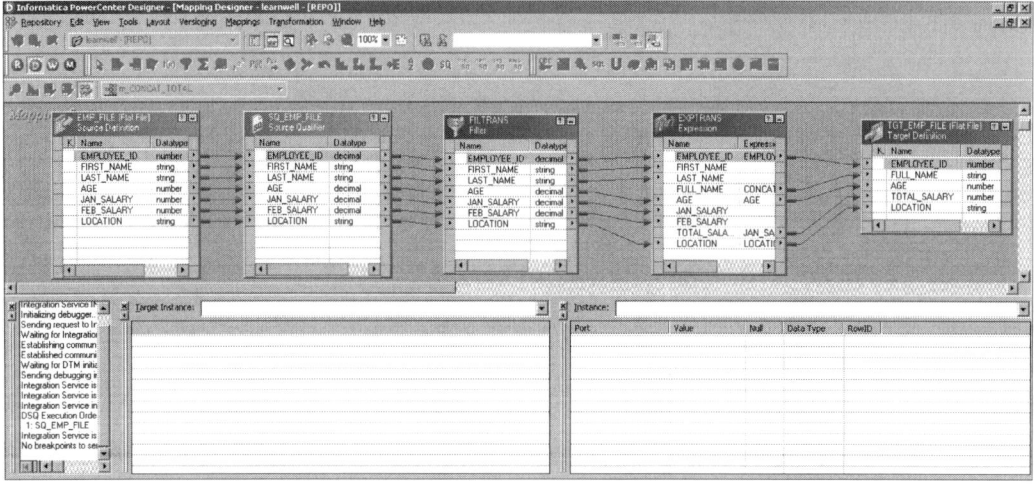

The output panel gets divided into the following sections:

- **Notification**: This section will show you general information about the debugger execution.

- **Target instance**: This section will show you the data as it reaches the target of your mapping. If your mapping contains multiple targets, all the targets will be displayed in this section in the drop-down list, as shown in the preceding screenshot. You can select the target for which you wish to see the data from the dropdown.

- **Instance**: This section will show you the data when it reaches different transformations of your mapping. If your mapping contains multiple transformations, all the transformations will be displayed in this section in the dropdown, as shown in the preceding screenshot. You can select the transformation for which you wish to see the data from the dropdown. The debugger shows you the data in each transformation as per the logic you coded in the mapping.

We have completed the setup for the debugger; now click on **Next Instance** to start the debugger.

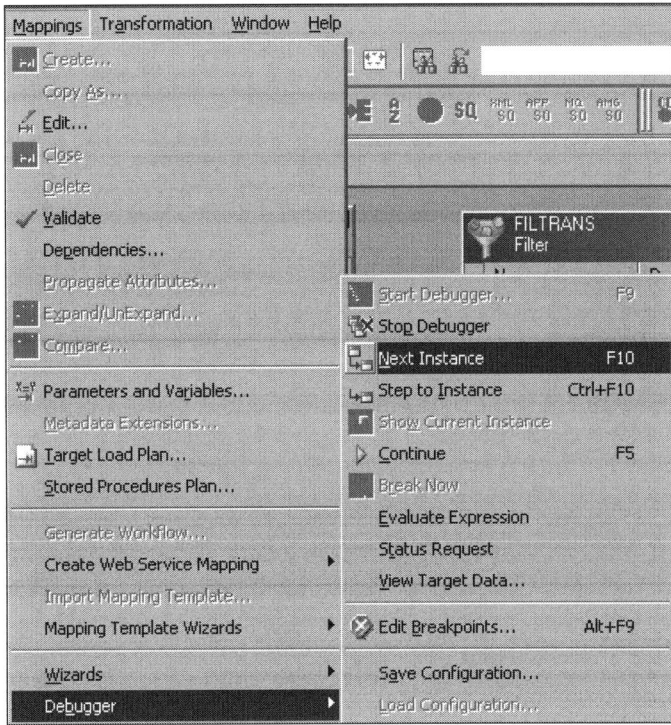

The debugger will start showing you the movement of the data from each transformation under the instance, and then in the target under the target instance at the end.

Keep pressing **Next Instance** (*F10*) to move the data toward the next instance in your mapping flow.

Once all the data reaches the target, the debugger will automatically shut down.

If you have very big mapping, and traversing through every transformation is a tough task, you can actually select particular transformations at a particular interval to understand and narrow the issue down. This can be achieved using breakpoints.

To set a breakpoint, click on **Edit Breakpoint**, as shown in the following screenshot:

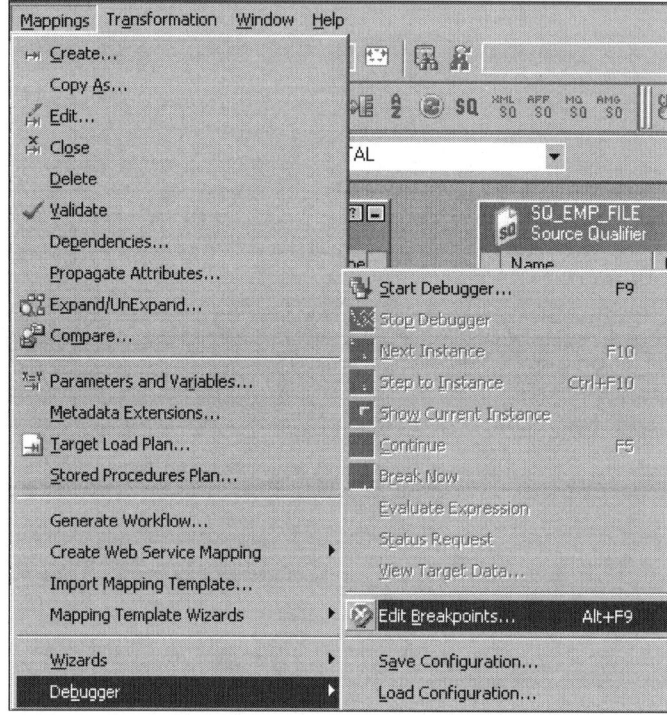

A new window will let you add breakpoints. Click on **Add** to add a new breakpoint to the debugger. You can set few more properties in this window.

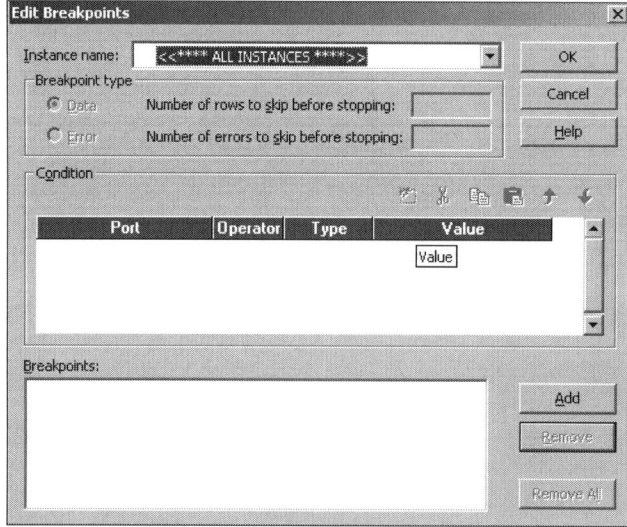

As you must have noticed, the debugger is the best way to find the issues in the data movement across the mapping. So, whenever you face some issues related to data loading in the target or mismatches in the targets, start a debugger and solve your issue.

Reuse me please – reusable transformation

As you are aware, source and targets are reusable components, that is, you work on sources in the Source Analyzer and targets in the Target Designer, respectively. Also, you must be aware that you cannot edit sources and targets in the Mapping Designer, and they can be edited in Source Analyzer and Target Designer, respectively.

Sources and targets are called reusable components because you can use the same source and target in multiple mappings. We can reuse the source or target across multiple mappings only if the metadata requirement of both the mappings is exactly the same. In this case, metadata means the number of columns, their data type, their data size, indexes, constraints, and so on. Even if there are small changes, you cannot reuse the components.

On the same lines, if we have the same logic to implement across multiple mappings, we can use the reusable transformations, which allow us to reuse the same transformation across mappings. You can only reuse the transformation if the metadata requirements in the mappings are exactly the same. Even if there is a small difference, the reusable transformations will not work as there can be mismatch in the processing.

There are two ways in which you can create reusable transformations:

- Using the Transformation Developer
- Making existing transformations reusable

Using Transformation Developer

To use Transformation Developer, perform the following steps:

1. In the designer, navigate to **Tools | Transformation**.

2. Click on **Transformation | Create**.

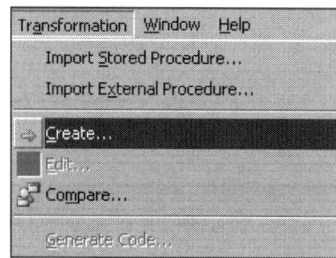

3. Select the transformation type you wish to create from the list of transformations. We are creating an expression transformation as an example. Click on **Create** and then click on **Done**.

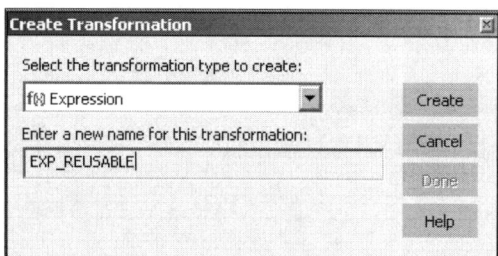

The transformation will appear on the screen. Also, you will see the transformation added to your navigator under **Transformations**, as shown in the following screenshot:

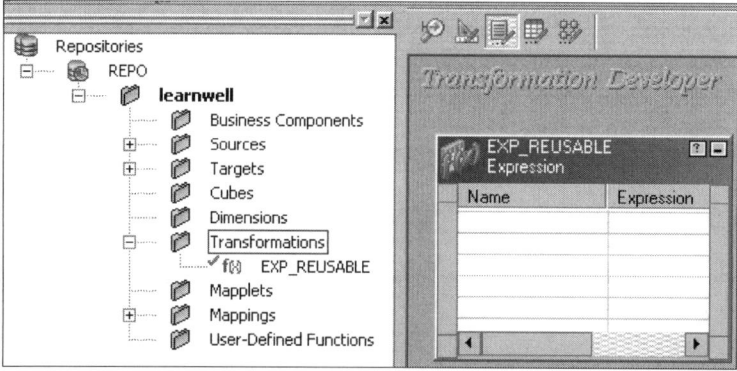

Now, you can drag-and-drop the transformation in the mapping in the Mapping Designer in order to use it as a reusable component.

You will see that you cannot edit the reusable transformation in the Mapping Designer. To edit the reusable transformation, you need to use Transformation Developer.

Making existing transformation reusable

In the earlier section, we saw how to use a new transformation as a reusable transformation. Consider that you already have a transformation that you wish to use in another mapping, but as it is nonreusable, you are not able to do so. To solve this issue, we have an option using which you can make an existing nonreusable transformation reusable. Perform the following steps to do this:

1. Open the mapping containing the transformation you wish to make reusable in the Mapping Designer. We are using an existing mapping containing an expression transformation in order to make it reusable.

2. Double-click on the transformation in order to view the properties of the transformation. You will see an option, **Make reusable**. Click on the box, as shown in the upcoming screenshot.

    A warning message will pop up mentioning that the process is irreversible.

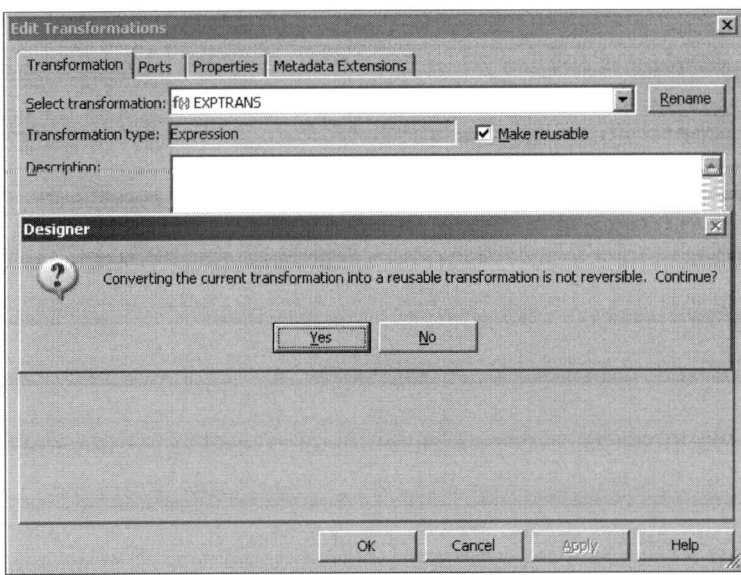

You can see that the transformation is now added under **Transformation** in the navigator, which indicates that the transformation can be reused; you can reuse this in other mappings too.

Mapplet

In the previous section, we saw how to make a transformation reusable. Going further, you might also like to reuse logic that was implemented using multiple transformations. The group of transformations that can be reused is called as mapplets.

Mapplets can be created in the Mapplet Designer in Informatica PowerCenter Designer. Mapplets allow you to reuse groups of transformations in multiple mappings. As is the case with reusable transformations, in order to use mapplets, the metadata requirements of the mappings should be exactly the same.

You can use the Mapplet Designer to create mapplets with new transformations or use existing transformations.

To create a new mapplet, perform the following steps:

1. In the designer, navigate to **Tools | Mapplet Designer**, as shown in the following screenshot. Then, click on **Create**.

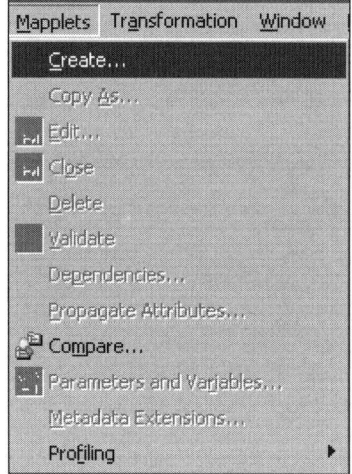

2. Specify the name of new mapplet as MPLT_REUSABLE.
3. Add the transformations in the mapplet as per your logic. We are using filter and expression transformation to create sample logic.
4. Click on **Transformations** and create mapplet input and mapplet output and name them MPLT_INPUT and MPLT_OUTPUT, respectively.

5. Place the mapplet input before the filter and the mapplet output after the expression. These will act as the source and target for the mapplet. Drag-and-drop the columns from the expression transformation to `MPLT_OUTPUT` and drag-and-drop the columns from filter transformation back to `MPLT_INPUT`, as shown in the following screenshot:

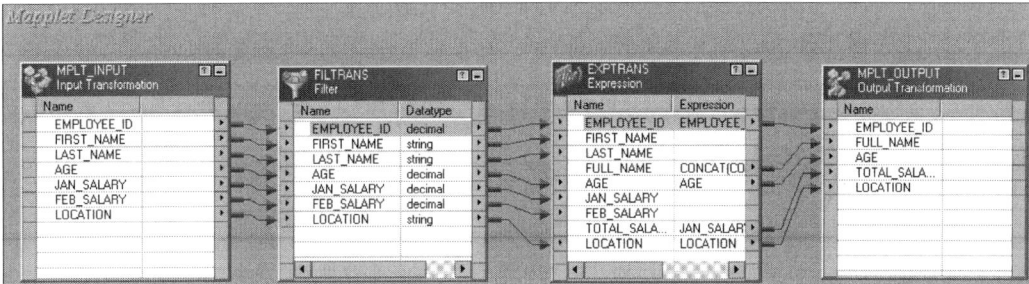

6. Press *Ctrl + S* to save the mapplet, and you will be able to see the mapplet added under mapplets in the navigator.

7. You can now drag-and-drop the mapplet in the Mapping Designer in order to use it as reusable components. Drag-and-drop the mapplet into the Mapping Designer and link the columns from the source qualifier to input ports of the mapplet and drag-and-drop the output ports from the mapplet to the Target Designer, as shown in the following screenshot:

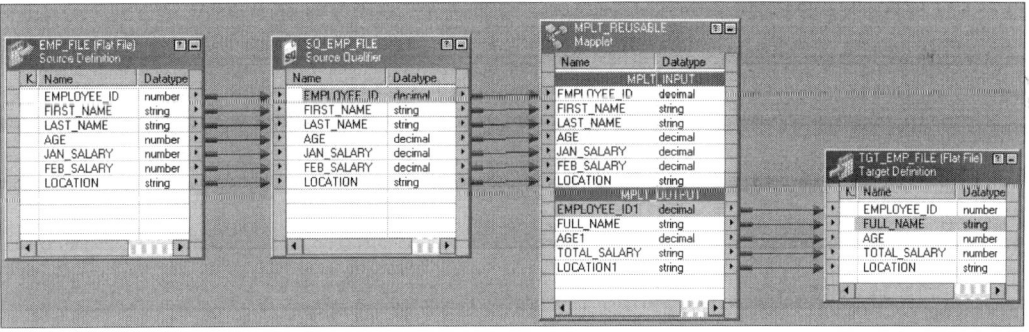

If you wish to reuse the logic that was implemented using multiple transformations in an existing mapping, you can simply copy the existing transformations from the Mapping Designer and paste it in the Mapplet Designer. This is the easiest way to use the existing group of transformations.

As you might have noticed, mapplet serves two purposes—first, it allows you to reuse your existing transformation and second, it makes your mapping look simpler by replacing multiple components with a single component.

Managing constraints – the target load plan

While you work on multiple mappings in a complex scenario, situations might demand that you put multiple data flows in a single mapping in order to justify the performance and the complexity. A sample mapping depicting the preceding statement is shown in the following screenshot:

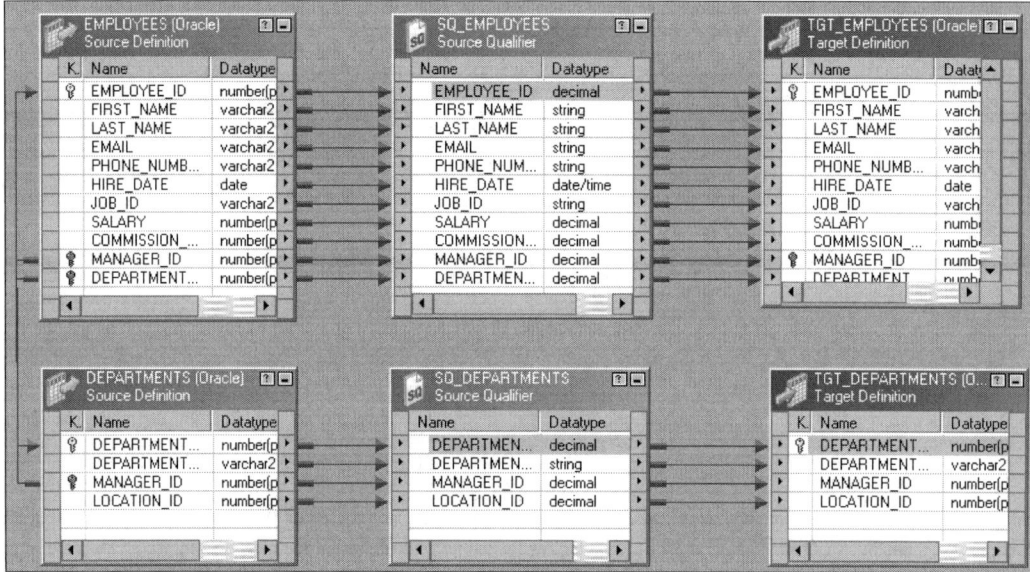

If you execute the mapping, the session might fail because of the primary key and foreign key violation. As the `Employee` and `Department` tables have dependencies on each other, when you run the mapping containing both the flows, the process might fail if the data violates the dependency.

To avoid the issue, Informatica PowerCenter contains a utility called the target load plan—how do you plan to load the data into multiple targets in a mapping? We can load the data in a particular sequence in multiple targets in a mapping in order to avoid failure due to constraints.

Consider that the EMPLOYEES table data depends on the DEPARTEMNTS data because of the primary key and foreign key constraints. So, to satisfy the referential integrity, the DEPARTMENTS table should be loaded first. The target load order is useful when you wish to handle referential integrity while inserting, deleting, or updating data in tables that have the primary key and foreign key relationships.

To set the target load plan in a mapping, perform the following process:

1. In the designer, navigate to **Tools** | **Mapping Designer** | **Mapping** | **Target Load Plan**, as shown in the following screenshot:

2. New window will pop up, as shown in the following screenshot:

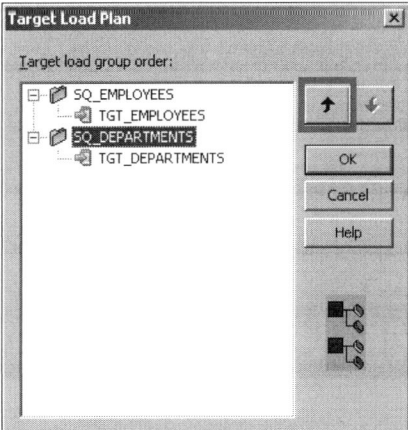

To set the target load plan, just move the target load group using the arrow provided in the window. To load the DEPARTMENTS table before the EMPLOYEES table, select SQ_DEPARTMENTS and click on the up arrow, as shown in the preceding screenshot.

This will make the DEPARTMENTS table load before the EMPLOYEES table is loaded, and we can avoid failure.

When we use the target load plan, Informatica PowerCenter actually restricts the extraction of the data from the source qualifier. It waits for the first flow in the selected sequence to finish loading the data and then starts extracting the data from the second source qualifier for its loading.

I hate hardcoding – parameters and variables

When you work on any technology, it is always advised that your code be dynamic. This means that you should use the hardcoded values as less as possible in your code. It is always recommended that you use the parameters or the variable in your code so that you can easily pass these values and don't need to change the code frequently. We will discuss this concept in more detail in the *Parameters file* section in *Chapter 5, Using the Workflow Manager Screen – Advanced*.

In this section, we will discuss how to use parameters and variables on the PowerCenter Designer screen.

The value of a variable can change between the session run. The value of a parameter will remain constant across the session runs. The difference is very minute, so you should define parameters and variables properly, as per your requirements.

Consider a filter transformation where you have defined the filter condition as LOCATION='USA'. As you have used hardcoded values in the filter conditions, it is always recommended that you pass the value using a parameter or variable.

Follow these steps to use variables or parameters:

1. In the designer, navigate to **Tools | Mapping Designer | Mapping | Parameters and Variables**, as shown in the following screenshot:

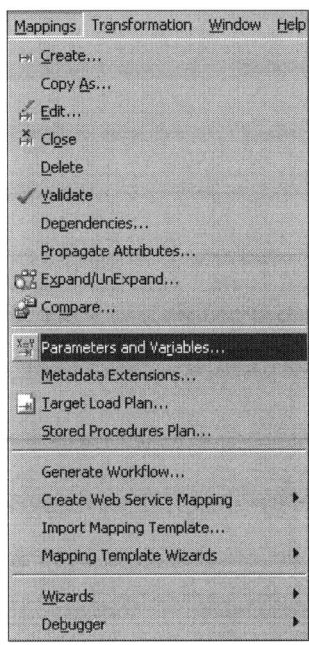

2. A new window will pop up allowing you to provide parameters and variables, as shown in the following screenshot. Add a new parameter or variable depending on your requirement. For our reference, we are creating a $$LOCATION. $$ parameter that is used as a mapping level variable or parameter. From the dropdown, you can choose whether you wish to make it a parameter or a variable. Then, click on **OK**.

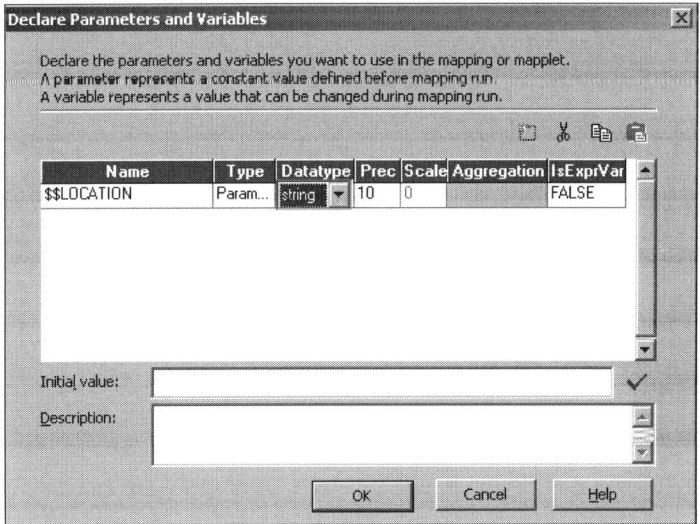

3. Once you define the parameter or variable at the mapping level, you can use them in the transformations. Take a look at the following screenshot:

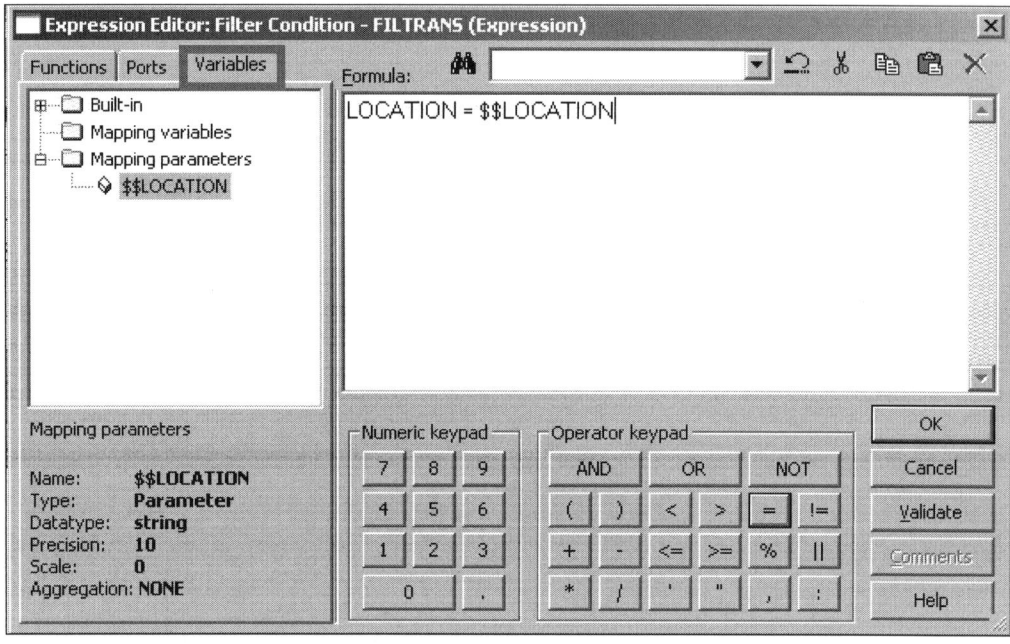

With this, we have defined a parameter or a variable at the mapping level and used it in the transformations in order to avoid hardcoding.

Comparing objects

Informatica PowerCenter allows you to compare objects that are present within repository. You can compare sources, targets, transformations, mapplets and mappings in the PowerCenter Designer under **Source Analyzer**, **Target Designer**, **Transformation Developer**, **Mapplet Designer**, and **Mapping Designer**, respectively. You can compare the objects in the same repository or in multiple repositories.

Perform the following steps to compare two objects. We are using two sources and comparing them as an example:

1. In the designer, navigate to **Tools | Source Analyzer | Sources | Compare**, as shown in the following screenshot:

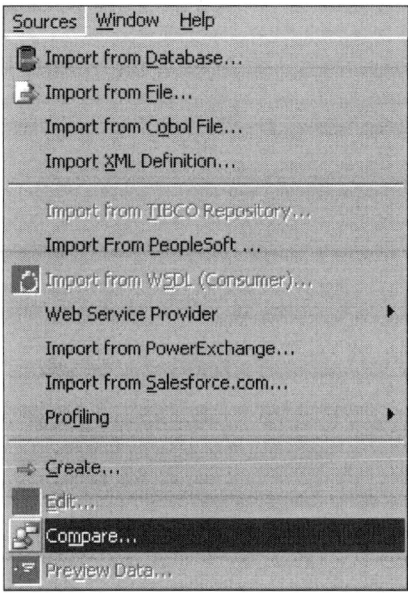

2. Select **Source 1** and **Source 2**, which you wish to compare, as shown in the following screenshot:

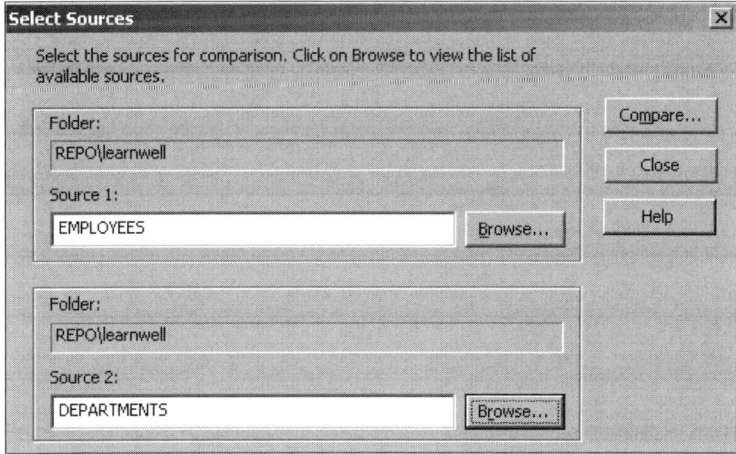

3. Click on **Compare**.

4. You can check out the different types of comparison options of the two sources. The Informatica PowerCenter comparison utility gives you the option to check out the differences between the repository and versions in the **General** tab. The table tab allows you to check out the differences between the owner name and the database type. The **Column** tab allows you to see the differences in the column and other properties related to columns such as data type, precision, and other constraints. Similar to this, when you compare targets and mappings, you can check out the differences using the **Compare Object** functionality.

This can be helpful in the analysis of the components and to understand the difference between the newer and the existing components.

Summary

We started the chapter with the debugger, which helps you debug the errors in your mapping. Using the debugger, you can pinpoint the error in your mapping using which you can easily resolve issues. Next, we discussed the reusable transformation that allows you to reuse the transformation across mappings. Reusable transformations are very important, as they save the time and effort required to recreate the same transformations.

Moving on, we talked about mapplets, which allow you to reuse groups of transformations that make your mapping simpler by replacing multiple transformations with a single component. Also, mapplets save your time and effort by allowing you to reuse existing components. Next in the line was the target load plan using which you can set the priority of loading the target tables in a single mapping. This is useful while loading the data and maintaining the constraints. We also saw some details about the parameters and variables that we will discuss in more details in *Chapter 5, Using the Workflow Manager Screen – Advanced*. We finished the chapter by comparing the objects functionality, which allows you to compare two components, which is very helpful in understanding and maintaining the versions on the repository.

With this, we have seen all the basic and advanced topics on the Informatica PowerCenter Designer screen. The more you practice, the better you will get at building your logic. As you must understand by now, practice is the only option if you wish to gain expertise and understand the nuances of the Informatica PowerCenter tool.

In the next chapter, we will take our discussion to a very important data warehousing concept, that is, **Slowly Changing Dimensions (SCD)**. We will use the wizard feature that is available on designer screens in order to understand the different types of SCDs that are available.

3

Implementing SCD – Using Designer Screen Wizards

Slowly Changing Dimensions (SCD), as the name suggests, allows you to maintain changes in the Dimension table in Datawarehouse. Before you read this chapter, make sure that you have a complete understanding of data warehousing concepts, especially SCD. Also, make sure you know the SCD1, SCD2, and SCD3 types. For your reference, we have described each SCD in detail in this chapter. For more details, refer to *The Data Warehouse Toolkit*, *Ralph Kimball*, *Wiley India Private Limited*. Before we move ahead with the implementation of the SCD in Informatica Power Center, let's discuss the different types of SCDs.

Note that we are talking about the general SCDs in our discussion, that is, SCD1, SCD2, and SCD3. Apart from these, there will always be Hybrid SCDs, which you will come across as well. Hybrid SCDs are nothing but a combination of multiple SCDs that serve your complex business requirements.

The various types of SCDs are described as follows:

- **Type 1 Dimension mapping (SCD1)**: This keeps only the current data and does not maintain historical data.

>  Use SCD1 mapping when you do not want to keep the history of the previous data.

- **Type 2 Dimension/Version Number mapping (SCD2)**: This keeps current as well as historical data in the table. SCD2 allows you to insert new records and changed records using a new column (PM_VERSION_NUMBER) by maintaining the version number in the table to track the changes. We use a new PM_PRIMARYKEY column to maintain the history.

Use SCD2 mapping when you want to keep the full history of the dimension data and track the progression of changes using a version number.

- **Type 2 Dimension/Flag mapping**: This keeps the current as well as historical data in the table. SCD2 allows you to insert new records and changed records using a new column (PM_CURRENT_FLAG) by maintaining the flag in the table to track the changes. We use a new PRIMARY_KEY column to maintain the history.

 Use SCD2 mapping when you want to keep the full history of dimension data and track the progression of changes using a flag.

- **Type 2 Dimension/Effective date range mapping**: This keeps current as well as historical data in the table. SCD2 allows you to insert new records and changed records using two new columns (PM_BEGIN_DATE and PM_END_DATE) by maintaining the date range in the table to track the changes. We use a new PRIMARY_KEY column to maintain the history.

 Use SCD2 mapping when you want to keep the full history of dimension data and track the progression of changes using **Start Date** and **End Date**.

- **Type 3 Dimension mapping**: This keeps the current as well as historical data in the table. We maintain only partial history by adding a new PM_PREV_COLUMN_NAME column; that is, we do not maintain full history.

 Use SCD3 mapping when you wish to maintain only partial history.

Let's take an example to understand the different SCDs.

Consider that there is a LOCATION column in the EMPLOYEE table and you wish to track the changes in the location of the employees. Consider a record for the 1001 employee ID that is present in your EMPLOYEE dimension table. STEVE was initially working in India and then was shifted to USA. We want to maintain the history in the LOCATION field.

EMPLOYEE_ID	NAME	LOCATION
1001	STEVE	INDIA

Your `datawarehouse` table should reflect the current status of `STEVE`. To implement this, we have different types of SCDs.

Take a look at the following table of type SCD1:

PM_PRIMARY_KEY	EMPLOYEE_ID	NAME	LOCATION
100	1001	STEVE	USA

As you can see, `INDIA` will be replaced with `USA`, so we end up having only current data, and we lose historical data. Now, if `STEVE` is again shifted to `JAPAN`, the `LOCATION` data will be replaced from `USA` to `JAPAN`, as follows:

PM_PRIMARY_KEY	EMPLOYEE_ID	NAME	LOCATION
100	1001	STEVE	JAPAN

The advantage of SCD1 is that we do not consume a lot of space to maintain the data; the disadvantage is we don't have the historical data.

Take a look at the following table of type SCD2, where we have added the version number:

PM_PRIMARYKEY	EMPLOYEE_ID	NAME	LOCATION	PM_VERSION_NUMBER
100	1001	STEVE	INDIA	0
101	1001	STEVE	USA	1
102	1001	STEVE	JAPAN	2
200	1002	MIKE	UK	0

As you can see, we are maintaining the full history by adding new records to maintain the history of the previous records. We add two new columns in the table, that is, `PM_PRIMARYKEY` to handle the issues of duplicate records in the primary key in the `EMPLOYEE_ID` (supposed to be the primary key) column, and `PM_VERSION_NUMBER` to understand the current and historical records.

The following SCD2 table has the flag column added to it:

PM_PRIMARYKEY	EMPLOYEE_ID	NAME	LOCATION	PM_CURRENT_FLAG
100	1001	STEVE	INDIA	0
101	1001	STEVE	USA	1

As you can see, we are maintaining the full history by adding new records to maintain the history of the previous records. We add two new columns in the table, that is, PM_PRIMARYKEY to handle the issues of duplicate records in the primary key in the EMPLOYEE_ID column, and PM_CURRENT_FLAG to understand the current and history record.

Again, if STEVE is shifted, the data would look like this:

PM_PRIMARYKEY	EMPLOYEE_ID	NAME	LOCATION	PM_CURRENT_FLAG
100	1001	STEVE	INDIA	0
101	1001	STEVE	USA	0
102	1001	STEVE	JAPAN	1

The following table of type SCD2 shows you the data range added to it:

PM_PRIMARYKEY	EMPLOYEE_ID	NAME	LOCATION	PM_BEGIN_DATE	PM_END_DATE
100	1001	STEVE	INDIA	01-01-14	31-05-14
101	1001	STEVE	USA	01-06-14	99-99-9999

As you can see, we are maintaining the full history by adding new records to maintain the history of the previous records. We add three new columns in the table, that is, PM_PRIMARYKEY to handle the issues of duplicate records in the primary key in the EMPLOYEE_ID column and PM_BEGIN_DATE and PM_END_DATE to understand the versions in the data.

The advantage of SCD2 is that you have the complete history of the data, which is a must for data warehouses, whereas the disadvantage of SCD2 is that it consumes a lot of space.

Take a look at the following SCD3 table:

PM_PRIMARYKEY	EMPLOYEE_ID	NAME	LOCATION	PM_PREV_LOCATION
100	1001	STEVE	USA	INDIA

As you can see, we are maintaining the history by adding a new column to maintain the history. An optional PM_PRIMARYKEY column can be added to maintain the primary key constraints. We add a new PM_PREV_LOCATION column in the table to store the changes in the data. As you can see, we added a new column to store data as against SCD2, where we added rows to maintain the history.

If STEVE is now shifted to JAPAN, the data changes to:

PM_PRIMARYKEY	EMPLOYEE_ID	NAME	LOCATION	PM_PREV_LOCATION
100	1001	STEVE	JAPAN	USA

As you can see, we lost INDIA from the data warehouse, and that is why we say we are maintaining partial history.

 To implement SCD3, decide how many versions of a particular column you wish to maintain. Based on this, the columns will be added in the table.

SCD3 is best when you are not interested in maintaining the complete history but are interested in maintaining only partial history. The drawback of SCD3 is that it doesn't store the full history.

At this point, you should be very clear with the different types of SCD. We need to practically implement these concepts in Informatica PowerCenter. Informatica PowerCenter provides a utility called wizard to implement the SCD. Using this wizard, you can easily implement any SCD. In the upcoming chapters, we will learn how to use the wizard to implement SCD1, SCD2, and SCD3.

Before you proceed to the next section, make sure you have a proper understanding of the transformations in Informatica PowerCenter. You should be clear about the source qualifier, expression, filter, router, lookup, update strategy, and sequence generator transformations. The wizard creates a mapping using all these transformations to implement the SCD functionality.

When we implement SCD, there will be some new records that will need to be loaded into the target table, and there will be some existing records for which we need to maintain the history.

 The record that appears for the first time in the table will be referred to as the NEW record, and the record for which we need to maintain the history will be referred to as the CHANGED record. Based on the comparison of the source data with the target data, we will decide which one is the NEW record and which one is the CHANGED record.

To start, we will use a sample file as our source and an Oracle table as our target in order to implement SCDs. Before we implement an SCD, let's talk about the logic that will serve our purpose, and then we will fine-tune the logic for each type of SCD:

1. Extract all records from the source.

2. Look up at the target table and cache all the data.

3. Compare the source data with the target data to flag the NEW and CHANGED records.

4. Filter the data based on the NEW and CHANGED flags.

5. Generate the primary key for every new row inserted into the table.

6. Load the NEW record into the table and update the existing record, if needed.

Based on the specific SCD, the preceding logic will be modified to a certain extent.

SCD1 – I hate history!

To implement SCD1 using wizard, perform the following steps:

1. In the designer, navigate to **Tools | Mapping Designer | Mapping | Wizard | Slowly Changing Dimensions**, as shown in the following screenshot:

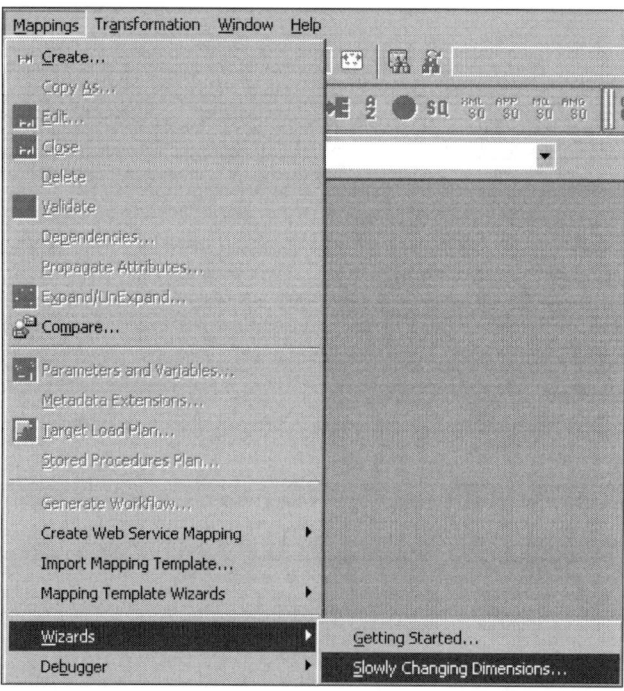

2. A new window will pop up, asking you the name (m_SCD1) of the new SCD mapping. Select **Type 1 Dimension - keep most recent values in the target**, as we are implementing SCD1. Click on **Next** as follows:

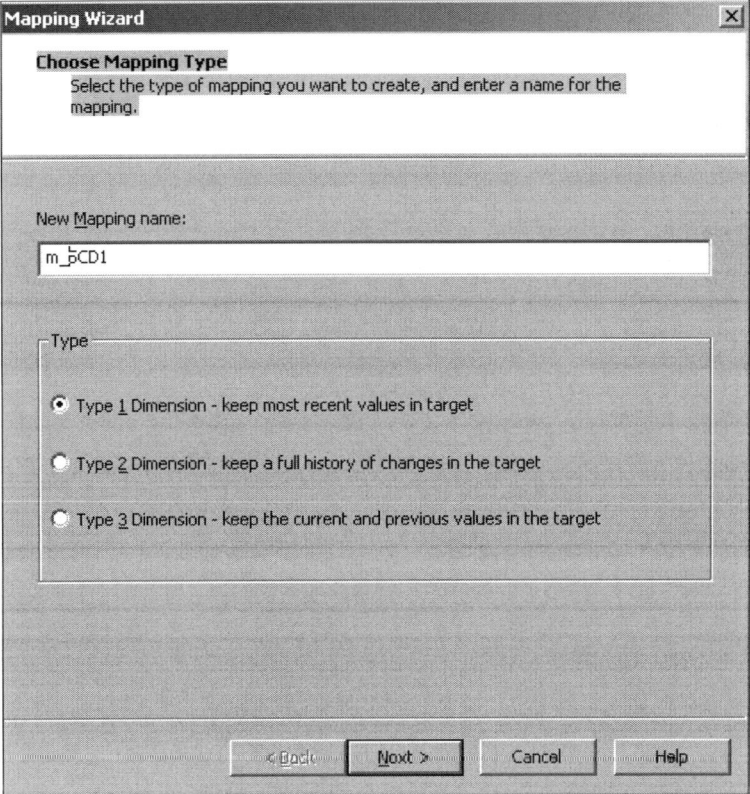

3.   The next screen will ask you to select the source. Select a source from the dropdown. All the sources present in your repository will be listed in this drop-down list. We are using EMP_FILE.txt as the source file for our reference. Also, specify the name of the target you wish to create. We will name the target as EMPLOYEE_SCD1 in this book for our reference. Click on **Next**.

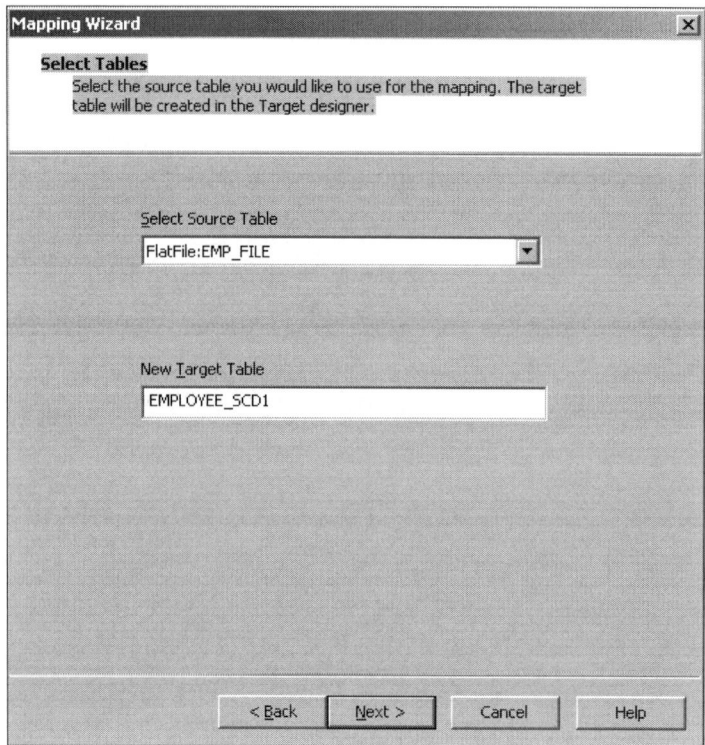

4.   In the next window, select **EMPLOYEE_ID** as **Logical Key Field**. This specifies which column will be used to check for the existence of data in the target. Make sure that the column you use is the Key column of the source. Also, add **LOCATION** under **Fields** to compare the changes. This specifies the column for which you wish to maintain the history. Click on **Finish**.

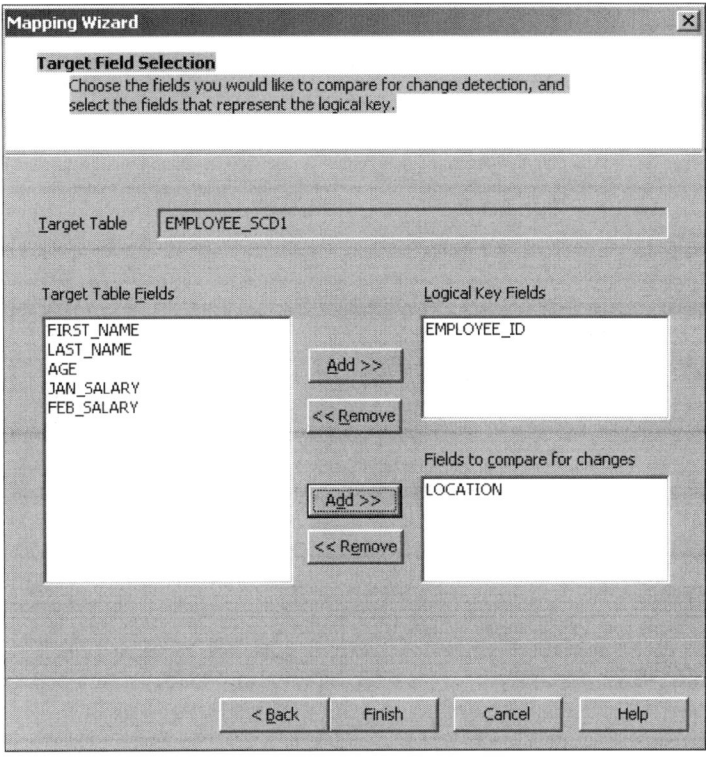

5. The wizard creates a complete mapping in your Mapping Designer Workspace. Make necessary changes to the mapping if required. An example of what your mapping could look like is as follows:

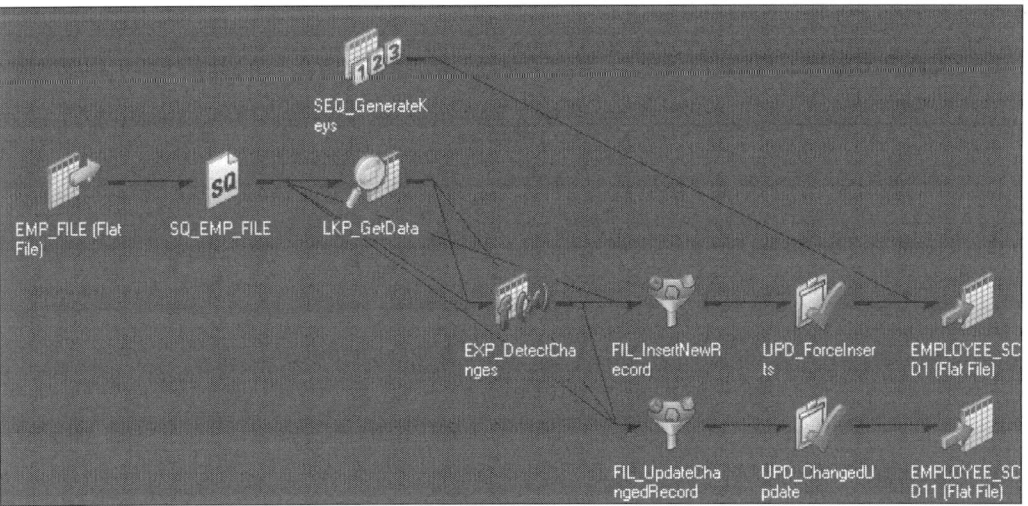

Before we proceed further, we need to make some points clear:

- As we have used flat file as a source, the Informatica PowerCenter wizard generates the target as a file as well. We cannot maintain SCD on files, so make sure you change the target type to the database. We will be changing this to the Oracle table as a reference. You can do this in the Target Designer. Drag the target (EMPLOYEE_SCD1) created by the wizard in the Target Designer, double-click to open the properties, and change the database type of Oracle. This will change the type of target from the file to Oracle. Once you modify the target table to the Oracle database, the mapping will look like the following figure:

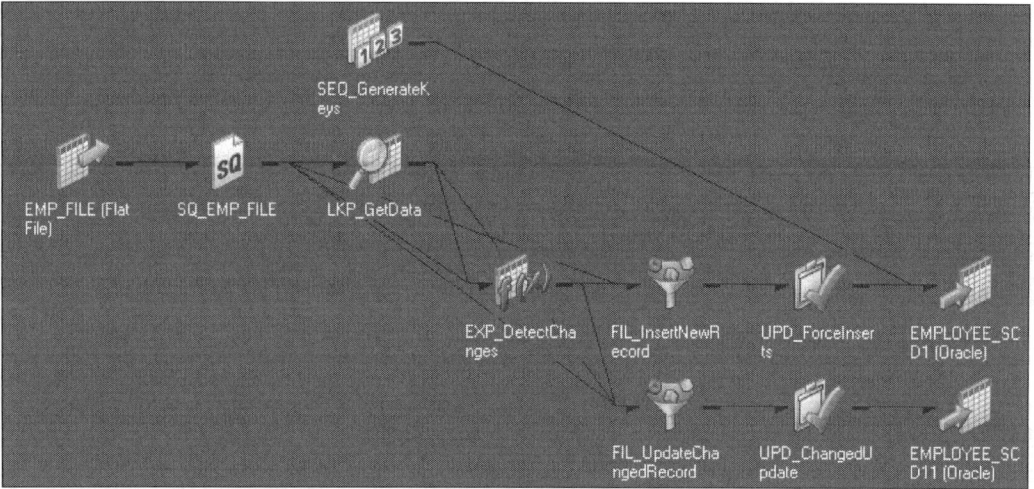

- The wizard creates two instances of the same Oracle target table in the mapping. Load the data from the NEW and CHANGED flows, respectively. Understand clearly that these two structures refer to the same Oracle table EMPLOYEE_SCD1. Even though the name (EMPLOYEE_SCD1 and EMPLOYEE_SCD11) is different in the view, when you double-click on the target instances in the **Table** tab, you can see **Table Name** as EMPLOYEE_SCD1.

As we are done with the mapping, it's time to analyze it. It is very important to understand each component of the mapping.

The Informatica PowerCenter SCD1 mapping uses a lookup transformation to look up the data in the target table and uses expression transformation to compare the target data with the source data. Based on the comparison, the expression transformation marks a record as a NEW flag or a CHANGED flag. The mapping is divided into two flows:

- The FIL_InsertNewRecord filter transformation allows only the NEW record to pass further and filters the records marked as CHANGED from the first flow. It passes new records to UPD_ForceInserts, which inserts these records into the target. The sequence generator generates the primary key for each NEW record.

- The FIL_UpdateChangedRecord filter transformation allows only the CHANGED record to pass further and filters the records marked as NEW from the second flow. It passes the changed records to UPD_ChangedUpdate, which replaces existing rows in the target to reflect the latest changes.

Let's understand each transformation that is used in the SCD1 mapping:

- **The source qualifier** (SQ_EMP_FILE): This extracts the data from the file or table you used as the source in the mapping. It passes data to the downstream transformations, that is, lookup, expression, and filter transformation.

- **Lookup** (LKP_GetData): This is used to look up the target table. It caches the existing data from the EMPLOYEE_SCD1 table.

  The EMPLOYEE_ID=IN_EMPLOYEE_ID condition in the **Condition** tab will compare the data with the source table and the target table. Based on the comparison, it passes the required data to the expression transformation.

- **Expression** (EXP_DetectChanges): This receives the data from the upstream transformation, and based on the comparison, it creates two flags, which are NewFlag and ChangedFlag. In our case, we are using the LOCATION field for comparison.

  For every record that comes from a source, if there is no matching record in target, we can flag that record as NewFlag; that is, the EMPLOYEE_ID != EMPLOYEE_ID condition signifies NewFlag. If no matching record is present for EMPLOYEE_ID in the target, it signifies that PM_PRIMARYKEY will not be available. So, the lookup transformation will return NULL for the PM_PRIMARYKEY column.

For every record that comes from a source, if there is a matching record in the target and if the location from source does not match the location for a particular EMPLOYEE_ID from the target, we can flag that record as ChangedFlag, that is, EMPLOYEE_ID = EMPLOYEE_ID AND LOCATION != PM_PREV_LOCATION:

  ○ The wizard created the condition for NewFlag as IIF(ISNULL(PM_PRIMARYKEY), TRUE, FALSE)

  ○ The condition for ChangedFlag is IIF(NOT ISNULL(PM_PRIMARYKEY) AND (DECODE(LOCATION,PM_PREV_LOCATION,1,0)=0), TRUE, FALSE)

Based on the condition, it passes the data to downstream filter transformations.

- **Filter** (FIL_InsertNewRecord): This filters the records that come from an upstream expression transformation and are marked as ChangedFlag; it only allows records with NewFlag to get passed to the UPD_ForceInserts update strategy.

- **Filter** (FIL_UpdateChangedRecord): This filters the records that come from an upstream expression transformation and are marked as NewFlag; it only allows records with ChangedFlag to get passed to the UPD_ChangedUpdate update strategy.

- **Update strategy** (UPD_ForceInserts): This uses the DD_INSERT condition to insert data into the target, which is EMPLOYEE_SCD1.

- **Update strategy** (UPD_ChangedUpdate): This uses the DD_UPDATE condition to overwrite the existing LOCATION field into the EMPLOYEE_SCD11 target instance.

- **Sequence generator** (SEQ_GenerateKeys): This generates a sequence of values for each row marked as NewFlag, which is then incrementally loaded into the target by 1. It populates the value into PM_PRIMARYKEY in the EMPLOYEE_SCD1 target instance.

- **Target** (EMPLOYEE_SCD1): This is the target table instance that accepts the NewFlag records into the target table.

- **Target** (EMPLOYEE_SCD11): This is the target table instance that accepts the ChangedFlag records into the target table.

SCD2 (version number) – I need my ancestors!

To implement SCD2 using the wizard, perform the following steps:

1. In the Designer, navigate to **Tools | Mapping Designer | Mapping | Wizard | Slowly Changing Dimensions**, as shown in the following screenshot:

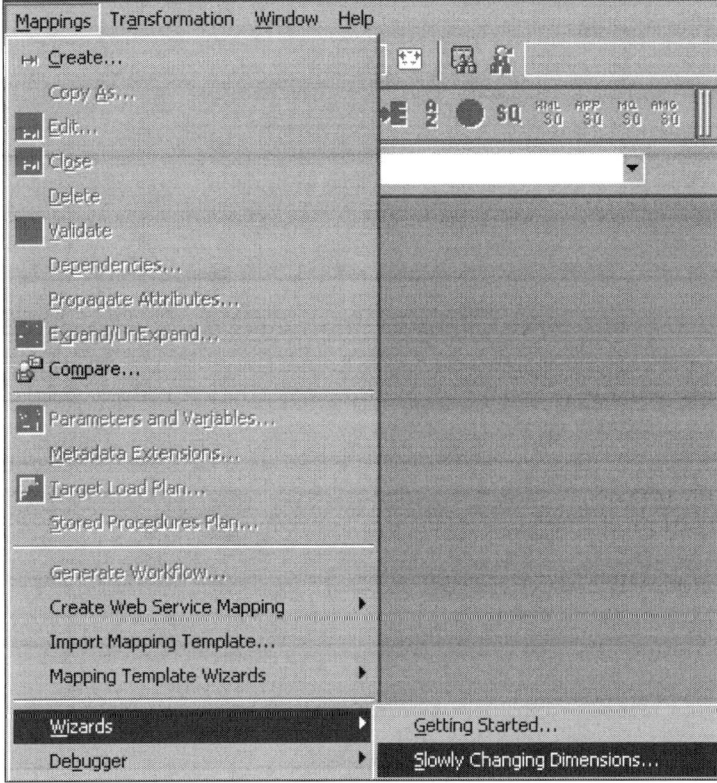

A new window will pop up, asking you the name of the new SCD mapping (m_SCD2_VERSION_NUMBER). Also, select the type of SCD you wish to implement. Select **Type 2 Dimension - keep a full history of the changes in the target**, as we are implementing SCD2 using a version number. Click on **Next**.

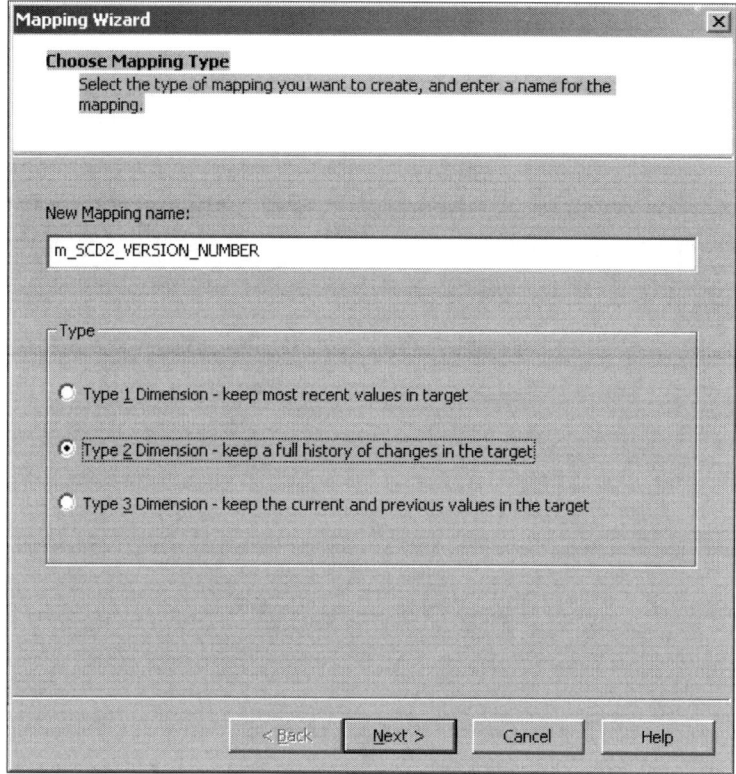

2. The next screen will ask you to select the source. Select a source from the drop-down list. We are using EMP_FILE.txt as the source file for our reference. Also, specify the name of the target you wish to create. We will name the target EMPLOYEE_SCD2_VERSION_NUMBER in this book for our reference. Then, click on **Next**.

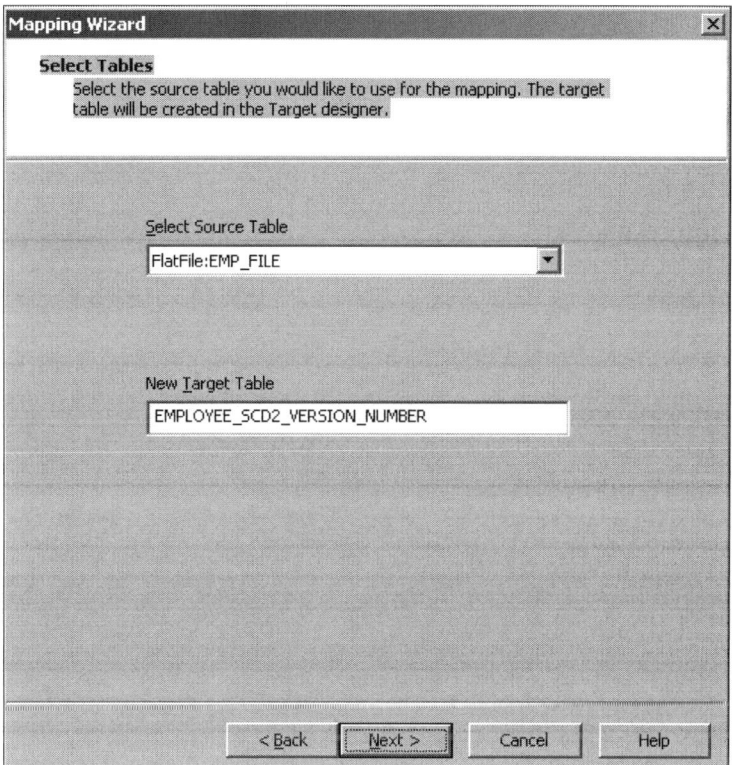

3. In the next window, select EMPLOYEE_ID as **Logical Key Field**. Also, add LOCATION under **Fields** to compare the changes, and then click on **Next**.

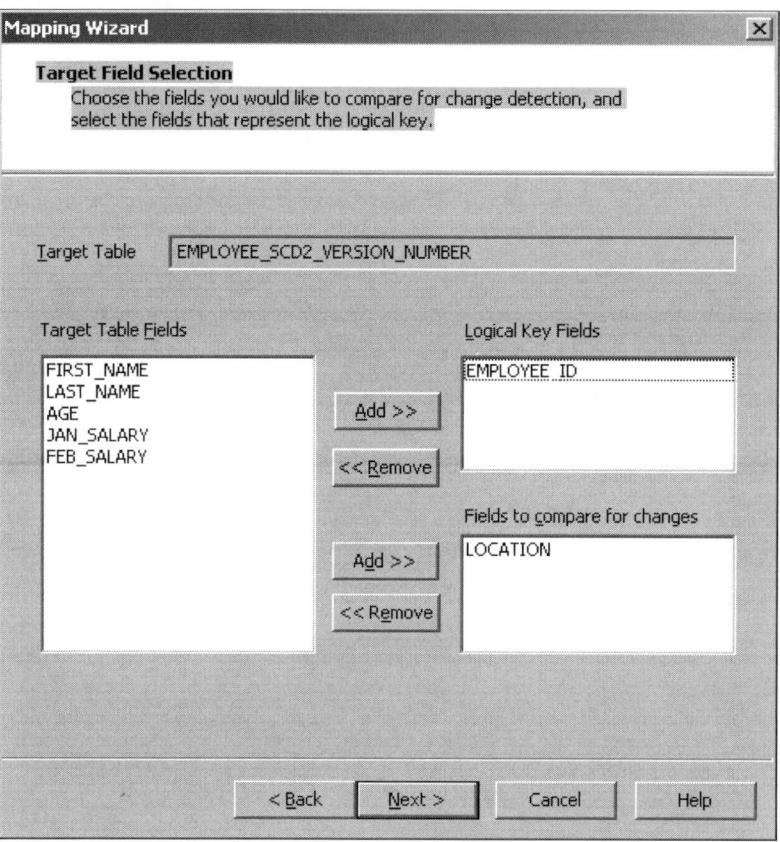

4. The next screen asks you to choose the option to maintain the history in the target. Select **Keep the 'version' number in separate column** and click on **Finish**.

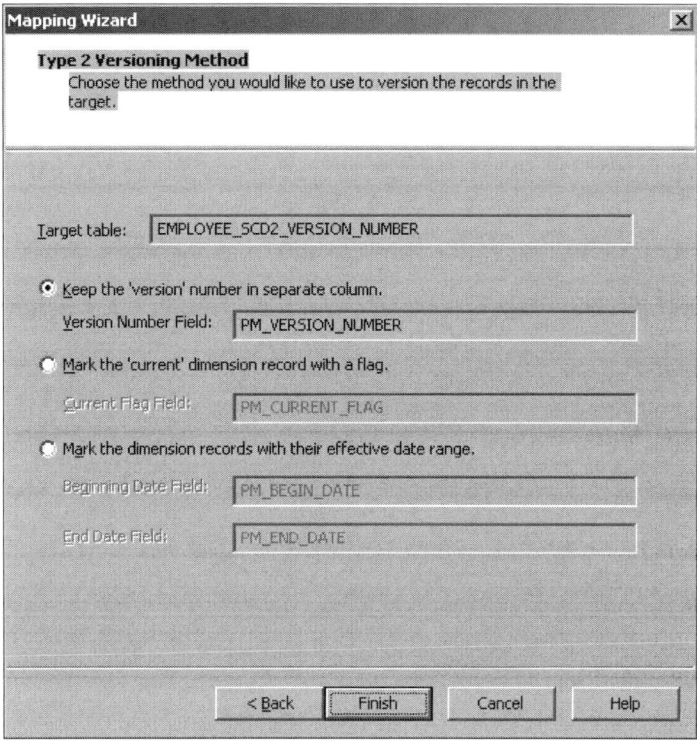

5. The wizard creates a complete mapping in your Mapping Designer Workspace. Make the necessary changes in the mapping, if required.

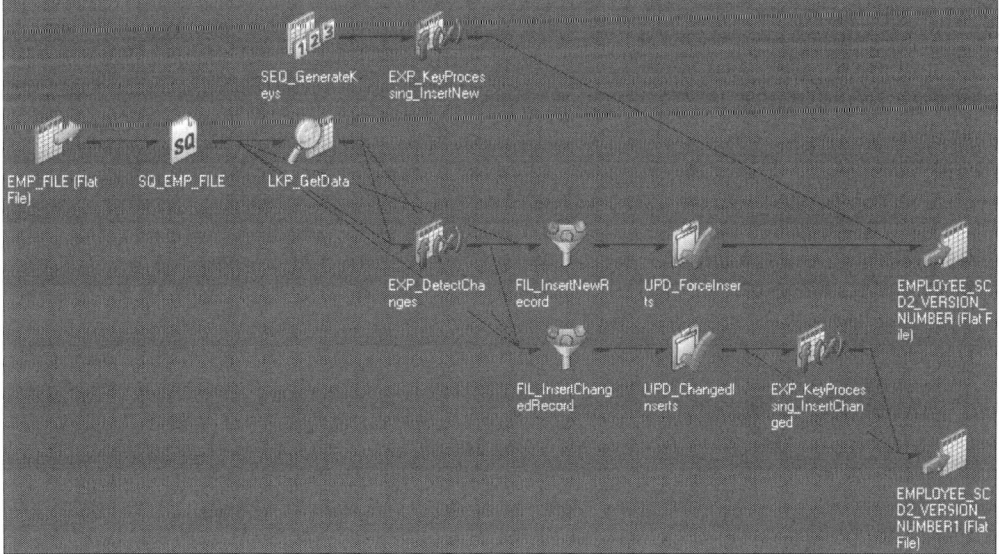

6. Change the target data type from the flat file to `Oracle` table, as shown in the following screenshot:

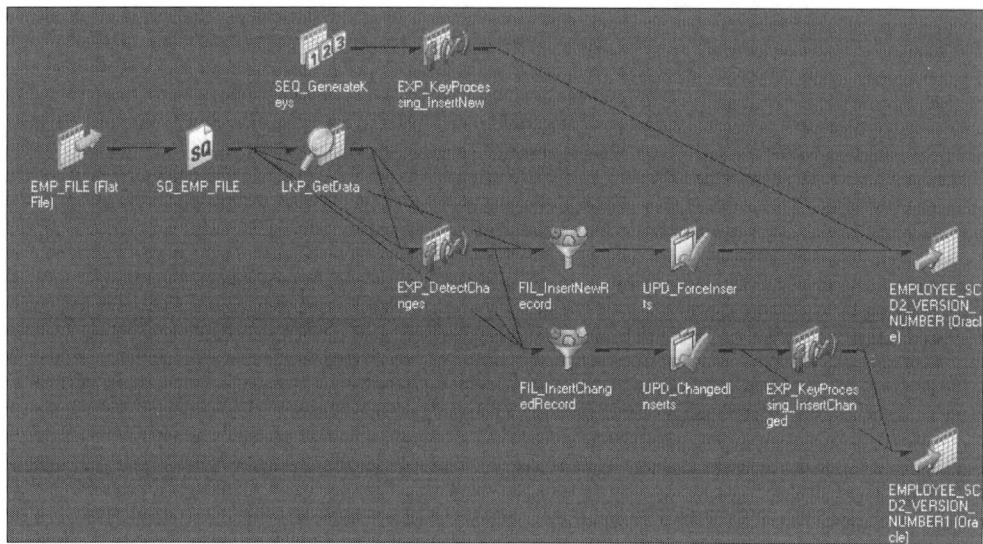

When we create an SCD2 mapping using a version number, the wizard creates two additional columns in the target table:

- `PM_PRIMARY_KEY`: The wizard generates the primary key for each row to be inserted into target. Note that `EMPLOYEE_ID` will not be the primary key in the table.

- `PM_VERSION_NUMBER`: The wizard generates a version number for each row inserted into table; this allows us to differentiate between current and historical records.

The Informatica PowerCenter SCD2 mapping uses a `0` lookup transformation to look up the data in the target table and uses the `EXP_Detect_Changes` expression transformation to compare the target data with the source data. Based on the comparison, the expression transformation marks a record as `NewFlag` or `ChangedFlag` using a flag. The mapping is divided into the following two flows:

- The `FIL_InsertNewRecord` filter transformation allows only the `NewFlag` record to pass further and filters the `ChangedFlag` record from the first flow. It passes new records to `UPD_ForceInserts`, which inserts these records into the target. The sequence generator, which is `SEQ_generateKeys`, generates the primary key for each `NewFlag` record. The `EXP_KeyProcessing_InsertNew` expression transformation multiplies the primary key value by `1000` and loads `0` as the version number for each new row into the target, which is `EMPLOYEE_SCD2_VERSION_NUMBER`.

- The FIL_InsertChangedRecord filter transformation allows only the ChangedFlag record to pass further and filters the records marked as NewFlag from second flow. It passes the changed records to UPD_ChangedUpdate, which replaces existing rows in the target to reflect the latest changes. The expression transformation, which is EXP_KeyProcessing_InsertChanged, increments both the primary key and version number by 1 and loads them into the target instance, which is EMPLOYEE_SCD2_VERSION_NUMBER1.

Let's work through each transformation that is used in the SCD2 mapping:

- **Source qualifier** (SQ_EMP_FILE): This extracts the data from the file or table that you used as a source in the mapping. It passes data to the downstream transformations, that is, lookup, expression, and filter transformation.

- **Lookup** (LKP_GetData): This is used to look up the target table. It caches the existing data from EMPLOYEE_SCD2_VERSION_NUMBER. The EMPLOYEE_ID=IN_EMPLOYEE_ID condition will compare the data with the source table and target table. It passes the data based on the comparison with the expression transformation.

- **Expression** (EXP_DetectChanges): This receives the data from an upstream transformation and based on that, it creates two flags, which are NewFlag and ChangedFlag:

  - **Condition for NewFlag**: IIF(ISNULL(PM_PRIMARYKEY), TRUE, FALSE)

  - **Condition for ChangedFlag**: IIF(NOT ISNULL(PM_PRIMARYKEY) AND (DECODE(LOCATION,PM_PREV_LOCATION,1,0)=0), TRUE, FALSE)

  It passes the data to downstream filter transformations.

- **Filter** (FIL_InsertNewRecord): This filters the records that come from an upstream expression transformation and are marked as ChangedFlag; it only allows records with NewFlag to get passes to the UPD_ForceInserts update strategy.

- **Filter** (FIL_UpdateChangedRecord): This filters the records that come from an upstream expression transformation and are marked as NewFlag; it only allows records with ChangedFlag to get passed to the UPD_ChangedInserts update strategy.

- **Update strategy** (UPD_ForceInserts): This uses the DD_INSERT condition to insert data into the target, which is EMPLOYEE_SCD2_VERSION_NUMBER.

- **Update strategy** (UPD_ChangedInserts): This uses the DD_UPDATE condition to overwrite existing LOCATION value into the target instance, which is EMPLOYEE_SCD2_VERSION_NUMBER1.

- **Sequence generator** (SEQ_GenerateKeys): This generates a sequence of values for each new row marked as NewFlag, which incrementally comes into the target by 1. It populates the value into the PM_PRIMARYKEY column in the EMPLOYEE_SCD2_VERSION_NUMBER target.

- **Expression** (EXP_KeyProcessing_InsertNew): This multiplies NEXTVAL generated by the sequence generator by 1000 using the NEXTVAL*1000 condition. Note that you can change this number as per your requirement. Using 1000 here means that we can maintain a 1000 history of a particular record.

- **Expression** (EXP_KeyProcessing_InsertChanged): This is used to increment the primary key by 1 and also increment the version number by 1 for every changed record.

- **Target** (EMPLOYEE_SCD2_VERSION_NUMBER): This is the target table instance that accepts new records into the target table.

- **Target** (EMPLOYEE_SCD2_VERSION_NUMBER1): This is the target table instance that accepts changed records into the target table.

SCD2 (flag) – flag the history

To implement SCD2 by maintaining the flag, perform the following steps:

1. In the designer, navigate to **Tools** | **Mapping Designer** | **Mapping** | **Wizard** | **Slowly Changing Dimensions**, as shown in the following screenshot:

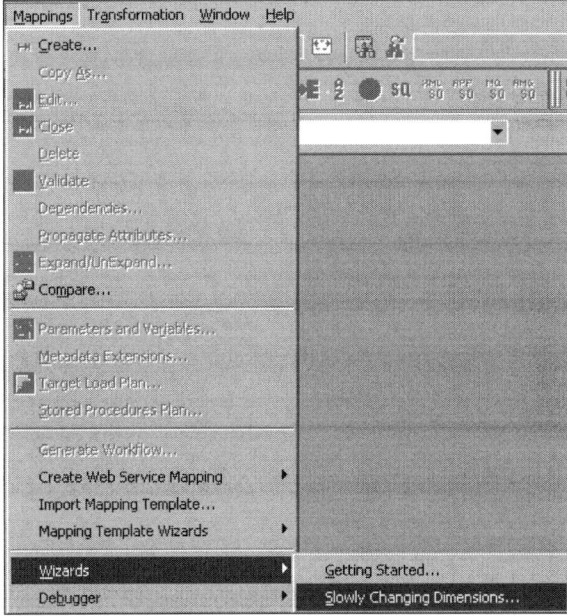

A new window will pop up, asking you the name (m_SCD2_FLAG) of the new SCD2 mapping. Select **Type 2 Dimension - keep a full history of the changes in the target**, as we are implementing SCD2, and click on **Next**.

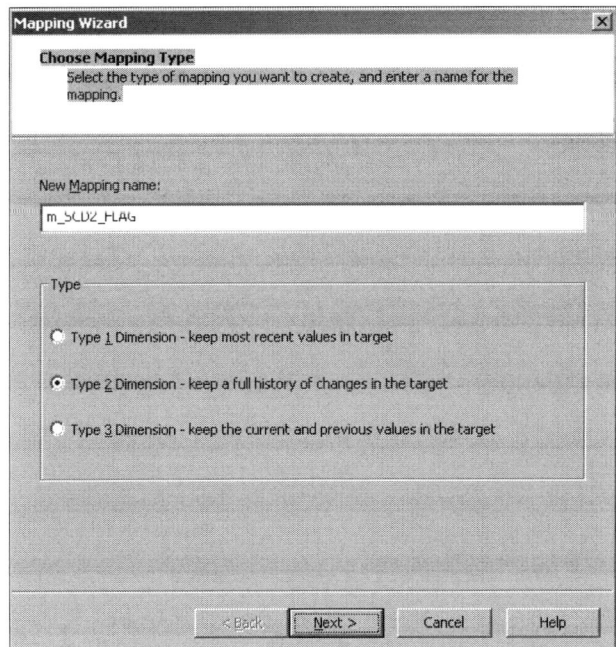

2. The next screen will ask you to select the source. Select a source from the drop-down list. We are using `EMP_FILE.txt` as the source file for our reference. Also, specify the name of the target you wish to create. We will name the target `EMPLOYEE_SCD2_FLAG` in this book for our reference. Then, click on **Next**.

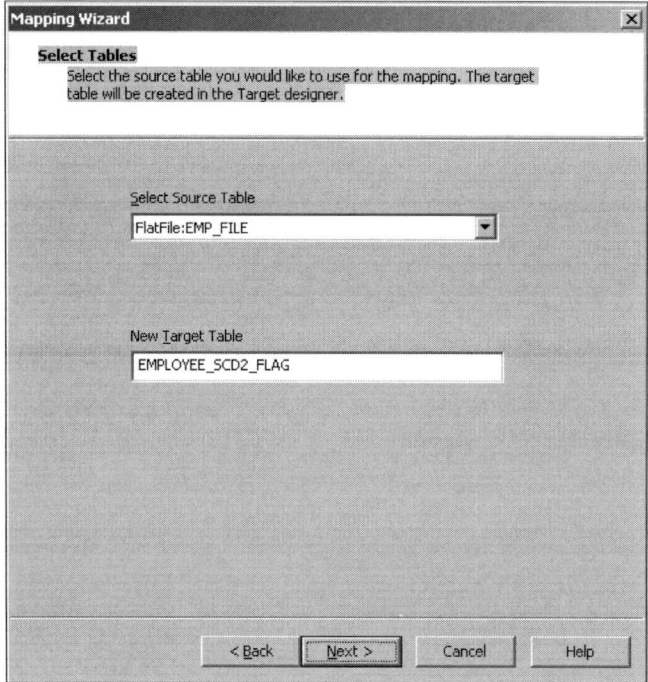

3. In the next window, select `EMPLOYEE_ID` as **Logical Key Field**. Also, add `LOCATION` under **Fields** to compare the changes, and click on **Next**.

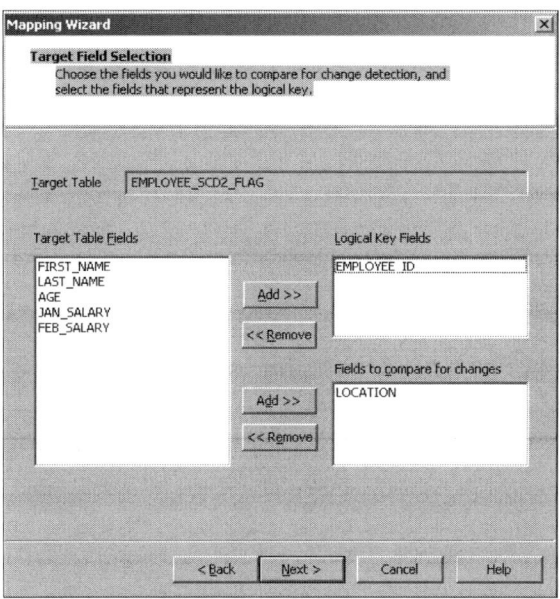

4. The next screen asks you to choose the option to maintain the history in the target. Select **Mark the 'current' dimension record with a flag**, and click on **Finish**.

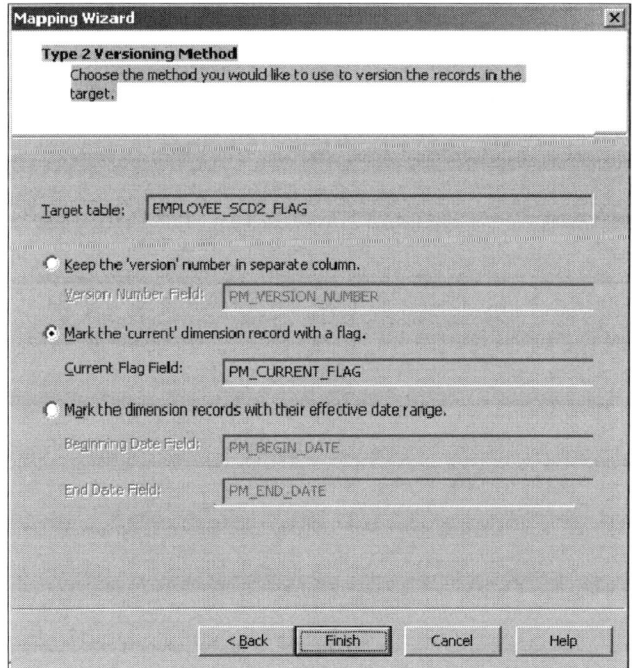

5. The wizard generates a complete mapping in your Mapping Designer Workspace. Make the necessary changes to the mapping, if required.

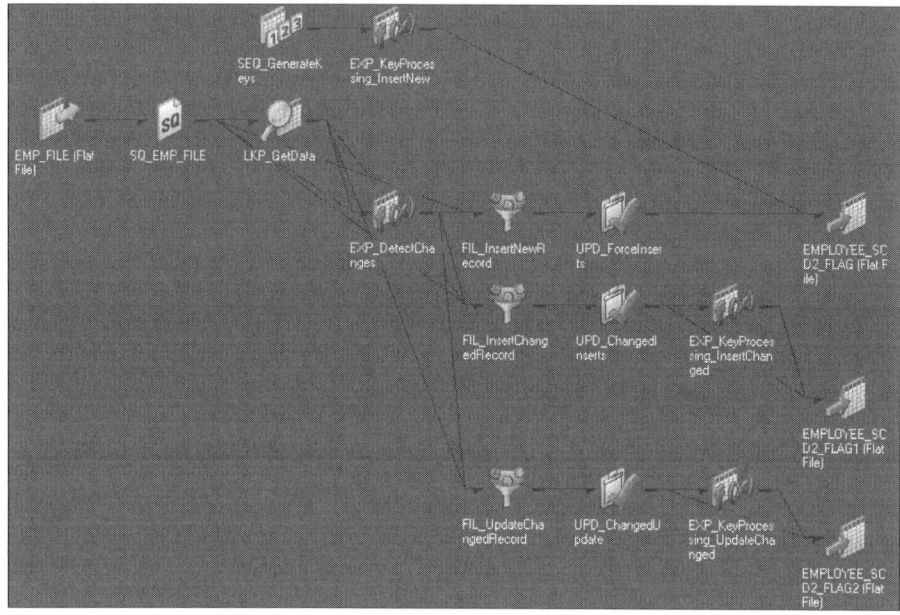

6. Change the target data type from the flat file to `Oracle` table, as shown in the following figure:

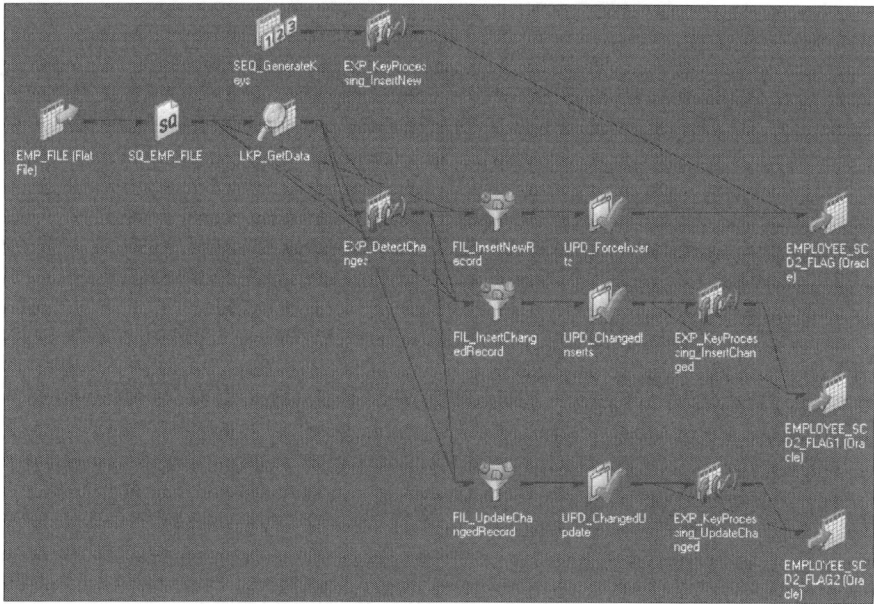

When we create a mapping using the flag option, the wizard creates the following two additional columns in the target table:

- PM_PRIMARY_KEY: The wizard generates the primary key for each row to be inserted into the target. Please note that EMPLOYEE_ID will not be the primary key in the table.

- PM_CURRENT_FLAG: The wizard loads 1 for each new record inserted into the table and marks all history records as 0; this will allow us to differentiate between current and historical records.

The Informatica PowerCenter SCD2 mapping uses the LKP_GetData lookup transformation to look up the data in the target table and uses the EXP_DetectChanges expression transformation to compare the data with the source data. Based on the comparison, the expression transformation marks a record as NewFlag or ChangedFlag. The mapping is divided into three flows:

- The FIL_InsertNewRecord filter transformation allows only the NewFlag record to pass further and filter the ChangedFlag record from the first flow. It passes new records to UPD_ForceInserts, which inserts these records into the target. The SEQ_GenerateKeys sequence generator generates the primary key for each NewFlag record. The EXP_KeyProcessing_InsertNew expression transformation multiplies the NEXTVAL value by 1000 and loads 1 as the current flag for each new row.

- The FIL_InsertChangedRecord filter transformation allows only the ChangedFlag record to get passed to UPD_ChangedInserts, which inserts changed records into the target, which is EMPLOYEE_SCD2_FLAG1. The EXP_KeyProcessing_InsertChanged expression transformation increments the primary key by 1 and loads the current flag as 1 to indicate that the updated row contains the current data.

- The FIL_UpdateChangedRecord filter transformation passes the primary key of the previous value for every ChangedFlag record to UPD_ChangedUpdate, which updates changed records in the target, which is EMPLOYEE_SCD2_FLAG2. The EXP_KeyProcessing_UpdateChanged expression transformation changes the current flag to 0 to indicate the row doesn't contain the current data anymore.

Let's work through each transformation that is used in the SCD2 mapping:

- **Source qualifier** (SQ_EMP_FILE): This extracts the data from the file or table that you used as the source in the mapping. It passes data to the downstream transformations, that is, lookup, expression, and filter transformation.

- **Lookup** (LKP_GetData): This is used to look up the target table. It caches the existing data from EMPLOYEE_SCD2_FLAG. The EMPLOYEE_ID=IN_EMPLOYEE_ID condition will compare the data with the source and target table. It passes the data based on the comparison with the expression transformation.

- **Expression** (EXP_DetectChanges): This receives the data from the upstream transformation and based on that, it creates two flags, which are NewFlag and ChangedFlag:

    ○ **Condition for NewFlag**: IIF(ISNULL(PM_PRIMARYKEY), TRUE, FALSE)

    ○ **Condition for ChangedFlag**: IIF(NOT ISNULL(PM_PRIMARYKEY) AND (DECODE(LOCATION,PM_PREV_LOCATION,1,0)=0), TRUE, FALSE)

  Based on the condition, it passes the data to downstream filter transformations.

- **Filter** (FIL_InsertNewRecord): This filters the records that come from the upstream expression transformation and are marked as ChangedFlag; it only allows records as NewFlag to get passed to the UPD_ForceInserts update strategy.

- **Filter** (FIL_InsertChangedRecord): This filters the records that come from the upstream expression transformation and are marked as NewFlag; it only allows records as ChangedFlag to get passed to the UPD_ChangedInserts update strategy.

- **Filter** (FIL_UpdateChangedRecord): This filters the records that come from the upstream expression transformation and are marked as NewFlag; it only allows records marked as ChangedFlag to pass. For every record marked as ChangedFlag, the filter passes the primary key of the previous version to the UPD_ChangedUpdate update strategy.

- **Update strategy** (UPD_ForceInserts): This uses the DD_INSERT condition to insert the data into the EMPLOYEE_SCD2_FLAG target instance.

- **Update strategy** (UPD_ChangedInserts): This uses the DD_INSERT condition to insert data into target instance EMPLOYEE_SCD2_FLAG1.

- **Update strategy** (UPD_ChangedUpdate): This uses the DD_UPDATE condition to overwrite the existing LOCATION value into the target, which is EMPLOYEE_SCD2_FLAG2.

- **Sequence generator** (SEQ_GenerateKeys): This generates a sequence of values for PM_PRIMARYKEY for each row marked as NewFlag into the target, incrementing the value by 1.

- **Expression** (EXP_KeyProcessing_InsertNew): This multiplies NEXTVAL generated by the sequence generator by 1000 using the NEXTVAL*1000 condition. Note that you can change this number as per your requirement. Using 1000 here means that we can maintain a 1000 history of a particular record. This creates a current flag of 1 for each NewFlag record to load into the PM_CURRENT_FLAG column in the target.

- **Expression** (EXP_KeyProcessing_InsertChanged): This is used to increment the primary key by 1 using the PM_PRIMARYKEY + 1 condition. It also creates a current flag of 1 for each NewFlag record to load the PM_CURRENT_FLAG column in the target.

- **Expression** (EXP_KeyProcessing_UpdateChanged): This is used to set PM_CURRENT_FLAG to 0 for the record marked as Changed, indicating that the record is no longer current.

- **Target** (EMPLOYEE_SCD2_FLAG): This is the target table instance that accepts new records into the target table.

- **Target** (EMPLOYEE_SCD2_FLAG1): This is the target table instance that accepts changed records into the target table.

- **Target** (EMPLOYEE_SCD2_FLAG2): This is the target table instance that allows updates to existing records into the target table.

SCD2 (date range) – marking the dates

To implement SCD2 by maintaining flags, perform the following steps:

1. In the designer, navigate to **Tools | Mapping Designer | Mapping | Wizard | Slowly Changing Dimensions**, as shown in the following screenshot:

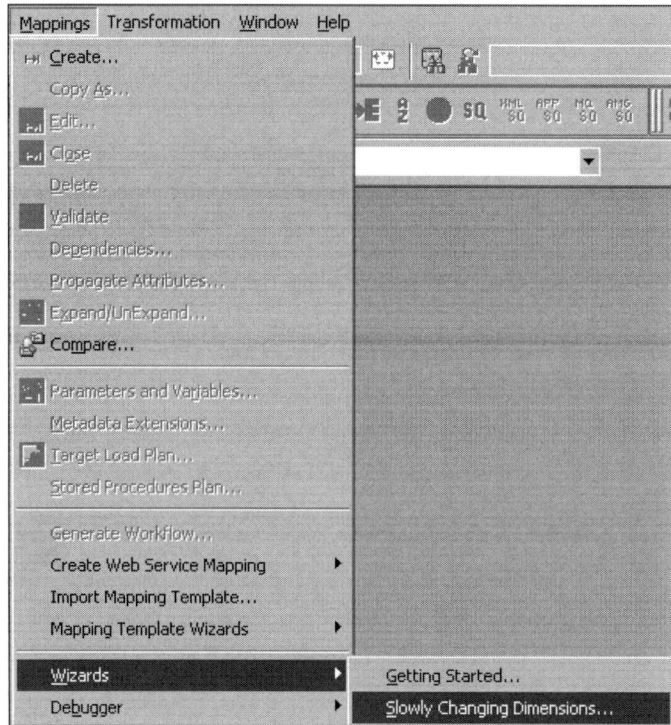

A new window will pop up, asking you the name (m_SCD2_DATE_RANGE) of the new SCD mapping. Select **Type 2 Dimension - keep a full history of the changes in the target**, as we are implementing SCD2, and click on **Next**.

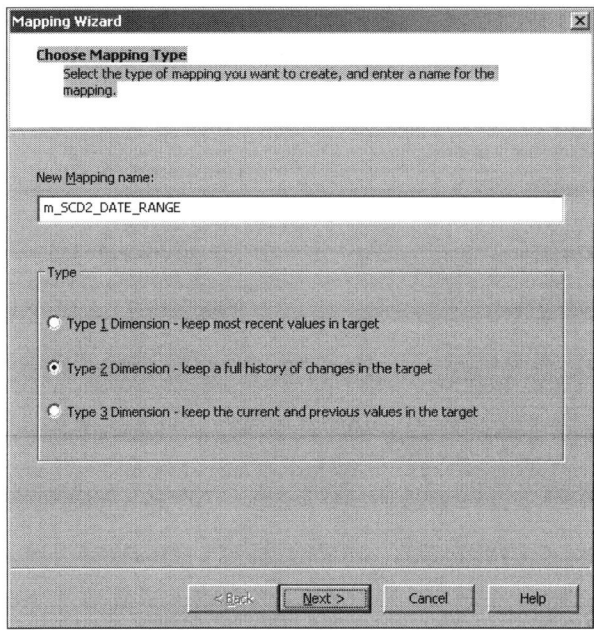

2. The next screen will ask you to select the source. Select a source from the drop-down list. We are using `EMP_FILE.txt` as the source file for our reference. Also, specify the name of the target you wish to create. We will name the target `EMPLOYEE_SCD2_DATE_RANGE` in this book for our reference. Then, click on **Next**.

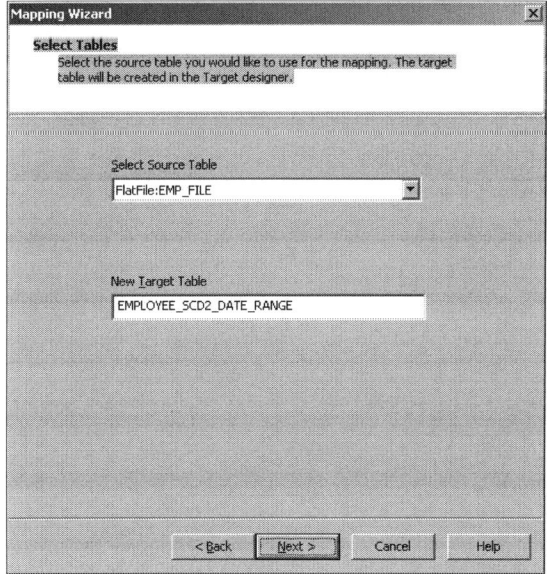

3. In the next window, select EMPLOYEE_ID as **Logical Key Field**. Also, add LOCATION under **Fields** to compare the changes, and click on **Next**.

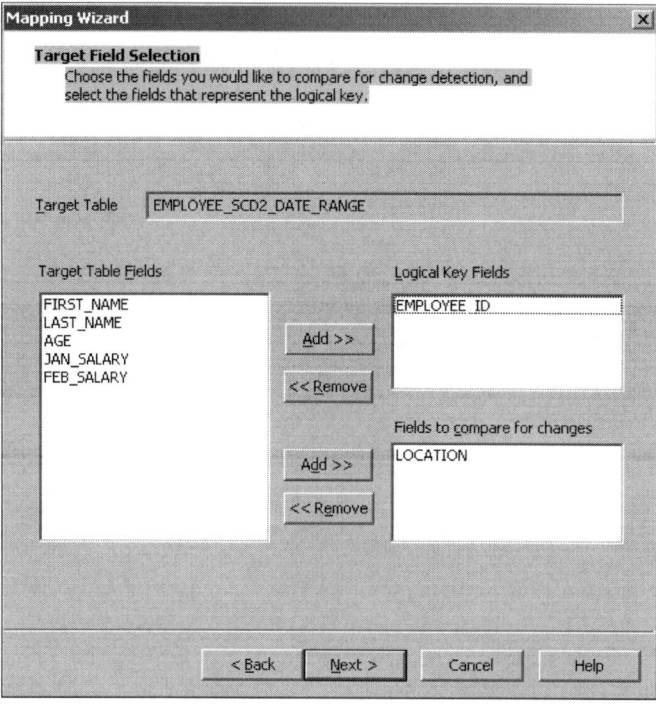

4. The next screen asks you to choose the option to maintain the history in the target. Select **Mark the dimension records with their effective date range** and click on **Finish**.

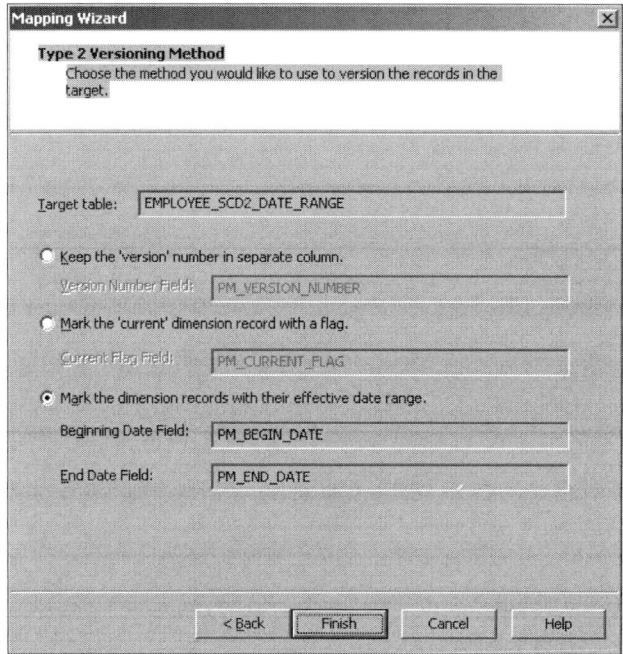

5. The wizard generates a complete mapping in your Mapping Designer Workspace. Make the necessary changes to the mapping if required.

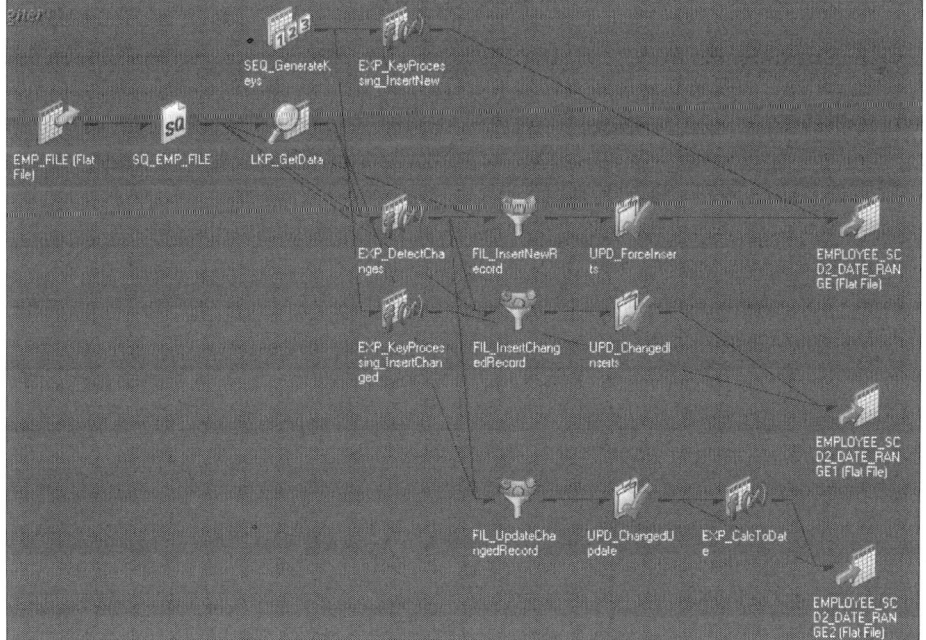

6. Change the target data type from the flat file to the `Oracle` table, as shown in the following figure:

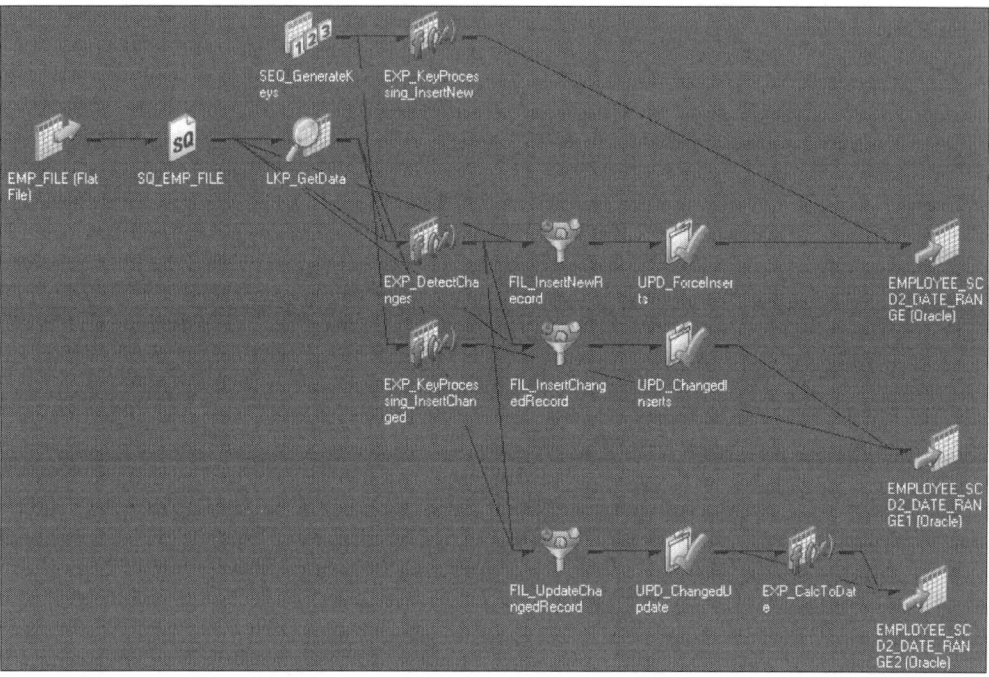

When we create a mapping using this option, the wizard create three additional columns in the target table:

- `PM_PRIMARY_KEY`: The wizard generates the primary key for each row to be inserted into the target. Note that `EMPLOYEE_ID` will not be the primary key in the table.

- `PM_BEGIN_DATE`: The wizard loads `SYSTEMDATE` for each `NewFlag` and `ChangeFlag` record inserted into the table.

- `PM_END_DATE`: The wizard loads `SYSTEMDATE` for each updated record inserted into the table, indicating the end date of the record.

The Informatica PowerCenter SCD2 mapping uses the LKP_GetData lookup transformation to look up the data in the target table and uses the EXP_DetectChanges expression transformation to compare the data with the source data. Based on the comparison, the expression transformation marks a record as NewFlag or ChangedFlag. The mapping is divided into three flows:

- The FIL_InsertNewRecord filter transformation allows only the NewFlag record to pass further and filter ChangedFlag from the first flow. It passes the NewFlag records to UPD_ForceInserts, which inserts these records into the EMPLOYEE_SCD2_DATE_RANGE target instance. The SEQ_GenerateKeys sequence generator generates the primary key for each NewFlag record. The EXP_KeyProcessing_InsertNew expression transformation loads SYSTEMDATE into the PM_BEGIN_DATE column and leaves PM_END_DATE as null. This indicates that the new record has been added from the date loaded in PM_BEGIN_DATE.

- The FIL_InsertChangedRecord filter transformation allows only the ChangedFlag record to get passed to UPD_ChangedInserts, which inserts changed records in the EMPLOYEE_SCD2_DATE_RANGE1 target instance. For every ChangedFlag record, the EXP_KeyProcessing_InsertChanged expression transformation loads SYSTEMDATE into the PM_BEGIN_DATE column and leaves PM_END_DATE as null. This indicates that the changed record has been added, and the changed row now contains the current data.

- The FIL_UpdateChangedRecord filter transformation passes the primary key of the previous value for every ChangedFlag record to UPD_ChangedUpdate, which inserts changed records into the target, which is EMPLOYEE_SCD2_DATE_RANGE2. The EXP_CalcToDate expression transformation loads SYSTEMDATE into PM_END_DATE to indicate that the row now contains the historical data.

Let's understand each transformation that is used in the SCD2 mapping:

- **Source qualifier** (SQ_EMP_FILE): This extracts the data from the file or table that you used as the source in the mapping. It passes data to the downstream transformations, that is, lookup, expression, and filter transformation.

- **Lookup** (LKP_GetData): This is used to look up the target table. It caches the existing data from EMPLOYEE_SCD2_DATE_RANGE. The EMPLOYEE_ID=IN_EMPLOYEE_ID condition will compare the data with the source table and target table. It passes the data based on the comparison with the expression transformation.

- **Expression** (EXP_DetectChanges): This receives the data from the upstream transformation and based on that, it creates two flags, which are NewFlag and ChangedFlag:

    ◦ **Condition for NewFlag**: IIF(ISNULL(PM_PRIMARYKEY), TRUE, FALSE)

    ◦ **Condition for ChangedFlag**: IIF(NOT ISNULL(PM_PRIMARYKEY) AND (DECODE(LOCATION,PM_PREV_LOCATION,1,0)=0), TRUE, FALSE)

    Based on the condition, it passes the data to downstream filter transformations.

- **Filter** (FIL_InsertNewRecord): This filters the records that come from the upstream expression transformation and are marked as ChangedFlag; it allows records with NewFlag to get passed to the UPD_ForceInserts update strategy.

- **Filter** (FIL_InsertChangedRecord): This filters the records that come from the upstream expression transformation and are marked as NewFlag; it allows records with ChangedFlag to get passed to the UPD_ForceInserts update strategy.

- **Filter** (FIL_UpdateChangedRecord): This filters the records that come from the upstream expression transformation and are marked as NewFlag; it allows records with ChangedFlag to get passed to the UPD_ChangedUpdate update strategy. For each row marked as ChangedFlag, it passes the primary key of the previous version to UPD_ChangedUpdate.

- **Update strategy** (UPD_ForceInserts): This uses the DD_INSERT condition to insert data into the EMPLOYEE_SCD2_DATE_RANGE target instance.

- **Update strategy** (UPD_ChangedInserts): This uses the DD_INSERT condition to insert data into the EMPLOYEE_SCD2_DATE_RANGE1 target instance.

- **Update strategy** (UPD_ChangedUpdate): This uses the DD_UPDATE condition to overwrite the existing LOCATION value into the EMPLOYEE_SCD2_DATE_RANGE2 target instance.

- **Sequence generator** (SEQ_GenerateKeys): This generates a sequence of values for each new row marked as NewFlag that comes into target, getting incremented by 1. It passes the value to EXP_KeyProcessing_InsertNew.

- **Expression** (EXP_KeyProcessing_InsertNew): This loads the generated value in the PM_PRIMARYKEY column in the EMPLOYEE_SCD2_DATE_RANGE target instance. It loads SYSTEMDATE into the PM_BEGIN_DATE column in the target, marking the start of the record.

- **Expression** (EXP_KeyProcessing_InsertChanged): This loads the generated value in the PM_PRIMARYKEY column in the EMPLOYEE_SCD2_DATE_RANGE1 target instance. It loads SYSTEMDATE into the PM_BEGIN_DATE column in the target, marking the start of the record in the EMPLOYEE_SCD2_DATE_RANGE1 target instance.

- **Expression** (EXP_CalcToDate): This uses SYSTEMDATE to update the PM_END_DATE column in the EMPLOYEE_SCD2_DATE_RANGE2 target instance in an existing record, indicating that the record is not current anymore.

- **Target** (EMPLOYEE_SCD2_DATE_RANGE): This is the target table instance that accepts new records in the target table.

- **Target** (EMPLOYEE_SCD2_DATE_RANGE1): This is the target table instance that accepts changed records in the target table.

- **Target** (EMPLOYEE_SCD2_DATE_RANGE2): This is the target table instance that allows updates to existing records in the target table.

SCD3 – store something, if not everything!

To implement SCD3 using wizard, perform the following steps:

1. In the designer, navigate to **Tools | Mapping Designer | Mapping | Wizard | Slowly Changing Dimensions**, as shown in the following screenshot:

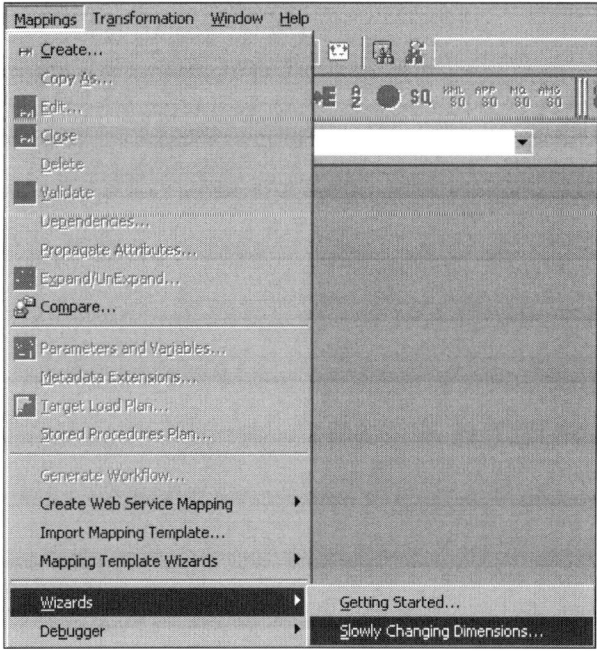

2. A new window will pop up, asking you the name (m_SCD3) of the new SCD mapping. Also, select the type of SCD you wish to implement. Select **Type 3 Dimension - keep the current and previous value in the target**, as we are implementing SCD3, and click on **Next**.

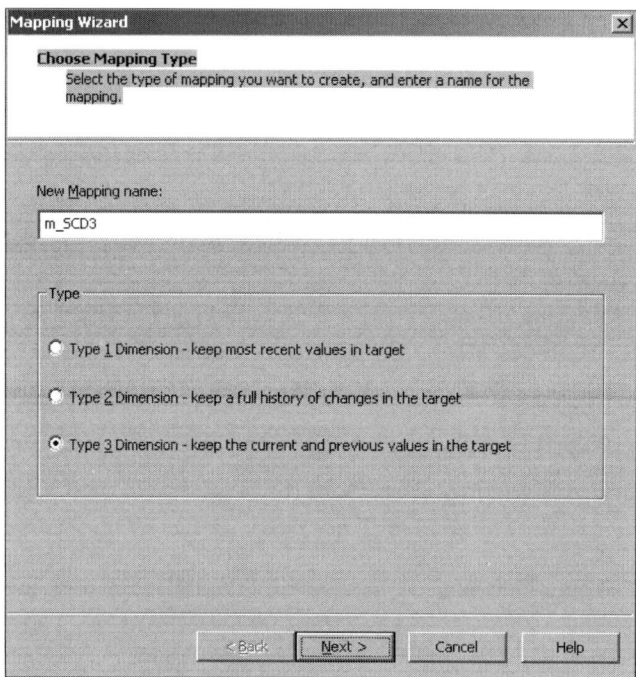

3. The next screen will ask you to select the source. Select a source from the dropdown. We are using EMP_FILE.txt as the source file for our reference. We will name the target as EMPLOYEE_SCD3 in this book for our reference. Then, click on **Next**.

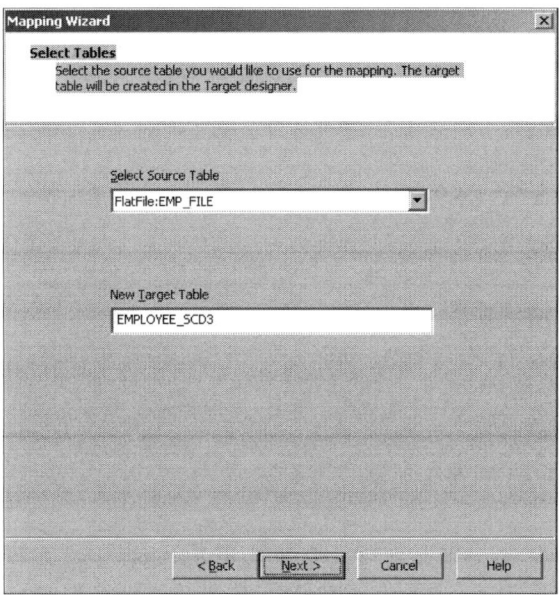

4. In the next window, select EMPLOYEE_ID as **Logical Key Field**. Also, add LOCATION under **Fields** to compare the changes and click on **Next**.

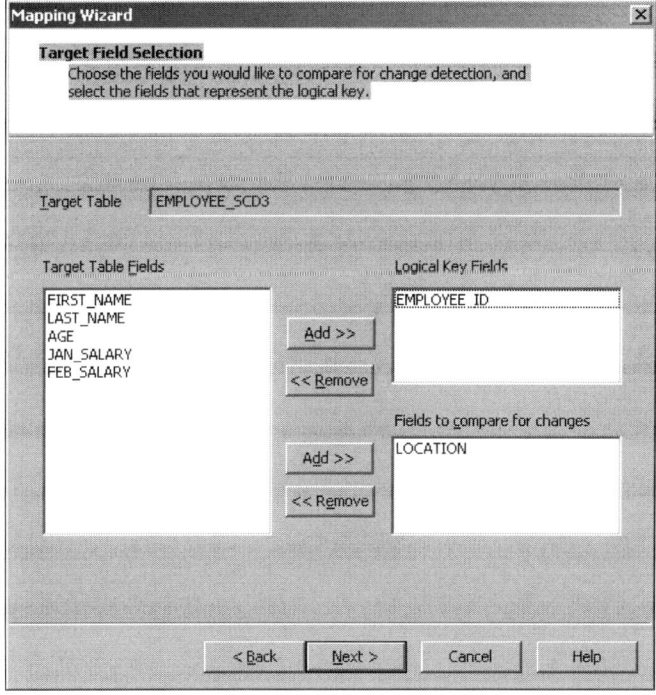

5. In the next window, select the target columns that you wish to compare in order to detect changes. In our case, the LOCATION column in the target will be compared against PM_PREV_LOCATION. You can select a PM_EFFECT_DATE optional field to understand the loading of new or changed records, and click on **Finish**.

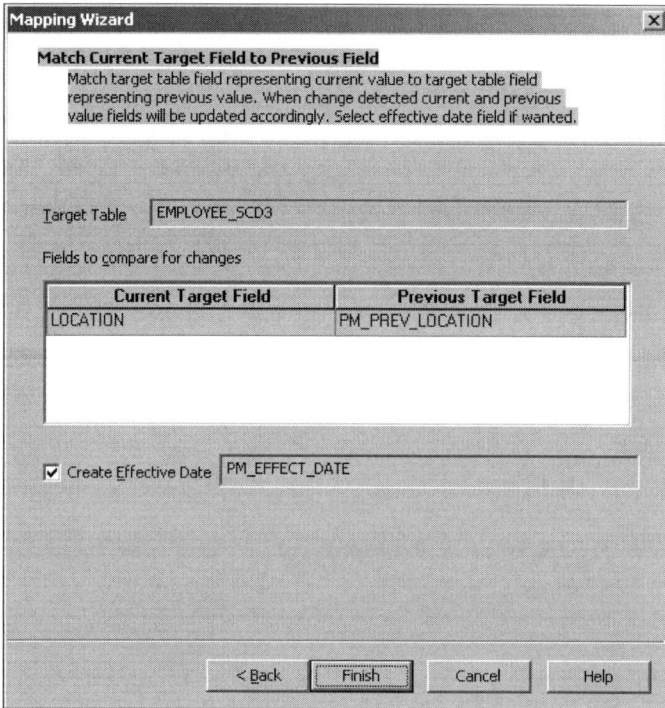

6. The wizard generates a complete mapping in your Mapping Designer Workspace. Make the necessary changes to the mapping if required.

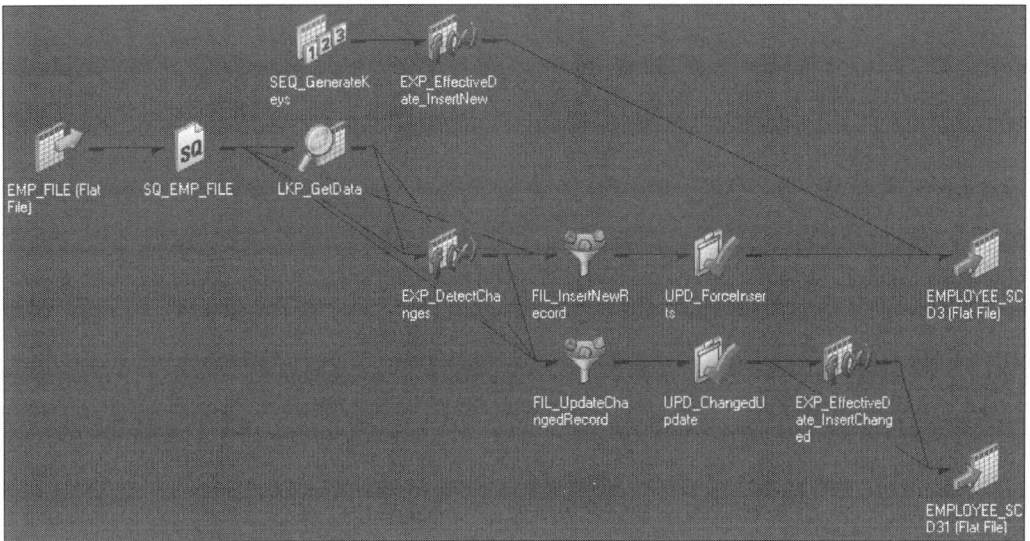

7. Change the target data type from the flat file to the `Oracle` table, as shown in the following figure:

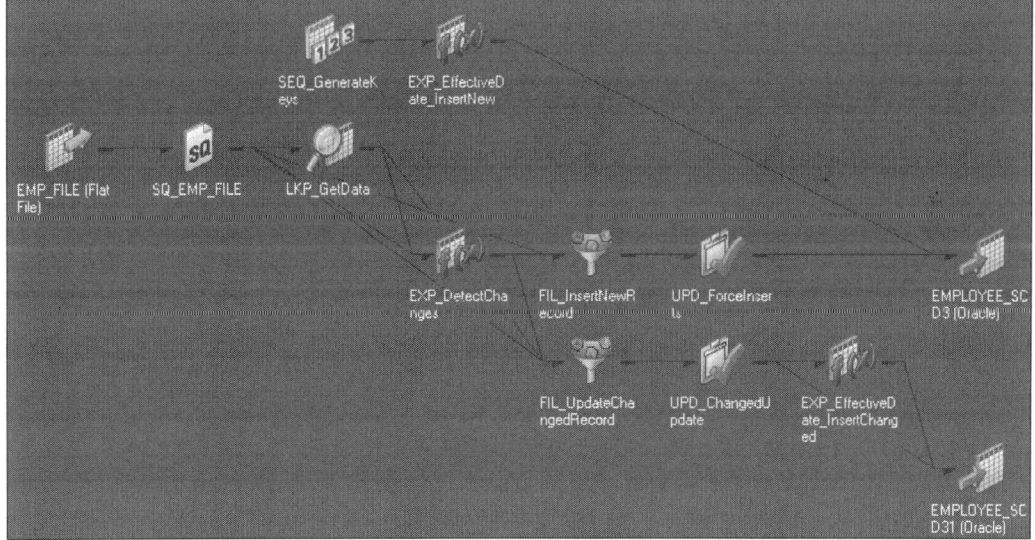

When we create the mapping using this option, the wizard creates three additional columns in the target table:

- PM_PRIMARY_KEY: The wizard generates the primary key for each row to be inserted into target. Note that EMPLOYEE_ID will not be the primary key in the table.

- PM_PREV_columnName: For every column for which we maintain the history, the wizard generates a previous column. In our case, we wish to maintain the history for the LOCATION field, so the wizard creates another column, which is PM_PREV_LOCATION.

- PM_EFFECT_DATE: This is an optional field; the wizard loads SYSTEMDATE in this column to indicate insertions or updates to the record in the table.

The Informatica Power Center SCD2 mapping uses the LKP_GetData lookup transformation to look up the data in the Target table and uses the EXP_DetectChanges expression transformation to compare the target data with the source data. Based on the comparison, the expression transformation marks a record as NewFlag or ChangedFlag. The mapping is divided into two flows:

- The FIL_InsertNewRecord filter transformation allows only NewFlag record to pass further and filter the ChangedFlag record from the first flow. It passes new records to UPD_ForceInserts, which inserts these records into the target. The SEQ_GenerateKeys sequence generator generates the primary key for each NewFlag record. If you select to create the PM_EFFECT_DATE column option in the wizard, the EXP_EffectiveDate_InsertNew expression transformation loads SYSTEMDATE into the PM_EFFECT_DATE column to indicate the loading of new records.

- The FIL_UpdateChangedRecord filter transformation allows only the ChangedFlag record to pass further. The current data is passed from the SQ_EMP_FILE source qualifier, and the previous data is taken from the target by using a lookup transformation to load the data in PM_PREV_LOCATION. It passes changed records to UPD_ChangedUpdates, which updates changed records in the target. If you select to create the PM_EFFECT_DATE column in the wizard, the expression transformation EXP_EffectiveDate_InsertChanged updates SYSTEMDATE in the PM_EFFECT_DATE column to indicate that new records have been updated.

Let's work through each transformation that is used in the SCD2 mapping:

- **Source qualifier** (SQ_EMP_FILE): This extracts the data from the file or table that you used as the source in the mapping. It passes data to the downstream transformations, that is, lookup, expression, and filter transformation.

- **Lookup** (LKP_GetData): This is used to look up the target table. It caches the existing data from EMPLOYEE_SCD3. The EMPLOYEE_ID=IN_EMPLOYEE_ID condition will compare the data with the source table and target table. It passes the data based on the comparison with the expression transformation.

- **Expression** (EXP_DetectChanges): This receives the data from the upstream transformation and based on that, it creates two flags, which are NewFlag and ChangedFlag. The conditions for both the flags are as follows:
    - ○ NewFlag: IIF(ISNULL(PM_PRIMARYKEY), TRUE, FALSE)
    - ○ ChangedFlag: IIF(NOT ISNULL(PM_PRIMARYKEY) AND (DECODE(LOCATION,PM_PREV_LOCATION,1,0)=0), TRUE, FALSE)

    Based on the condition, it passes the data to downstream filter transformations.

- **Filter** (FIL_InsertNewRecord): This filters the records that come from the upstream expression transformation and are marked as ChangedFlag; it allows records with NewFlag to get passed to the UPD_ForceInserts update strategy.

- **Filter** (FIL_UpdateChangedRecord): This filters the records that come from the upstream expression transformation and are marked as NewFlag; it allows records with ChangedFlag to get passed to the UPD_ChangedUpdate update strategy. It uses the value of the LOCATION field that is returned from LKP_GetData to load PM_PREV_LOCATION.

- **Update strategy** (UPD_ForceInserts): This uses the DD_INSERT condition to insert data into the EMPLOYEE_SCD3 target instance.

- **Update strategy** (UPD_ChangedUpdate): This uses the DD_UPDATE condition to overwrite the existing LOCATION field into the EMPLOYEE_SCD3 target instance. It passes data to EXP_EffectiveDate_insertChanged in order to load PM_PREV_LOCATION in the target.

- **Sequence generator** (SEQ_GenerateKeys): This generates a sequence of values for each new row marked as NewFlag that comes into the target, getting incremented by 1. It passes the generated value to EXP_KeyProcessing_InsertNew.

- **Expression** (EXP_EffectiveDate_InsertNew): This transformation is created by the wizard only if you selected to load the PM_EFFECT_DATE option in the wizard. It loads the generated value in the PM_PRIMARYKEY column into the target, which is EMPLOYEE_SCD3. It loads SYSTEMDATE into the PM_EFFECT_DATE column in the target, marking the start of the record.

- **Expression** (EXP_EffectiveDate_InsertChanged): This transformation is created by the wizard only if you selected to load the PM_EFFECT_DATE option in wizard. It loads the generated value in the PM_PRIMARYKEY column in the EMPLOYEE_SCD32 target instance. It loads SYSTEMDATE into the PM_EFFECT_DATE column in the target in order to indicate that the record has been updated.

- **Target** (EMPLOYEE_SCD3): This is the Target table instance that accepts new records into the target table instance.

- **Target** (EMPLOYEE_SCD31): This is the Target table instance that accepts updates to the existing row in the target table instance.

With this, we saw in detail how to implement the different types of SCDs. Note that we have learned how to implement SCD using wizard. You can also manually create the mapping in order to get more practice and better hands-on experience.

Summary

In this chapter, we specifically concentrated on a very important feature—SCD. We talked about the different types of SCDs, that is, SCD1, SCD2, and SCD3. We saw in detail how to use different transformations to achieve the SCD functionality. At the beginning of the chapter, we used an example to understand the different types of SCDs. We learned how to maintain only current data in SCD1. We checked for different forms of SCD2 mapping, that is, using version number, flag, and date range. We checked how SCD3 maintains partial data. We also checked how wizard creates different columns in different types of SCD mapping.

4
Finishing the Development – Using the Workflow Manager Screen Basics

In the previous chapters, we discussed the Informatica PowerCenter Designer screen in detail. This chapter marks the beginning of another client tool called Workflow Manager. Informatica PowerCenter Workflow Manager lets you execute the Informatica code. By now, you must be clear that we create a skeleton of the data flow in the mapping that contains the source for the target flow. Workflow Manager allows us to execute the mapping; in other words, we actually make the data flow from the source to the target when we execute the process called workflow in Workflow Manager.

Basically, Workflow Manager contains a set of instructions, which we define as a workflow. The basic building block of workflow is tasks. As we have multiple transformations in designer screen, we have multiple tasks in Workflow Manager screen. When you create a workflow, you add tasks to it as per your requirement and execute the workflow to see the status in the monitor.

Using Workflow Manager

As we discussed in *Chapter 1, Starting the Development Phase – Using the Designer Screen Basics*, the designer client screen is divided into five sections. Similar to this, Workflow Manager Screen is also divided into five sections called navigator, toolbar, workspace, output panel, and status bar. See *Chapter 1, Starting the Development Phase – Using the Designer Screen Basics* for a detailed description.

Informatica PowerCenter Workflow Manager has the following tools that you can use to create and execute workflows and tasks:

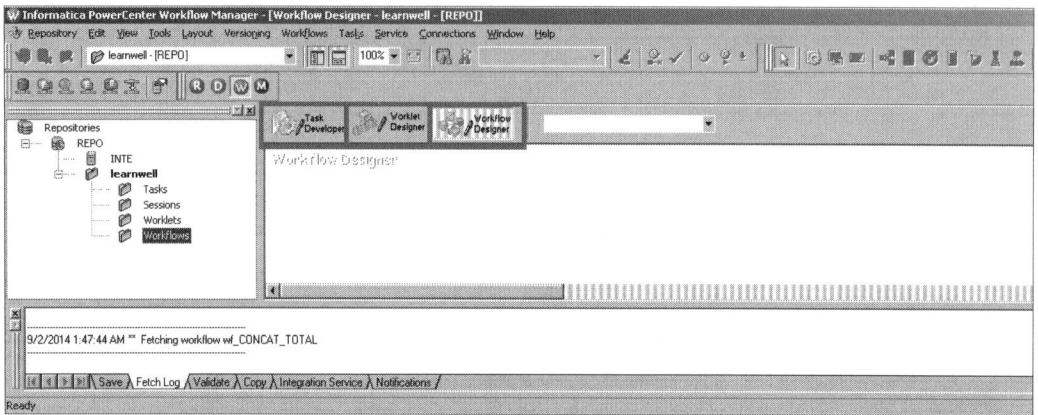

The tools are as follows:

- **Task Developer**: Using this component, you can create different types of tasks that you wish to add to your workflow. The tasks created in **Task Developer** are reusable tasks.
- **Worklet Designer**: A group of reusable tasks is defined as Worklet. You can create Worklet on **Worklet Designer**.
- **Workflow Designer**: A workflow can be created in **Workflow Designer**. Add different tasks to the workflow by connecting links.

Creating a workflow

A workflow is combination of multiple tasks connected with links that trigger in a proper sequence to execute a process. Every workflow contains a start task along with other tasks. When you execute the workflow, you actually trigger the **Start** task, which in turn triggers other tasks that are connected in the flow.

The following figure shows you a sample workflow:

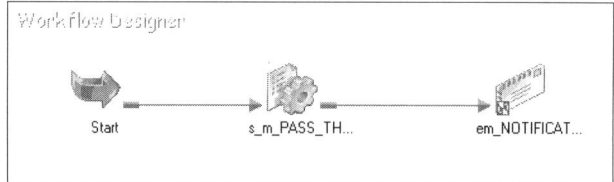

Informatica PowerCenter provides options to create Workflow manually and automatically; these options are discussed in the upcoming sections.

Creating a workflow manually

To create a workflow manually, perform the following steps:

1. In the Workflow Manager, navigate to **Workflows | Create**.

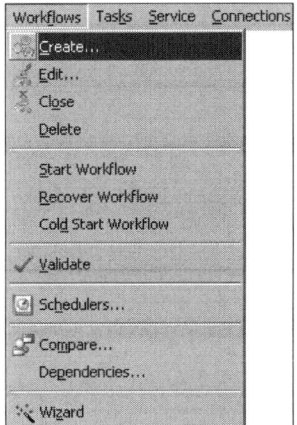

2. Specify the name of the workflow. Please read the naming conventions to be followed while working on the PowerCenter tool. Use `http://dw-learnwell.com/Informatica_naming_conventions.php` to download the naming convention document. The name of the workflow should be `wf_WORKFLOWNAME`. Then, and click on **OK**. We are using `wf_PASS_THROUGH` as the workflow name for our reference.

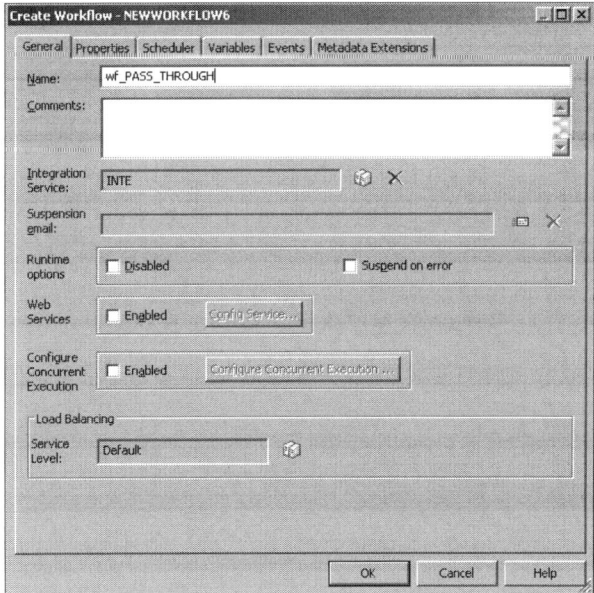

A start symbol appears on the screen in Workflow Manager. Also, the wf_PASS_ THROUGH workflow appears under the navigator, as shown in the following screenshot:

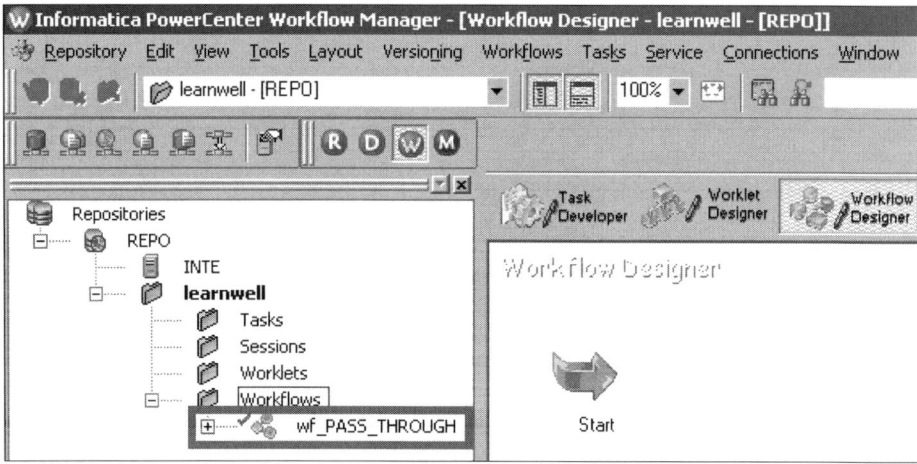

With this, we have learned how to add the start task as a first step to creating the workflow. In the next section, we will create the workflow directly from designer screen.

Creating a workflow automatically

Informatica PowerCenter provides a utility to create the workflow directly from the designer client tool. This feature lets you create a workflow for a particular mapping from designer screen. To create a workflow from designer screen, perform the following steps:

1. In the designer, open the mapping for which you wish to generate the workflow. Navigate to **Mappings | Generate Workflow**.

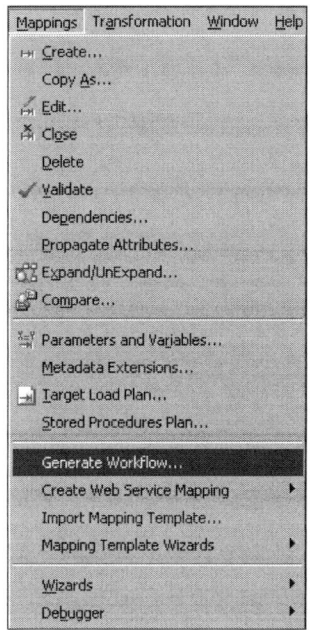

2. On the next screen, select the appropriate option for your session task that will be created. By default, you create workflows with nonreusable sessions.

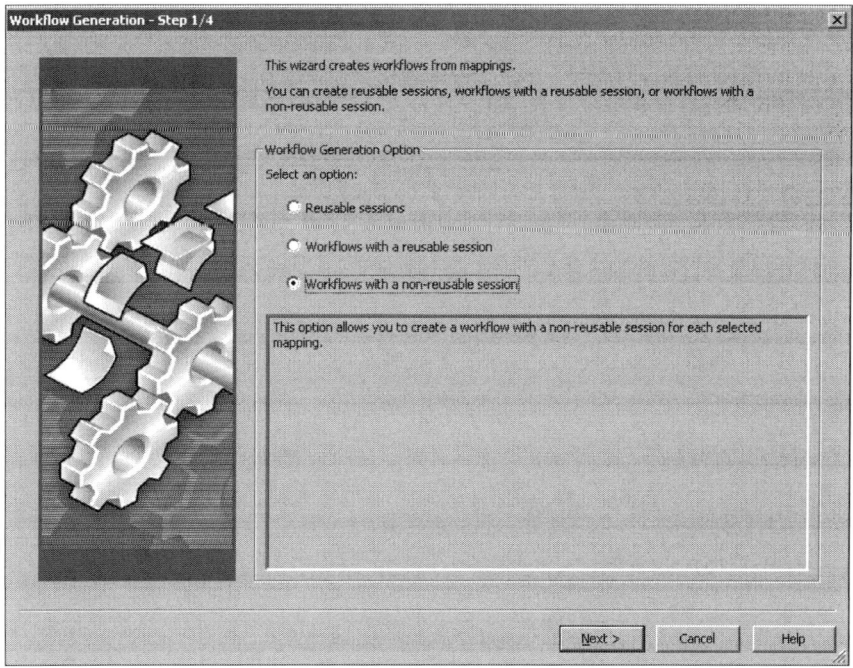

3.   On the next screen, select **Integration Service** (if you have multiple services available) from the drop-down list. Also, specify **Connection Object**. For our reference, we have selected **Oracle** as our source and target in the mapping below the Oracle database. Specify the name of the workflow and the session task. We are using `wf_PASS_THROUGH_EMPLOYEE` and `s_m_PASS_THROUGH_EMPLOYEE` as our workflow and session task name. Now, click on **Next**.

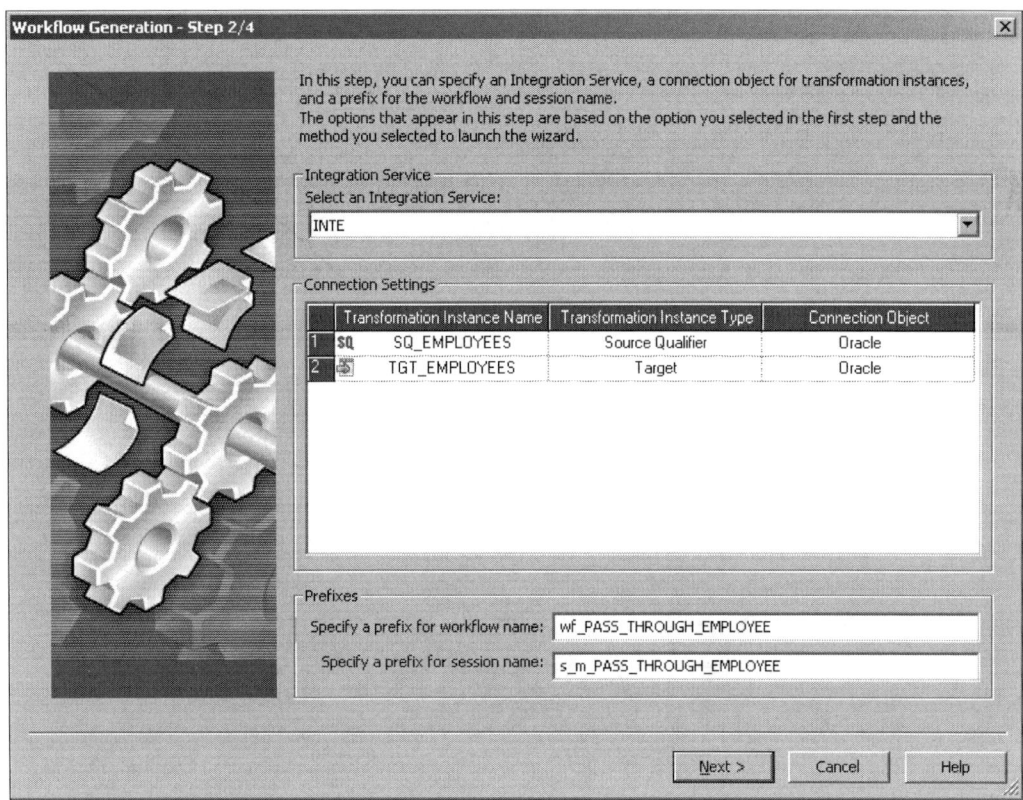

4. On the next screen, you can modify the workflow and session task details. Usually, you need not change anything unless you see any conflict. Then, click on **Next**.

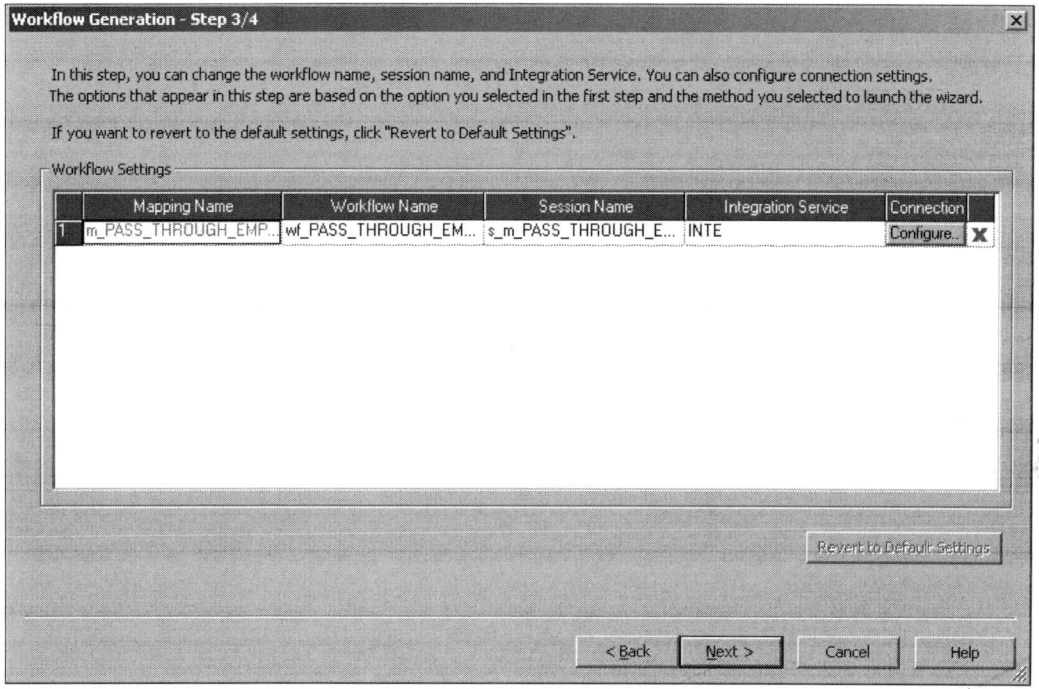

5. The next window gives you a confirmation that the workflow has been created successfully. Click on **Finish**.

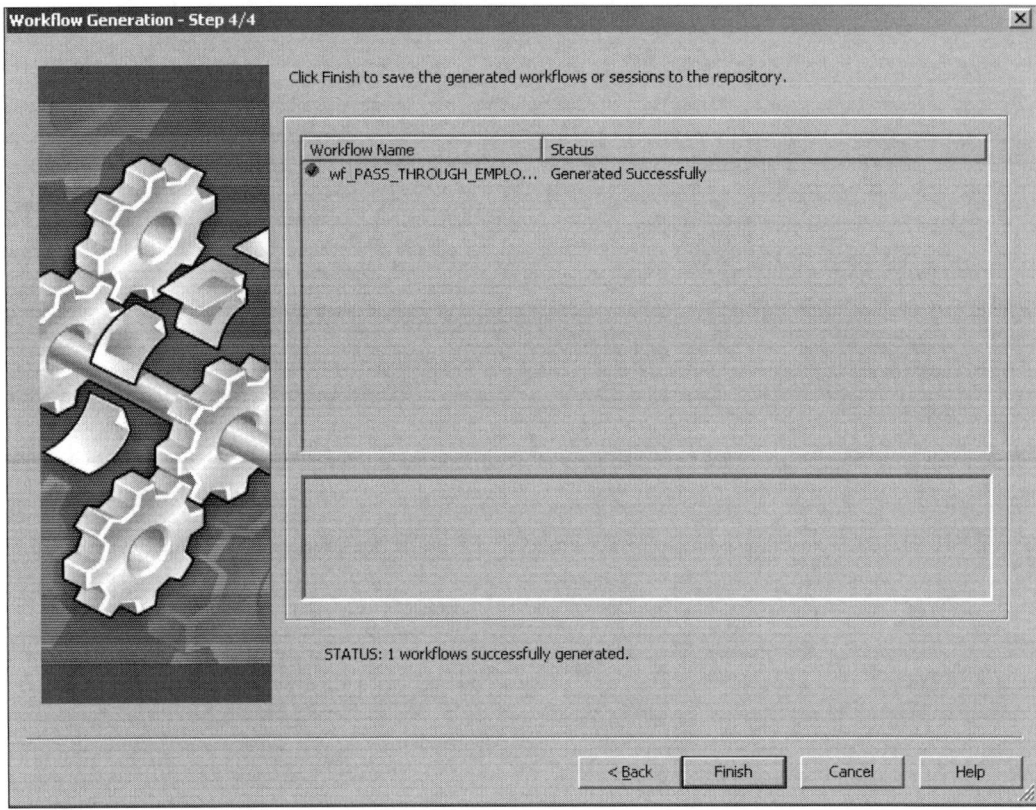

PowerCenter will generate a workflow with a start task and session task in Workflow Manager. Open the Workflow Manager screen to check the workflow. If you are already connected to Workflow Manager, disconnect the repository and connect again to see the workflow under the navigator.

Adding tasks in a workflow

Once you create a workflow, you can add multiple tasks to the workflow. You can directly add the task by creating it in Workflow Manager, or you can create the task in the Task Developer and use it in the workflow.

Adding tasks to the workflow directly

To add a task to the workflow, perform the following steps:

1. In Workflow Manager, navigate to **Task** | **Create**.

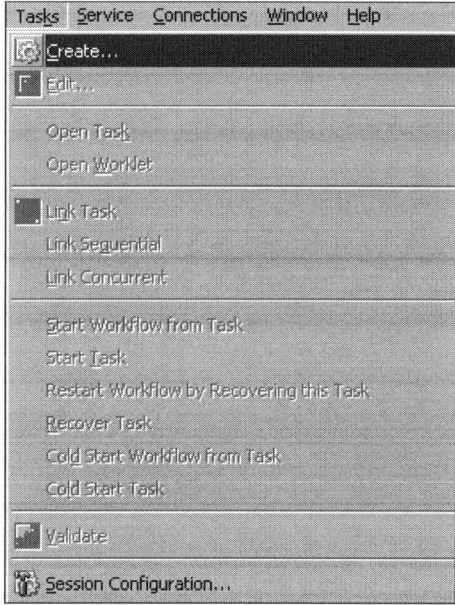

2. Select the type of task from the drop-down list you wish to add to the workflow, and specify the name of the task. The selected task will appear on the screen. Read the naming convention. For our reference, we are creating the session task. The name of the session task should be `s_mappingname`. Click on **OK**.

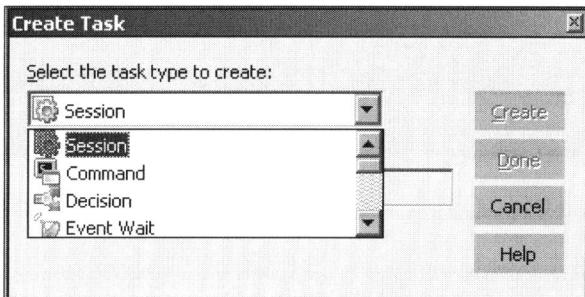

Note that we will discuss all the tasks in detail in the next chapter.

3. If you create a session task, another window will pop up, asking you to select the mapping that you wish to associate with the session. The window displays a list of all the valid mappings present in your repository. Select the appropriate mapping and click on **OK**.

We are selecting m_PASS_THROUGH_EMPLOYEE for our reference.

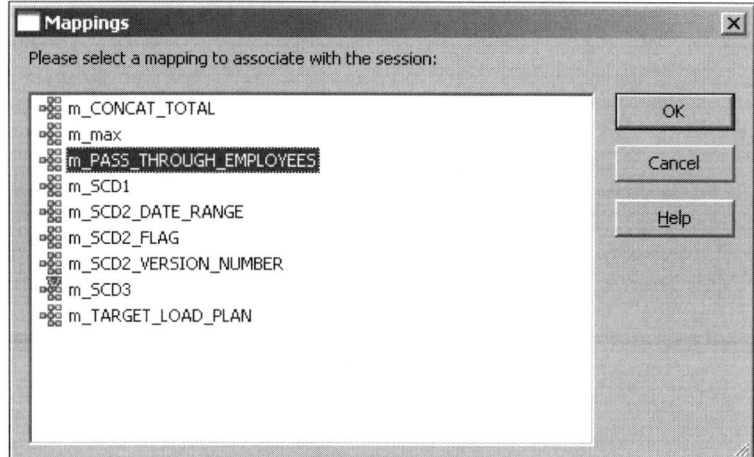

The session task appears in the workspace, as shown in the following screenshot:

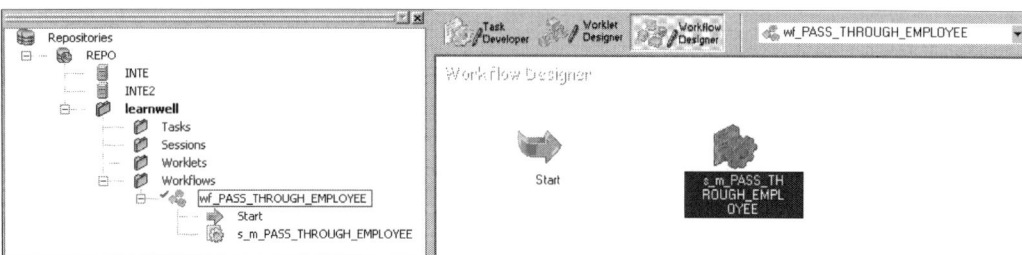

Also, as you can see in the preceding screenshot, s_m_PASS_THROUGH_EMPLOYEE is added to the navigator.

Note that every task will have a different appearance, and based on the task you select to create, the icon will appear in the workspace.

 You can associate only one mapping in one session. Also, you cannot change the mapping once you associate the mapping with the session. If you mistakenly associate a wrong mapping, delete the session task, create a new one, and assign the correct mapping.

Creating nonreusable tasks – Task Developer

In the preceding section, we saw how to create nonreusable tasks in Workflow Manager. As mentioned, we can create reusable tasks in Task Developer. Follow these steps to create the tasks in **Task Developer**:

1. In Workflow Manager, click on **Task Developer**.

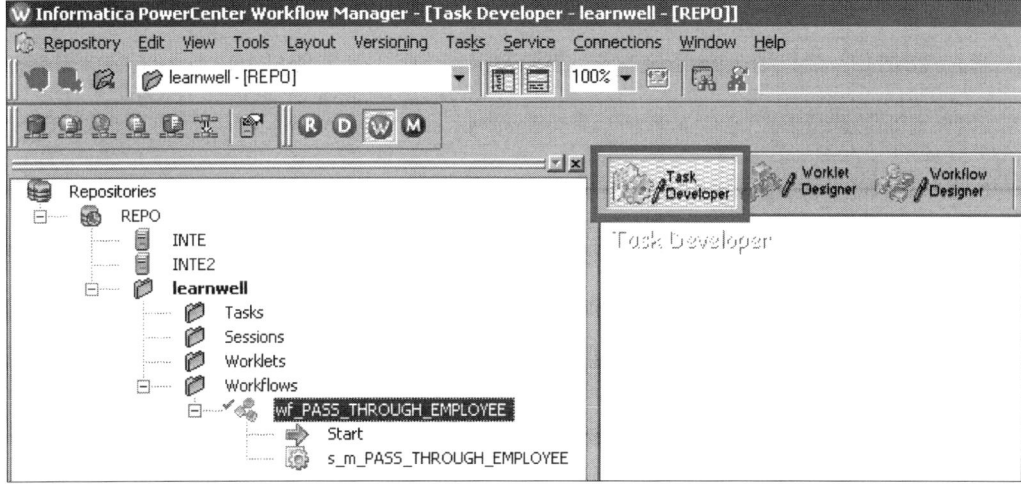

2. In Task Developer, navigate to **Task | Create**.

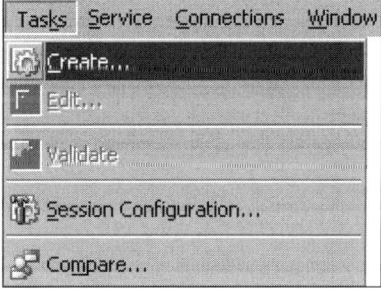

3. Select the required task from the drop-down list, provide the name of the task, click on **Create**, and then click on **Done**.

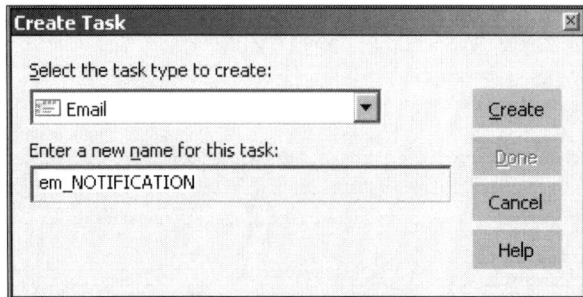

For our reference, we are using the **Email** task with the em_NOTIFICATION name.

The selected task will appear in Task Developer, as shown in the following screenshot:

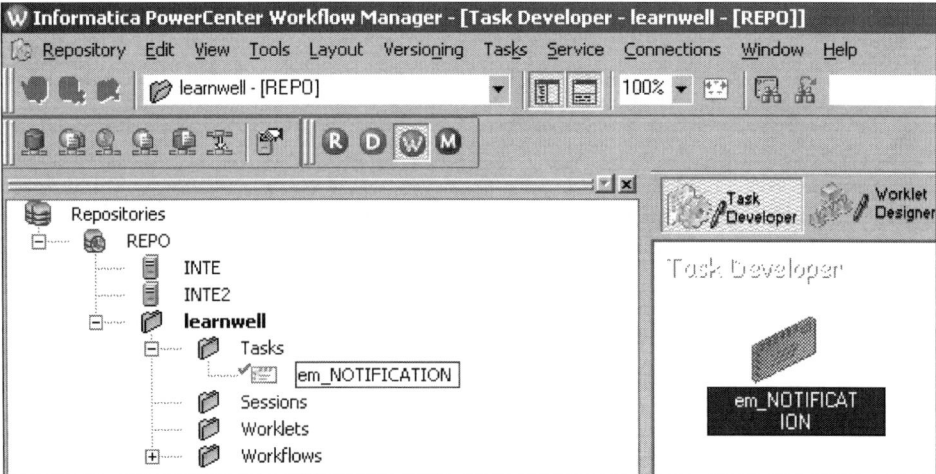

The task will also get added under **Tasks** in the navigator. This indicates that a reusable task is created in the repository.

Adding tasks to the workflow – Task Developer

If you have created a task earlier in Task Developer, you can use these tasks in Workflow Manager. Open the navigator and drag the appropriate task to the workspace where you workflow is already open; the task will appear in the workspace.

To add the reusable task created in the previous step to Workflow, drag-and-drop the em_NOTIFICATION task to the workspace. The task will appear in the workflow, as shown in the following screenshot:

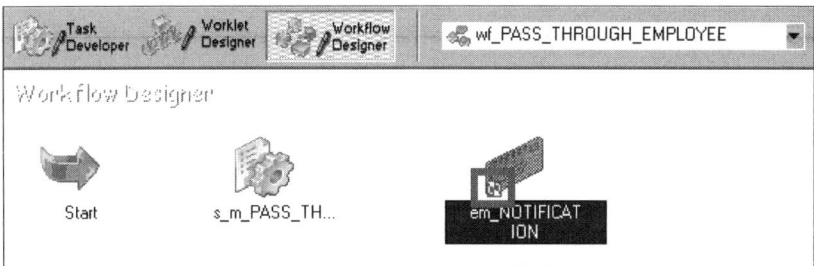

A small icon under em_NOTIFICATION indicates that this is a reusable task.

 Tasks created in Workflow Manager are nonreusable, and tasks created in Task Developer are reusable, that is, you can use these tasks in multiple workflows.

Working with the session task – basic properties

Before we can execute the workflow and make the data flow from the source to the target in a mapping, we need to configure some basic properties in a session task. These properties enable the session task to pick the data from the source and load it into the target.

 Mapping is only the structural representation of the source and target requirement; actual data movement happens with the properties we define in the session task.

To define the properties, you need to perform a series of steps. In Workflow Manager, open the workflow containing the session task. Double-click on the session task, click on **Mapping**, and then click on **Source**.

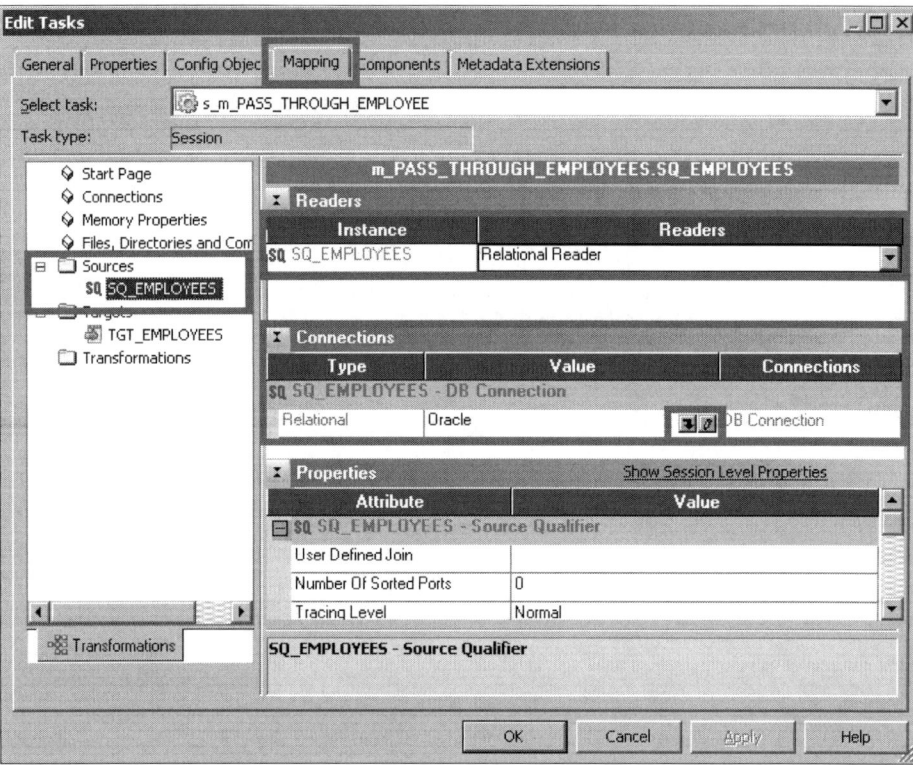

The **Mapping** tab of the session task lets you define the properties for the source and the target. Let's discuss the options in detail:

- **Readers**: As we are using the Oracle table as our source, the property is mentioned as relational reader. This signifies that our source is a table from where we are extracting the data. If your source is flat file, the property will change to **File Reader**.

- **Connections**: Assign the connection for the database, as shown in the preceding screenshot. If your source is **File**, the connections option will be disabled, as we need not define connections for files. Note that we will be discussing how to add connection objects later in this chapter.

- **Properties**: Scroll through the properties, and make changes if required. If you are using **File** as **Source**, you need to define the location of the file in your system under the source file directory. Also, specify the name of the file under the **Source** filename if you use flat file as a source, as shown in the following screenshot:

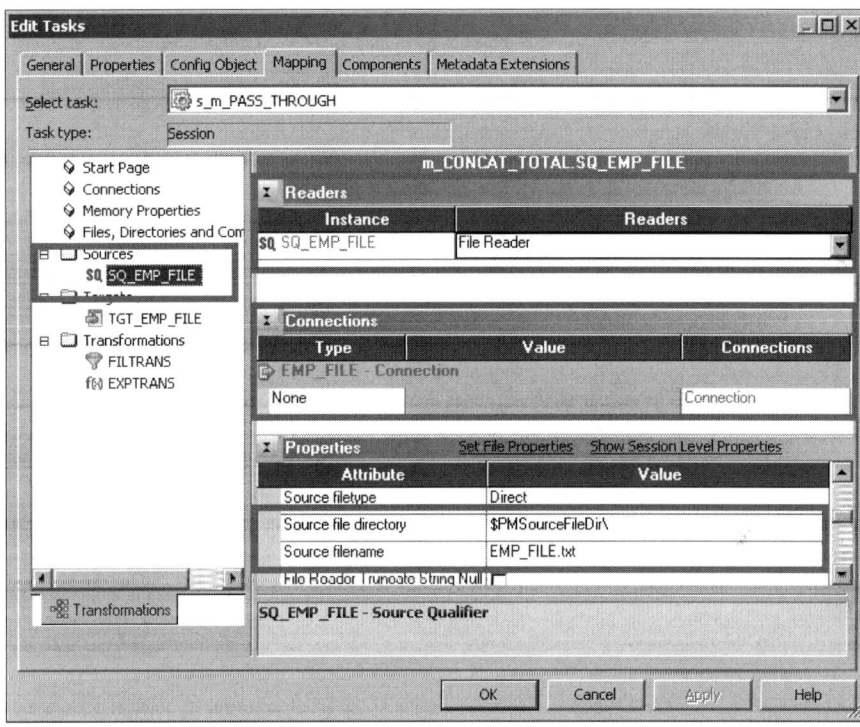

Clicking on **Target** will bring you to the following screen:

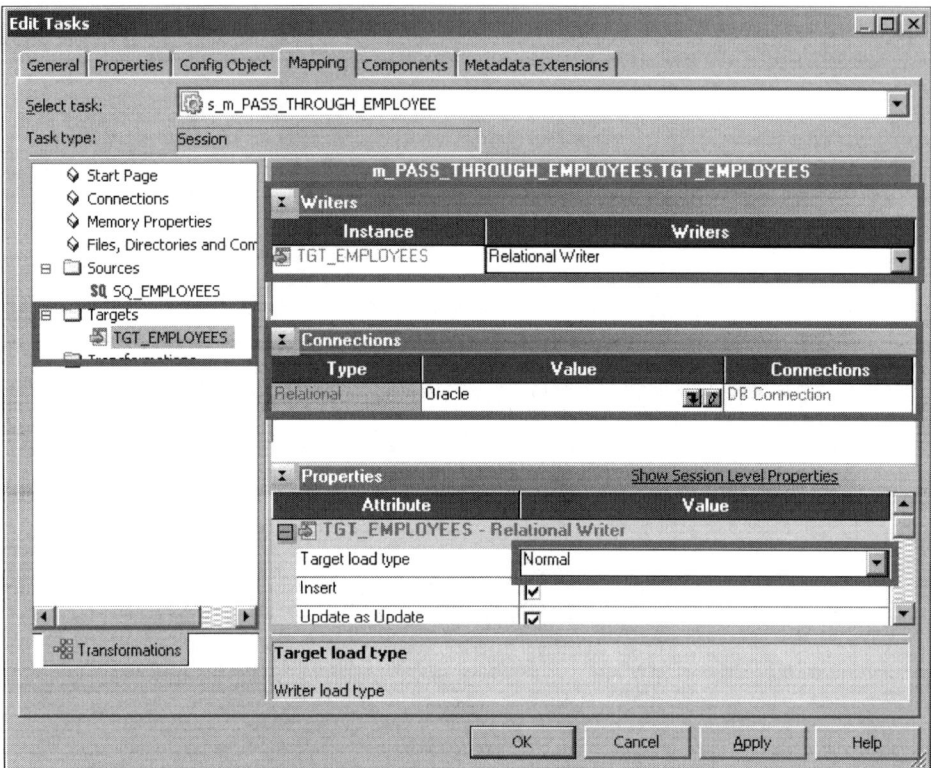

Let's discuss the options in detail:

- **Writers**: As we are using the Oracle table as the target, the property is mentioned as a relational writer. This signifies that our target is the table where we wish to load the data. If we use target as flat file, the property will change to **File Writer**.

- **Connection**: Assign **Target Connection** for the database, as shown in the preceding screenshot. If your target is **File**, the **Connections** option will be disabled, as we need not define the connection for files.

- **Properties**: The target load type is a very important aspect while loading the data. The target load type is of two types: **Normal** and **Bulk**. Selecting the property as bulk allows faster loading into the target. You cannot use the property as bulk if you have a primary key or other constraints in your target table. As our target table has keys defined, we are using a normal property.

Scroll through the properties and make changes if required. If we use **File** as **Target**, we need to define the location of the file in your system under the **Output** file directory. Also, specify the name of the file under **Output** filename if you use flat file as target, as shown in the following screenshot:

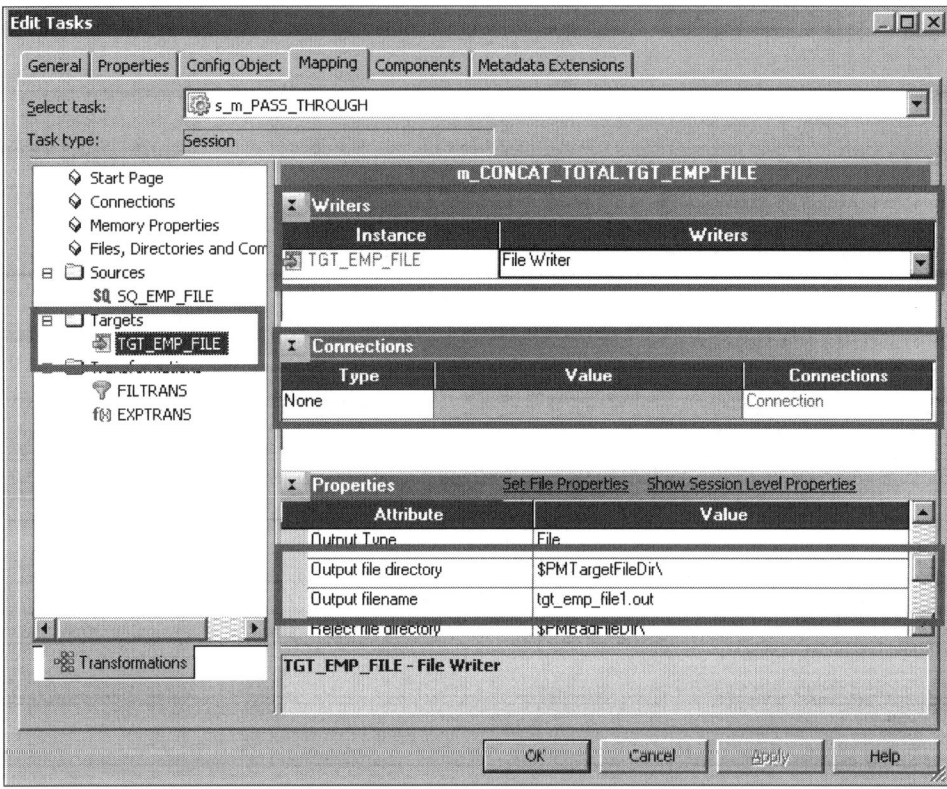

If you are using the lookup transformation in your mapping, you will need to define the file path or table connection for lookup. Click on **Lookup** under **Transformations** and define the **Connection** details, as shown in the upcoming screenshot.

Lookup Sql Override, as indicated in the following screenshot, is a property that is available if you are using lookup transformation to look up a table. When you use lookup transformation to look up a table, it generates a default query to extract the data from the table and bring in Informatica PowerCenter. You can modify the default query generated by the lookup transformation, which is referred to as a lookup SQL override. Using this property, you can save time by eliminating unwanted records while extracting itself.

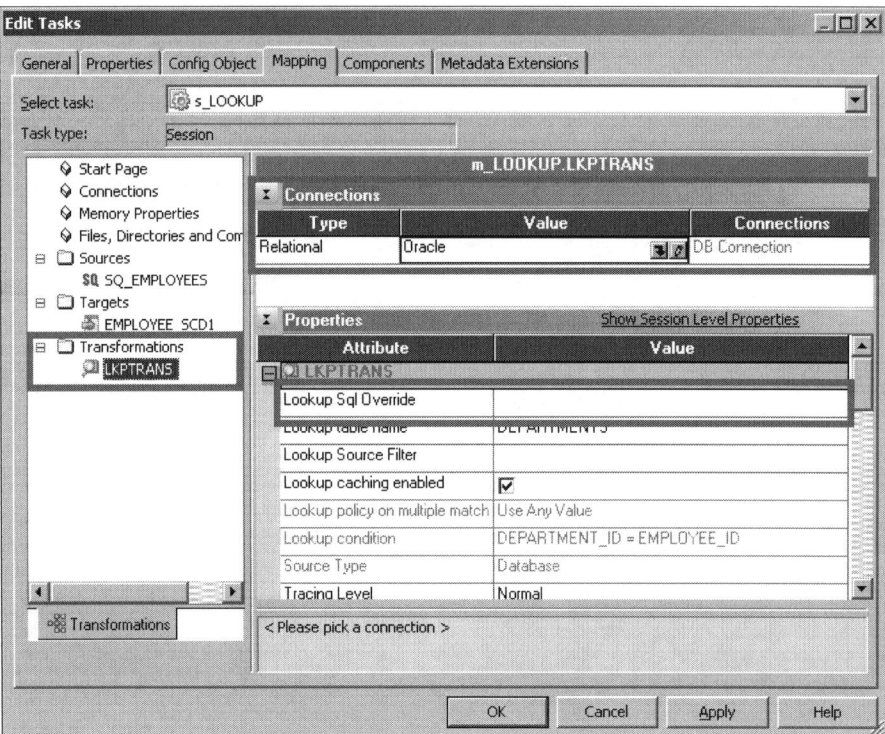

If you use lookup transformation to look up a file, you will need to define
`LookupFileDirectory` and `LookupFileName`, as shown in the following screenshot:

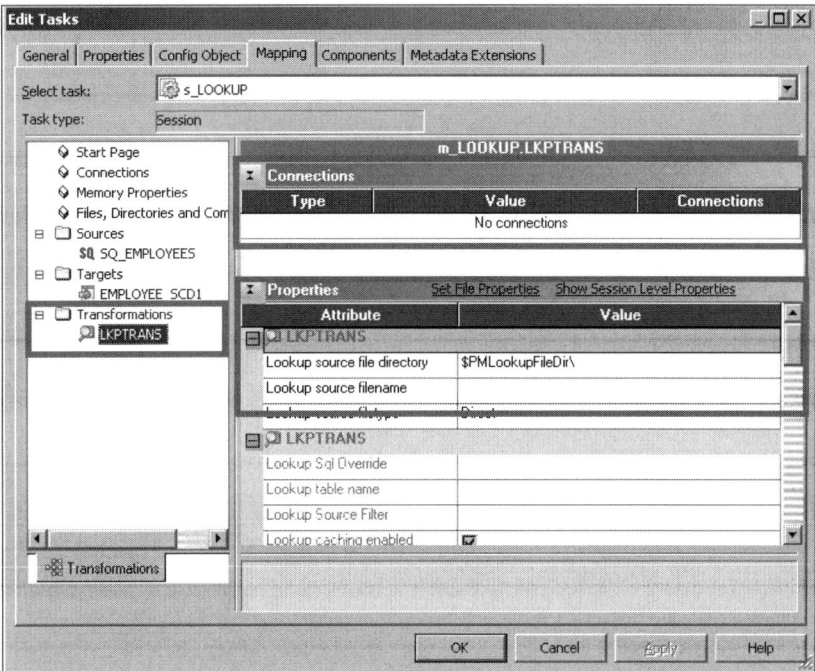

We will discuss other properties of session tasks in detail in the next chapter.

Connecting the tasks – links

At this point, we have learned how to create the workflow and add reusable and
nonreusable tasks. Before you execute the workflow, you need to connect the start
task to other tasks that are present in the workflow. We use the link task to connect
tasks. Link tasks are also used to define a condition if you have multiple branches in
the workflow. Links control the flow of the workflow if you have multiple branches.

To use the link, perform the following steps:

1. Open Workflow Manager and navigate to **Tasks | Link**.

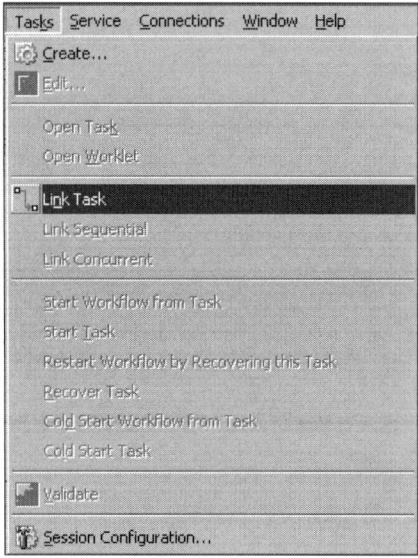

   Alternatively, you can use the icon to create the link, as shown in the following screenshot:

2. In the Workflow Manager workspace, click on the **Start** task and drag the task you wish to connect.

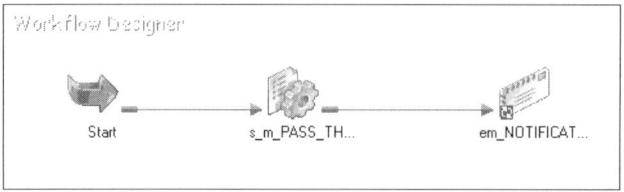

This results in a link between the tasks, as shown in the preceding screenshot. Note that you can connect any two tasks using the link task.

Assigning Integration Service to a workflow

When you create a workflow, Informatica assigns an Integration Service to the workflow in order to enable the data movement from source to target. If you have created multiple Integration Services under the repository, you can change the Integration Service assigned to particular workflow. You might need to change the Integration Service if the assigned Integration Service is not available due to certain reasons. Follow these steps to assign an Integration Service:

1. In Workflow Manager, open the workflow for which you wish to assign an Integration Service.

2. Navigate to **Workflow | Edit**.

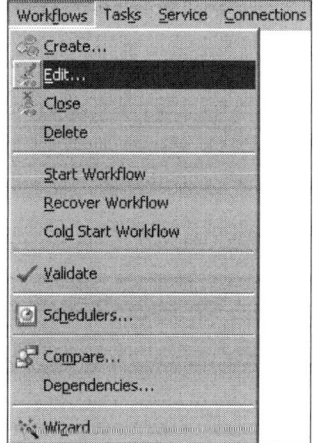

3. A new window will pop up, as shown in the following screenshot. Click on the icon that allows you to select the Integration Service.

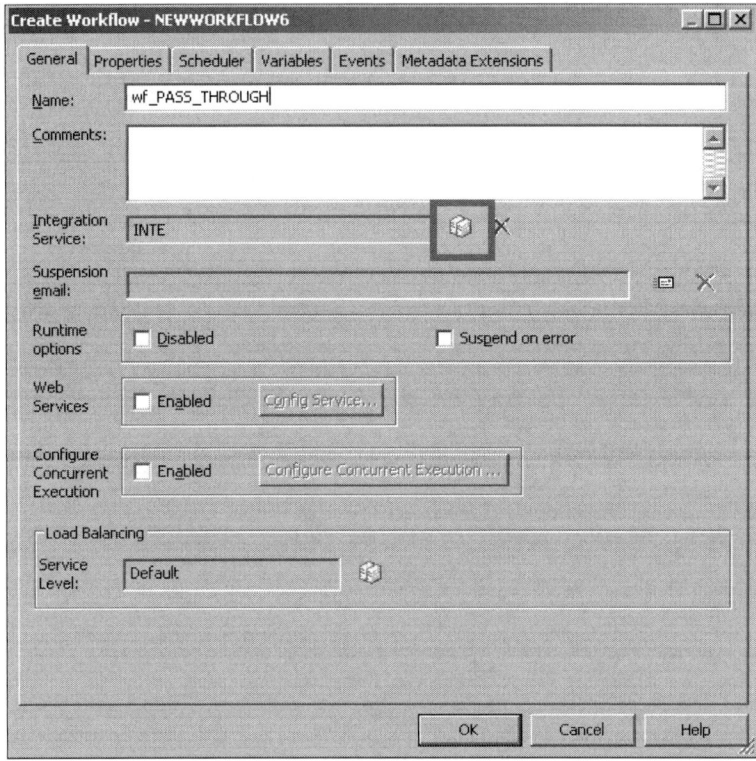

A window with a list of all the Integration Services will appear.

4. Select the Integration Service and click on **OK**. Click on **OK** again. The new service will be assigned to the workflow.

Deleting a workflow

We might need to discard some of the workflows that are not required any longer. Make sure you check the usability or dependability of the workflow you are deleting. There are various ways in which you can delete a workflow:

- To delete a workflow, select the workflow in the navigator and press the *Delete* button

- To delete a workflow that is currently opened in a workspace, navigate to **Workflow** | **Delete**:

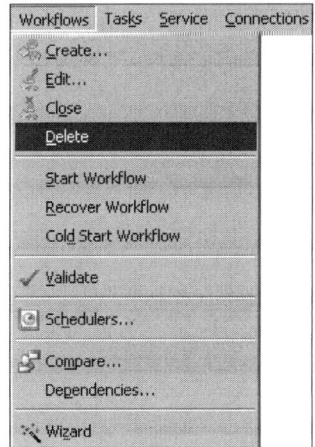

When you delete a workflow, all the associated nonreusable tasks are deleted from the repository. Reusable tasks remain in the repository.

Trigger – starting a workflow

Before you start the workflow, make sure the workflow is valid. Note that you can either create a complete workflow that can be executed, or you can create a part of the workflow.

Running the complete workflow

To run Workflow Manager, perform the following steps:

1. In Workflow Manager, open the workflow you wish to execute in the workspace.

2. Navigate to **Workflows | Start Workflow**.

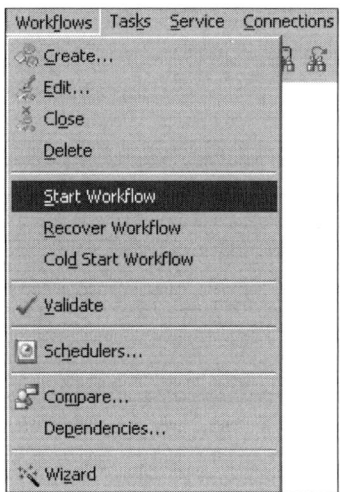

The workflow will start the execution, and the status can be checked in Workflow Manager.

Running a part of the workflow

If you wish to execute only a part of the workflow, select the task from which you wish to execute the workflow. Right-click on the task, and click on **Start Workflow from task**.

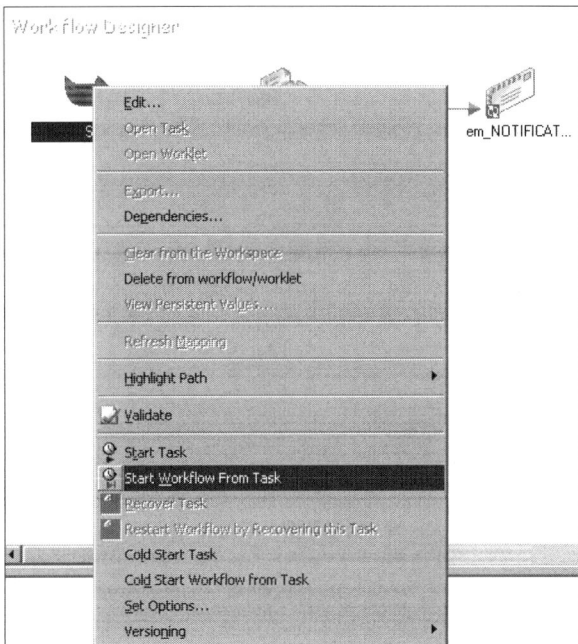

Running a task

Apart from running the workflow, Informatica PowerCenter allows you to run only a particular task. This feature is specifically important when you are in the development phase of your project and you wish to check each component before you run the complete workflow. To run a task, perform the following steps:

1. In Workflow Manager, open the workflow containing the task.

2. Right-click on the task you wish to execute and click on **Start Task**.

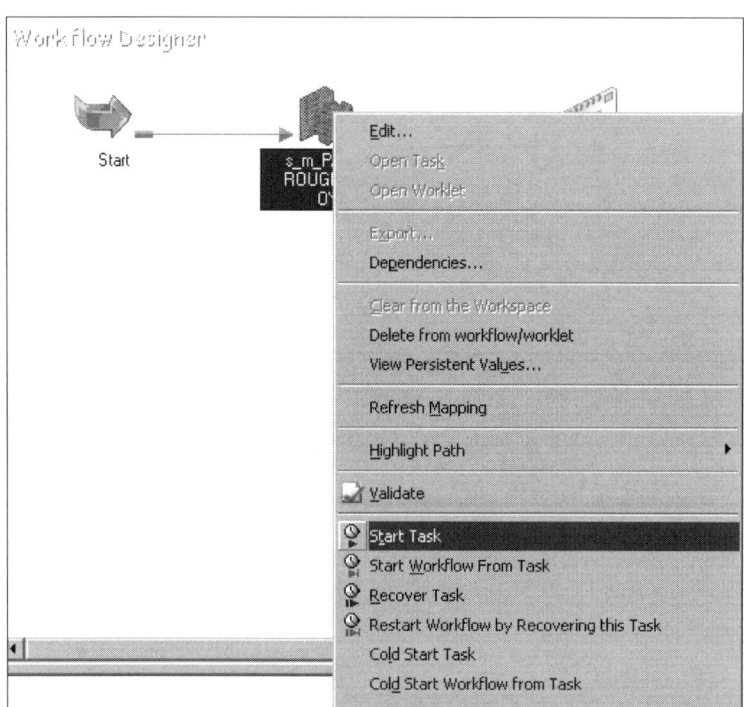

You can check the status of the task in the Workflow Monitor. You will see that only the selected task is executed.

Working with connection objects

At this stage, you must be aware that we will need to define the database connections in Workflow Manager before we can define the connection in the workflow. Defining the connection is necessary in order to make the data flow from the actual database table to Informatica.

If we use **File** for **Source** or **Target**, we need to define the path location for the source or file. However, if we are using the database table as our source, target, or lookup transformation, we will need to define the database connection that we discussed in the *Working with session task* section of this chapter. Before you can assign the connection in the session task, you need to configure the connection object in the workflow. This is similar to adding the database connection object in the PowerCenter Designer.

There are various types of connection objects that Informatica PowerCenter supports:

- **Relation connection**: As mentioned previously, before you can define connection values in a session task, you need to add the connection under Workflow Manager. You can create a connection for any type of relational database, such as Oracle, SQL, DB2, and so on.

- **FTP connection**: You can create a File Transfer Protocol connection to transfer the files.

- **External loader connection**: Informatica supports an external loader that directly loads the data from files to database tables. The external loader eliminates the need to run SQL commands to insert data into the table.

- **Queue connection**: These connections enable the processing of message queues.

- **Application connection**: You can create connections to enable session tasks and extract the data from or load the data into applications such as Salesforce, PeopleSoft, Siebel, and TIBCO.

Note that apart from the relational connection, all other connection objects are rarely required based on your project requirements. So, you might be more interested in learning relational database first.

Creating a connection object

To create a new connection object in Workflow Manager, click on **Connections** in Workflow Manager and select the type of connection you wish to create.

Configuring a relational database

To create a new relational database connection, perform the following steps:

1. In Workflow Manager, navigate to **Connections | Relational**, as shown in the preceding screenshot.

2. On the next screen, click on **New** to add a new connection.

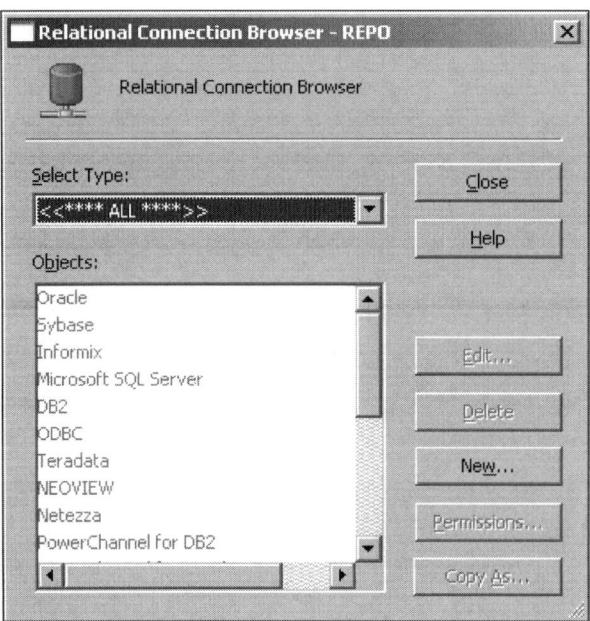

3. Select the database subtype and click on **OK**. For our reference, we are selecting **Oracle**.

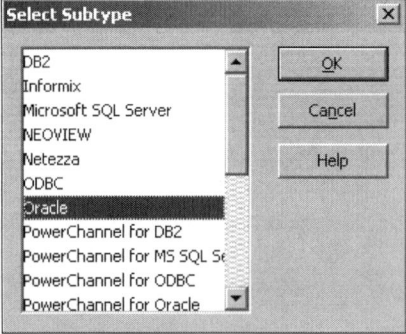

4. On the next screen, you can define all the properties. Define the properties and click on **OK**, and then click on the close button to get the connection added to your repository.

Note that you need to have all the details available with you before you can configure the relational database connection object:

- **Database name**: This specifies the name of the database, for example, Oracle, SQL Server, and so on. In our case, we are using Oracle.

- **Database type**: This specifies the type of the database, for example, Oracle, SQL Server, and so on. In our case, we are using Oracle.

- **Database user name**: This mentions the name of the database user who has proper authentication to read from and write into the database table. We are using HR as the username for our reference.

- **Password**: This mentions the password for the user you mentioned under the database username. We are using the password as HR for our reference.

- **Connect string**: This mentions the connection string that transfers the data to the table. For our reference, we are using XE as the connection string.

- **Database code page**: This selects the code page associated with your database.

The details that need to be filled in are shown in the following screenshot:

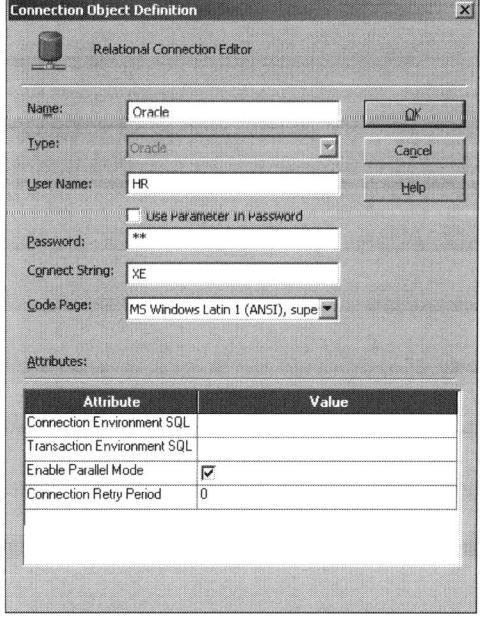

This will add the connection to your Workflow Manager screen in the repository. Now, you can use the connection in your session task.

Summary

We can summarize this chapter by saying that we learned about the complete development of Informatica, that is, we learned about designer screen and the Workflow Manager screen. By now, you should be able to create the mapping and workflows.

In this chapter, we learned how to work on the Workflow Manager screen. We learned how to create the workflow, add tasks, and link the tasks. We saw various options to create workflows and tasks. We learned how to create reusable and nonreusable tasks in Task Developer.

Then, we discussed how to run the workflow. We checked how to run a complete workflow and how to run part of a workflow and an individual task. The last section of the chapter talked about connection objects. We discussed the different types of connection objects present in Informatica. We also discussed the frequently used connection, that is, relation connection, in detail.

In the next chapter, we are going to talk about the various types of tasks and high-level properties of the Workflow Manager screen.

5

Using the Workflow Manager Screen – Advanced

In the previous chapter, we discussed the basics of the Workflow Manager screen. In this chapter, we will take forward what we covered in the previous chapter. We will talk about the advanced topics of the Workflow Manager screen. We will start the chapter with a discussion on various tasks. As mentioned in the previous chapter, tasks are the basic building blocks of Workflow Manager. Later in the chapter, we will discuss worklet, parameter files, scheduling, and so on.

Working with tasks

As mentioned in the previous chapter, tasks are the basic building blocks of workflows. Every task has a different functionality, as every transformation has a different functionality. We need to use tasks as per our requirement in the workflow or worklet. Tasks can be created as reusable or as nonreusable.

You can create reusable tasks in Task Developer and nonreusable tasks in Workflow Manager.

Before we talk about each task in detail, let's take a look at the different tasks that we have:

Name of task	Details
Session task	This is used to execute a mapping.
Email task	This is used to send success or failure e-mail notifications.
Command task	This is used to execute Unix shell or Perl scripts or commands. It can also be used to execute DOS commands in Windows.
Timer task	This is used to add some time gap or delay between two tasks.
Assignment task	This is used to assign a value to a workflow variable.
Control task	This is used to control the flow of the workflow by stopping or aborting the workflow in the case of an error.
Decision task	This is used to check the status of multiple tasks and hence control the execution of the workflow based on the condition defined in the decision task.
Event Wait task	This is used to wait for a particular event to occur. Usually, it is called the file watcher task.
Event-Raise task	This is used to trigger user-defined events.
Link task	This is used to link tasks to each other. You can also define conditions in the link to control the execution of the workflow.

Before we move on, let's talk about an important topic. Consider that we have two workflows: `wf_WORKFLOW1` and `wf_WORKFLOW2`. The `Wf_WORKFLOW1` workflow contains the session task and the command task. We have a requirement in which `wf_WORKFLOW1` triggers `wf_WORKFLOW2` upon successful completion.

For the session task and the command task, `wf_WORKFLOW1` will be called the parent workflow.

For `wf_WORKFLOW2`, `wf_WORKFLOW1` will be called the top-level workflow, because `wf_WORKFLOW1` triggers `wf_WORKFLOW2`.

Configuring a task

In the previous chapter, we discussed how to create tasks in Workflow Manager and Task Developer. After we create a task, we can configure the options in the **General** tab of every task as shown in the following screenshot:

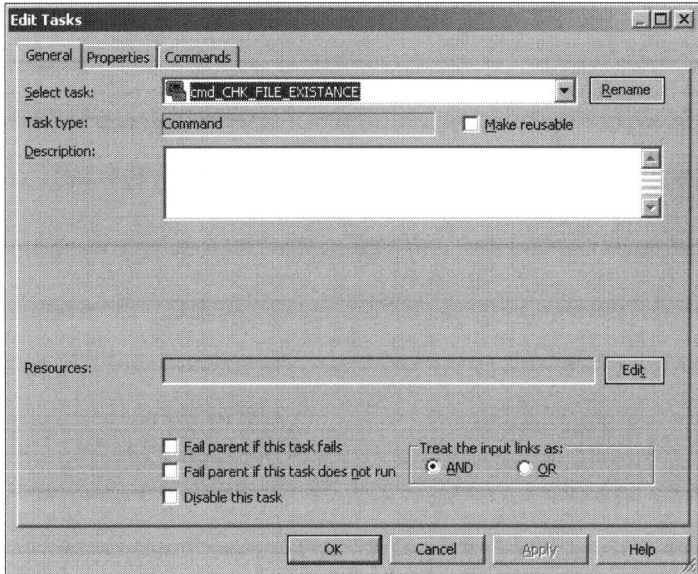

Every task has properties that are similar to how we control the workflow in the **General** tab:

- **Fail parent if this task fails**: When you check this option, the workflow or worklet will fail if the task in that workflow or worklet fails

- **Fail parent if this task does not run**: When you check this option, the workflow or worklet will fail if the task in that workflow or worklet does not run

- **Disable this task**: When you check this option, the task in the workflow or worklet will become invisible, and it will not run in a sequence

- **Treat input link as**: When you check this option, Informatica PowerCenter will run the task if all or one of the input link conditions become true

The session task

In the previous chapter, we discussed the basic properties of the session task.

The Session task is used to execute a mapping. It is the most widely used task among all the tasks of Workflow Manager. As you must have seen earlier, there are lots of properties that we can define in the session task. In the previous chapter, we discussed some of these properties, for example, the **Mapping** tab of the Session task. We learned how to provide the source, target, and lookup transformation details required to move the data. We will discuss the remaining properties in this chapter.

Tabs of the session task

Double-click on the session task to see the various tabs, as shown in the following screenshot:

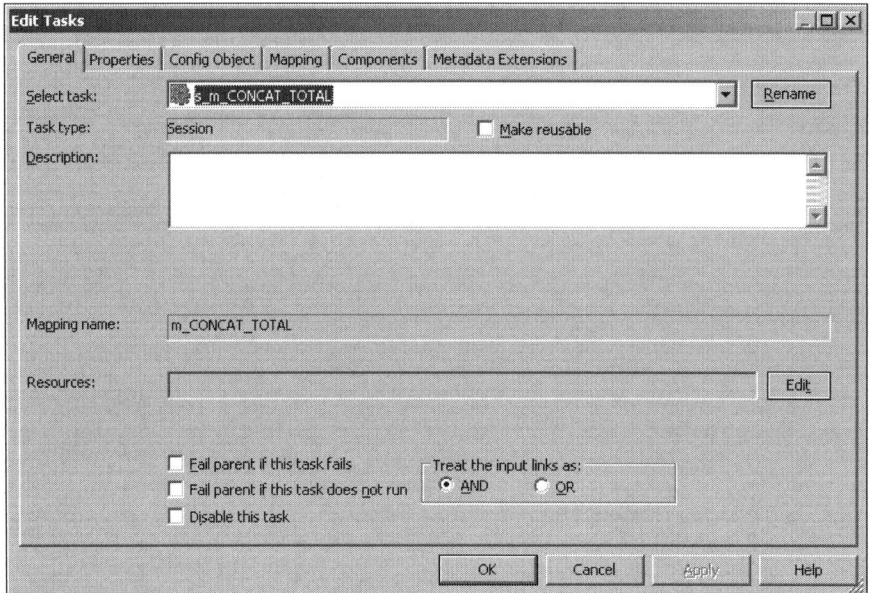

The various tabs of the session task are as follows:

- **General**: As discussed in the preceding section, you can define the session name, rename the session name, and mention the description and other tasks related properties, as shown in the preceding section. We have discussed the **General** tab properties in the preceding section.

- **Properties**: You can define the session log's filename, commit interval, test load setting, recovery settings, and other performance-related properties. The following screenshot shows you the **General Options** properties that can be defined under the **Properties** tab:

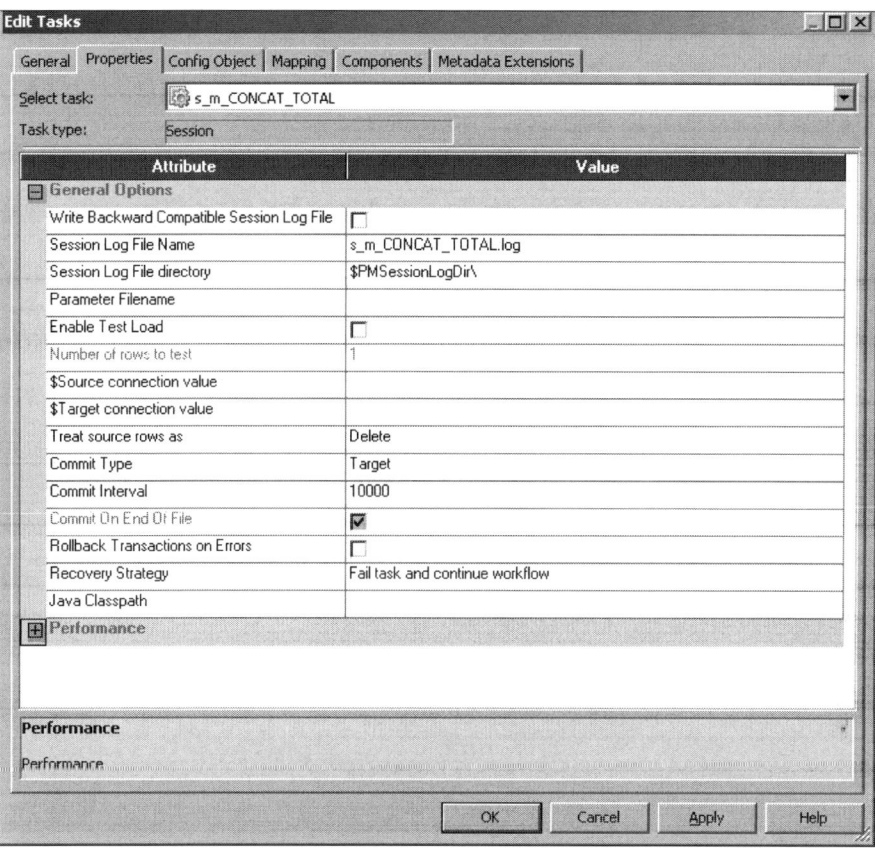

The description of the property shown in the preceding screenshot is as follows:

Property	Description
Write Backward Compatible Session Log File	You can select this option if you wish to write the generated session logs to a file. If you select this option, Informatica PowerCenter creates a log file, else it generates a normal session log file.
Session Log File Name	With this, you can define the session log filename. The default session log filename is SESSION_NAME. log. You can also define the parameters in this option. We will discuss the parameter file in detail later in the chapter. When you define the parameter, pass the value from the parameter file.
Session Log File Directory	With this, you can define the session log file directory. You can also define the parameters in this option. When you define the parameter, pass the value from the parameter file.
Parameter Filename	If you use the parameters and variables in your code, you need to pass the values from the parameter file. You can define the parameters' filename and path here.
Enable Test Load	You can select this option to allow only a few records to pass through the mapping. This option is useful when you are in the testing phase of your project.
Number of rows to test	When you select the **Enable Test Load** option, you can define the number of records you wish to flow from **Mapping**. Suppose you have 10,000 records to process. You can check the **Enable Test Load** option and mention the number of records you wish to test. So, if you define 100 records, Informatica will only process 100 records out of the 10,000 records.
$Source connection value	You can define the **Database Connection** value here. Consider that your database connection's name is ORACLE. If you define ORACLE at this place, you can select $Source in the **Mapping** tab for the source connection.
$Target connection value	You can define the **Database Connection** value here. Consider that your database connection's name is ORACLE. If you define ORACLE at this place, you can select $Target in the **Mapping** tab for the target connection.

Property	Description
Treat source rows as	This property allows you to treat records as `INSERT`, `UPDATE`, `DELETE`, or `DATA DRIVEN` for the records that come from a source. The default property is `INSERT`, which indicates all the records that come from a source will be inserted into the target.
	The **DATA DRIVEN** property is selected when you use the update strategy transformation in **Mapping**. We will talk about the update strategy transformation in *Chapter 7, The Lifeline of Informatica – Transformations*.
Commit Type	You can select either a source-based or a target-based commit type. The default property is the target-based commit type.
	If you select a source-based commit type, Informatica commits the data into the target-based commit type for commit interval and flush latency intervals. Flush latency is the time interval for which you wish to commit the data. If you define the flush latency as 5 seconds and the commit interval as 10,000, Informatica will commit the data to the target-based commit type for whichever interval it reached first. Flush latency is a property defined by the Informatica PowerCenter administrator. So, you need not be worried about how to set up this property. In most cases, data is committed based on the commit interval, so we don't use the flush latency property frequently.
	If you select the target-based commit type, Informatica commits the data based on the commit interval.
Commit On End Of File	This option is selected by default. This property indicates that the records will be committed to the target. If the file contains a smaller number of records, then the commit interval is defined.
Rollback Transactions on Errors	When you select this option, Informatica will roll back the records at the next commit interval. This only happens if there is a nonfatal error.

Property	Description
Recovery Strategy	Using this property, you can recover the session task if the session happens to fail. Various options are available in this property, which you can select based on your requirement: • **Fail session and continue the workflow**: If you select this option, you cannot recover your session task. The session will fail if it encounters an error but will continue the workflow. • **Restart Task**: If you select this option, the session task restarts when the workflow is recovered after a failure. • **Resume from last checkpoint**: If you select this option, Informatica saves the start of the session task and resumes the session from the last checkpoint.
Java Classpath	Use this option if you wish to use different types of Java packages in a Java transformation.

The following screenshot shows you the **Performance** properties that can be defined under the **Properties** tab:

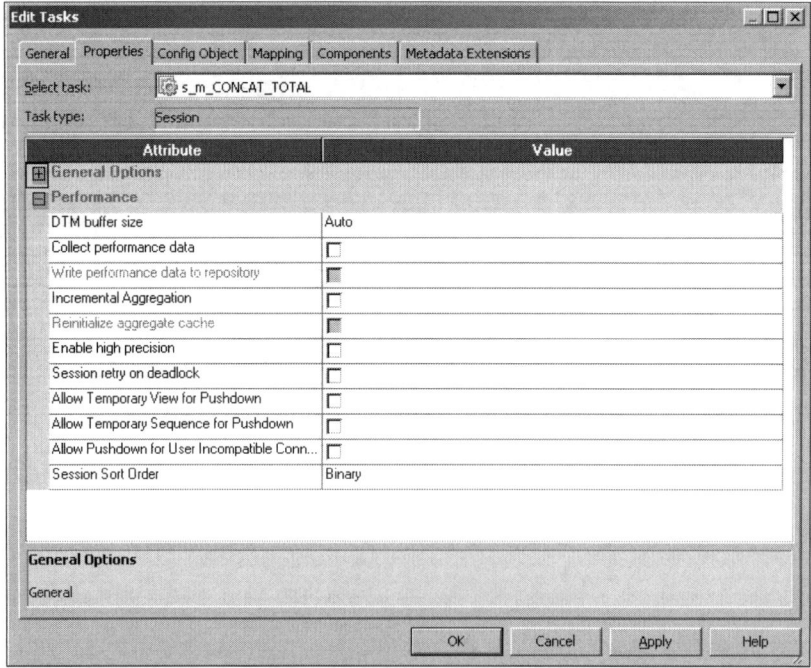

The description of the properties shown in the preceding screenshot is as follows:

Property	Description
DTM buffer size	This indicates how much memory you wish to assign for the DTM processes. When you create a session, Informatica assigns a specific value for the DTM. You can make the value **Auto**, so Informatica keeps on increasing the value automatically, if required.
Collect performance data	If you select this option, Informatica collects the performance data as it runs the session. Usually, you do not select this option unless you really need to find the performance. This option can actually hamper your performance in some way, because it takes some time to collect the performance details. So, unless it's very important, do not check this option.
Write performance data to repository	You can save the performance collected for the session run to the repository so that you can check the details later. This again hampers the performance, so unless required, do not check this option.
Incremental Aggregation	If you wish to make use of incremental aggregation, check this option.
	We will discuss this in more detail later in the chapter.
Reinitialize aggregate cache	If you are using incremental aggregation, you can use this option. When you use incremental aggregation, Informatica stores the data of the previous run in the cache memory. If you wish to reinitialize the value, select this option.
	We will discuss this in more detail later in the chapter.
Enable high precision	If you select this option, Informatica processes the decimal data to a precision of 28. Usually, you leave this option unchecked.
Session retry on deadlock	If you select this option, Informatica tries to load the data into target if it finds the deadlock. So, instead of giving an error, it tries to load the data again.
	This option is available only for normal load and not for bulk load setting.
Allow Temporary View for Pushdown	If you select this option, Informatica creates a temporary view in the database when you use the **Pushdown** feature.
	Pushdown optimization is a feature that we will discuss with performance in the next chapter.

Property	Description
Allow Temporary Sequence for Pushdown	If you select this option, Informatica creates a temporary sequence in the database when you use the **Pushdown** feature.
Allow Pushdown for User Incompatible Connections	This property indicates that the user through which you are accessing the database used in the session has read permission. If the user does not have the read permission, the session task fails.
Session Sort Order	You can select the sort order for your session. The default sort order is binary.

In the **Config Object** tab, you can select the **Advanced** setting, **Log Options**, the **Error handling** properties, and **Partitioning Options**.

The advanced settings under the **Config Object** tab are shown in the following screenshot:

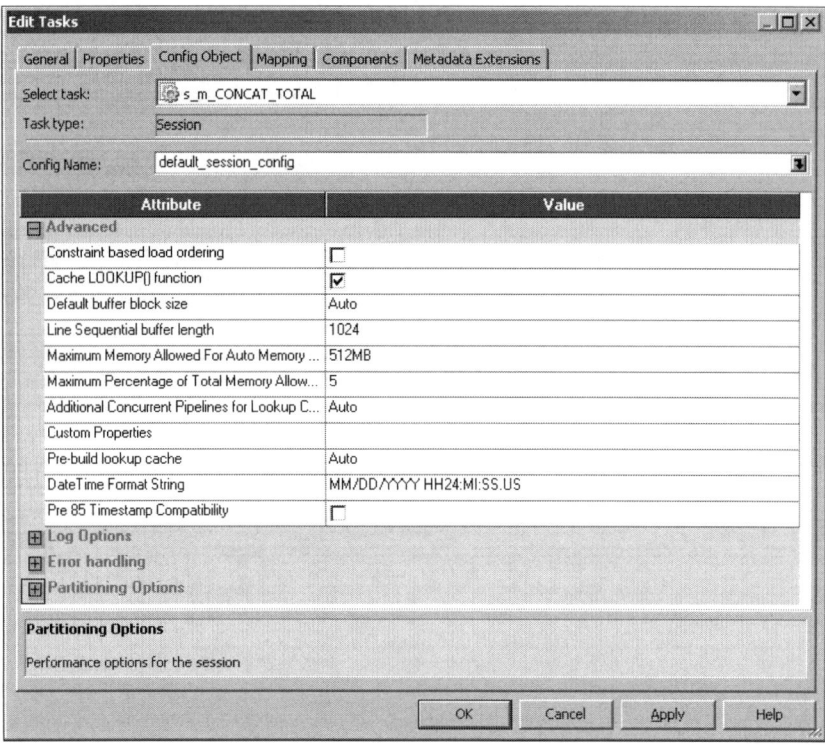

The description of the properties shown in the preceding screenshot is as follows:

Property	Description
Constraint based load ordering	If you check this option, the data is loaded into the target based on the relationship between the primary key and the foreign key wherever possible.
Cache LOOKUP() function	This property is related to the lookup transformation functionality. By default, lookup transformation performs a row-by-row operation. If you check this option, Informatica overrides mapping level lookup settings.
Default buffer block size	This option specifies the size of the buffer block you wish to assign for the data cache and index cache movement from the source to the target. By default, it is set to **Auto**, so the size is automatically increased as required.
Line Sequential Buffer Length	This property is related to the number of bytes in an individual record in a flat file. The default value is 1024 bytes. If your records have a larger byte length, increase the value as per the requirement.
Maximum Memory Allowed For Auto Memory Attributes	This setting is related to the amount of memory allocated to the session cache at runtime.
Maximum Percentage of Total Memory Allowed for Auto Memory Attributes	This setting is related to the percentage of memory allocated to the session cache at runtime.
Additional Concurrent Pipelines for Lookup Cache Creation	This setting is related to the creation of concurrent caches by creating an additional pipeline for the lookup transformation. By default, the value is set to **Auto**, which indicates that the value will be decided at runtime. Informatica caches the data either concurrently or sequentially. If you set this property to 0, Informatica processes the lookup cache sequentially.
Custom Properties	You can customize some of the default properties for the session. Usually, we need not change the settings.

The **Log Options** setting under the **Config Object** tab is shown in the following screenshot:

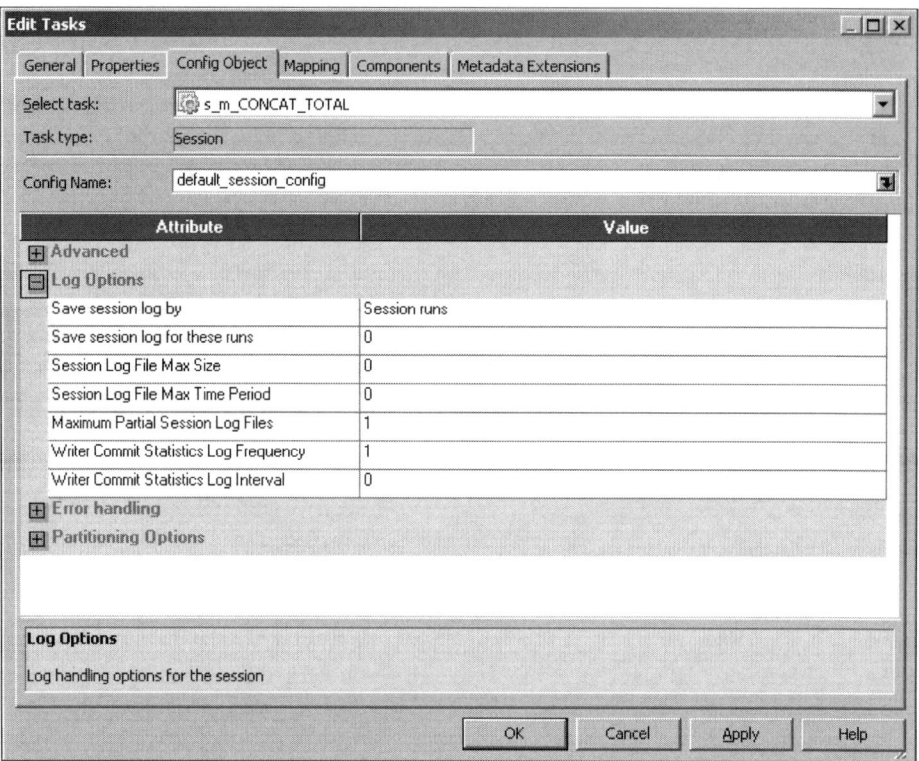

The description of the property shown in the preceding screenshot is as follows:

Property	Description
Save session log by	You have the option to save the session log file by either session runs or timestamp.
	When you set the option as a session run, Informatica saves a specific number of session log files. You can set the number of log files to be saved in the **Save Session Log for These Runs** option.
	When you set the option as **Timestamp**, Informatica saves the session log file by appending the timestamp to the log filename.
	When you save the history of session log files, you can use the files to compare the files in case of any errors.

Property	Description
Save session log for these runs	This option allows you to define the number of session log files you wish to save in order to maintain the history of log files. By default, the session log files are overwritten. The maximum number of history you can maintain is 2,147,483,647.
Session Log File Max Size	With this, you can define the maximum size of the session log file. If the log file size exceeds the value defined in this property, a new log file is created. The default value is 0.
Session Log File Max Time Period	With this, you can define the maximum number of hours for which the information is written for a session log file. If the maximum time exceeds the value defined in this property, a new log file is created. The default value is 0.
Maximum Partial Session Log Files	With this, you can define the maximum number of log files to be saved. If the number of files exceeds the value defined in this property, the oldest file is overwritten.
Writer Commit Statistics Log Frequency	With this, you can define the frequency at which the commit statistics are written to the session log. The default value is 1.
Writer Commit Statistics Log Interval	With this, you can define the time interval at which the commit statistics are written to the session log. The time is defined in minutes.

The **Error handling** properties under the **Config Object** tab is shown in the following screenshot:

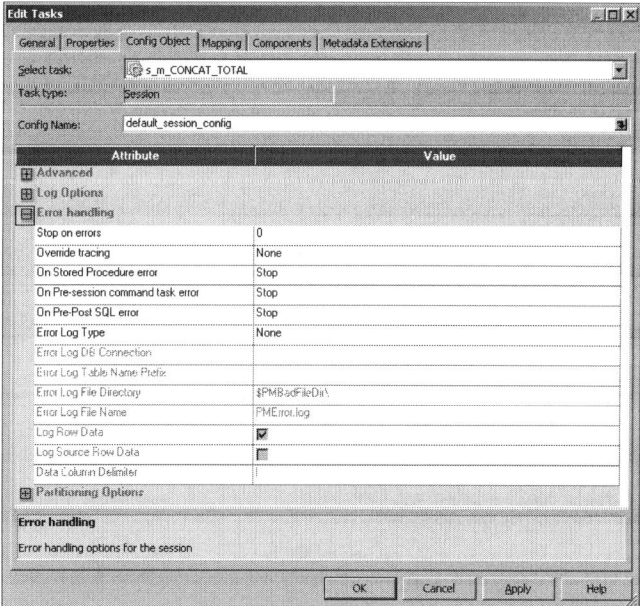

The description of the property shown in the preceding screenshot is as follows:

Property	Description
Stop on errors	This option defines the number of errors till you do not wish to fail the workflow. If you set this as 5, Informatica will keep on running till it encounters 5 error rows. On sixth error record, Informatica will fail the workflow.
Override tracing	You can override the tracing level set in the mapping. If you defined the tracing level as **Terse** in **Mapping** and you selected the **Normal Tracing** level in **Session**, Informatica will take the tracing level as normal and reject the setting in the mapping. Various options that are available are **None**, **Terse**, **Normal**, **Verbose Initialization**, and **Verbose Data**.
On Stored Procedure error	You can select this option to define what should happen if there is any pre- or post-session stored procedure error. If you select the **Stop** option, the session will fail if it encounters an error in the stored procedure. If you select the **Continue** option, the session will continue even if it encounters an error in **Stored Procedure**.
On Pre-session command task error	You can use this option when you use the **Pre-session Command** task in the **Session** task. If you select the **Stop** option, the session will fail if it encounters an error in the pre-session command. If you select the **Continue** option, the session will continue even if it encounters an error in the pre-session command.
On Pre-Post SQL error	You can use this option when you use a pre- or post- SQL command in the session task. If you select the **Stop** option, the session will fail if it encounters an error in the pre- or post- SQL command. If you select the **Continue** option, the session will continue even if it encounters an error in the pre- or post- SQL command.
Error Log Type	You can use this option to define the type of error log to be generated. The available options are **Flat File**, **Relational Database**, or **None**. The default setting is set to **None**.
Error Log DB Connection	If you select **Error Log Type** as **Relational Database**, this option gets enabled. You can specify the **Database Connection** details for **Error Log**.
Error Log Table Name Prefix	With this, you can mention the table name you created to store the error logs.

Property	Description
Error Log File Directory	If you select the error log type as **Flat File**, this option gets enabled. You can specify the file directory details for the error log.
Error Log File Name	With this, you can mention the name of the error log file.
Log Row Data	If you select this option, you can save the row-level transformation data into the log.
Log Source Row Data	If you select this option, you can save the source-row-level data into the log. The data is not saved by default.
Data Column Delimiter	You can define the delimiters to be used when saving the row data and source row data. The default delimiter is the (	) pipeline.

The **Partitioning Options** property under the **Config Object** tab is shown in the following screenshot:

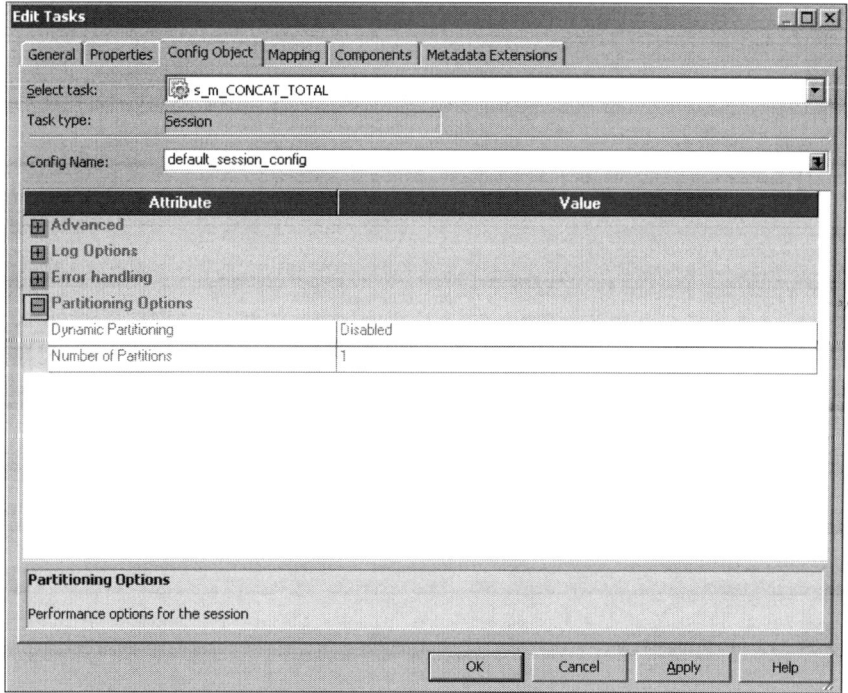

The description of the property shown in the preceding screenshot is as follows:

Property	Description
Dynamic Partitioning	You can enable the partitioning option for which you run the process. The default setting is disabled. This is available only if you have the partitioning license available.
	The various options available are **Based on number of partitions, Based on number of nodes in grid, Based on source partitioning,** and **Based on number of CPUs.**
Number of Partitions	You can define the number of partitions you wish to set.

Edit Tasks also has the following tabs:

- **Mapping**: With this you can define the session, target, and lookup transformation path or connection. We discussed this tab in the previous chapter.

- **Components**: With this, you can define pre- or post- Command and Email tasks. This acts as a replacement for the Command and Email tasks.

The **Components** tab is shown in the following screenshot:

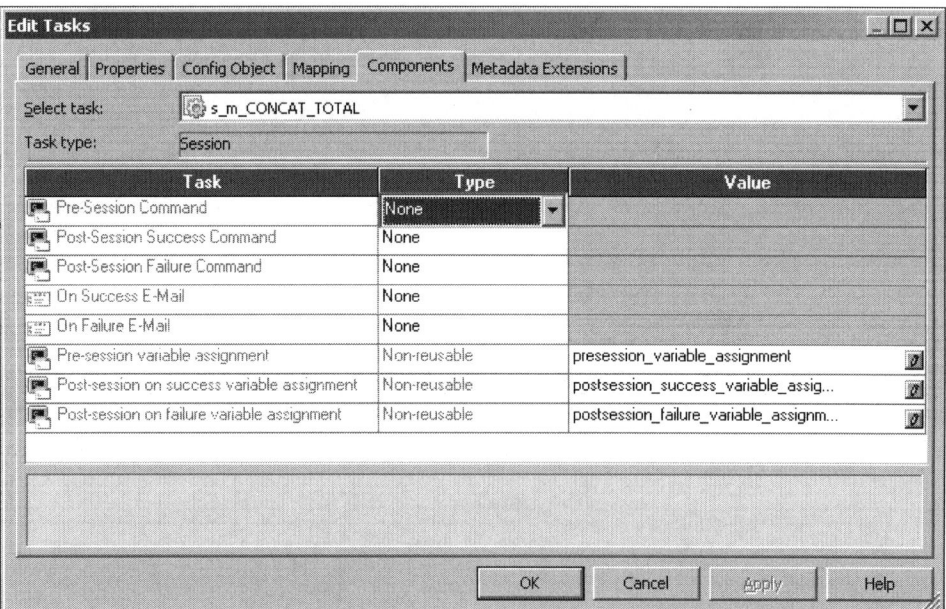

The description of the property shown in the preceding screenshot is as follows:

Property	Description
Pre-Session Command	You can use this option as a replacement for the command task used before the session task. You can define reusable or nonreusable types and also define the shell command you wish to mention in the command task. Informatica executes the pre-session command before it executes the session task.
	We will talk about the command task in detail later in the chapter.
Post-Session Success Command	You can use this option as a replacement for the post-session success command task used after the session task. You can define reusable or nonreusable types and also define the shell command you wish to mention in the command task. Informatica executes the post-session command after the successful completion of the session task. You need not define any condition in the link.
Post-Session Failure Command	You can use this option as a replacement for the post-session failure command task used after the session task. You can define reusable or nonreusable types and also define the shell command you wish to mention in the command task. Informatica executes the post-session command if the session task fails.
On Success E-mail	You can use this option as a replacement for the post-session success Email task used after the Session task. You can define reusable or nonreusable types and also define the e-mail properties you wish to mention in the Email task. Informatica executes the Post-Session E-mail after the successful execution of the session task.
On Failure E-mail	You can use this option as a replacement for the post-session failure Email task used after the Session task. You can define reusable or nonreusable types and also define the e-mail property you wish to mention in the Email task. Informatica executes the post-session e-mail if the session task fails.
Pre-session variable assignment	You can assign values to various parameters and variables used in the mapping and session before the session is executed.
Post-session on success variable assignment	You can assign values to various parameters and variables used in the workflow and worklet after the session is executed successfully.
Post-session on failure variable assignment	You can assign values to various parameters and variables used in the workflow and worklet if the session task fails.

The **Metadata Extensions** tab helps define metadata-extension-related properties. Usually, we do not use this tab. It is used to define general information related to the workflow or to define the project-level information that can be used in future for reference purposes.

Creating a session task

To create a session task in Workflow Manager or Task Developer, perform the following steps:

1. In **Workflow Manager** or **Task Developer**, navigate to **Tasks | Create**.

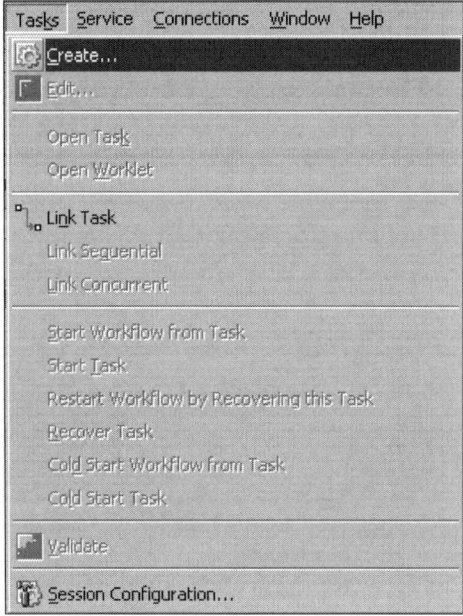

 This step is the first step to be performed when creating any task.

2. From the list of tasks, select the **Session** task and specify the name of the session task as s_TASK_NAME. For our reference, we are using the session task name as s_CONCAT_TOTAL or s_m_CONCAT_TOTAL, where m_CONCAT_TOTAL is the mapping name for which we are creating the session. Click on **Create**.

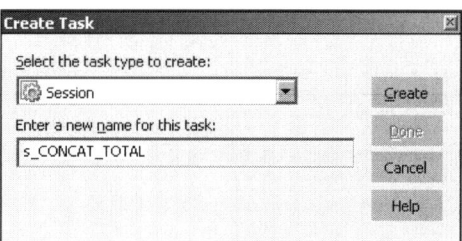

3. In the next window, select the mapping you wish to associate in the session. When you run the session, it makes the data flow from the source to the target in the mapping you selected. Note that once you associate a mapping to a session, you cannot change the mapping. Click on **OK**, and then click on **Done**.

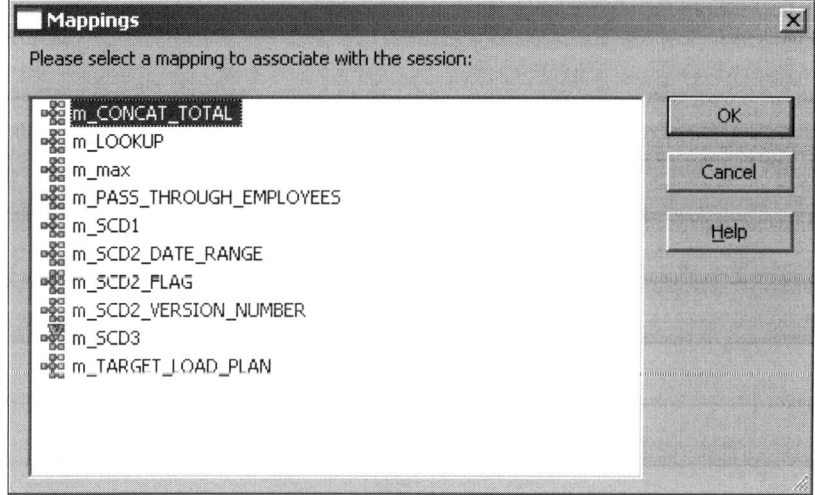

The session task appears in Workflow Manager or Task Developer. Use the Link task to connect the start task to the session task:

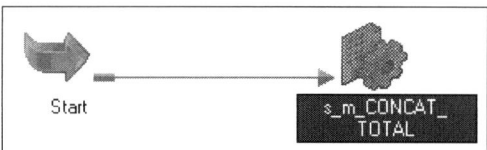

The command task

The command task is used to execute shell scripts or standalone shell commands. You can define one or more commands or scripts in a command task. If you define multiple command or scripts in the same command task, the task executes the commands in a sequence.

You can define Unix/Perl commands for Unix servers or DOS commands for Windows servers. If your Informatica server is installed on a Unix operating system, you will be able to execute Unix commands. If the Informatica server is installed on Windows, you can use DOS commands.

Creating a command task

To create a command task in Workflow Manager or Task Developer, perform the following steps:

1. In Workflow Manager or Task Developer, navigate to **Tasks | Create** (refer to the screenshot shown in the *Creating a Session task* section).

2. From the list of tasks, select the **Command** task and specify the name of the command task, which is cmd_TASK_NAME. For our reference, we are using the command task name as cmd_COPY_FILE. Click on **Create**, and then click on **Done**.

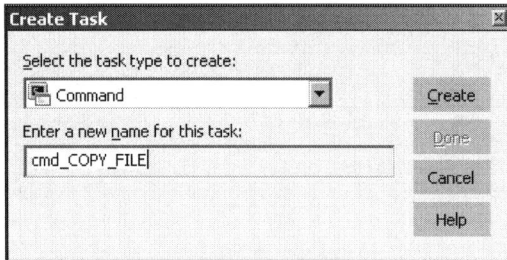

The task appears in Workflow Manager or Task Developer. Use the link task to connect the start task to the command task.

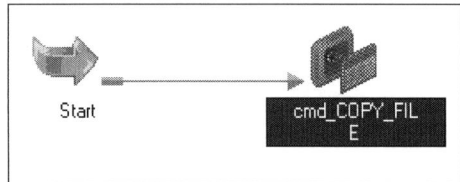

3. Double-click on the command task to open the task in the edit view. Click on **Commands**.

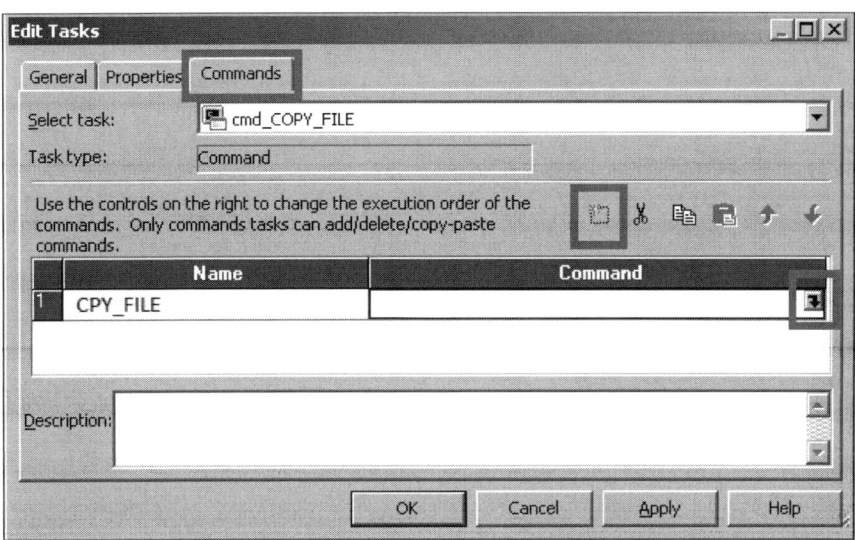

Add a new command by clicking on the **Add a new Command** option, as shown in the preceding screenshot. In the **Name** column, enter the name of the command. For our reference, we are using COPY_FILE as the command name.

4. Click on the edit button to open **Command Editor** and write the command that you wish to execute. If you wish to execute Unix scripts, write the Unix script's path and name, otherwise simply define the Unix command. Click on **OK** to close the edit view.

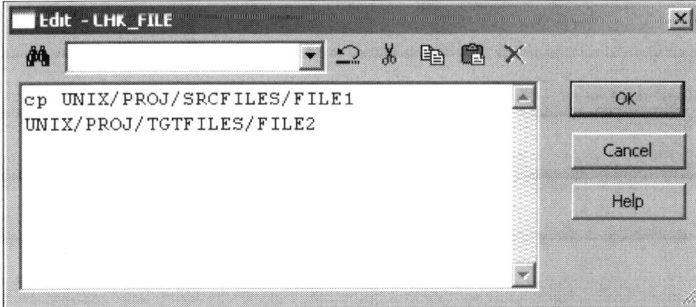

A sample Windows command is indicated in the following screenshot:

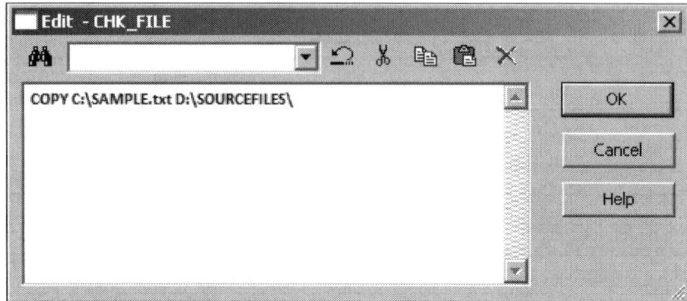

The e-mail task

The Email task is used to send success or failure e-mail notifications. You can use the Email task to send e-mail notifications to inform about the success or failure of a particular part of a workflow. You can use your mail server to send e-mail notifications. Your admin team will configure the mail server with Informatica to send e-mail notifications. Once you configure your mail server with Informatica, when an e-mail task gets triggered, the e-mail is sent directly from your mailbox.

You can configure the Email task to send e-mail notifications, or you can also configure the session task to send e-mail notifications. We have discussed the latter option in the session task.

Creating an e-mail task

To create an Email task in Workflow Manager or Task Developer, follow these steps:

1. In Workflow Manager or Task Developer, navigate to **Tasks | Create**.
2. From the list of tasks, select the Email task and specify the name of the Email task, which is em_TASK_NAME. For our reference, we are using the Email task name as em_FAILURE_NOTIFICATION. Click on **Create**, and then click on **Done**.

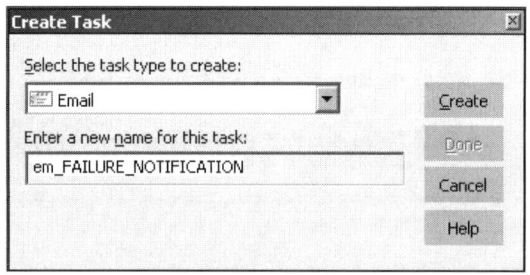

The task appears in Workflow Manager or Task Developer. Use the Link task to connect the start task to the Email task:

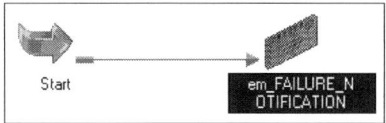

3. Double-click on the Email task to open the task in the edit view. Click on **Properties**.

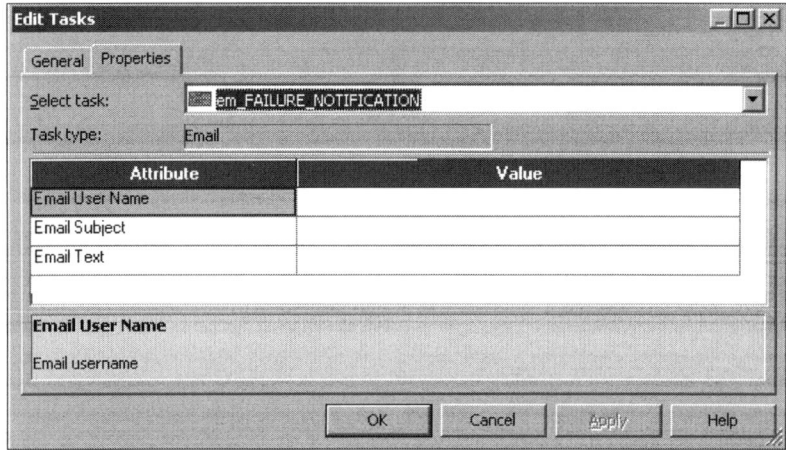

4. Click on **OK** to close the edit view.

5. Add the details in the Email task as follows:

    ○   **The Email user name**: Mention the name of the e-mail address to which you wish to send e-mail notifications. If you wish to send an e-mail to multiple users, separate the e-mail IDs by comma.

    ○   **Subject**: Enter the subject of the e-mail you wish to send.

    ○   **Text**: Click to open the e-mail editor to enter the text that you wish to send with the e-mail. You can attach the log file, workflow name, repository name, and so on using the variables available in the e-mail task editor.

The assignment task

The assignment task is used to assign a value to user-defined variables in Workflow Manager.

Before you can define a variable in the assignment task, you need to add the variable in Workflow Manager. To add a variable to the Workflow, perform the following steps:

1. In Workflow Manager, open the workflow for which you wish to define user-defined variables. Navigate to **Workflow | Edit | Variables**.

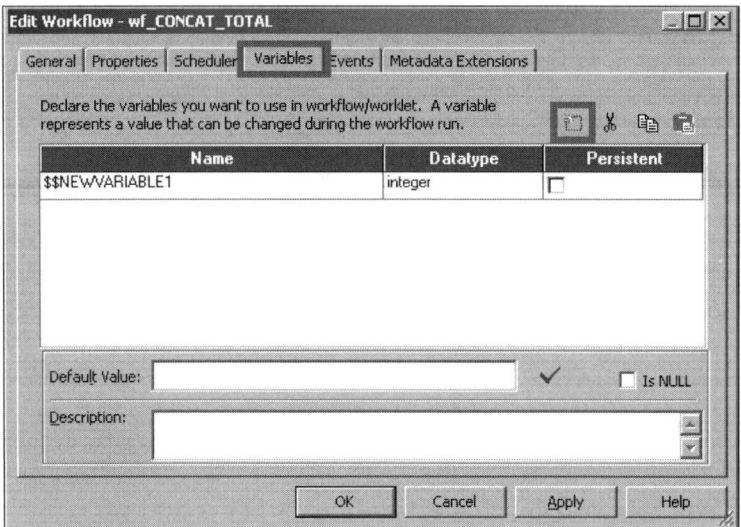

2. Click on the **Add a new variable** option to add new variables to the workflow, as shown in the preceding screenshot.

    A new variable is created, as shown in the preceding screenshot. The new variable that is created is $$NEWVARIABLE1. You can change the name of the variable and its data type.

Creating an assignment task

To create an assignment task in Workflow Manager, follow these steps:

1. In Workflow Manager, navigate to **Task | Create**.

2. From the list of tasks, select **Assignment Task** and specify the name of the assignment task, which is amt_TASK_NAME. For our reference, we are using the assignment task's name as amt_ASSIGN_VALUE. Then, click on **Done**.

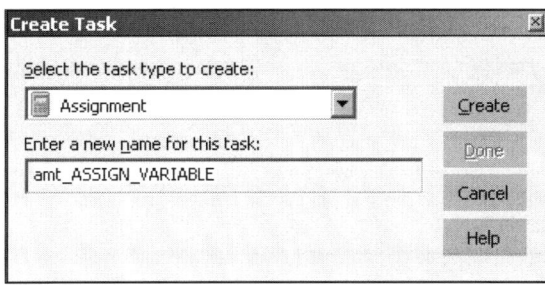

The task appears in Workflow Manager. Use the link task to connect the start task to the assignment task.

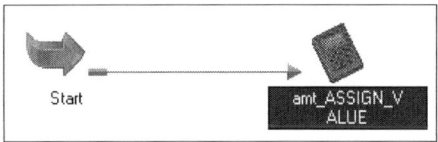

3. Double-click on the assignment task to open the task in the edit view. Navigate to **Expressions | Add a new Expression**.

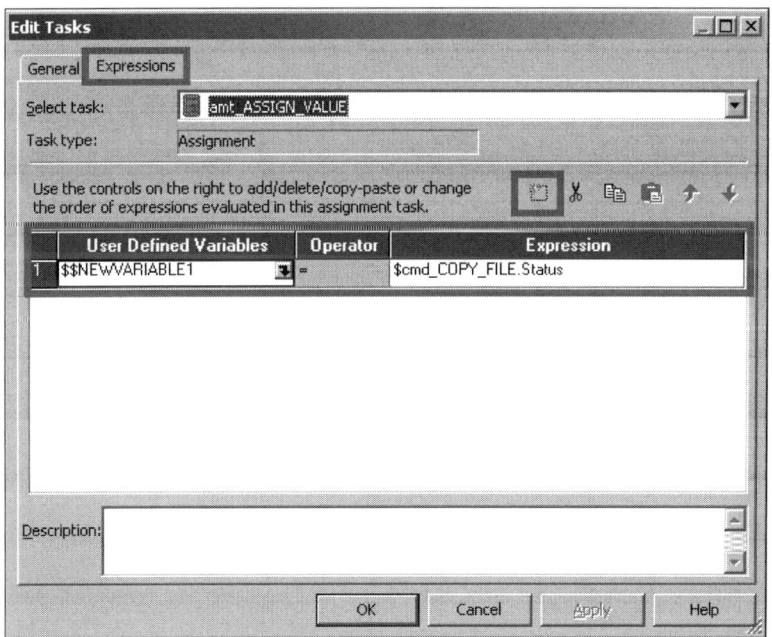

Select the user-defined variable you added at the Workflow level. We have added $$NEWVARIABLE1.

4. Assign the value that you wish to assign to the variable. We have assigned the status of the `cmd_COPY_FILE` command task from the **Expressions** tab in the assignment task, as shown in the preceding screenshot. Then, click on **OK**.

The timer task

The timer task is used to add a time gap between the executions of two tasks. In other words, you can specify the time in the timer task to wait before the process triggers the next task in the workflow. Also, another option in the timer task allows you to start the next task after a particular time gap in the workflow.

The timer task has two types of settings:

- **Absolute Time**: This option enables you to specify the time when you want the next task to start in the workflow.

- **Relative Time**: This option enables you start the next task by comparing the start time of the timer task. If you mention **Relative time** as **10 minutes**, Informatica PowerCenter will wait for 10 minutes at the timer task before it triggers the next task in the workflow.

Creating a timer task

To create a timer task in Workflow Manager, perform the following steps:

1. In Workflow Manager, navigate to **Tasks** | **Create**.

2. From the list of tasks, select the **Timer** task and specify the name of the timer task, which is `tm_TASK_NAME`. For our reference, we are using the Timer task's name as `tm_TIME_GAP`. Click on **Create**, and then click on **Done**.

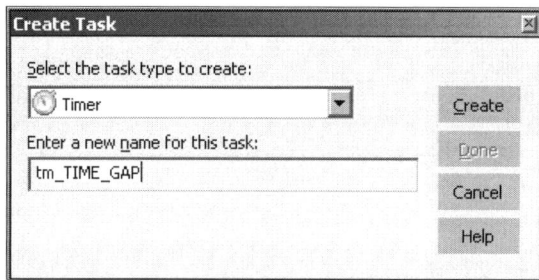

The timer task appears in Workflow Manager. Use the link task to connect the start task to the timer task.

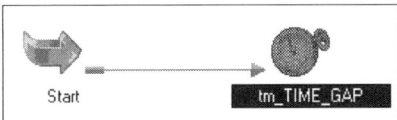

3. Double-click on the Timer task to open the task in the edit view. Click on **Timer**. Based on your requirement, select the **Relative time** or **Absolute time** option. Then, click on **OK**.

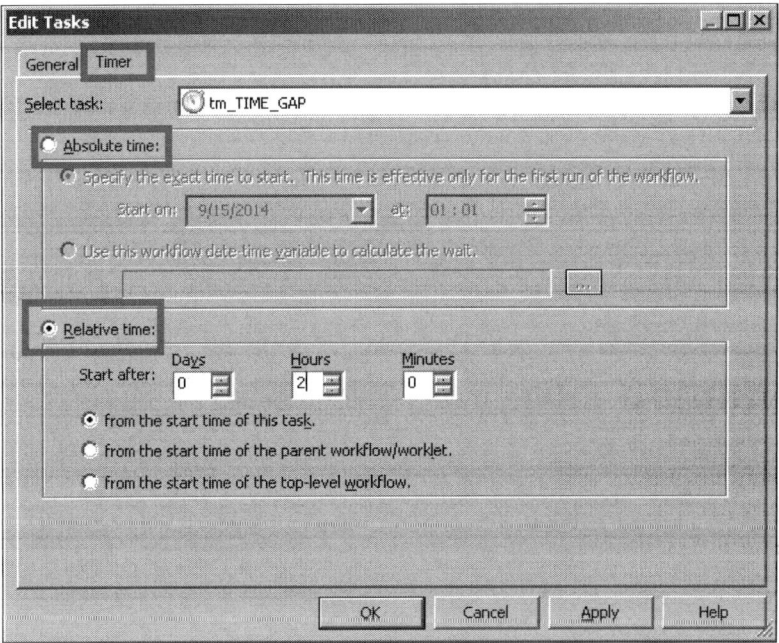

For reference, we have selected **Relative time** in the preceding screenshot. Based on the selection, our timer task will start the execution after 2 hours from the end of previous task.

The control task

The control task is used to control the execution of the workflow. You can stop, abort, or fail the parent workflow or top-level workflow by defining the appropriate condition in the control task.

The control task acts as a green signal or red signal. If you use a control task in a branch in the workflow and if everything is moving smoothly, that is, there are no issues with the process, the control task will not even get triggered. It will act invisible. However, if the process catches up with the issue, the control task will take control, and based on the option you select in the properties, it will stop, abort, or fail the workflow or the top-level workflow.

Creating a control task

To create a control task in Workflow Manager, perform the following steps:

1. In Workflow Manager, navigate to **Task | Create**.

2. From the list of tasks, select the **Control** task and specify the name of the control task, which is cntl_TASK_NAME. For our reference, we are using the control task name as cntl_ABORT_WORKFLOW. Click on **Create**, and then click on **Done**.

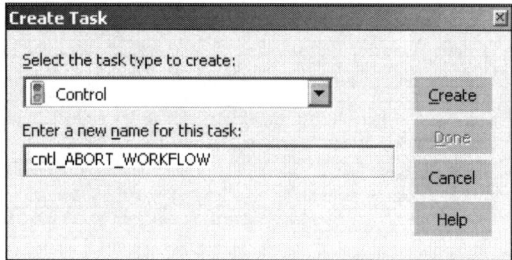

The control task appears in Workflow Manager. Use the link task to connect the start task to the control task.

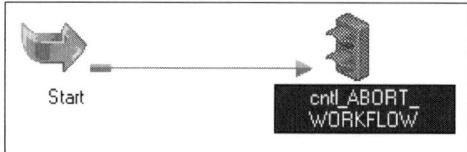

3. Double-click on the control task to open the task in the edit view. Click on **Properties**.

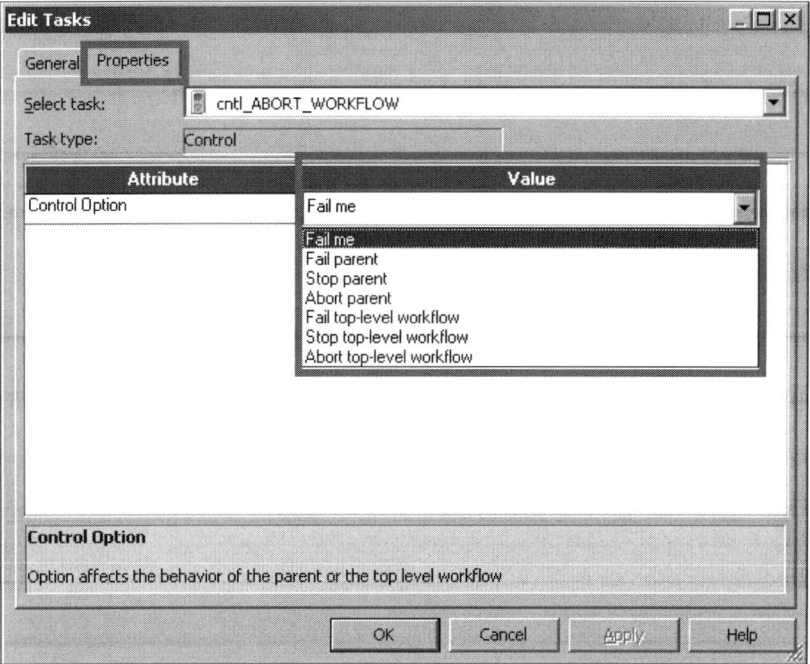

4. Select a particular option from the drop-down list as per your requirements. The various options are present in the control task properties:

  ° **Fail Me**: If you select this option, the control task will show you the **FAILED** status in Workflow Monitor if the task is triggered.

  ° **Fail Parent**: If you select this option, the workflow will fail and you will see the status as **FAILED** in Workflow Monitor.

  ° **Stop Parent**: If you select this option, the workflow will stop, and you will see the status as **STOPPED** in Workflow Monitor.

  ° **Abort Parent**: If you select this option, the Workflow will abort and you will see the status as **ABORTED** in Workflow Monitor.

  ° **Fail Top-Level Workflow**: If you select this option, the top-level workflow will fail and you will see the status as **FAILED** in Workflow Monitor.

     ° **Stop Top-Level Workflow**: If you select this option, the top-level workflow will stop and you will see the status as **STOPPED** in Workflow Monitor.

     ° **Abort Top-Level Workflow**: If you select this option, the top-level workflow will abort and you will see the status as **ABORTED** in Workflow Monitor.

The decision task

You can control the execution of the workflow by defining the condition in the decision task. The decision task allows you to specify the condition using which you can control the execution of branches in a workflow. In other words, you can check the condition of multiple tasks, and based on that, you can decide whether you wish to trigger the next task or not.

Consider the workflow shown in the next screenshot. As you can see, the session task should be triggered only if the two tasks before the decision task are successful. We can define the condition in the two link tasks, but the problem in that case will be that the session task will be triggered even if one task is successful. This issue can be resolved using the decision task. You can define the condition in the decision task that will make the session task execute only if the two tasks are successful.

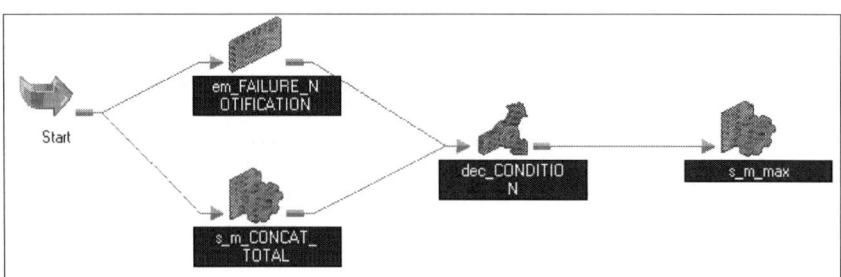

Creating a decision task

To create a decision task in Workflow Manager, follow these steps:

1. In Workflow Manager, navigate to **Tasks | Create**.

2. From the list of tasks, select the **Decision** task and specify the name of the decision task, which is `dec_TASK_NAME`. For our reference, we are using the decision task named `dec_CONDITION`. Click on **Create**, and then click on **Done**.

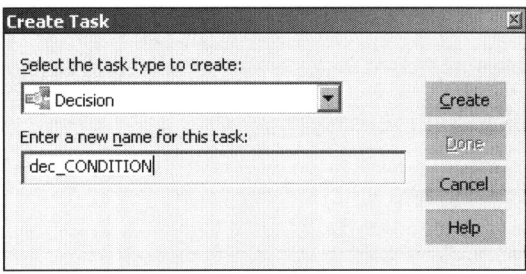

The decision task appears in Workflow Manager. Use the link task to connect the start task to the control task. In our case, we are implementing a scenario where the `s_m_max` session task should be triggered only after the successful execution of the `em_FAILURE_NOTIFICATION` Email task and the `s_m_CONCAT_TOTAL` session task, as shown in the preceding screenshot:

3. Double-click on the decision task to open the task in the edit view. Click on **Properties** and mention the condition under **Value**. As per our requirement, we have defined the condition as `$em_FAILURE_NOTIFICATION.Status = SUCCEEDED AND $s_m_CONCAT_TOTAL.Status = SUCCEEDED`. Now, click on **OK**.

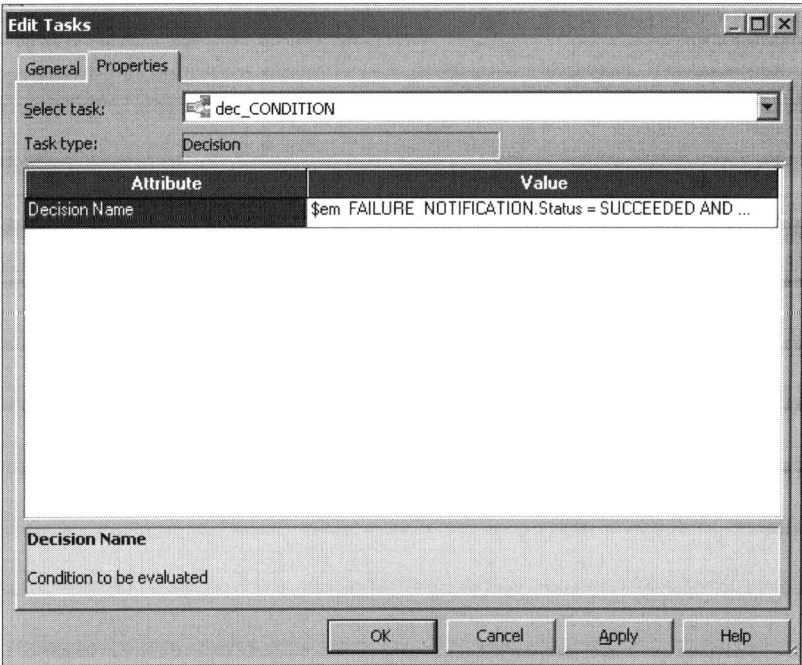

Event tasks – event wait and event raise

An event is simply a functionality that you wish to implement in a workflow. Informatica PowerCenter has some system-defined events, and you can define user-defined events as well.

There are two types of events:

- **The Event Wait task**: This is the task that waits for a particular event to occur. You can define the event for which the Event Wait task should wait. Once triggered, the Event Wait task will wait infinitely for the specified event. As soon the event occurs, the Event Wait succeeds and triggers the next task in the workflow.

  In the Event Wait task, you can define system-defined events (predefined events) or user-defined events.

- **Event Raise task**: As opposed to Event Wait, the Event Raise task triggers a particular event in the workflow.

  You can define only user-defined events in the Event Raise task.

Informatica PowerCenter events can be of two types—predefined or user-defined:

- **Predefined events**: These are also referred to as system-defined events. They are generally called file-watch events. You can use these events to wait for a specified file at a specific location. Once the file arrives at the path mentioned, the Event Wait or File Watcher triggers the rest of the tasks in the workflow.

- **User-defined events**: You can create an event of your own based on the requirement. An Event Raise task is nothing but a sequence of tasks in the workflow. To use a user-defined task, define the event under the workflow.

Before you can use user-defined events under event tasks, you need to create the event at the workflow level. Perform the following steps to add the event to the workflow:

1. Open the workflow in the Workflow Manager for which you wish to add a user-defined event, and then navigate to **Workflow** | **Edit** | **Events**.

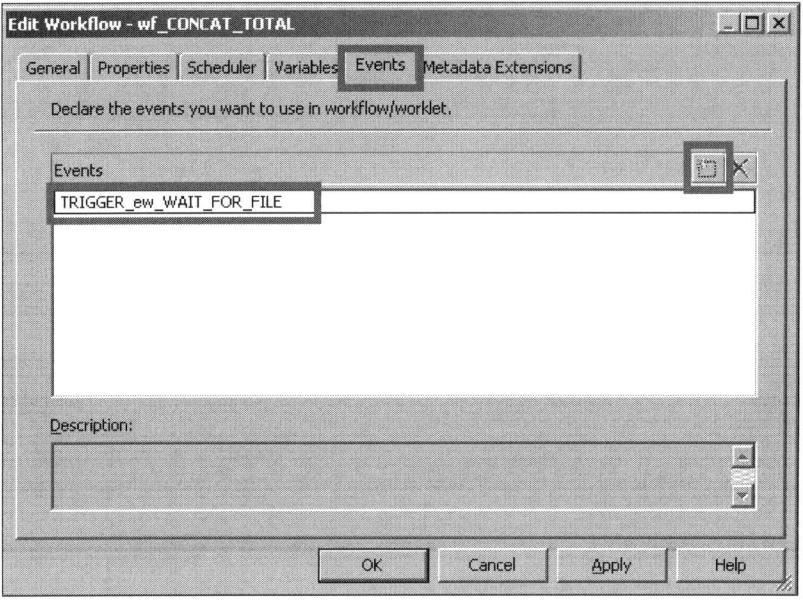

2. Add a new event, as shown in the preceding screenshot. Then, click on **OK**.

Creating an event (wait/raise) task

To create an Event Wait or Event Raise task in Workflow Manager, perform the following steps:

1. In Workflow Manager, navigate to **Task | Create**.

2. From the list of tasks, select the **Event Wait** or **Event Raise** task and specify the name of the task, which is ew_TASK_NAME or er_TASK_NAME. For our reference, we are using the Event Wait task name as ew_WAIT_FOR_FILE and the Event Raise task name as er_TRIGGER_TASK. Click on **Create**, and then click on **Done**.

The dialog box for the Event Wait task is shown as follows:

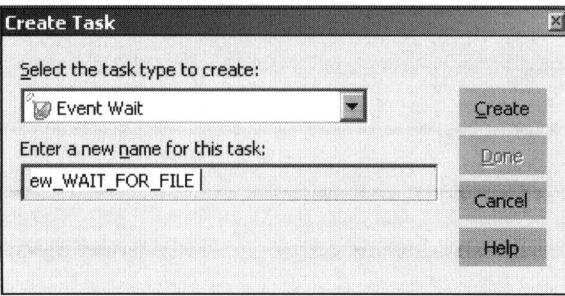

The dialog box for the Event Wait task is shown as follows:

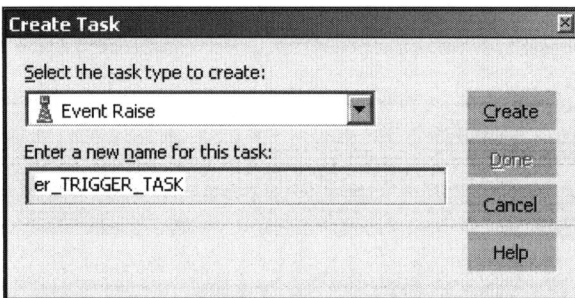

The Event (Wait/Raise) task appears in Workflow Manager. Use the link task to connect the start task with the event tasks.

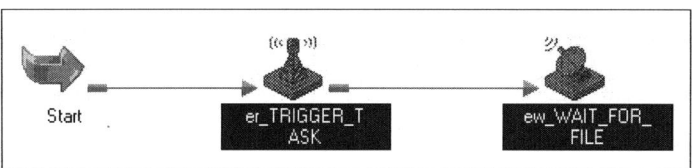

Note that you can use the Event Wait and Event Raise tasks individually as well. We have used both the tasks together for reference purposes.

3. Double-click on the Event Raise task and click on **Properties**. Add a new user-defined event, as shown in the following screenshot:

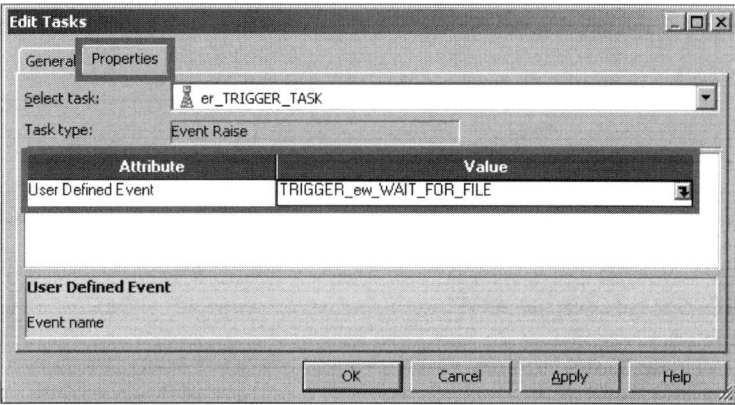

4. Double-click on the Event Wait task to open the task in the edit view. If you wish to use the **Predefined** task, specify the path and filename in the option. If you wish to use the **User-Defined** name, click on the add new event option. Then, click on **OK**.

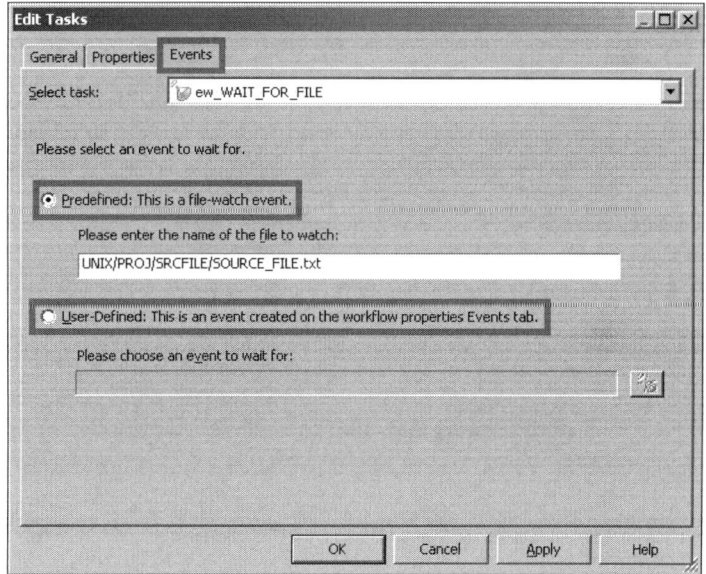

For our reference, we have added a predefined event called the file-watch event. We have added UNIX/PROJ/SRCFILES/SOURCE_FILE.txt as the event wait file.

The link task

The link task is used to control the execution of the workflow. You can have multiple branches in the workflow that can be triggered using the link task. By now, you must have understood that we use the link task to connect two tasks and also connect the start task with other tasks in a workflow. You can define the condition in the link task using which you can control the flow of the workflow.

You can define various conditions based on the tasks from which you are connecting the link.

Creating a link task

To create a Link task to connect two tasks, follow these steps:

1. In Workflow Manager, navigate to **Task | Link task**.

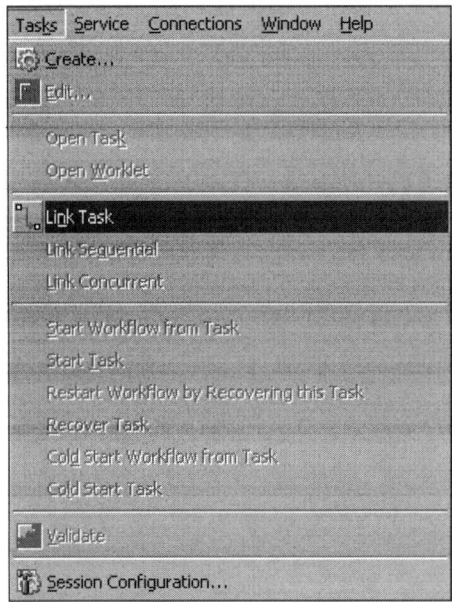

2. Drag the link between the tasks you wish to link.

Worklets – groups of tasks

Group of tasks that can be reused in multiple workflows are called worklets. Worklets are similar to mapplets in Mapping Designer. As you know from the previous chapter, you use mapplets instead of multiple transformations; similarly, you can use worklets instead of multiple tasks. When you wish to reuse the functionality implemented using multiple tasks, a worklet is your answer. As reusing a reusable task itself is a rare occurrence, you do not frequently reuse the logic of individual tasks, which makes using a worklet a more rare occurrence in Informatica. Worklets can surely save your time, as you can reuse an existing functionality. Similar to workflows, worklets should also start with a Start task.

Creating a worklet

To create a worklet, perform the following steps:

1. In Worklet Manager, navigate to **Worklets** | **Create**.

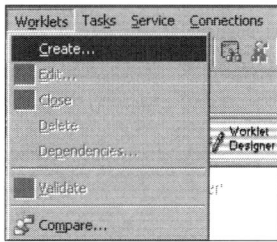

2. Specify the name of the worklet. For our reference, we are using the worklet name `wlt WORKLET`; then, click on **Done**.

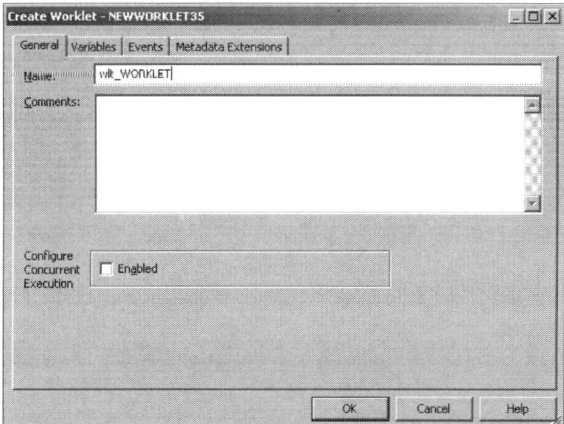

The start task appears in Worklet Manager.

3. Drag the existing reusable task from the navigator under **Sessions** or **Tasks** to your worklet. We have dragged the existing reusable session, which is `s_m_CONCAT_TOTAL`, to the worklet. Use the link task to connect the start task to the session task.

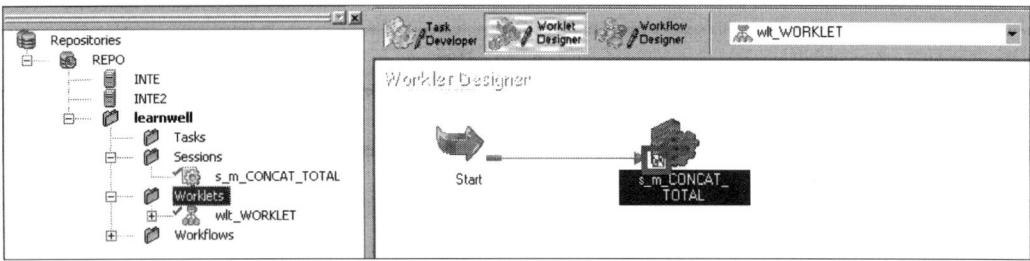

The small green icon at the bottom of session task, which is indicated in the preceding screenshot, represents it as a reusable task. The worklet gets added to the navigator under worklets.

Schedulers

Scheduling is one of the most important aspects of any technology we use. We need to schedule the process so that the process regularly gets executed at the specified interval. Using the schedule, you can define the frequency with which you wish to execute the workflow. Based on the frequency you have defined, the workflow will automatically get triggered. Informatica PowerCenter comes with an internal scheduler. To create a schedule, perform the following steps:

1. Open the workflow in the Workflow Manager for which you wish to define a scheduler, and navigate to **Workflows | Schedulers**.

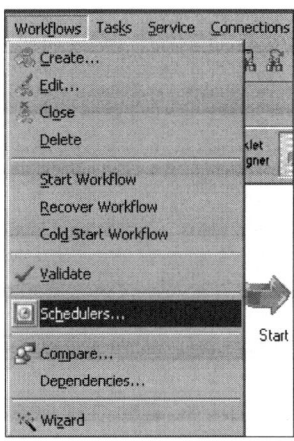

2. In the new window, you can add a scheduler. Then, click on **New**.

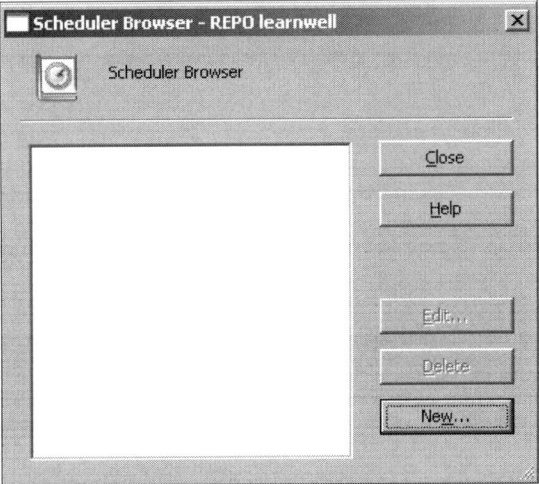

3. In the new window, specify the name of the scheduler as per your requirement, and click on **Schedule**.

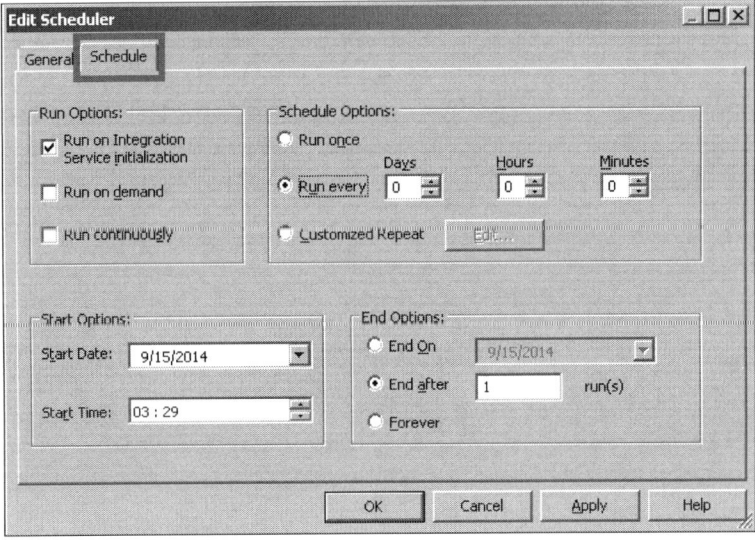

Various options present on the schedule screen are described as follows:

Option	Description
Run on Integration Service initialization	When you check this option, the workflow will get triggered as per your defined schedule. When you check this option, various options under the schedule option get enabled, and you can specify the time at and frequency with which you wish to execute the workflow.
Run on demand	When you check this option, you can run the workflow manually.
Run continuously	When you check this option, the workflow will keep on running continuously from the time you define as the start time.
Run once	This option indicates that the workflow will run only once at the scheduled time.
Run Every	When you check this option, you can schedule the workflow to run at a particular interval. If you wish to run the workflow every day, mention **1** under **Days** and define **Start data** and **End date**.
Customized Repeat	With this, you can customize the schedule with which you wish to run your workflow. This option is helpful in scenarios where you might only need to run your workflow on Mondays.
Start Date/Start Time	This option indicates the date at and the time from which you wish to schedule your workflow.
End On	This option indicates the date till which you wish to schedule your workflow.
End after	This option indicates the number of times you wish to let the workflow run.
Forever	If you check this option, the schedule will keep on running forever with no end date.

File List – the indirect way

File List is a concept that provides you with an easier way to merge the data and load it into the target. As the name suggests, it is specifically related to flat files. This is an indirect way of passing the source file. We saw earlier that we can define the source path and the source file name under the mapping tab in the session task. There is another property in the session task called the **Source File** type, where you can select the **Direct** or **Indirect** option, as shown in the following screenshot:

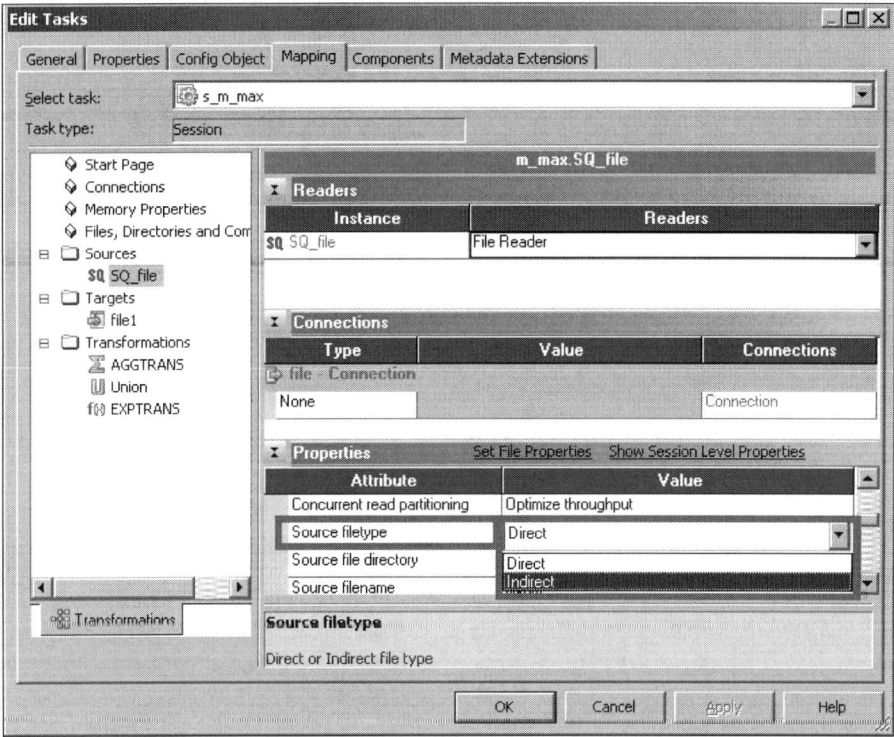

When we select **Source filetype** as **Direct**, Informatica directly goes to the defined **Source file directory** path and extracts the data from the filename defined in the **Source filename** option. When you select **Source filetype** as **Indirect**, Informatica reads the data from the file mentioned indirectly. Let's look at an example to understand this concept.

Consider that you have been provided with three source files with the same structure but different data. The names of the source files are `C:/FILE1.txt`, `D:/FILE2.txt`, and `E:/FILE3.txt`. The requirement is to merge the data into a target file. You can achieve the requirement using union transformation, which we are going to discuss in *Chapter 7, The Lifeline of Informatica – Transformations*, in the *Union transformations* section. The indirect file type concept helps you achieve the same requirement in an easier way. Remember to implement the File List concept—the files you are willing to merge should have exactly the same data type. To implement the file list, we will create another file with a name such as `FILE_LIST.txt`. Then, add the names of all the three files with the path in `FILE_LIST.txt`, as follows:

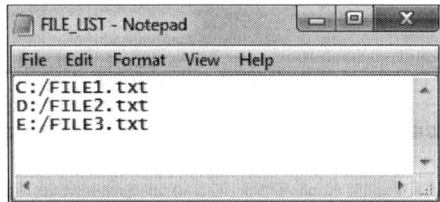

Define the properties in the session task for **Indirect** file type, as shown in the following screenshot:

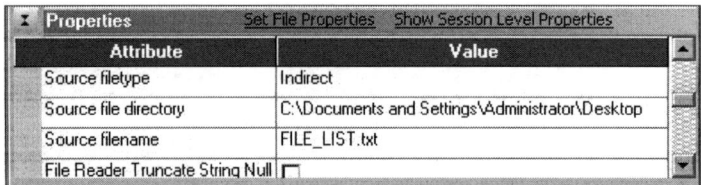

The mapping will be as simple as Source - Source Qualifier - Target.

When you define **Source filetype** as **Indirect**, Informatica reads the name of the files from `FILE_LIST.txt` and extracts the data one by one from the files mentioned in `FILE_LIST.txt`. This way, the data will be appended in the target.

Incremental aggregation

This concept is related to Aggregator transformation. When you have data, which in increasing but the existing data remains constant, you can utilize the incremental aggregation functionality to achieve the output faster and enhance the performance. When you select the **Incremental Aggregation** option in the **Session** properties, Informatica saves the result of the last run in the cache and replaces the value in the next run and hence enhances the performance. To understand this concept, let's look at an example.

Consider that you have a file containing the salary of employees, and you wish to get the sum of the salaries of all the employees. Then, consider that we have three employees in the month of JAN, six employees in the month of FEB, and nine employees in the month of MARCH, as shown in the following screenshot:

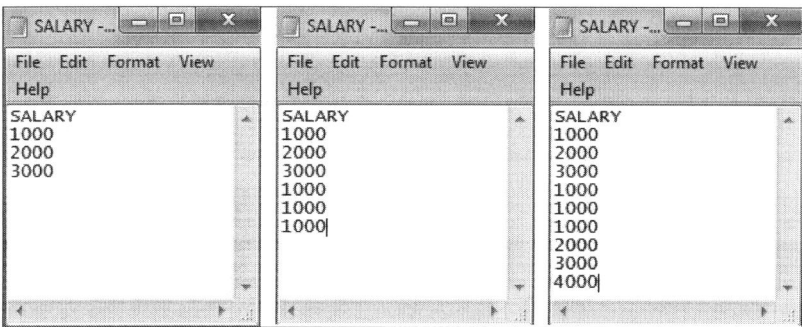

As you can see, the data in the file is increasing—the first file has the data of employees present in the month of JAN, the second file has the data of employees in the month of FEB, and the third file has the data for MARCH. To get the sum of the salaries of all the employees, we will use the Aggregator transformation. As the number of records is increasing, the time taken for the calculation will also increase. Also, note that the previous data does not change; only the new data is added to the file. To save time, we use the concept of incremental aggregation. This option is present in the session task, as shown in the screenshot of the **Properties** tab in the preceding *Tabs of Session task* section.

When you run the file for the month of JAN, the Aggregator transformation will calculate the value of three records and give the corresponding output, which is 6000 in our case. When you do not check the **Incremental Aggregation** option, Informatica again calculates the six records in the file for the month of FEB and gives you the result, which is 9000 in our case. If you use the **Incremental Aggregation** option, the aggregator cache will save the value of the last run, which is 6000. When you run the same process for the month of FEB, Informatica replaces the first three records of the file with the value stored in the cache and adds new records to get the result. This results in faster calculation, as the number of records to be calculated reduces.

The basic criterion in order to use incremental aggregation is that the data from the previous run should remain the same.

If the records from the previous run change, the result will be incorrect, as Informatica will not consider the changed value and will replace that value with the value stored in the cache. To handle this, make sure that you check the **Reinitialize aggregate cache** box. When you check this option, Informatica reinitializes the aggregate cache value and stores the new value. It is important to note that you need to uncheck the **Reinitialize aggregate cache** option if your data is not changing, otherwise it will always keep on reinitializing the cache, which will indirectly hamper the performance.

The parameter file – parameters and variables

It is always a best practice of coding that you should never hardcode the values. The same applies to Informatica as well. It is always better to pass the values using parameters or variables instead of hardcoding them. When you define parameters or variables in the code, you need to pass the values to those parameters and variables. Parameter files serve this purpose. Any value that you hardcode can be passed through a parameter file. You can define the parameter file at the session level and the workflow level.

You must have noticed the system defined $PMSourceFileDir\ or $PMTargetFileDir\ variables. Similar to them, we can define the user-defined variables. You can define the variable at both the mapping level and the workflow level.

> If the value that is passed remains constant across the session run, it is called the parameter, and if the value changes across the session run, it is called the variable.

Let's take a look at an example to understand the parameter file. You are aware that Informatica has three different repositories to cater to the need of three regions. Let's say we have three repositories—REPO_DEV, REPO_TEST, and REPO_PROD—that serve development, testing, and production regions, respectively. Also, we have three Oracle databases corresponding to three regions, which are ORACLE_DEV, ORACLE_TEST, and ORACLE_PROD, respectively. When you start the coding in the development region under REPO_DEV, you will hardcode the database connection value to ORACLE_DEV. Your code is working successfully, and when you want to deploy the code to the test region, you will need to manually replace the database connection value with ORACLE_TEST. Changing the code after the testing is not allowed. The same case applies when you wish to deploy the code from the test to the production.

The solution comes as a parameter file. Parameter files serve the purpose of passing the value based on the region in which you are running the code. We are defining the parameter file to pass the value for the source database connection ($DBCONNECTION1), target file name ($TGTFILENAME), e-mail recipient ($EMAILUSER), and a mapping-level variable for location ($$LOCATION). We are using examples of a session-level variable, workflow-level variable, and mapping-level variable so that you understand clearly how they work.

Defining session-level variables

The variables that are defined under the session task are called session-level variables. There are various values that can be passed via variables, such as the source, target database connection value, source/target filename, source/target file path, session log file name/path, and so on. The session task does most of the work in the Workflow Manager screen and hence has been assigned special privileges. To pass the value through a variable, simply replace the hardcoded value with a variable of your choice. As shown in the following screenshot, we are using a database connection variable as $DBCONNECTION1:

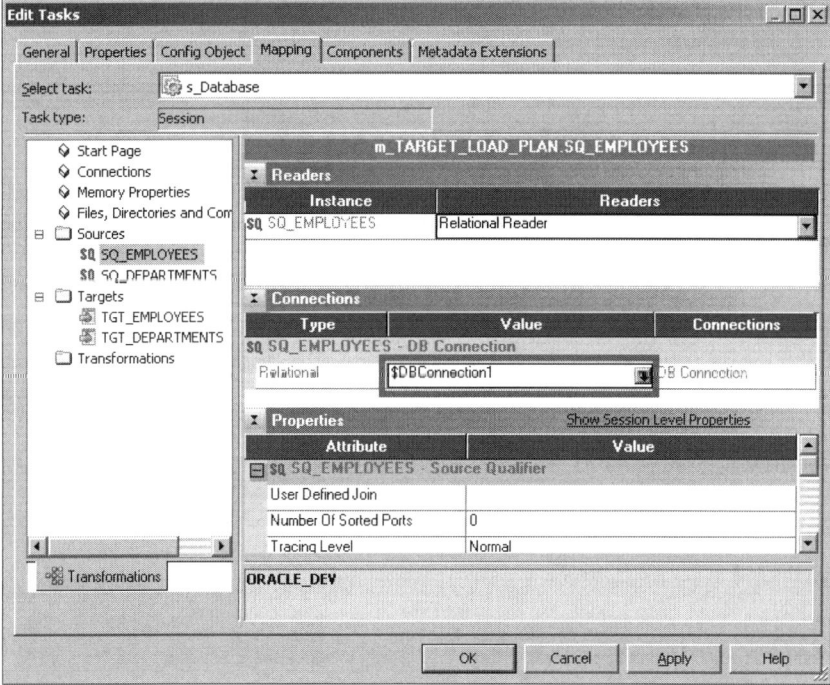

Similarly, assign the value to the target filename ($TGTFILENAME). As we define the target filename under the session task, it will be referred to as a session-level variable.

Defining workflow-level variables

The variables that are defined under various tasks are called workflow-level variables. Note that you can define the session-level variables under the workflow as well as in the parameter file. In our case, we are passing the e-mail user value as variable. To assign the value, simply replace the hardcoded value with the variable in the Email task, as shown in the following screenshot:

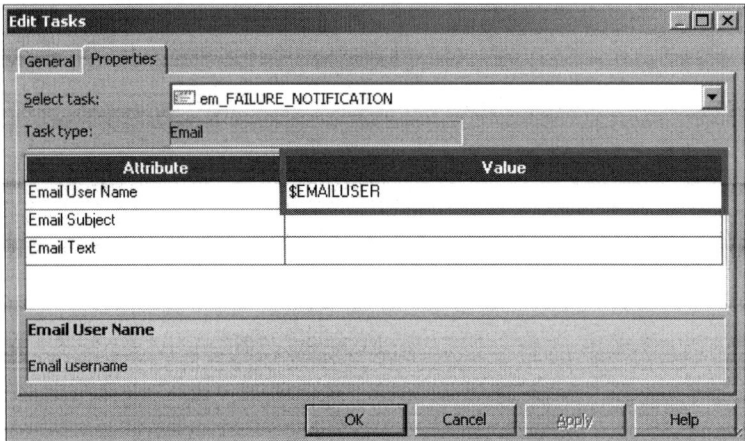

Defining mapping-level variables

As mentioned earlier, you can define variables for the hardcoded values in the mapping inside transformations as well. You need to define parameters or variables under **Mapping** before you can use them in transformations, otherwise the mapping will become invalid. To add the value, perform the following steps:

1. Open the mapping for which you wish to add variables in Mapping Designer, and navigate to **Mappings | Parameters and Variables**.

2. In the next screen, click on **Add a new variable to this table**. Define the variable as **select the type as Parameter and Variable** based on your requirement. Now, click on **OK**.

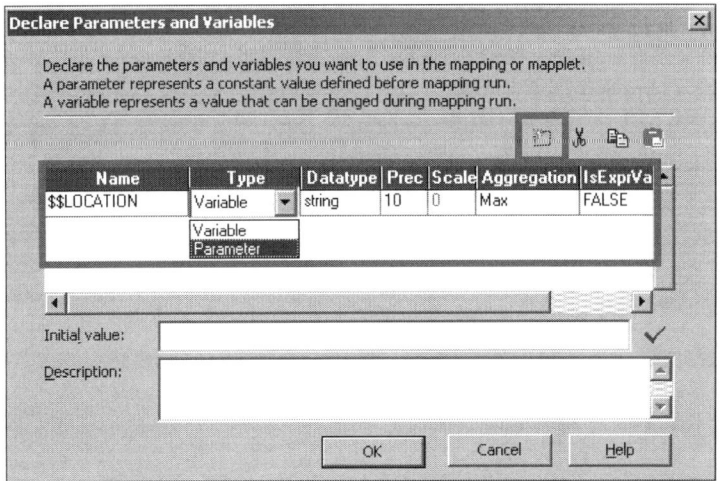

As you can see, the mapping-level variables are always defined as $$.

3. Open the transformation for which you wish to assign a variable or parameter. We are using filter transformations to pass the value.

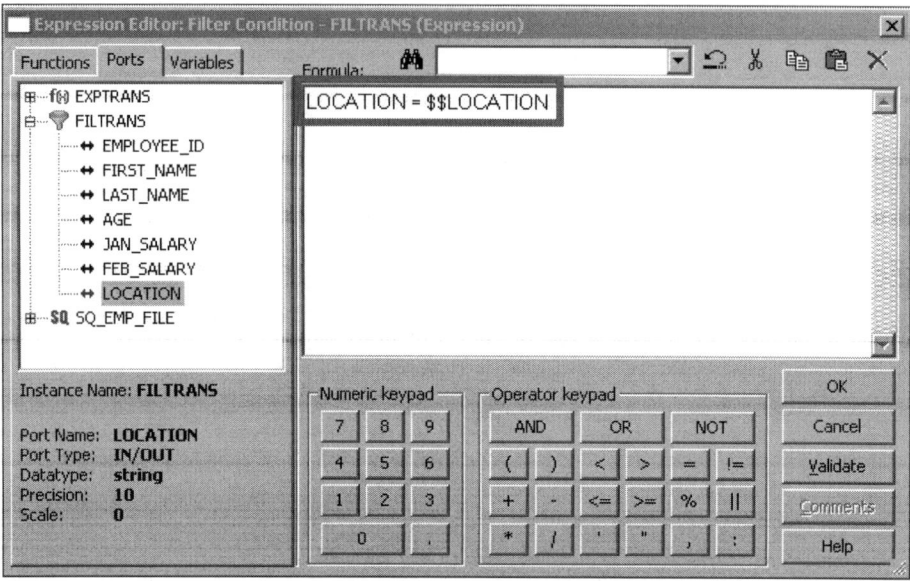

As you can see, we have assigned $$LOCATION to filter the condition.

With this, we are done with defining the variable or parameters. Next, we will see how to pass the values to them using the parameter file.

Creating the parameter file

A parameter file is nothing but a simple .txt file that contains the value of the variable to be passed to variables. A sample parameter file for the variable defined in the preceding steps is as follows:

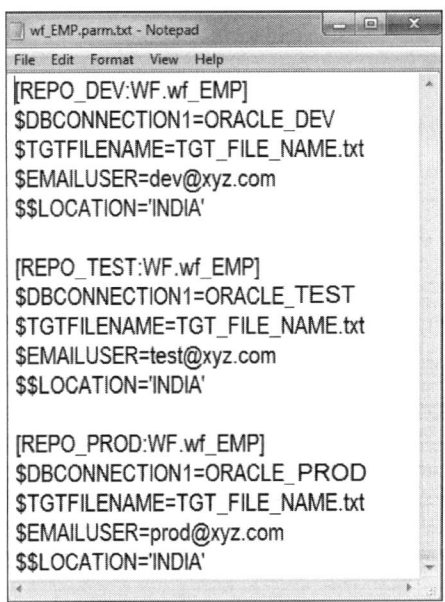

As you can see, the parameter file contains the values of the variables to be replaced in the three regions. Informatica matches the repository name against the name of the repository defined in the parameter file and replaces the values of the variables internally before it runs the workflow. The name of workflow for which you defined the parameter file is wf_EMP. So, if you are running workflow in the production region, Informatica will match the REPO_PROD repository name with the same name in the parameter file and internally replace the variables with the value and execute the workflow with the replaced values.

Mentioning the parameter file at the workflow level

To define the parameter file at the workflow level, open Workflow Manager and navigate to **Workflow | Edit | Properties**. Specify the path and name of the parameter file for the attribute, as indicated in the following screenshot:

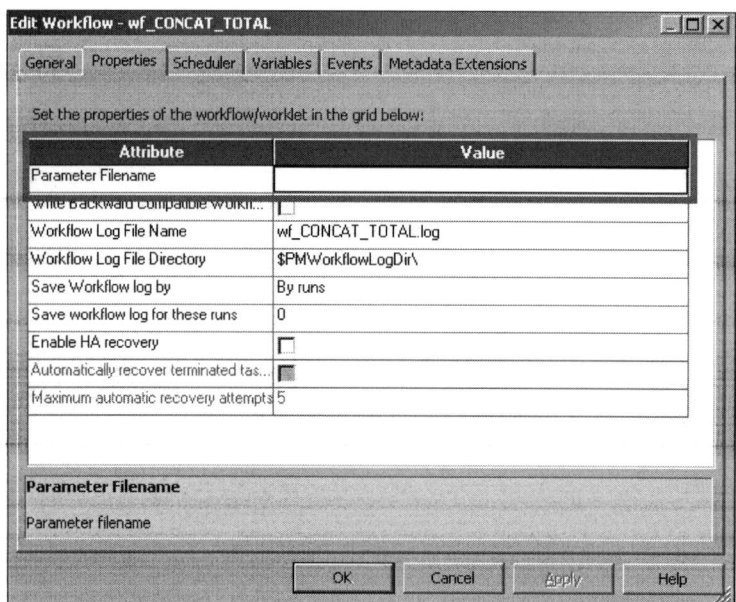

Mentioning the parameter file at the session level

To define the parameter file at the session level, open the session in Workflow Manager, double-click on the session task, and click on **Properties**. Specify the path and name of the parameter file for the attribute, as indicated in the following screenshot:

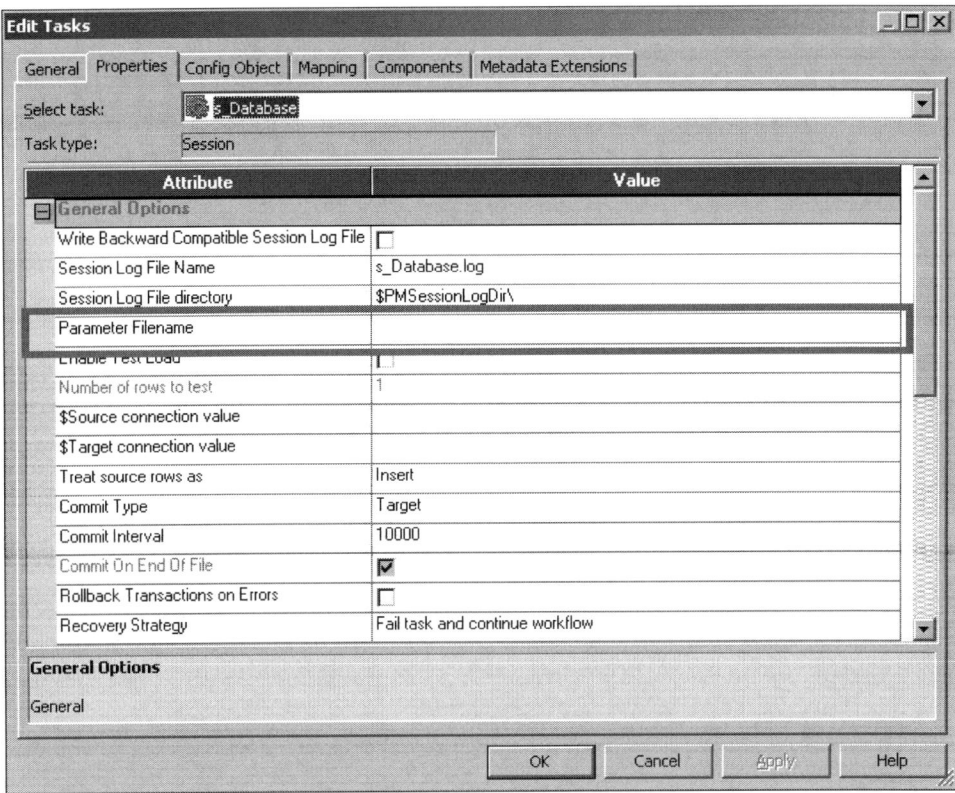

We have learned how to use the parameters and variables, create the parameter file, and define the parameter file. Another importance of the parameter file is that if the value of any variable is changing, you need not modify the code; simply change the value in the parameter file, and the changed value will take effect the next time you run the code.

Also, note that parameter files can also be used to replace the value for an individual session run. Parameter files can also be defined at the folder level as against at the repository level, as seen earlier. It is not mandatory that you define the workflow for all three regions. A sample parameter file for an individual session run (s_m_EMP_PASS_THROUGH) defined at the folder level (learnwell) is shown in the following screenshot:

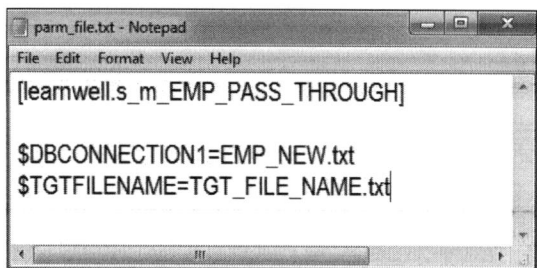

Summary

In this chapter, we talked about the various aspects of the Workflow Manager screen. We saw the detailed properties of the session task. We also saw the various tasks present in Workflow Manager. We learned how to create tasks and use them in a workflow.

We also learned how to work with worklets, which are groups of tasks that allow us to reuse the existing functionality that was implemented. We also talked about schedulers, which help us schedule the workflow to run at specific intervals. Later in the chapter, we talked about another topic called the file list, which provides us with a simpler way of merging the data with multiple files. Next, we covered incremental aggregation, which allows us to process the aggregate calculations faster by storing the value of the previous run. Last, we discussed the parameters file using which we can easily pass the values of variables and parameters.

In the next chapter, we are going to talk about our third client tool—the workflow monitor—where we will talk about looking at different views of monitoring workflows. We will also discuss logs and how to rectify errors using log files.

6
Monitoring Your Code – Using the Workflow Monitor Screen

In the previous chapter, we discussed some advanced topics on the Workflow Manager screen. Before we jump into this chapter, you now have an understanding of the various aspects of Informatica PowerCenter Designer and the Workflow Manager screen. This chapter will help you get a clear understanding about the Informatica PowerCenter Workflow Monitor screen. At this stage, you must be very clear on the basic usage of the Designer and Workflow Manager screen. We use the Workflow Monitor screen to check the status of the workflow that we executed in the Workflow Manager Screen. Apart from checking the status, the monitor screen serves various purposes, such as checking the statistics and understanding runtime details.

When you run the workflow, Workflow Monitor continuously receives information from Integration Services and other processes in order to display the information on the screen. The Workflow Monitor screen shows you the status of the workflow and the tasks being executed.

Using Workflow Monitor

The Workflow Monitor screen, as mentioned earlier, displays the status of the running workflow and tasks. It has two views to show the status – the **Gantt Chart** view and the **Task View**. You can select the view you wish to see. The Workflow Monitor screen can be seen in the following screenshot:

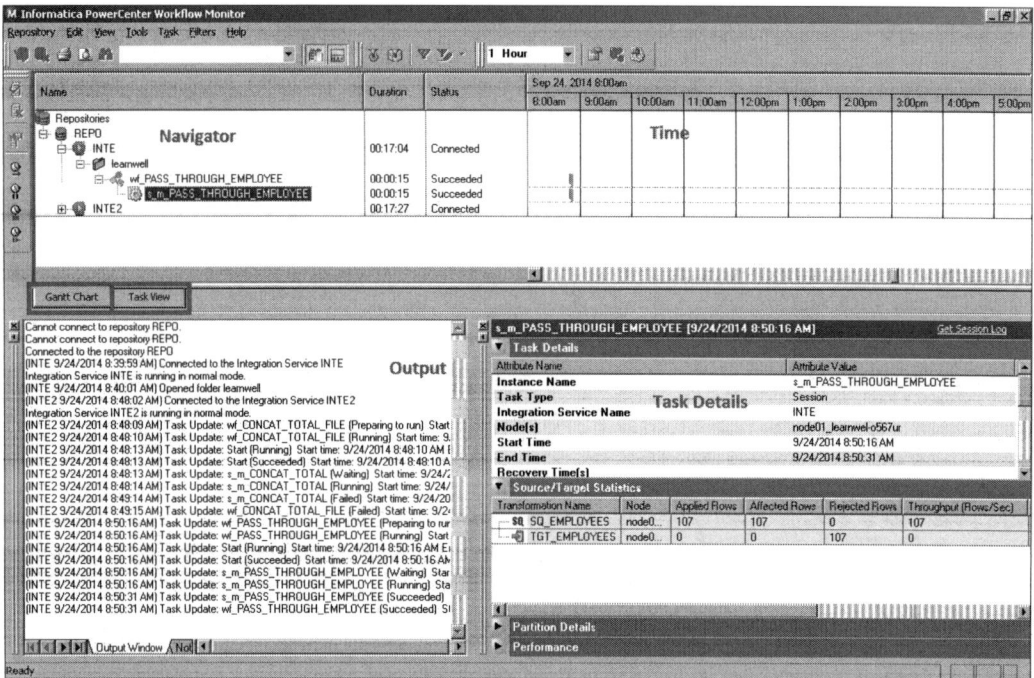

The screen is divided into the following sections:

- **Navigator**: This section of the screen displays various repositories, Integration Service, and the workflow names running at the instant. This section shows you all the objects that have been executed at least once.

- **Output**: This section displays various system-level information details received from Integration Service and repositories.

- **Time**: This section displays the timings of the execution of various workflows.

- **Gantt Chart view**: This view shows you the information of various workflow runs in a chronological order.

- **Task view**: This view shows you the information of various workflow runs in the report form.
- **Task details**: This section shows you the details of a task. It also shows you the source-to-target statistics and the performance and partition details, if selected.

Connecting to the Workflow Manager screen

When you open the Workflow Monitor screen, you need to connect to the repository and Integration Service to view the workflow and task status. You can view the Workflow Manager Screen through various ways:

- Under **All Programs**, navigate to **Informatica 9.5.1 | Client | PowerCenter Client | PowerCenter Workflow Monitor**
- From the Designer or Workflow Manager screen, click on the icon that represents Workflow Monitor (M)

Once you open the Workflow Monitor screen, perform the following steps to connect and view the workflow and task status:

1. Open the Workflow Monitor screen.
2. Right-click on the repository you wish to connect to (if you have multiple repositories available), and connect to it using the username and password. In our case, the repository is REPO.
3. Once you connect to the repository, the next step is to connect to Integration Service. This is done by right-clicking on the Integration Service you created. In our case, the Integration Service is INTE.
4. Select the workflow for which you wish to check the status. You can see the status if the workflow is executed at least once.
5. Select the view, which is **Gantt Chart** or the **Task View**, under which you wish to see the status of workflows and tasks.

Opening previous workflow runs

Apart from checking the status of the currently executing workflow, you can also check the status of the existing workflow runs in both **Gantt Chart** and the **Task View**.

In the navigator of Workflow Monitor, select the workflow for which you wish to see previous runs. Right-click on the workflow and click on **Open Latest 20 Run**, as shown in the following screenshot:

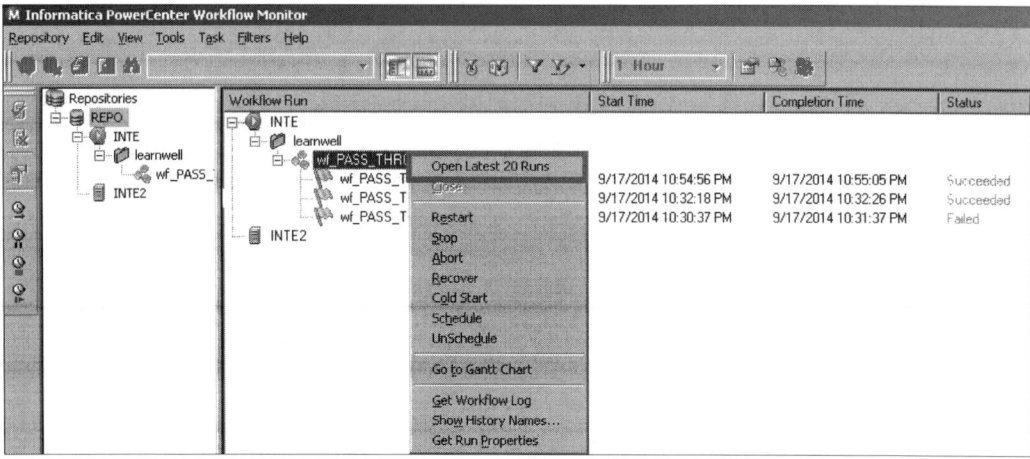

The list of latest 20 runs of the workflow will appear if available.

Running or recovering workflows or tasks

As mentioned earlier, the Workflow Monitor screen displays the workflow that is executed at least once. You can run or recover the workflow from the Workflow Monitor screen. To run or recover the workflow or task, right-click on the workflow/task in the navigator and select **Restart/Recover**.

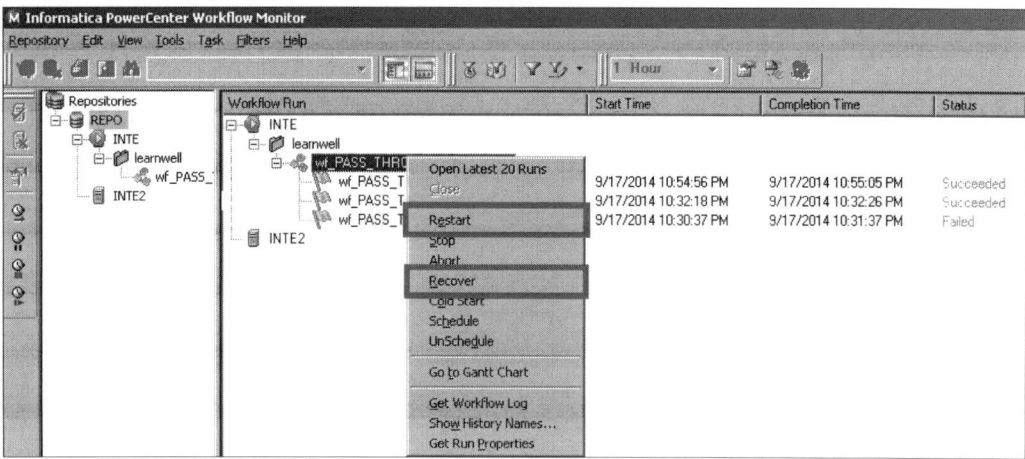

Stopping or aborting the workflow or task

You can stop or recover the workflow from the Workflow Monitor screen.

When you stop the process, Integration Service stops processing the scheduled tasks and all other processes of that workflow. However, it continues to process the currently running task. The process will stop once the current task execution is finished.

When you abort the task, it kills the DTM and hence, all the other processes get terminated. DTM in Informatica PowerCenter is called data transformation manager. This DTM does the work of managing and arranging all the prerequisites to run a session, such as checking the cache memory, checking the buffer memory, checking the table deadlock, and so on. Also, it helps generate the session log, execute pre-session and post-session SQL, and so on. To stop/abort the workflow or task, right-click on the workflow/task in the navigator and select **Stop/Abort**.

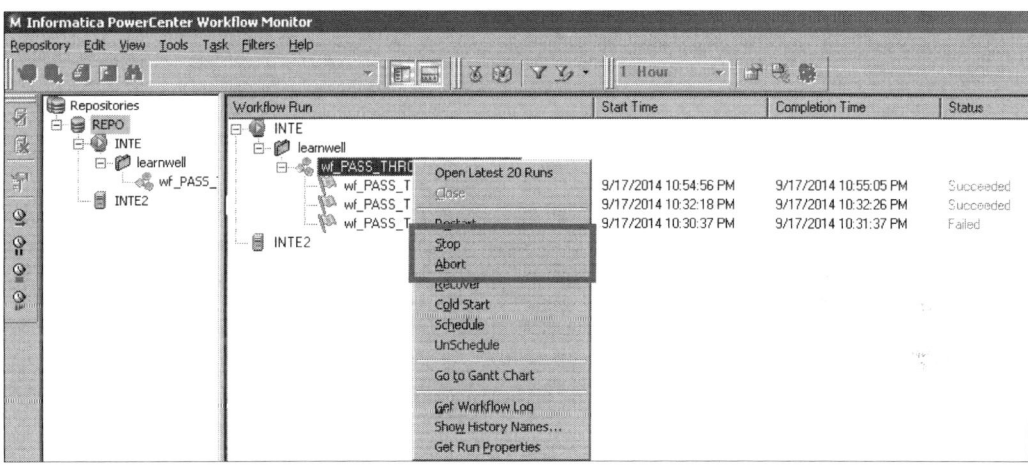

The status of workflows and tasks

Various statuses possible for workflows and tasks are as follows:

Status	Status for Workflow/Task	Description
Succeeded	Both	The process is completed successfully
Failed	Both	The process failed due to some error
Running	Both	The process is getting executed currently

Status	Status for Workflow/Task	Description
Preparing to Run	Workflow only	The process is waiting for Integration Service to run the workflow
Scheduled	Workflow only	The workflow is scheduled to run in the future
Stopped	Both	The workflow has been stopped manually
Stopping	Both	The Integration Service is in the process of stopping the workflow after manual selection
Aborted	Both	The workflow has been aborted manually
Aborting	Both	The Integration Service is in the process of aborting the workflow after manual selection
Disabled	Both	You manually selected to disable the workflow or task
Suspended	Workflow only	The workflow will show the suspended status because of the failure of the task. This status is available only if you selected **Suspend** on receiving an error.
Suspending	Workflow only	The Integration Service is suspending the workflow.
Terminated	Both	Integration Service is terminated due to some unexpected reasons.
Terminating	Both	Integration Service is stopping, aborting, or terminating the workflow.
Waiting	Both	Integration service is waiting for the resources that are required to execute the workflow.

Viewing the session log and workflow log

You can view the session and workflow log from the Workflow Monitor screen. When you run the workflow, the workflow log and session logfile is saved in the form of a file at the location that you defined in the session's properties. You can maintain the history of the logfiles by adding a timestamp or by saving the session run.

To get the workflow log for the workflow, right-click on the workflow in the navigator and select **Get Workflow Log**.

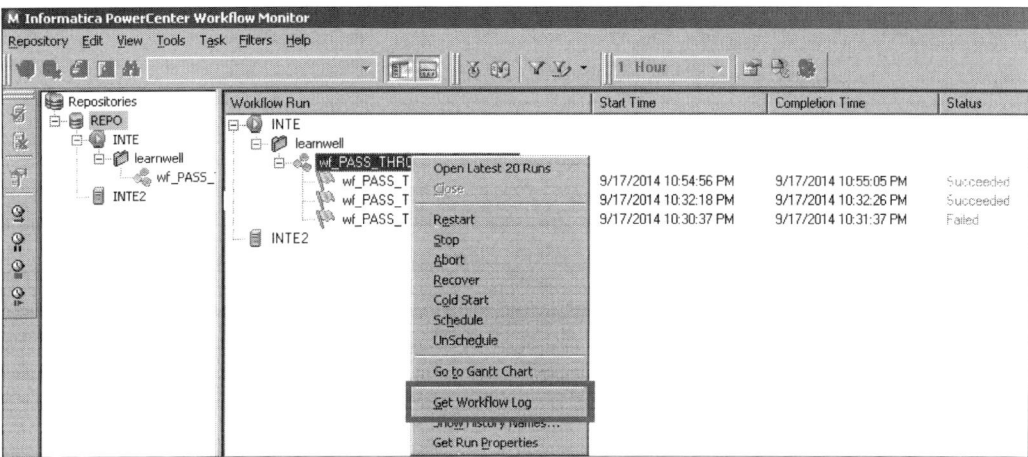

To get the session log for the workflow, right-click on the session task in the navigator and select **Get Session Log**.

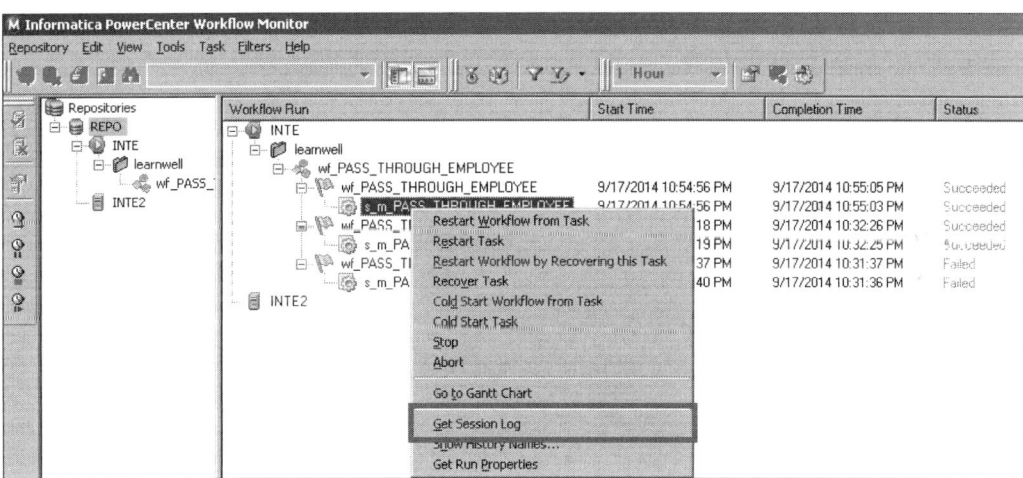

Working with the workflow log

When you select to generate the workflow log, another screen opens, which shows you the details related to the workflow run. Informatica PowerCenter writes all the details related to the execution of the workflow in the log. Using the Workflow log, you can check all the system-related information that was used in executing the workflow along with the error messages if any. The following screenshot shows the workflow log:

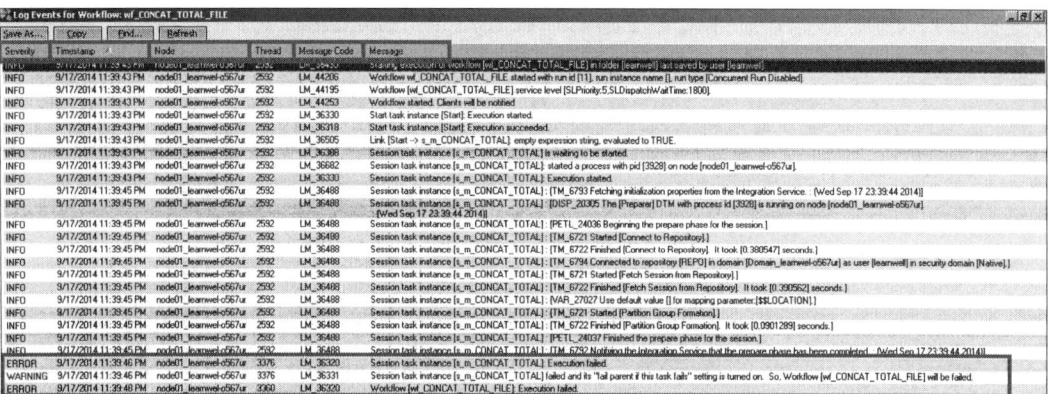

The following table describes the various option of the workflow log:

Option	Description
Severity	This shows you the status of the particular event that took place while executing the Workflow: • INFO: This indicates general system-level information • ERROR: This indicates the error that has occurred due to which the Workflow failed • WARNING: This indicates the process that was not executed as per expectations. The workflow might not fail because of warning.
Timestamp	This indicates the exact timing of the particular step that the workflow was running.
Node	This indicates the name of the node under which the workflow is executed.
Thread	This indicates the thread each step is using to execute. You can see the different threads in the session log.
Message Code	This indicates the system-defined message code. Usually in Informatica PowerCenter, we do not refer to message code.
Message	This shows you the detailed message, indicating the steps that occurred during the execution of the workflow.

Working with the session log

Similar to the workflow log, the session log also indicates the detailed level of information that provides you with a complete understanding of the process that occurred while the workflow was running. Session logs in Informatica give you the exact reason for the error that has occurred, using which you can debug the issue and correct the code. For example, in the following screenshot, the session log indicates the error as **The system cannot find the file specified**. This directly indicates that the file you wish to access does not exist. Check the details in the session task, correct the path, and your workflow will succeed.

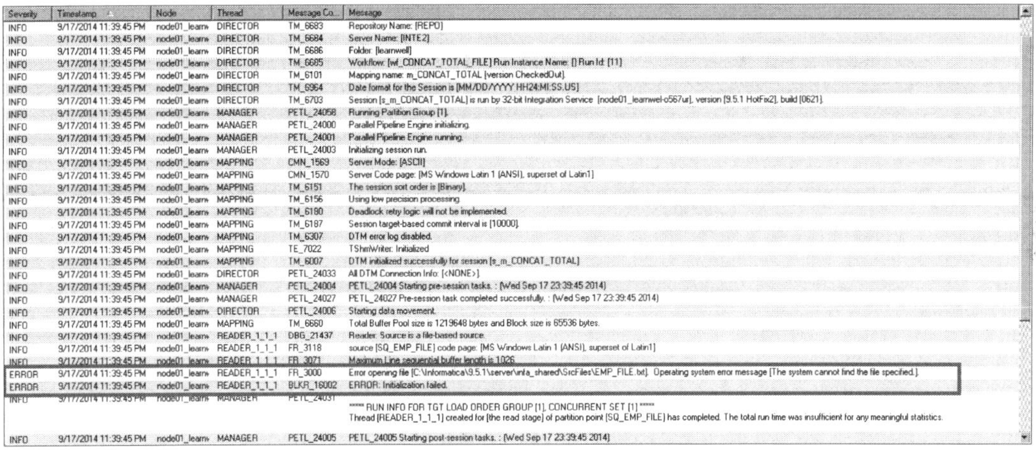

Viewing workflow run properties

Informatica PowerCenter Workflow Monitor indicates the workflow-level properties. To open the workflow run properties, right-click on the workflow and select **Get Run Properties**, as shown in the following screenshot:

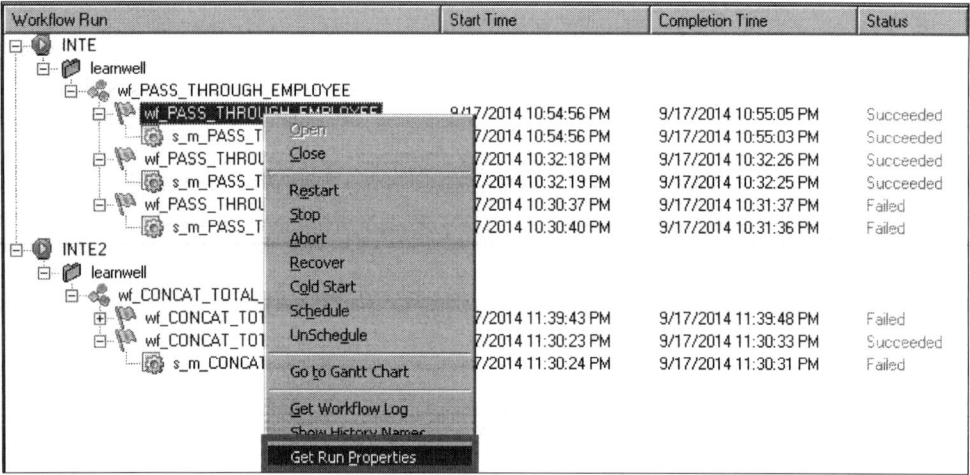

The workflow-level properties section will appear in the bottom-right section of the monitor screen, as shown in the following screenshot:

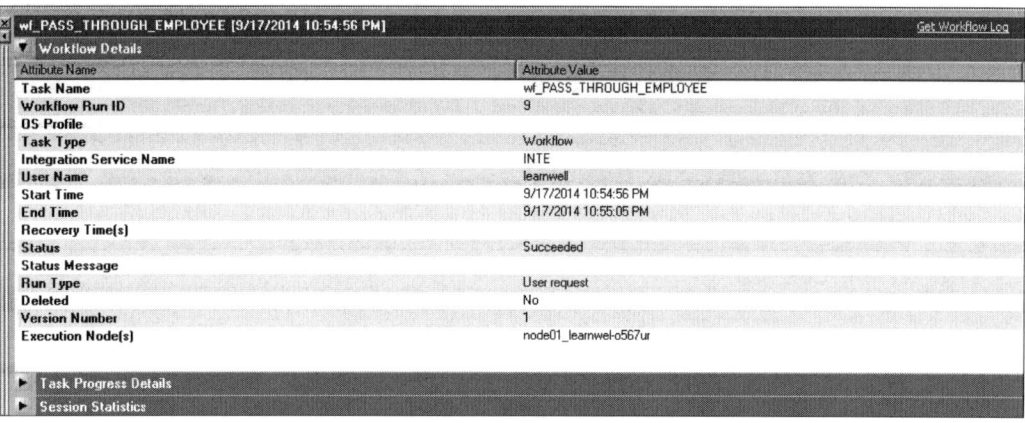

Various options under workflow run properties are as follows:

Properties	Description
Task Name	This indicates the name of the workflow.
Workflow Run ID	This indicates the ID of the workflow run.
OS Profile	This indicates the name of the operating system profile assigned to the workflow. Usually, it is empty.
Task Type	This indicates the type of task. The value can be a workflow, session, and so on. In this case, the value is workflow, because we are looking at the workflow run properties.
Integration Service Name	This indicates the name of Integration Services used to run the workflow.
User Name	This indicates the name of User Services used to run the workflow.
Start Time	This indicates the start time of the workflow.
End Time	This indicates the end time of the workflow.
Recovery Time(s)	This indicates the number of times the workflow has been recovered.
Status	This indicates the status of the workflow.
Status Message	This indicates the status message of the workflow.
Run Type	This indicates the method used to execute the workflow.
Deleted	This indicates whether the workflow is deleted. The value can be yes or no.
Version Number	This indicates the version number of the workflow.
Execution Node(s)	This indicates the nodes on which the workflow is running.

Viewing session run properties

Similar to workflow run properties, Informatica PowerCenter Workflow Monitor shows you the session-level run properties. To open the session run properties, right-click on the session and select **Get Run Properties**.

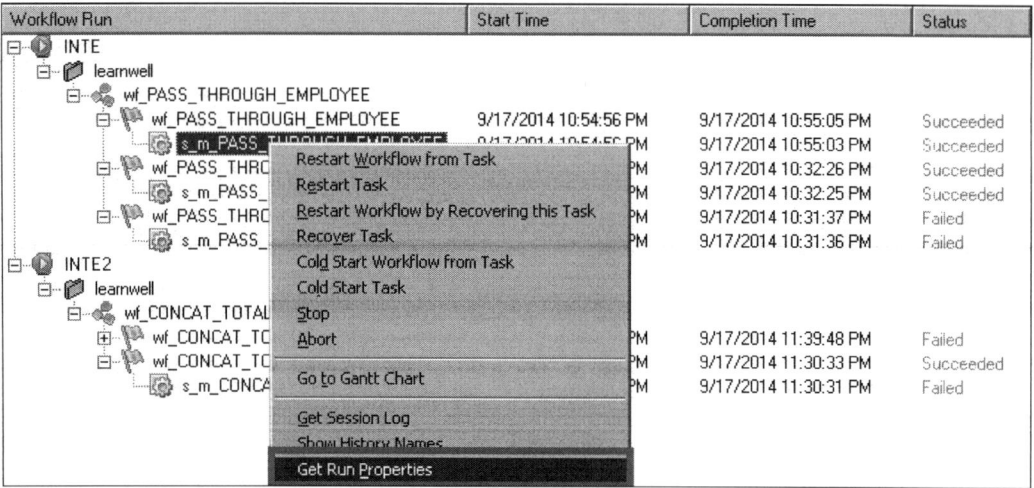

The session-level run properties section will appear in the bottom-right section of the monitor screen.

Properties of task details

Task details under session run properties are shown in the following screenshot:

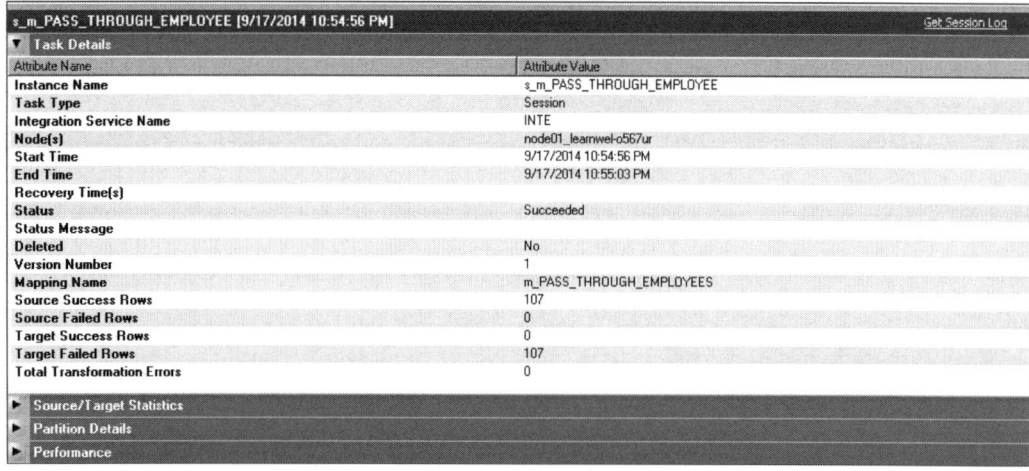

The various options under **Task Details** of the session run properties are as follows:

Properties	Description
Instance Name	This indicates the name of the session.
Task Type	This indicates the type of task. In this case, it is **Session**.
Integration Service Name	This indicates the name of Integration Services used to run the session.
Node(s)	This indicates the nodes on which the session is running.
Start Time	This indicates the start time of the session.
End Time	This indicates the end time of the session.
Recovery Time(s)	This indicates the number of times the session has been recovered.
Status	This indicates the status of the session task.
Status Message	This indicates the status message of the session task.
Deleted	This indicates whether the session is deleted. The value can be yes or no.
Version Number	This indicates the version number of the session task.
Mapping Name	This indicates the name of the mapping associated with the session task.
Source Success Rows	This indicates the number of records that are successfully extracted using the session task.
Source Failed Rows	This indicates the number of records that failed while extracting the data using the session task.
Target Success Rows	This indicates the number of records that were successfully loaded into the target using the session task.
Target Failed Rows	This indicates the number of records that failed to load into the target using the session task.
Total Transformation Errors	This indicates the number of transformation errors that occurred during the execution of the session task.

Properties of source/target statistics

Source/Target-level task details under session run properties are shown in the following screenshot:

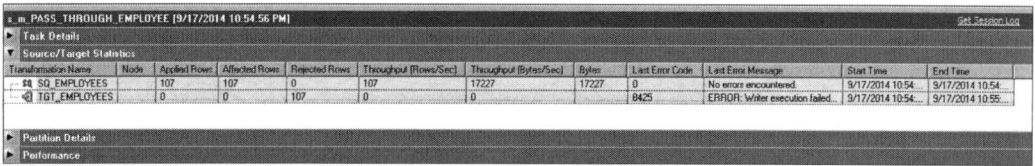

The various options under source/target statistics of session run properties are as follows:

Properties	Description
Transformation Name	This indicates the name of the source qualifier or target instance name in the mapping.
Node	This indicates the nodes on which a particular transformation is running.
Applied Rows	This indicates the number of records that were successfully extracted from a source for processing or the records that are successfully loaded into the target after the processing.
Affected Rows	This indicates the number of records successfully extracted from the source or successfully loaded into the target.
Rejected Rows	This indicates the number of records rejected while extracting from the source or the number of records rejected while loading into the target.
Throughput(Rows/Sec)	This indicates the rate at which the data is extracted from the source or the rate at which data is loaded into the target.
Throughput(Bytes/Sec)	This indicates the rate at which the data is extracted from the source per second or the rate at which the data is loaded into the target per second.
Bytes	This indicates the total number of bytes transferred while extracting and loading the data.
Last Error Code	This indicates the latest error code that occurred while extracting or loading into the target.

Properties	Description
Last Error Message	This indicates the latest error message that occurred while extracting or loading into the target.
Start Time	This indicates the start time of the extraction of data and the start time of the loading into the target.
End Time	This indicates the end time of the extraction of data and the end time of the loading into the target.

You can also view the partitioning- and performance-level details if you configure to get them.

Common errors

When you execute the session and workflow, there are certain common errors that you might face, as follows:

- **Source file not found**: This indicates that the source file is not available at the specified location. Make sure that you have placed the file in the correct folder.

- **Unable to generate the session log**: This might be due to an invalid session task or because you may have forgotten to specify the lookup filename and path in the session task.

- **Table or view not found**: This indicates the database table into which you are willing to load the data that is not available. Make sure that you have created the table before you load the data into it.

- **Communication link failure**: This indicates whether the network issues are affecting the Integration Service or repository.

- **Failed to allocate memory**: This indicates whether the memory required to execute the process is available.

- **Duplicate Primary/Foreign key**: This indicates that you are trying to load the duplicate data in the primary key in the table.

To know more about the common errors that we come across, refer to `http://docs.oracle.com/cd/E12102_01/books/AnyInstAdm784/ AnyInstAdmTroubleshooting3.html for more errors.`

Summary

In this chapter, we talked about various aspects of the Workflow Monitor screen. We started the chapter with a discussion on the various sections of the Workflow Monitor screen. We also saw the steps to connect to Workflow Monitor and you learned to check the status of the workflow and tasks. We checked how to restart and recover the workflow and task directly from Monitor Screen. We also checked the process to stop/abort the workflow. You learned how to check the workflow and session log. At the end of the chapter, we saw the workflow-level run properties and session-level run properties.

In the next chapter, we are going to talk about the different types of transformations available on the Informatica PowerCenter Designer screen.

7
The Lifeline of Informatica – Transformations

Transformations are the most important aspect of the Informatica PowerCenter tool. The functionality of any ETL tool lies in transformations. Needless to say, transformations are used to transform data. Informatica PowerCenter provides multiple transformations, each serving a particular functionality. Transformations can be created as reusable or nonreusable based on the requirement. The transformations created in Workflow Manager are nonreusable, and those created in the task developer are reusable. You can create a mapping with a single transformation or with multiple transformations.

When you run the workflow, Integration Services extracts the data in a row-wise manner from the source path/connection you defined in the session task and makes it flow from the mapping. The data reaches the target through the transformations you defined.

The data always flows in a row-wise manner in Informatica no matter what your calculation or manipulation is. So if you have 10 records in source, there will be 10 source to target flows while the process is executed.

Creating the transformation

There are various ways in which you can create the transformation in the Designer tool. They are discussed in the upcoming sections.

Mapping Designer

To create transformations using Mapping Designer, perform the following steps:

1. Open the mapping in Mapping Designer. Then open the mapping in which you wish to add a transformation, and navigate to **Transformation | Create**.

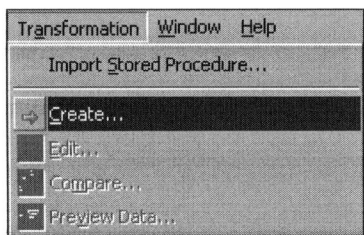

2. From the drop-down list of transformations, select the transformation you wish to create, and specify the name. Click on **Create**, and then click on **Done**.

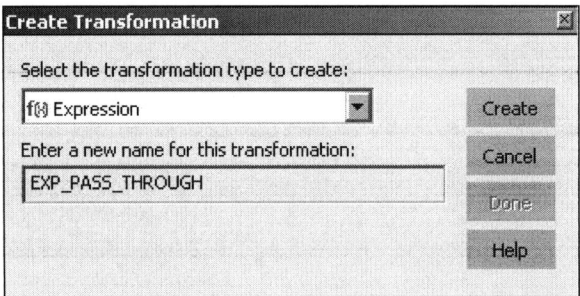

The transformation appears in the Mapping Designer Workspace. For reference, we have created an Expression transformation in the preceding image. You can create all other transformations in the same way.

The transformations you create in Mapping Designer are nonreusable, so you cannot use them in other mappings. However, you can change the transformation to reusable.

Mapplet Designer

To create the transformation in Mapplet Designer, perform the following steps:

1. Open the Mapplet in Mapplet Designer, and navigate to **Transformation | Create**, as shown in the preceding screenshot.

2. From the drop-down list of transformations, select the transformation you wish to create and specify the name.

Transformation Developer

To create the transformation in the designer, perform the following steps:

1. Open Transformation Developer and navigate to **Transformation | Create** as shown in Mapping Designer.

2. From the drop-down list of transformations, select the transformation you wish to create and specify the name as shown in Mapping Designer.

The transformations created in Transformation Developer are reusable, so you can use them across multiple mappings or mapplets.

With this basic understanding, we are all set to jump into the most important aspect of the Informatica PowerCenter tool, which is transformation.

The Expression transformation

Expression transformations are used for row-wise manipulation. For any type of manipulation you wish to perform on an individual record, use an Expression transformation. The Expression transformation accepts the row-wise data, manipulates it, and passes it to the target. The transformation receives the data from the input port and sends the data out from output ports.

Use Expression transformations for any row-wise calculation, such as if you want to concatenate the names, get the total salary, and convert it to uppercase. To understand the functionality of the Expression transformation, let's take a scenario.

Using flat file as the source, which we we created in *Chapter 1, Starting the Development Phase – Using the Designer Screen Basics*, concatenate FIRST_NAME and LAST_NAME to get FULL_NAME and TOTAL_SALARY from JAN_SALARY and FEB_SALARY of an individual employee.

We are using Expression transformation in this scenario because the value of FULL_NAME can be achieved by concatenating FIRST_NAME and LAST_NAME of an individual record. Similarly, we can get TOTAL_SALARY using JAN_SALARY and FEB_SALARY. In other words, the manipulation required is row-wise.

We are going to learn some basic aspects of transformations, such as ports in transformations, writing a function, and so on while we implement our first transformation using an expression.

Perform the following steps to achieve the functionality:

1. Create the source using flat file in **Source Analyzer** and the target in **Target Designer**. We will be using EMP_FILE as the source and TGT_EMP_FILE as the target.

2. Create a new m_EXP_CONCAT_TOTAL mapping in Mapping Designer, drag the source and target from the navigator to the workspace, and create the Expression transformation with the EXP_CONCAT_TOTAL name.

3. Drag-and-drop all the columns from the source qualifier to the Expression transformation. At this point, the mapping will look as shown in the following screenshot:

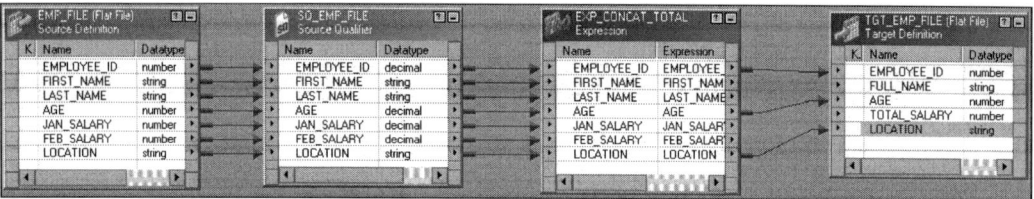

We have connected EMPLOYEE_ID, AGE, and LOCATION directly to the target as no manipulation is required for these columns.

At this step, we need to understand how to use the different types of ports in the transformation.

Ports in transformations

Transformations receive the data from input ports and send the data out using output ports. Variable ports temporarily store the value while processing the data.

Every transformation, with a few exceptions, has input and output ports as shown in the following screenshot:

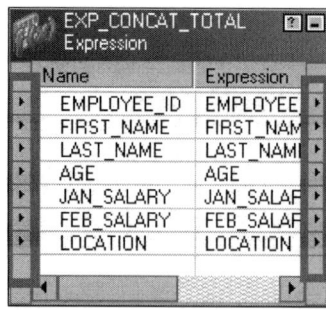

Double-click on the transformation and click on **Ports** to open the edit view and see the input, output, and variable ports.

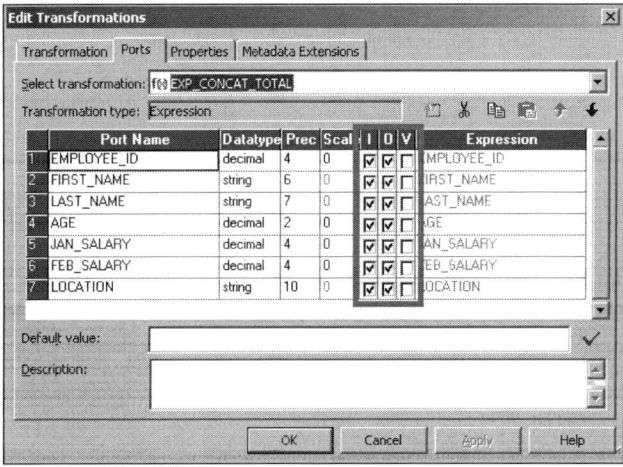

You can disable or enable input or output ports based on the requirement. In our scenario, we need to use the values that come from input ports and send them using an output port using concatenate, by writing the function in the expression editor.

Create two new output ports for FULL_NAME after LAST_NAME and TOTAL_SALARY after FEB_SALARY. We need to add the FULL_NAME port after LAST_NAME, because the FULL_NAME port will use the values in FIRST_NAME and LAST_NAME. To add a new port, double-click on the Expression transformation, click on **Ports**, and add two new output ports, as shown in the following screenshot:

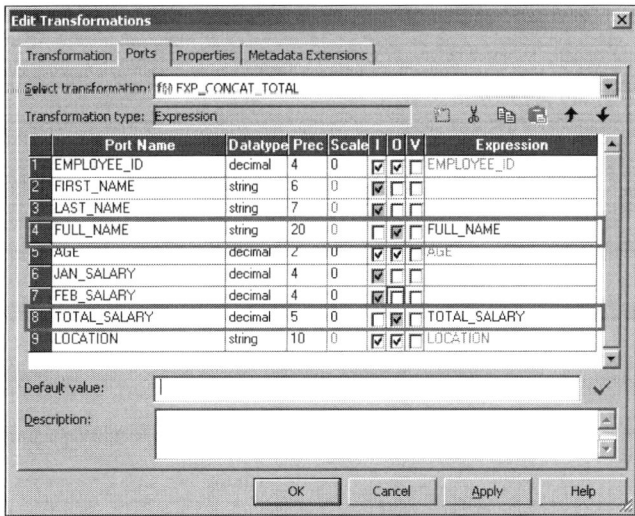

Make sure you define the proper data type and size of the new ports that are added. As you can see, we have disabled the input ports of FULL_NAME and TOTAL_SALARY. Also, as you must have noticed, we have disabled the output ports of FIRST_NAME, LAST_NAME, JAN_SALARY, and FEB_SALARY as we do not wish to pass the data from those ports to the output. This is as per the coding standards we follow in Informatica.

Once you disable the input ports of FULL_NAME and TOTAL_SALARY, you will be able to write the function for the port.

Using the expression editor

To manipulate the date, we need to write the functions in the ports. You can use the functions provided from the list of functions inside the expression editor:

1. Click on the icon shown in the following screenshot to open the expression editor.

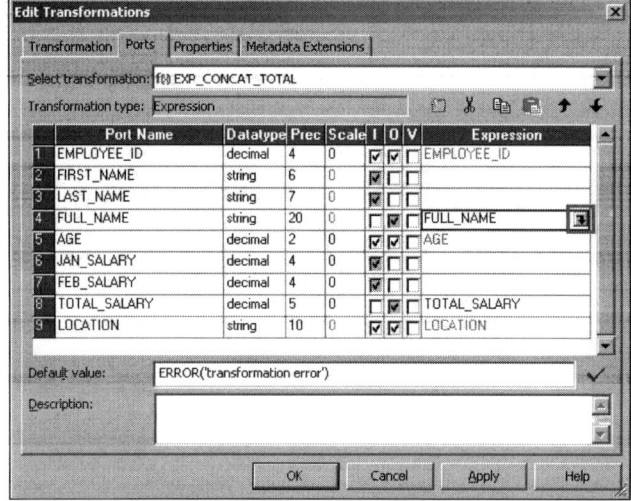

2. New windows where you can write the function will pop up . From the **Functions** tab, you can use these functions. Informatica PowerCenter provides all the functions that cater to the need of SQL/Oracle functions, mathematical functions, trigonometric functions, date functions, and so on.

    In our scenario, we need to use the CONCAT function. Double-click on the **Concat** function under the list of functions to get the function in the editor, as shown in the following screenshot:

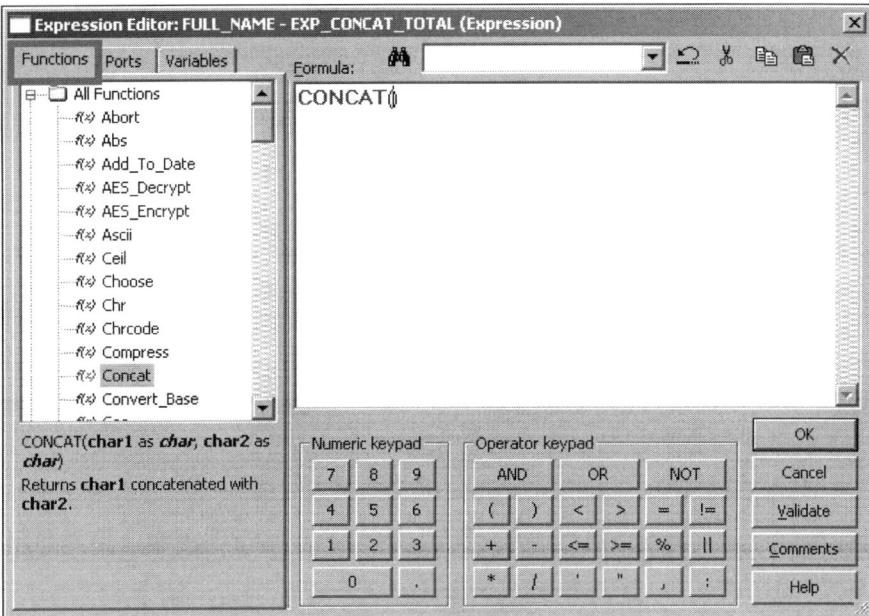

3. Click on **Ports** in the expression editor, and double-click on FIRST_NAME and LAST_NAME to get the function, as shown in the following screenshot:

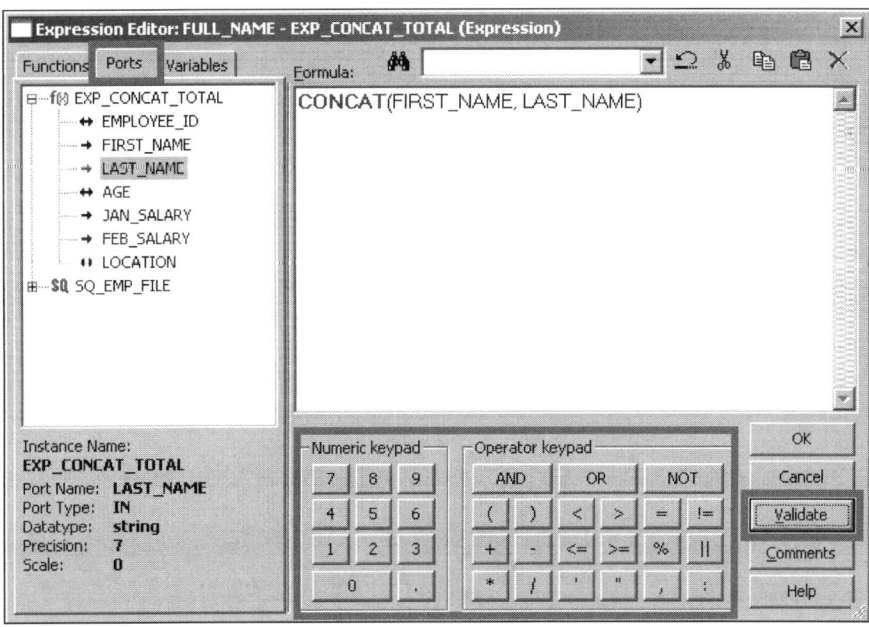

As you can see in the preceding screenshot, the expression editor provides **Numeric keypad** and **Operator keypad**, which can be used to write the functions.

Once you finish writing the function, click on **Validate** to make sure the function is correct syntactically. Then, click on **OK**.

Similarly, write the function to calculate TOTAL_SALARY; the function will be JAN_SAL+FEB_SAL.

4. Link the corresponding ports to the target, as shown in the following screenshot:

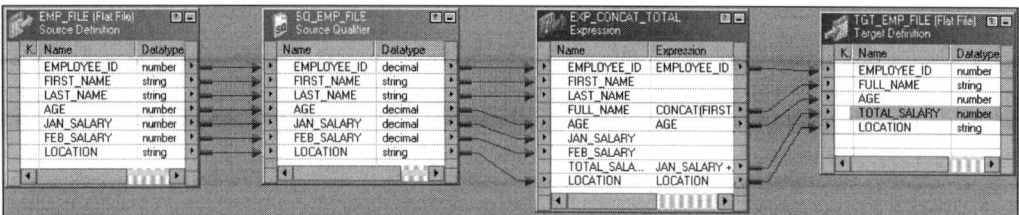

Save the mapping to save the metadata in the repository. With this, we are done creating the mapping using the Expression transformation. We have also learned about ports and how to use an expression editor. We discovered how to write functions in a transformation. These details will be used across all other transformations in Informatica.

The Aggregator transformation

The Aggregator transformation is used for calculations using aggregate functions in a column as opposed to the Expression transformation that is used for row-wise manipulation.

You can use aggregate functions, such as SUM, AVG, MAX, and MIN, in the Aggregator transformation.

Use the EMPLOYEE Oracle table as the source and get the sum of the salaries of all employees in the target.

Perform the following steps to implement the functionality:

1. Import the source using the EMPLOYEE Oracle table in Source Analyzer and create the TGT_TOTAL_SALARY target in Target Designer.

2. Create the `m_AGG_TOTAL_SALARY` mapping and drag the source and target from the navigator to the workspace. Create the Aggregator transformation with the `AGG_TOTAL_SAL` name.

3. As we need to calculate `TOTAL_SALARY`, drag only the `SALARY` column from the source qualifier to the Aggregator transformation.

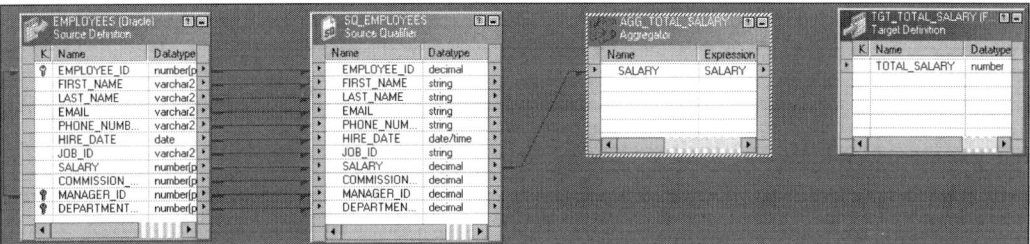

4. Add a new `TOTAL_SALARY` column to the Aggregator transformation to calculate the total salary, as shown in the following screenshot:

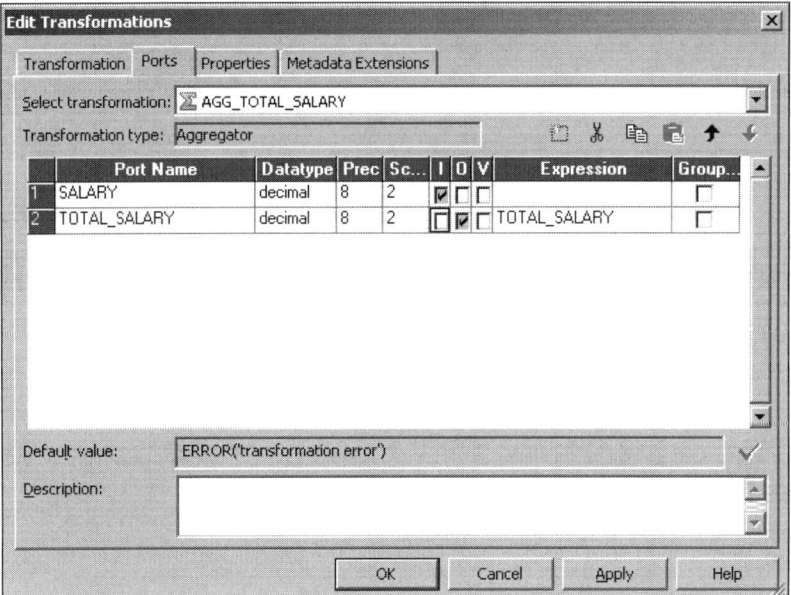

5. Add the function to the TOTAL_SALARY port by opening the expression editor, as described in the preceding section. The function we need to add to get the total salary is SUM(JAN_SAL).

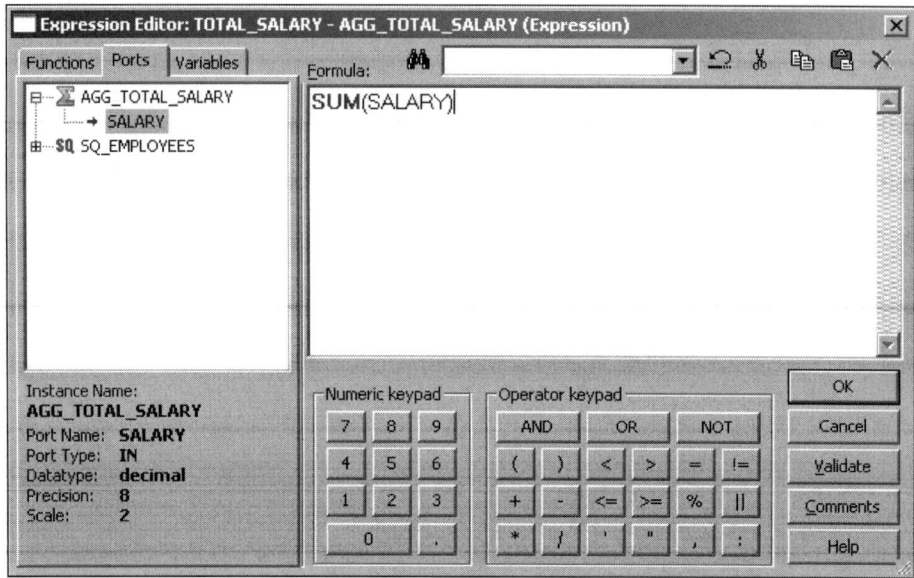

6. Connect the TOTAL_SALARY port to the target, as shown in the following screenshot:

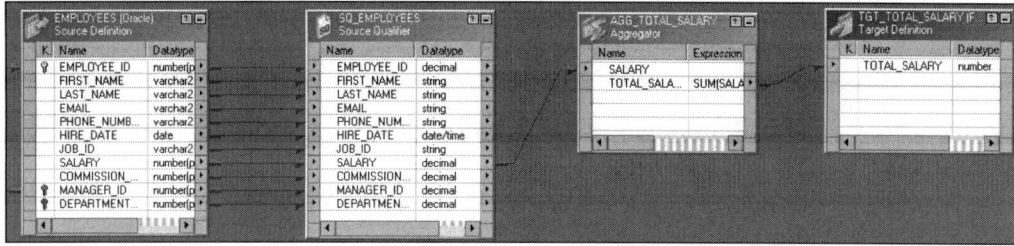

With this, we are done using the Aggregator transformation. When you use the Aggregator transformation, Integration Service temporarily stores the data in the cache memory. The cache memory is created because the data flows in a row-wise manner in Informatica and the calculations required in the Aggregator transformation are column-wise. Unless we temporarily store the data in the cache, we cannot calculate the result. In the preceding scenario, the cache starts storing the data as soon as the first record flows into the Aggregator transformation. The cache will be discussed in detail later in the chapter in the *Lookup transformation* section.

In the next section, we will talk about the added features of the Aggregator transformation. The Aggregator transformation comes with features such as group by and sorted input.

Using Group By

Using the **Group By** option in the Aggregator transformation, you can get the result of the aggregate function based on groups. Suppose you wish to get the sum of the salaries of all employees based on Department_ID, we can use the group by option to implement the scenario, as shown in the following screenshot:

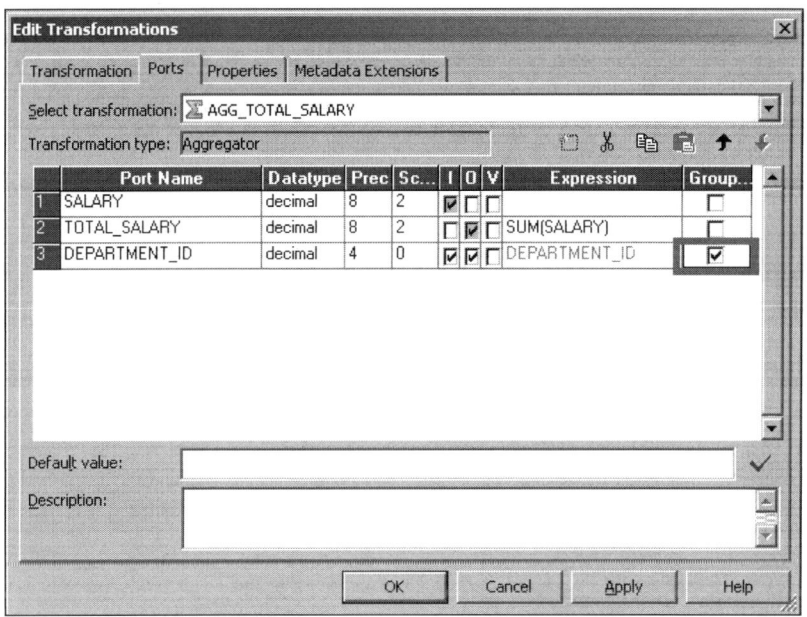

Using Sorted Input

It is always recommended that we pass the **Sorted Input** to the Aggregator transformation, as this will enhance performance. When you pass the sorted input to the Aggregator transformation, Integration Service enhances the performance by storing less data in the cache. When you pass unsorted data, the Aggregator transformation stores all the data in the cache, which takes more time. When you pass the sorted data to the Aggregator transformation, it stores comparatively less data. The aggregator passes the result of each group as soon as the data for a particular group is received.

Note that the Aggregator transformation cannot perform the operation of sorting the data. It will only internally sort the data for the purpose of calculations. When you pass the sorted data to the Aggregator transformation, check the **Sorted Input** option in the properties, as shown in the following screenshot:

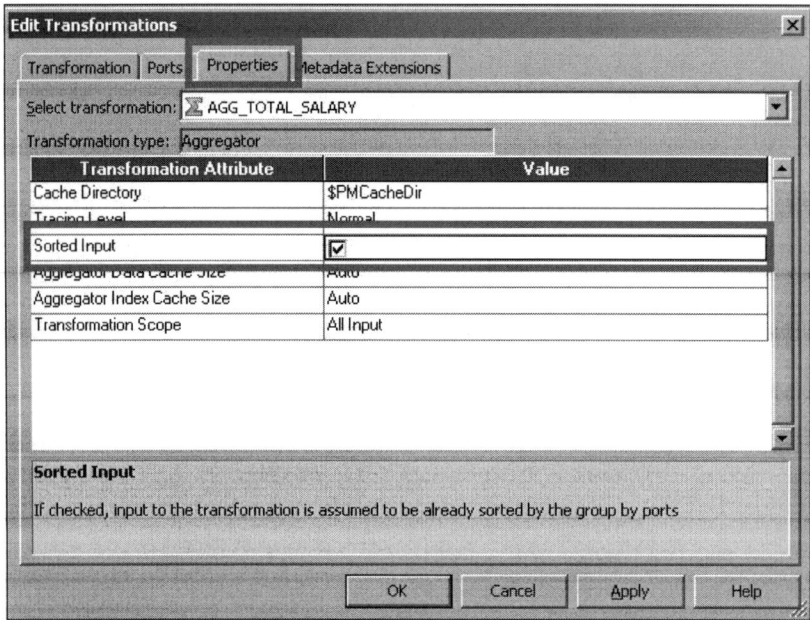

With this we have seen various option and functionality of Aggregator transformation.

The Sorter transformation

Sorter transformation is used to sort the data in an ascending or descending order based on single or multiple keys. A sample mapping showing Sorter transformation is displayed in the following screenshot:

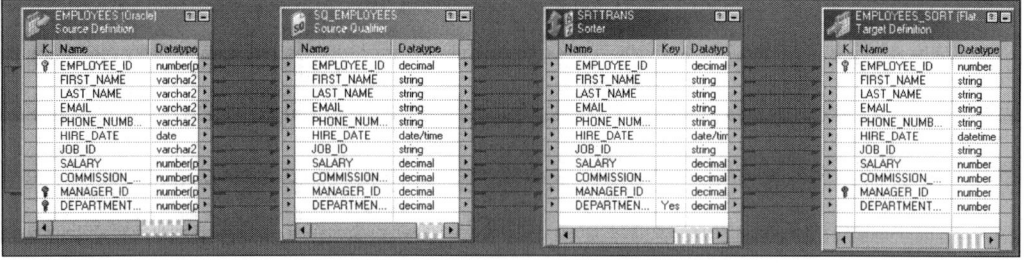

In this mapping, we wish to sort the data based on the DEPARTMENT_ID field. To achieve this, mark the key port for the DEPARTMENT_ID columns in the Sorter transformation and select from the drop-down list what you wish to have as the **Ascending** or **Descending** sorting, as shown in the following screenshot:

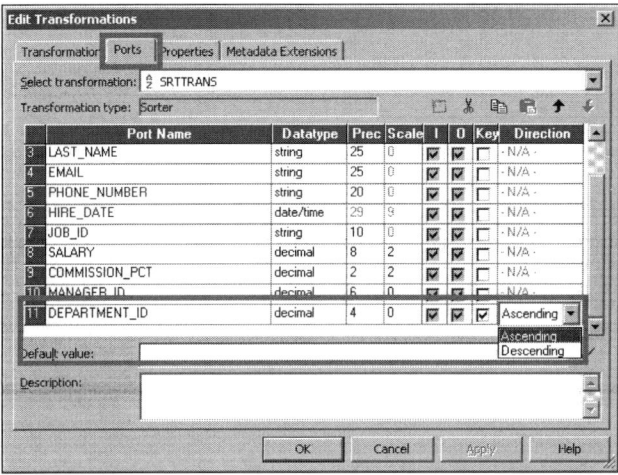

If you wish to sort the data in multiple columns, check the **Key** ports corresponding to the required port.

Apart from ordering the data in ascending or descending order, you can also use the Sorter transformation to remove duplicates from the data using the **Distinct** option in the properties. The sorter can remove duplicates only if the complete record is a duplicate and not just a particular column. To remove a duplicate, check the **Distinct** option in the Sorter transformation, as shown in the following screenshot:

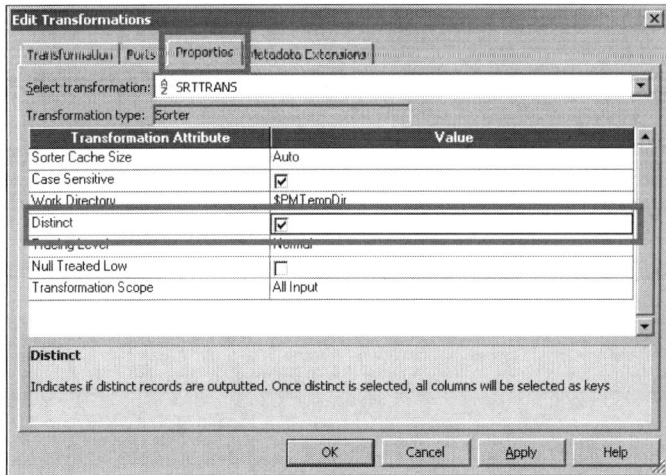

The Sorter transformation accepts the data in a row-wise manner and stores the data in the cache internally. Once all the data is received, it sorts the data in ascending or descending order based on the condition and sends the data to the output port.

The Filter transformation

Filter transformation is used to remove unwanted records from the mapping. You can define the filter condition in the Filter transformation, and based on the filter condition, the records will be rejected or passed further in the mapping.

A sample mapping showing the Filter transformation is given in the following screenshot:

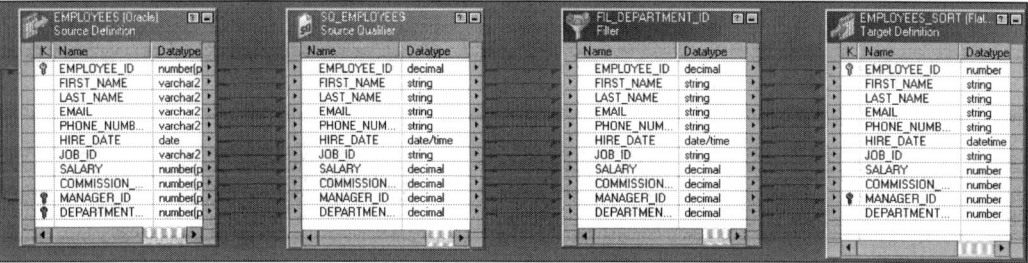

The default condition in Filter transformation is TRUE. Based on the condition defined, if the record returns TRUE, the Filter transformation allows the record to pass. For each record that returns FALSE, the Filter transformation drops the records.

To add the Filter transformation, double-click on the Filter transformation and click on the **Properties** tab, as shown in the following screenshot:

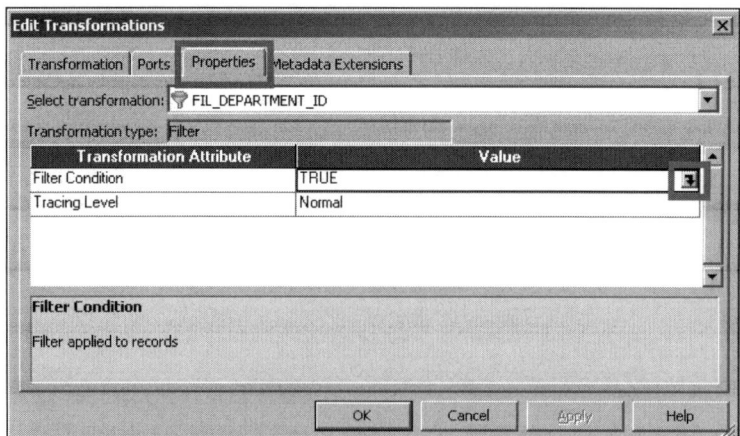

Click on the button shown in the preceding screenshot to open the expression editor and add the function for the filter condition. Then, add the required condition. We have used the condition as DEPARTMENT_ID=100; this will allow records with DEPARTMENT_ID as 100 to reach the target, and the rest of the records will get filtered.

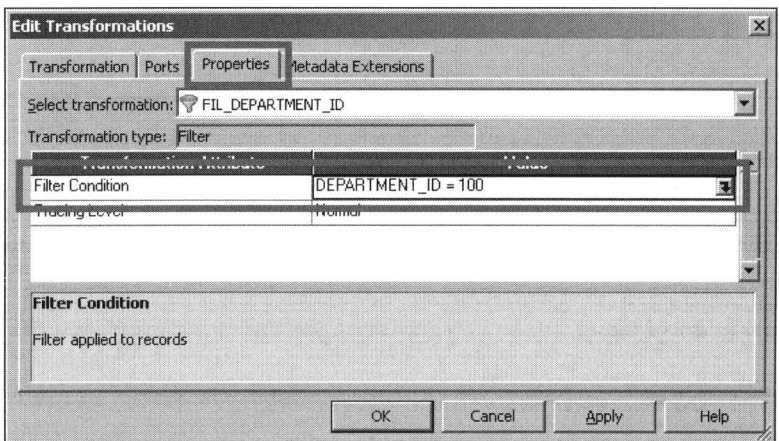

We have understood the functionality of Filter transformation in the above section and next we will talk about Router transformation, which can be used in place of multiple filters.

The Router transformation

Router transformation is single input to multiple output group transformation. Routers can be used in place of multiple Filter transformations. Router transformations accept the data through an input group once, and based on the output groups you define, it sends the data to multiple output ports. You need to define the filter condition in each output group.

A mapping using the Router transformation where we wish to load all records from LOCATION as INDIA in one target, records from UK in another target, and all other nonmatching records in the third target, is indicated in the following screenshot:

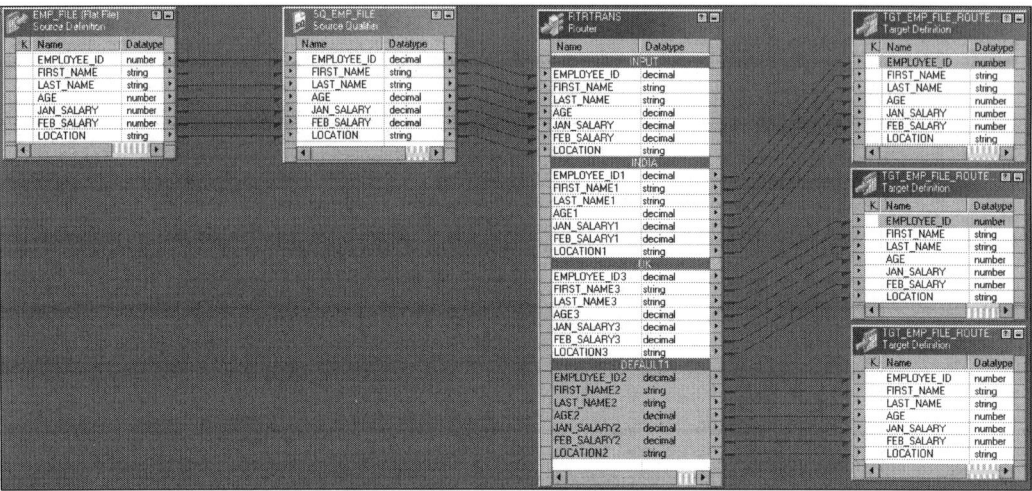

When you drag the columns to the router, the Router transformation creates an input group with only input ports and no output port. To add the output groups, click on the **Groups** tab and add two new groups. Enter the name of each group under the group name and define the filter condition for each group. Click on **OK** to create the output groups in the Router transformation.

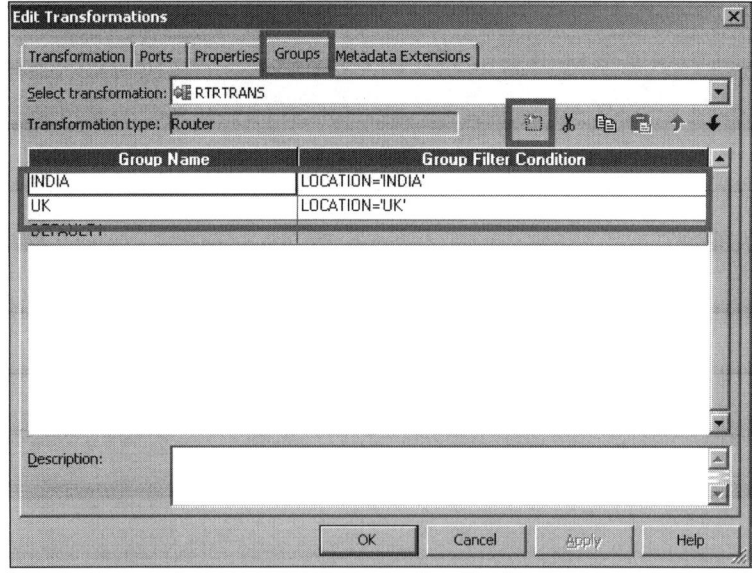

When you add the group, a **DEFAULT** group gets created automatically. All nonmatching records from the other groups will pass through the default group if you connect the **DEFAULT** group's output ports to the target.

When you pass the records to the Router transformation through the input group, the Router transformation checks the records based on the filter condition you define in each output group. For each record that matches, the condition passes further. For each record that fails, the condition is passed to the DEFAULT group.

As you can see, Router transformations are used in place of multiple Filter transformations. This way, they are used to enhance the performance.

The Rank transformation

The Rank transformation is used to get a specific number of records from the top or bottom. Consider that you need to take the top five salaried employees from the EMPLOYEE table. You can use the Rank transformation and define the property. A sample mapping indicating the Rank transformation is shown in the following screenshot:

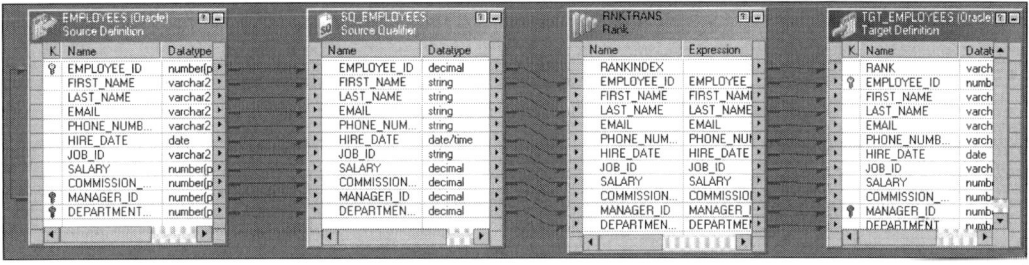

When you create a Rank transformation, a default RANKINDEX output port comes with the transformation. It is not mandatory to use the RANKINDEX port. We have connected the RANKINDEX port to the target as we wish to give the rank of EMPLOYEES based on their SALARY.

When you use a Rank transformation, you need to define the port on which you wish to rank the data. As shown in the following screenshot, we have ranked the data based on SALARY:

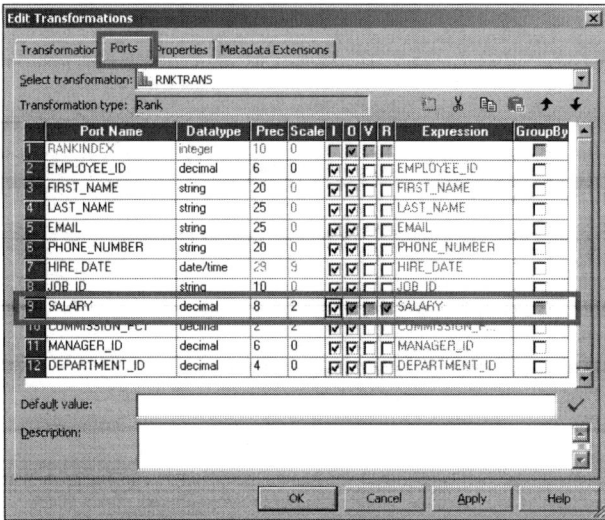

You cannot rank the data on multiple ports. Also, you need to define either the **Top** or **Bottom** option and the number of records you wish to rank in the **Properties** tab. In our case, we have selected **Top** and **5** to implement the scenario, as shown in the following screenshot:

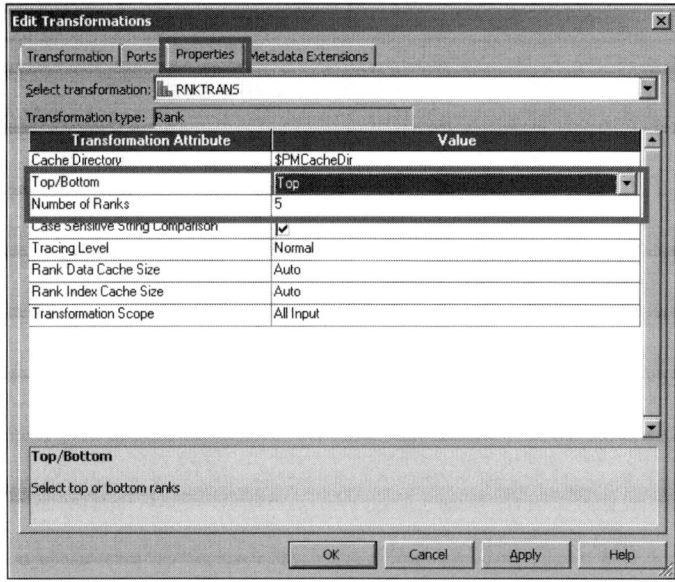

Rank transformations accept the data in a row-wise manner and store the data in the cache. Once all the data is received, it checks the data based on the condition and sends the data to the output port.

Rank transformations allow you to get the data based on a particular group. In the next section, we will talk about the group by key present in the Rank transformation.

Group by ranking

Rank transformation also provides a feature to get the data based on a particular group. Consider the scenario discussed previously. We need to get the top five salaried employees from each department. To achieve the functionality, we need to select the group by option, as shown in the following screenshot:

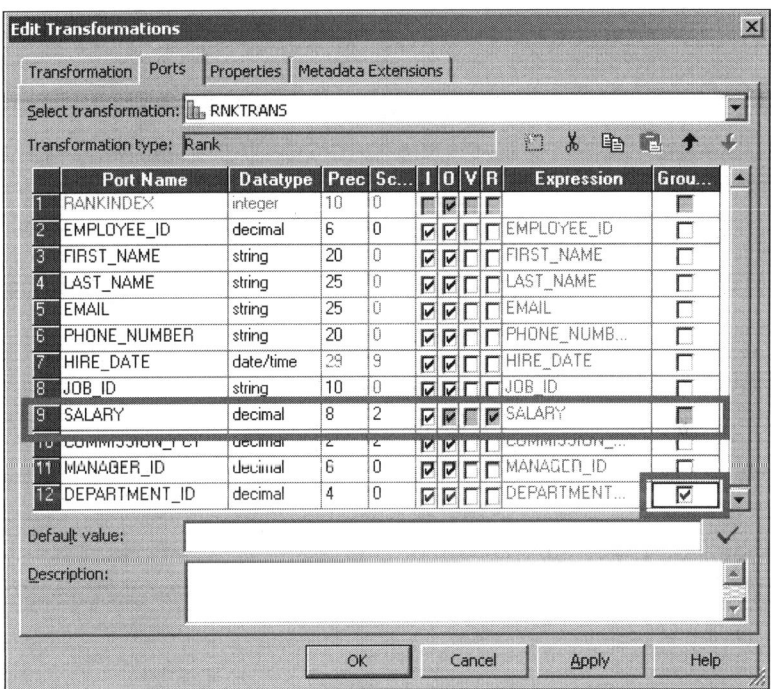

Next, we will talk about the default port of Rank transformations, rank index.

Rank index

When you create a Rank transformation, a default column called rank index gets created. If required, this port can generate numbers indicating the rank. This is an optional field that you can use if required. If you do not wish to use rank index, you can leave the port unconnected.

Suppose you have the following data belonging to the SALARY column in the source:

```
Salary
100
1000
500
600
1000
800
900
```

When you pass the data through a Rank transformation and define a condition to get the top five salaried records, the Rank transformation generates the rank index as indicated here:

```
Rank_Index, Salary
1,1000
1,1000
3,900
4,800
5,600
```

As you can see, the rank index assigns 1 rank to the same salary values, and 3 to the next salary. So if you have five records with 1000 as the salary in the source along with other values, and you defined conditions to get the top five salaries, Rank transformation will give all five records with a salary of 1000 and reject all others.

With this, we have learned all the details of Rank transformation.

The Sequence Generator transformation

Sequence Generator transformation is used to generate a sequence of unique numbers. Unique values are generated based on the property defined in the Sequence Generator transformation. A sample mapping showing the Sequence Generator transformation is shown in the following screenshot:

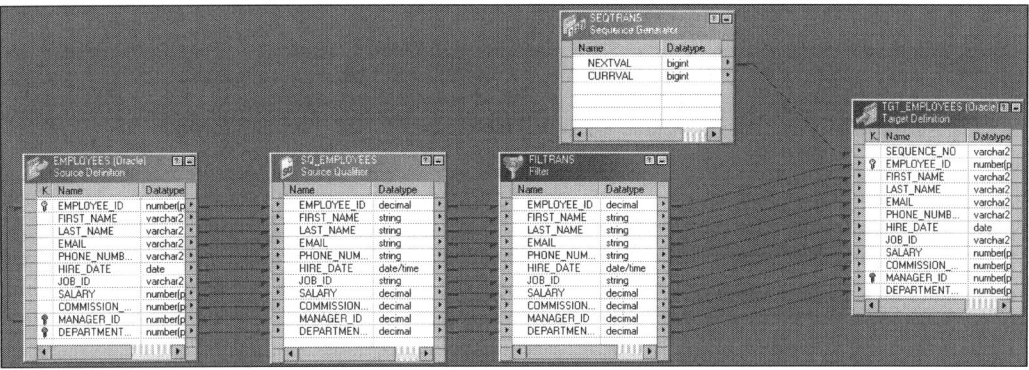

As you can see in the mapping, the Sequence Generator transformation does not have any input port. You need to define the start value, increment by value, and end value in the properties. Based on properties, the sequence generator generates the value. In the preceding mapping, as soon as the first record enters the target from the Source Qualifier transformation, NEXTVAL generates its first value, and so on for other records. The sequence generator is built to generate numbers.

Ports of the Sequence Generator transformation

The Sequence Generator transformation has only two ports, NEXTVAL and CURRVAL. Both the ports are output ports. You cannot add or delete any port in a sequence generator. It is recommended that you always use the NEXTVAL port first. If the NEXTVAL port is utilized, then use the CURRVAL port. You can define the value of CURRVAL in the properties of the Sequence Generator transformation.

Consider a scenario where we are passing two records to the transformation. The following events occur inside the Sequence Generator transformation. Also note that in our case, we have defined the start value as 0, the increment by value as 1, and the end value is the default in the property. Also, the current value defined in **Properties** is 1. The following is the sequence of events:

1. When the first record enters the target from the filter transformation, the current value, which is set to 1 in the **Properties** of the sequence generator, is assigned to the NEXTVAL port. This gets loaded into the target by the connected link. So for the first record, SEQUENCE_NO in the target is given the value of 1.

2. The sequence generator increments CURRVAL internally and assigns that value to the current value, 2 in this case.

3. When the second record enters the target, the current value that is set as 2 now gets assigned to NEXTVAL. The sequence generator gets incremented internally to give CURRVAL a value of 3.

So at the end of the processing of record 2, the NEXTVAL port will have a value of 2 and the CURRVAL port will have its value set as 3. This is how the cycle keeps on running till you reach the end of the records from the source.

It is slightly confusing to understand how the NEXTVAL and CURRVAL ports behave, but after reading the given example, you will have a proper understanding of the process.

Properties of the Sequence Generator transformation

There are multiple values that you need to define inside the Sequence Generator transformation. Double-click on the sequence generator and click on the **Properties** tab, as shown in the following screenshot:

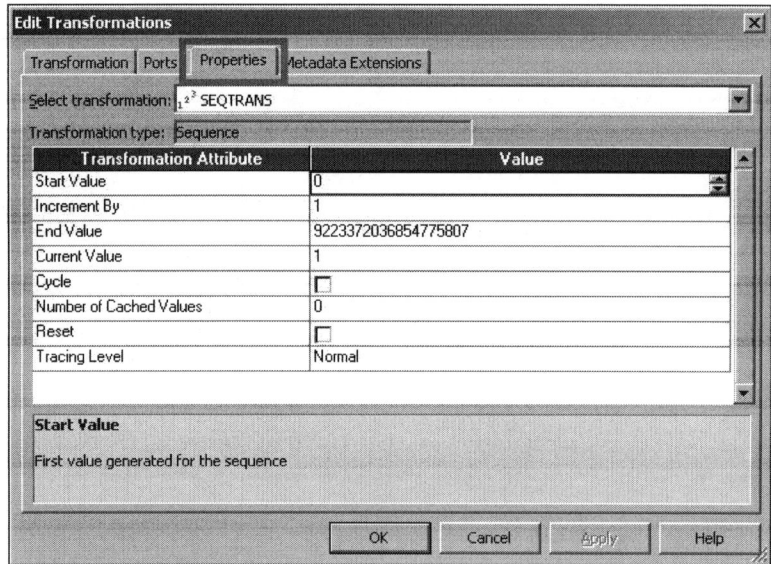

Let's discuss the properties in detail:

- **Start Value**: This comes into the picture only if you select the **Cycle** option in the properties. **Start Value** indicates the Integration Service that starts over from this value when the end value is reached after you have checked the cycle option.

  The default value is 0 and the maximum value is 9223372036854775806.

- **Increment By**: This is the value by which you wish to increment the consecutive numbers from the NEXTVAL port.

  The default value is 1 and the maximum value is 2147483647.

- **End Value**: This is the maximum value that the Integration Service can generate. If the Sequence Generator reaches the end value and is not configured for the cycle, the session will fail, giving the data overflow error. The maximum value is 9223372036854775807.

- **Current Value**: This indicates the value assigned to the CURRVAL port. Specify the current value that you wish to have as the value for the first record. As mentioned earlier, the CURRVAL port gets assigned to NEXTVAL, and the CURRVAL port is incremented.

  The CURRVAL port stores the value after the session is over, and when you run the session the next time, it starts incrementing the value from the stored value if you have not checked the reset option. If you check the reset option, Integration Services resets the value to 1. Suppose you have not checked the **Reset** option and you have passed 17 records at the end of the session; then, the current value will be set to 18, which will be stored internally. When you run the session the next time, it starts generating the value from 18.

  The maximum value is 9223372036854775807.

- **Cycle**: If you check this option, Integration Service cycles through the sequence defined. If you do not check this option, the process stops at the defined **End Value**.

  If your source records are more than the end value defined, the session will fail with an overflow error.

- **Number of Cached Values**: This option indicates how many sequential values Integration Services can cache at a time. This option is useful only when you are using reusable Sequence Generator transformations.

  The default value for nonreusable transformations is 0. The default value for reusable transformations is 1000. The maximum value is 9223372036854775807.

- **Reset**: If you do not check this option, Integration Service stores the value of the previous run and generates the value from the previously stored value. Otherwise, the integration will get reset to the defined current value and will generate values from the initial value that was defined. This property is disabled for reusable Sequence Generator transformations.

- **Tracing Level**: This indicates the level of detail you wish to write into the session log. We will discuss this option in detail later in the chapter.

With this, we have seen all the properties of the Sequence Generator transformation.

Let's talk about the usage of the Sequence Generator transformation:

- **Generating a primary/foreign key**: The sequence generator can be used to generate a primary key and foreign key. The primary key and foreign key should be unique and not null. The Sequence Generator transformation can easily do this, as seen here. Connect the NEXTVAL port to the targets for which you wish to generate the primary and foreign key, as shown in the following screenshot:

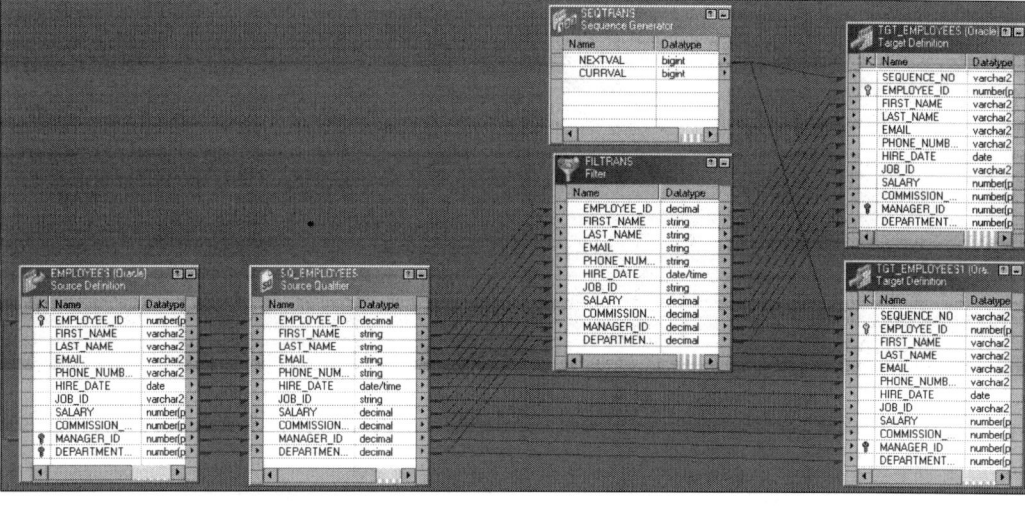

- **Replace the missing values**: You can use the Sequence Generator
  transformation to replace missing values by using IIF and ISNULL functions.
  Consider that you have some data with JOB_ID of an employee. Some
  records do not have JOB_ID in the table. Use the following function to replace
  these missing values. Make sure you are not generating NEXTVAL in a manner
  similar to existing JOB_ID in the data:

```
IIF( ISNULL (JOB_ID), NEXTVAL, JOB_ID)
```

The preceding function interprets whether JOB_ID is null and then assigns
NEXTVAL, otherwise it keeps JOB_ID as it is. The following screenshot indicates
these requirements:

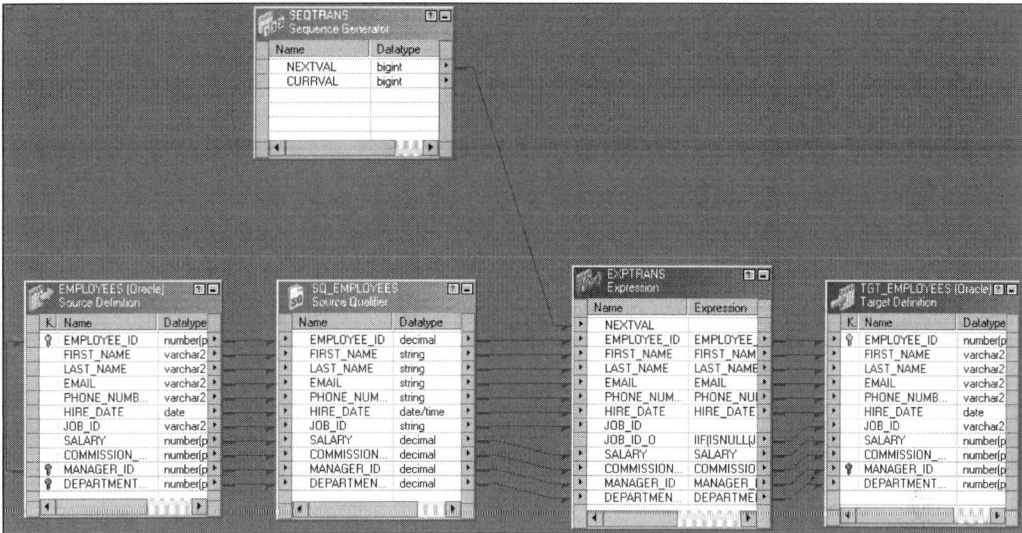

With this, we have learned all the options available in the Sequence Generator
transformation. Next, we will talk about Joiner transformations.

The Joiner transformation

Joiner transformation is used to join two heterogeneous sources. You can join data from the same source type as well. The minimum criteria to join the data are matching columns in both the sources. A mapping indicating the Joiner transformation is shown in the following screenshot:

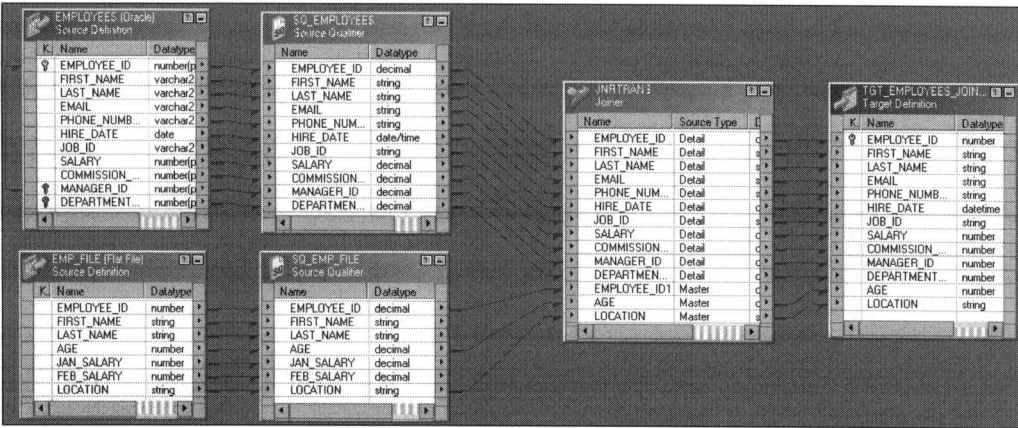

A Joiner transformation has two pipelines; one is called master and the other is called detail. One source is called the master source and the other is called detail. We do not have left or right joins like we have in the SQL database.

To use a Joiner transformation, drag all the required columns from two sources into the Joiner transformation and define the join condition and join type in the properties.

Master and detail pipeline

As mentioned in the preceding section, one source is called master and the other is called detail. By default, when you add the first source, it becomes the detail and the other becomes the master. You can decide to change the master or detail source. To make a source the master, check the **Master** port for the corresponding source, as shown in the following screenshot:

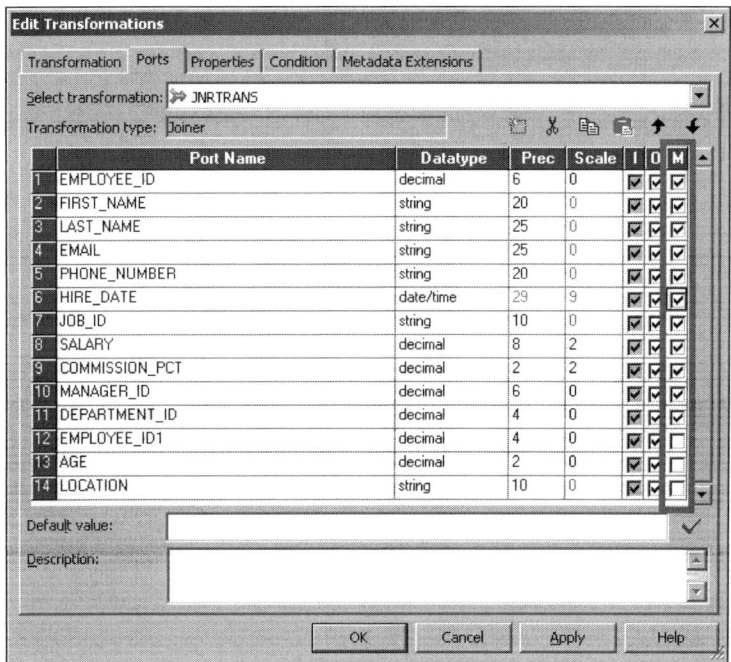

Always verify that the master and detail sources are defined to enhance the performance. It is always recommended that you create a table with a smaller number of records as the master and the other as the detail. This is because Integration Service picks up the data from the master source and scans the corresponding record in the details table. So if we have a smaller number of records in the master table, fewer iterations of scanning will happen. This enhances the performance.

Join condition

Join conditions are the most important condition to join the data. To define the join condition, you need to have a common port in both the sources. Also, make sure the data type and precision of the data you are joining is same. You can join the data based on multiple columns as well. Joining the data on multiple columns increases the processing time. Usually, you join the data based on key columns such as the primary key/foreign key of both the tables.

Joiner transformations do not consider NULL as matching data. If it receives NULL in the data, it does not consider them to be matching.

To define a join condition, double-click on the Joiner transformation, click on the **Condition** tab, and define the new condition.

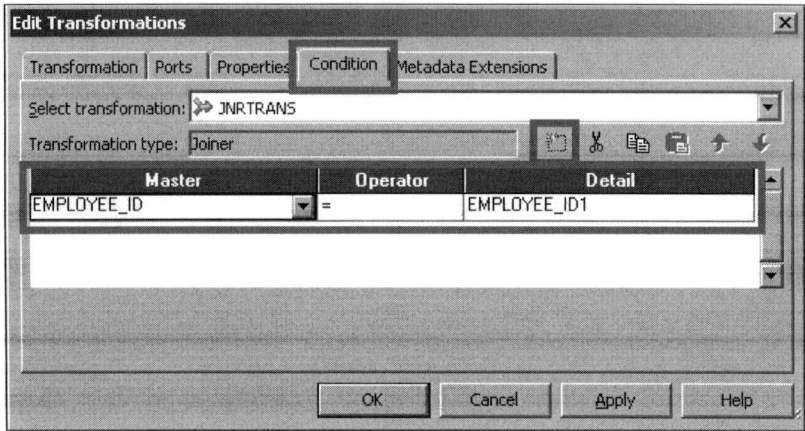

You can define multiple conditions to join two tables.

Join type

The Joiner transformation matches the data based on the join type defined. Similar to SQL, Joiner transformation use the join type to join the data. Let's discuss the join type in detail by taking the following example. We have two sources, the master source as EMPLOYEE_TABLE and the detail source as EMPLOYEE_FILE:

```
EMPLOYEE_TABLE (Master Source - Oracle`)
EMPLOYEE_ID,AGE
101,20
102,30
103,20
EMPLOYEE_FILE (Detail Source - Flat File)
EMPLOYEE_ID,SAL
101,1000
103,4000
105,2000
106,4000
110,5000
```

As you can see, we have created a table with fewer records as the master source to enhance performance. To assign the join type, double-click on the Joiner transformation and click on the **Properties** tab. Select the join type out of the four types from the drop-down list, as shown in the following screenshot:

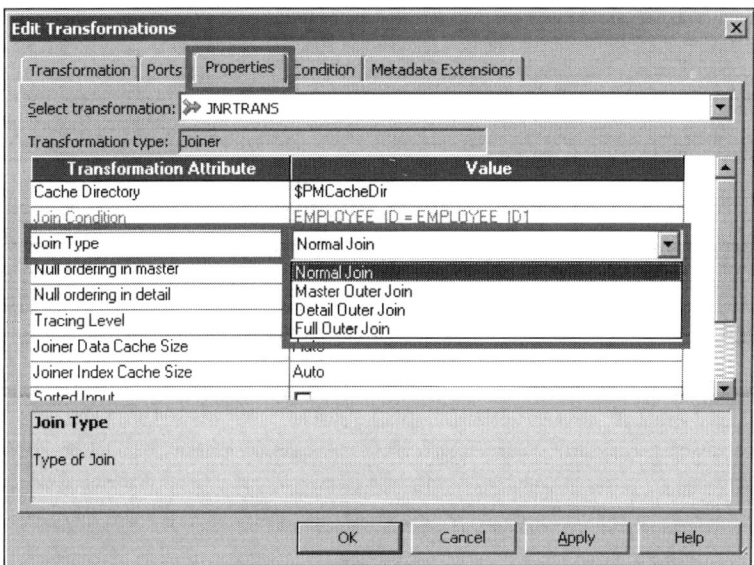

Normal join

When you define a normal join, Integration Service allows only matching records from both the master and detail source and discards all other records.

For the preceding scenario, we will set the join condition as EMPLOYEE_ID = EMPLOYEE_ID.

The result of the normal join for the previously-mentioned data is as follows:

```
EMPLOYEE_ID,AGE,SAL
101,20,1000
103,20,4000
```

All nonmatching records with a normal join will get rejected.

Full join

When you define a full join, Integration Service allows all the matching and nonmatching records from both the master and detail source.

The result of the full join for the previously mentioned data is as follows:

```
EMPLOYEE_ID,AGE,SAL
101,20,1000
102,30,NULL
103,20,4000
105,NULL,2000
106,NULL,4000
110,NULL,5000
```

Master outer join

When you define a master outer join, Integration Service allows all matching records from both the master and detail source and also allows all other records from the details table.

The result of the master outer join for the previously mentioned data is as follows:

```
EMPLOYEE_ID,AGE,SAL
101,20,1000
103,20,4000
105,NULL,2000
106,NULL,4000
110,NULL,5000
```

Detail outer join

We you define a detail outer join, Integration Service allows all matching records from both the master and detail source and also allows all other records from the master table.

The result of the detail outer join for the previously mentioned data is as follows:

```
EMPLOYEE_ID,AGE,SAL
101,20,1000
102,30,NULL
103,20,4000
```

With this, we have learned about the various options available in Joiner transformations.

Union transformation

The Union transformation is used to merge data from multiple sources. Union is a multiple input, single output transformation. It is the opposite of router transformations, which we discussed earlier. The basic criterion to use a Union transformation is that you should have data with the matching data type. If you do not have data with the matching data type coming from multiple sources, the Union transformation will not work. The Union transformation merges the data coming from multiple sources and does not remove duplicates, so it acts as the union of all SQL statements.

As mentioned, union requires data to come from multiple sources. Union reads the data concurrently from multiple sources and processes the data. You can use heterogeneous sources to merge the data using a Union transformation.

A mapping indicating the Union transformation is shown in the following screenshot:

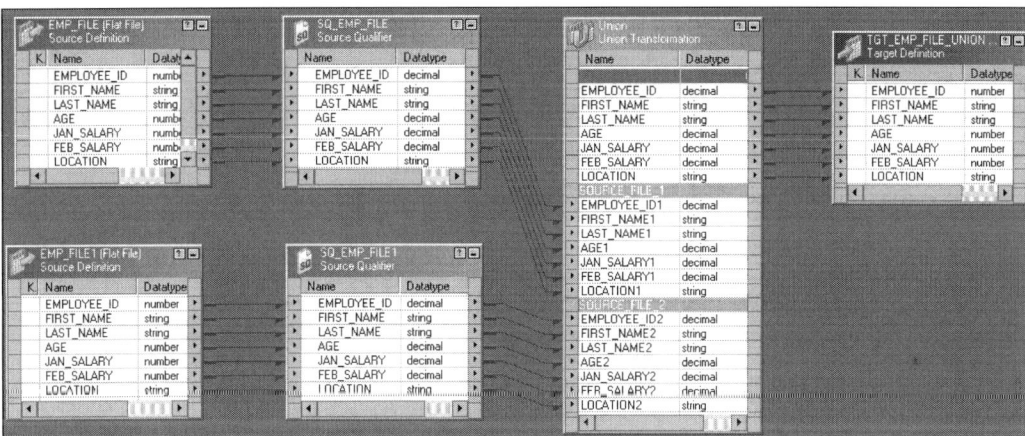

Working on Union transformation is a little different from other transformations. To create a Union transformation, perform the following steps:

1. Once you create a Union transformation, drag all the required ports from one source to the Union transformation. As soon you drag the port, the union creates an input group and also creates another output group with the same ports as the input.

2. Add the output groups from the **Group** tab in the Union transformation. Add as many groups as the input sources you have, as shown in the following screenshot:

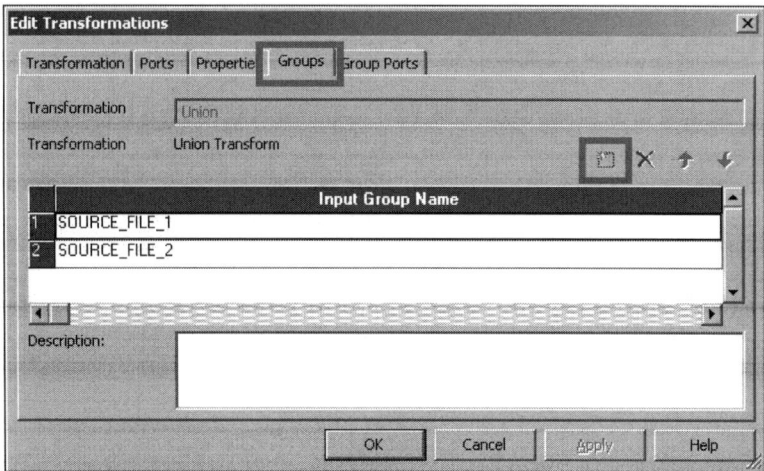

3. Once you add the groups, the Union transformation creates the groups with the same ports, as shown in the preceding mapping.

4. Link the ports from the other source to the input ports of the other group in the Union transformation.

With this, we have created a mapping using a Union transformation.

Source Qualifier transformation

Source Qualifier transformation act as virtual sources in Informatica. When you drag a relational table or flat file in Mapping Designer, the Source Qualifier transformation comes along with it. A source qualifier is the point where the Informatica processing actually starts. The extraction process starts from the source qualifier.

Note that it is always recommended that the columns of source and source qualifier match. Do not change the columns or their data type in the source qualifier. You can note the data type difference in the source definition and source qualifier, which is because Informatica interprets the data in that way itself.

To discuss the source qualifier, let's take an example of the Joiner transformation mapping we created earlier.

As you can see, there are two Source Qualifier transformations present in the mapping: one for flat file and the other for a relational database. You can see that we have connected only three columns from the Source Qualifier transformation of flat file to the Joiner transformation. To reiterate the point, all the columns are dragged from the source to source qualifier, and only three columns are linked to the Joiner transformation. This indicates that the source qualifier will only extract data that's related to three ports, not all. This helps in improving performance, as we are not extracting the unwanted columns' data.

In the same mapping, another Source Qualifier transformation is connected to a relational source. Multiple options are possible in this case. We will discuss each option in detail in the upcoming sections.

Viewing the default query

When you use the relational database as a source, the source qualifier generates a default SQL query to extract the data from the database table. By default, Informatica extracts all the records from the database table. To check the default query generated by Informatica, perform the following steps:

1. Double-click on the Source Qualifier transformation, click on the **Properties** tab, and select the SQL query.

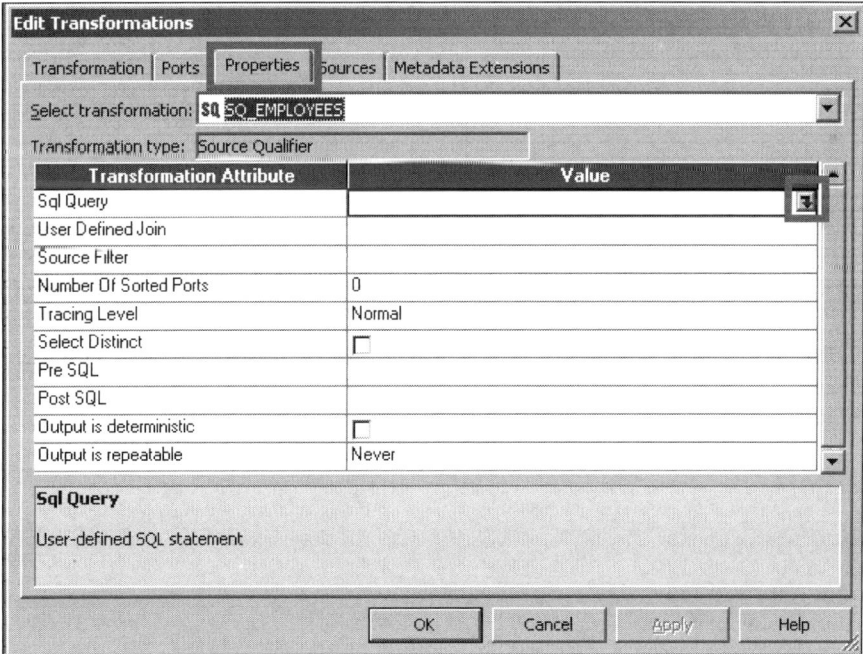

2. The SQL editor opens up. Click on the **Generate SQL** option. If required, specify the database username and password.

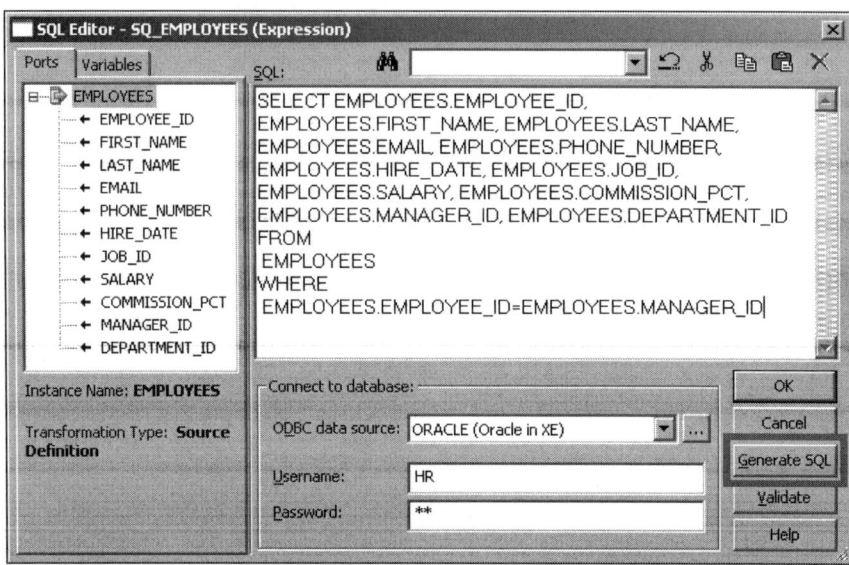

Informatica shows you the default query based on the links connected from the Source Qualifier transformation.

In the preceding screenshot, the WHERE clause in the SQL query (WHERE EMPLOYEES. EMPLOYEE_ID = EMPLOYEES.MANAGER_ID) signifies the self-referential integrity of the table. That means that every manager needs to be an employee.

Overriding the default query

We can override the default query generated by the Source Qualifier transformation. If you override the default query generated by the source qualifier, it is called an SQL override. You should not change the list of ports or the order of the ports in the default query. You can write a new query or edit the default query generated by Informatica. You can perform various operations while overriding the default query.

Using the WHERE clause

You can add the WHERE clause in the SQL query while you override the default query. When you add the WHERE clause, you reduce the number of records extracted from the source. This way, we can say that our Source Qualifier transformation is acting as a filter transformation. You can also define the WHERE condition in the source filter. If you define the source filter, you need not add the WHERE clause in the SQL query. You can add the source filter as shown in the following screenshot:

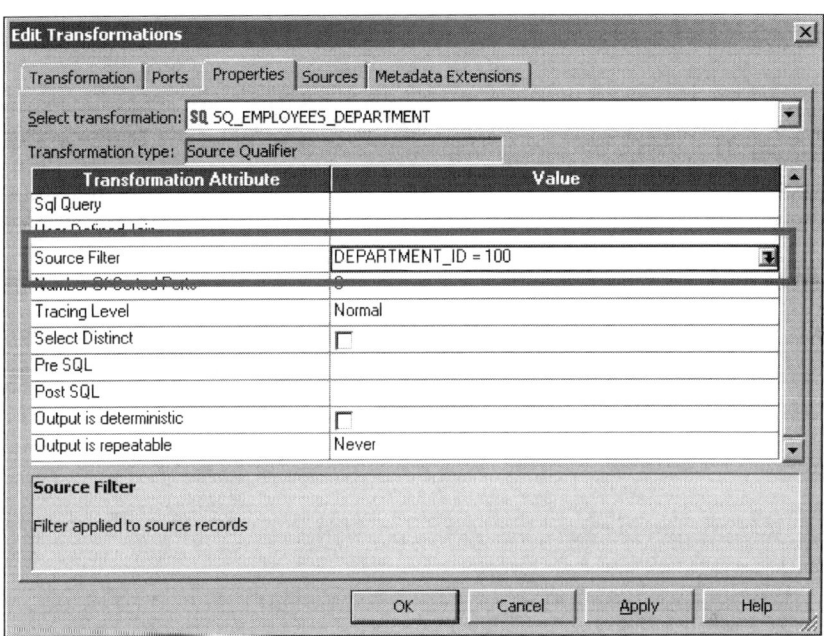

Joining the source data

You can use the Source Qualifier transformation to define the user-defined join types. When you use this option, you can avoid using the Joiner transformation in the mapping. When you use the Source Qualifier transformation to join the data from two database tables, you will not use the master or detail join. You will use the database-level join types, such as the left and right join.

We will use the EMPLOYEE and DEPARTMENT Oracle tables to join the data using the Source Qualifier transformation. Follow these steps to use the source qualifier to perform the join functionality:

1. Open Mapping Designer and drag the EMPLOYEE and DEPARTMENT Oracle tables into the mapping. Once you drag both the sources into Mapping Designer, delete the source qualifier of the DEPARTMENT table and drag all the columns from the DEPARTMENT source definition into the EMPLOYEE source qualifier, as shown in the following screenshot:

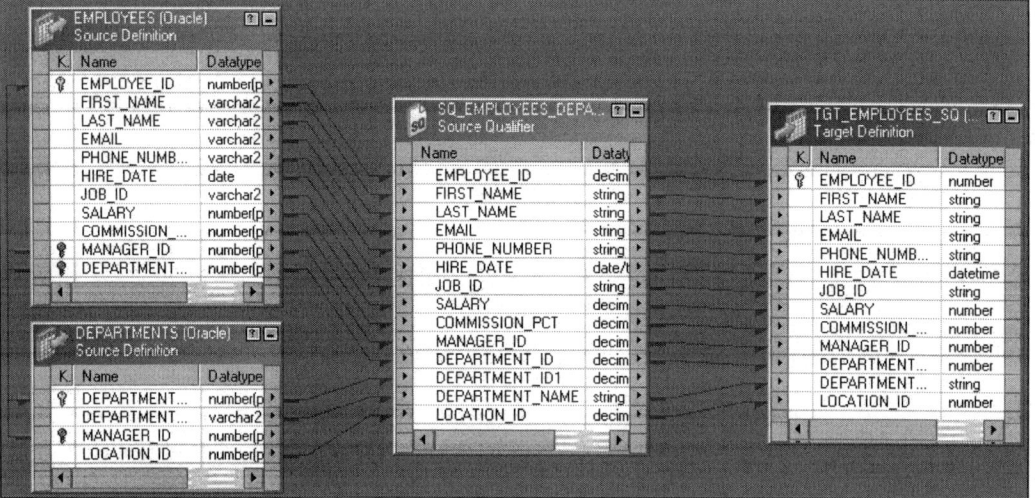

Link the required columns from the source qualifier to the target as per your requirement.

2. Open the **Properties** tab of the Source Qualifier transformation and generate the default SQL. Now, you can modify the default generated query as per your requirement, to perform the join on the two tables.

Using this feature helps make our mapping simple by avoiding the Joiner transformation and, in turn, helps in faster processing. Note that you cannot always replace a joiner with a source qualifier. This option can be utilized only if you wish to join the data at the source level and both your sources are relational tables in the same database and connection. You can use a single source qualifier to join the data from multiple sources; just make sure the tables belong to same database scheme.

Sorting the data

You can also use the Source Qualifier transformation to sort the data while extracting the data from the database table. When you use the sorted port option, Integration Service will add defined ports to the ORDER BY clause in the default query. It will keep the sequence of the ports in the query similar to the sequence of ports defined in the transformation. To sort the data, double-click on the Source Qualifier transformation, click on the **Properties** tab, and specify **Number Of Sorted Ports**, as shown in the following screenshot:

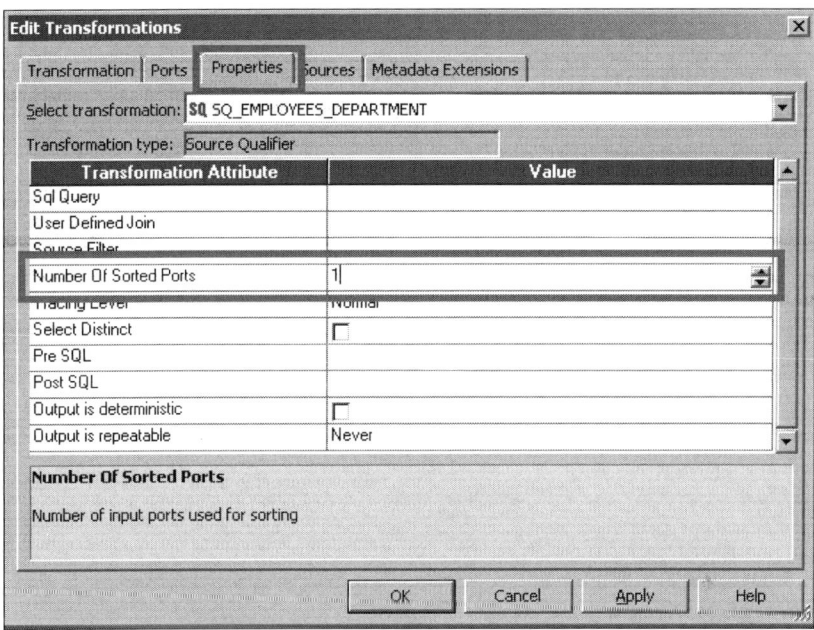

This will be possible only if your source is a database table and only if you wish to sort the data at the source level. If you wish to sort the data in between the mapping, you need to apply the Sorter transformation.

Selecting distinct records

You can use the source qualifier to remove the duplicates from the database tables using the select distinct option. By default, Integration Service extracts all the columns from the source in the default query. When you select the distinct option, Integration Service adds the SELECT DISTINCT statement into the query that it generates.

To add the distinct command in your query, double-click on the Source Qualifier transformation, click on the **Properties** tab, and check the **Select Distinct** option, as shown in the following screenshot:

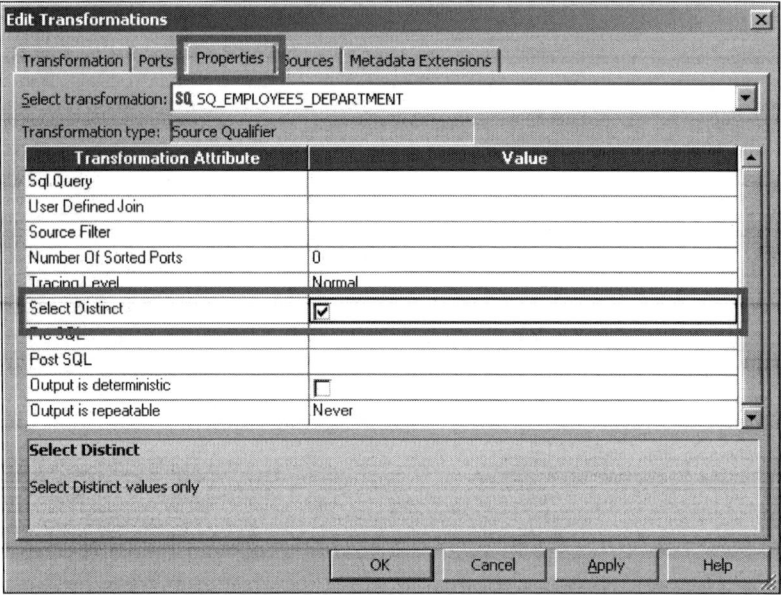

This will be possible only if your source is a database table and only if you wish to select unique records at the source level. If you wish to get unique records in between the mapping, you need to use the Sorter transformation, which also provides the ability to remove duplicates.

Classification of transformations

At this point, we have seen quite a few transformations and their functions. Before we look at the next transformations, let's talk about the classification of transformations. Based on their functionality, transformations are divided as follows.

Active and passive

This classification of transformations is based on the number of records in the input and output port of the transformation. This classification is not based on the number of ports or the number of groups.

If the transformation does not change the number of records in its input and output ports, it is said to be a passive transformation. If the transformation changes the number of records in the input and output ports of the transformation, it is said to be an active transformation. Also, if the transformation changes the sequence of records passing through it, it is classed as an active transformation, as with Union transformations. Let's take an example to understand this classification.

Consider the Expression transformation from the mapping we used in the example of Expression transformations, where we concatenated FIRST_NAME and LAST_NAME, as shown in the following screenshot:

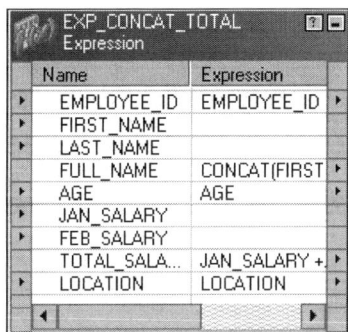

As you can see, the number of input ports is seven and the number of output ports is five. Say our source contains 10 records in the mapping. When we pass all the records to the transformation, the total records that will reach the input ports will be 10 and the total records that will reach the output ports will also be 10, so this makes Expression transformation passive. We are not concerned about the number of ports in the input and output.

Consider the example of filter transformations that filter out unwanted records, as this changes the number of records, it is an active transformation.

Connected and unconnected

A transformation is said to be connected if it is connected to any source, target, or any other transformation by at least one link. If the transformation is not connected by any link, it it classified as unconnected. Only the lookup and Stored Procedure transformations can be connected and unconnected, all other transformations are connected.

The Lookup transformation

The Lookup transformation is used to look up a source, source qualifier, or target to get the relevant data. You can look up flat file and relational tables. The Lookup transformation works on similar lines as the joiner, with a few differences. For example, lookup does not require two sources. Lookup transformations can be connected and unconnected. They extract the data from the lookup table or file based on the lookup condition.

Creating a Lookup transformation

Perform the following steps to create and configure a Lookup transformation:

1. In Mapping Designer, click on **Transformations** and create a Lookup transformation. Specify the name of the Lookup transformation and click on **OK**.

2. A new window will ask you to select **Source**, **Target**, or **Source Qualifier** that you wish to look up. You will get a list of all the sources, targets, and source qualifiers available in your repository. Click on the required component and then click on **OK**, as shown in the following screenshot:

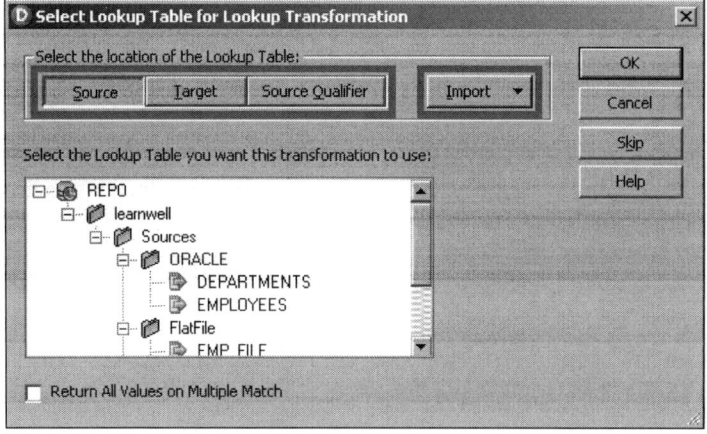

If the required source or target is not available in the repository, you can import it before you use it to look up. Click on the **Import** button to import the structure, as shown in the preceding screenshot.

The Lookup transformation with the same structure as the source, target, or source qualifier appears in the workspace.

Configuring the Lookup transformation

We have learned how to create a Lookup transformation in the previous section. Now we will implement a mapping similar to the one shown in the Joiner transformation using the Lookup transformation. We will use the EMPLOYEE Oracle table as the source and will look up the EMP_FILE flat file. Perform the following steps to implement the mapping:

1. Drag the EMPLOYEE table as the source in Mapping Designer and drag the target.

2. We have already created the Lookup transformation.

3. To get the relevant data based on the matching conditions of the EMPLOYEE table and the EMP_FILE file, drag the EMPLOYEE_ID column from the EMPLOYEE table to the Lookup transformation. Drag the corresponding columns from the EMPLOYEE source qualifier and Lookup transformation to the target, as shown in the following screenshot:

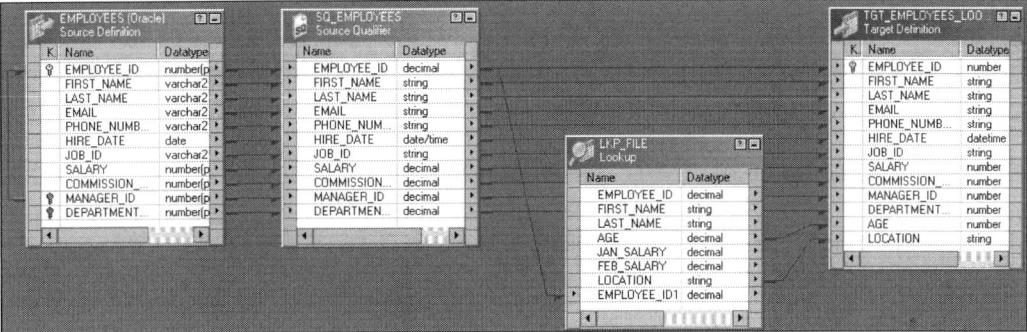

4. Click on the **Condition** tab and create a new condition, as shown in the following screenshot:

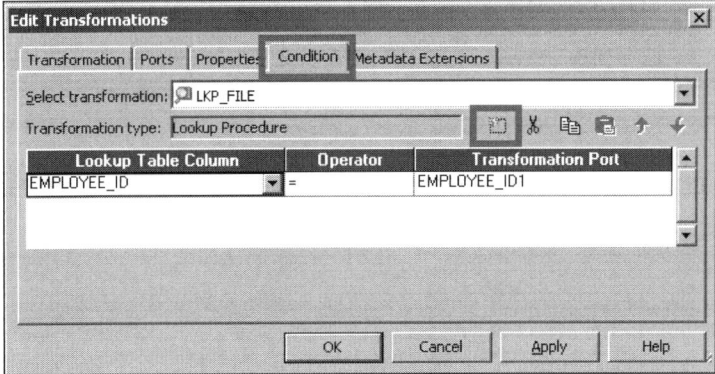

Setting up the Lookup transformation

When you create the Lookup transformation, you can configure it to cache the data. Caching the data makes the processing faster, as the data is stored internally after the cache is created. Once you choose to cache the data, the Lookup transformation caches the data from the file or table once. Then, based on the condition defined, the lookup sends the output value. As the data gets stored internally, processing becomes faster as it does not need to check the lookup condition in the file or database. Integration Service queries the cache memory instead of checking the file or table to fetch the required data.

When you choose to create the cache, Integration Service creates cache files in the $PMCacheDir default directory. The cache is created automatically and is also deleted automatically once the processing is complete. We will discuss what cache is later in the chapter.

Lookup ports

A Lookup transformation has four different types of ports. To view the ports of the Lookup transformation, click on its **Ports** tab.

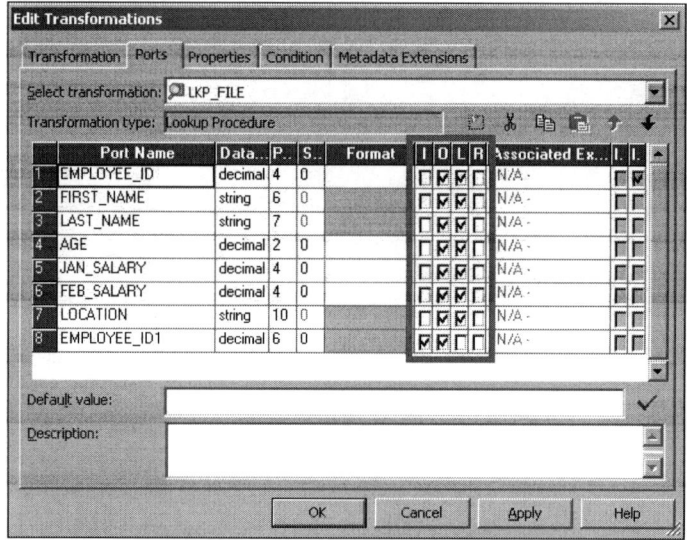

The ports are as follows:

- **Input Ports (I)**: The input ports receive the data from other transformations. This port will be used in the lookup condition. You need to have at least one input port.

- **Output Port (O)**: Output ports pass the data from the Lookup transformation to other transformations.

- **Lookup Port (L)**: Each column is assigned as the lookup and output port when you create the Lookup transformation. If you delete the lookup port from the flat file lookup source, the session will fail. If you delete the lookup port from the relational lookup table, Integration Service extracts the data with only the lookup port. This helps to reduce the data extracted from the lookup source.

- **Return Port (R)**: This is only used in the case of an unconnected Lookup transformation. It indicates which data you wish to return in the Lookup transformation. You can define only one port as the return port, and it's not used in the case of connected Lookup transformations.

Lookup queries

Similar to the Source Qualifier transformation, which generates a default query when you use the source as a relational database table, the Lookup transformation also generates a default query based on the ports used in the Lookup transformation. To check the default query generated by the Lookup transformation, click on the **Properties** tab and open **Lookup Sql Override**, as shown in the following screenshot:

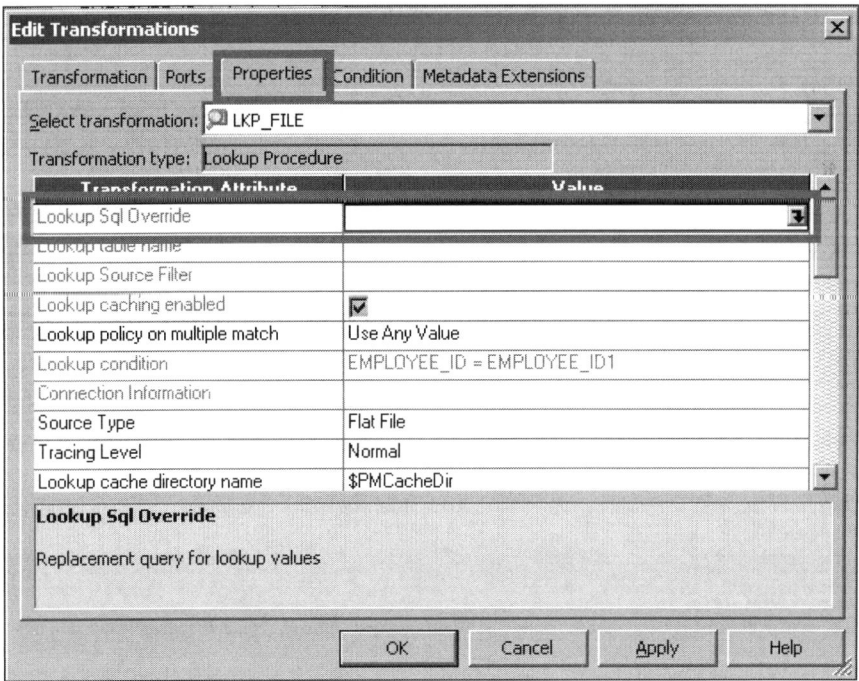

Similar to overriding the default SQL in the Source Qualifier transformation, you can override the default query generated by the Lookup transformation. If you override the default query generated by the Lookup transformation, it is referred to as a lookup SQL override.

Unconnected Lookup transformations

As mentioned, unconnected transformations are not connected to any other transformation, source, or target by any links. An unconnected Lookup transformation is called by another transformation with the :LKP function. Using the :LKP function, you can pass the required value to the input port of the Lookup transformation, and the return port passes the output value back to the transformation from which the lookup was called. A mapping using an unconnected Lookup transformation is as follows:

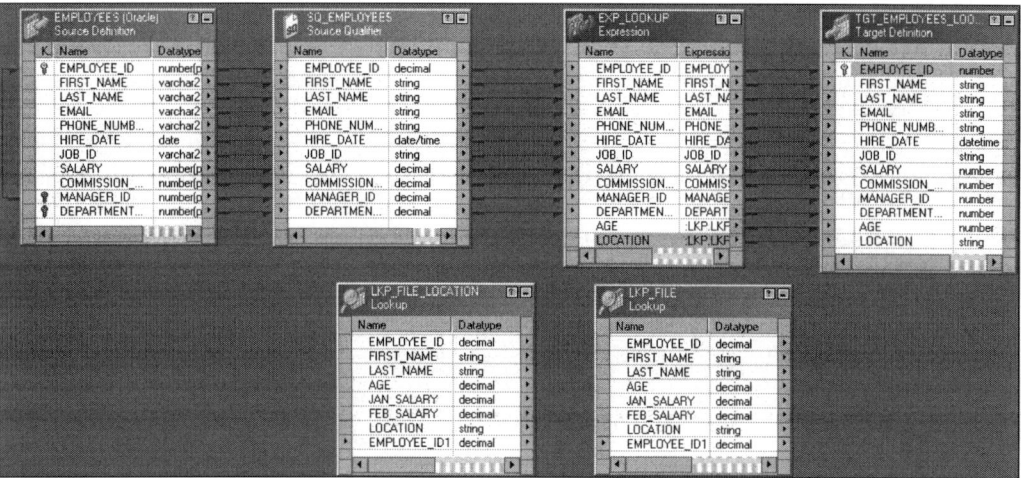

In the preceding mapping, we are implementing the same scenario that we implement using a connected Lookup transformation. Perform the following steps to implement this scenario:

1. Create an Expression transformation and drag all the ports from the Source Qualifier transformation to Expression transformation.

2. Create an EMPLOYEE_ID input port in the Lookup transformation that will accept the value of EMPLOYEE_ID using the :LKP function.

3. Create another AGE output port in the Expression transformation that is used to call an unconnected Lookup transformation using the :LKP function. Link the AGE port to the target. Write the :LKP.LKP_FILE(EMPLOYEE_ID) function in the expression editor of the AGE column, as shown in the following screenshot:

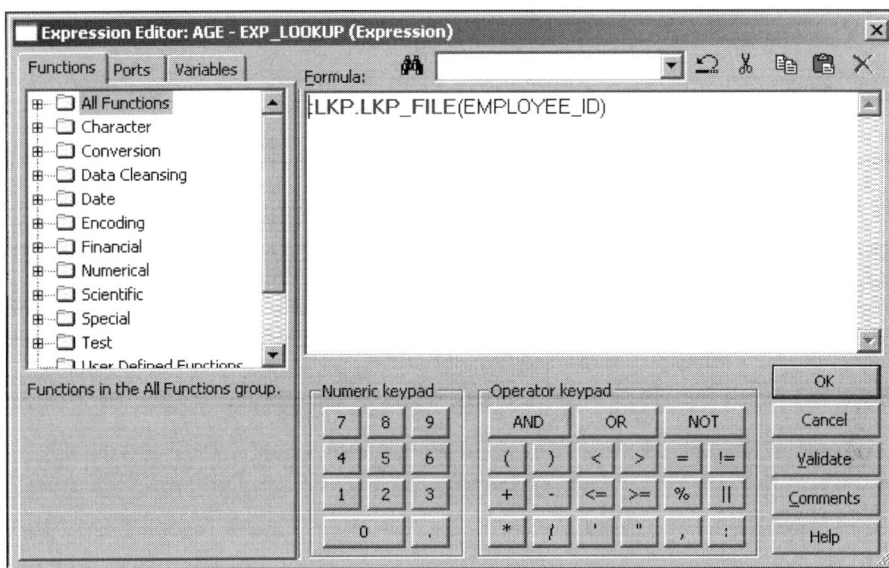

4. Double-click on the Lookup transformation, click on ports, and make AGE the return port, as shown in the following screenshot:

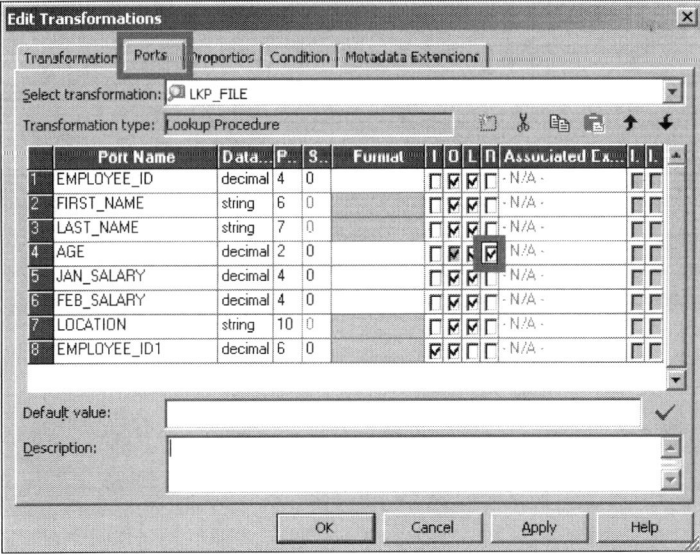

When you execute the mapping, row-wise data will flow from the source to the Expression transformation. The :LKP function passes the data to the Lookup transformation, which compares the data based on the condition defined in the **Condition** tab, which in turn returns the data from the **Return** port to the Expression transformation, from where the data is passed further in the mapping.

5. Similarly, add another LOCATION output port to the Expression transformation. Then, create another Lookup transformation. We cannot use the same Lookup transformation, as the unconnected Lookup transformation can return only one port. Follow the process described here to look up for the AGE port to complete the mapping.

We have seen the implementation of connected and unconnected Lookup transformations.

Lookup transformation properties

Let's discuss the properties of the Lookup transformation:

Property	Description
Lookup SQL override	This is similar to a SQL override. When you override the default query generated by the Lookup transformation to extract the data from relational tables, it is referred to as a lookup SQL override.
Lookup table name	This is the name of the table that you are looking up using the Lookup transformation.
Lookup source filter	Integration Service will extract only those records that satisfy the filter condition defined.
Lookup cache enabled	This property indicates whether Integration Service caches data during the processing. Enabling this property enhances performance.

Property	Description
Lookup policy on multiple match	You can decide to choose a particular value if the Lookup transformation returns multiple values based on the condition defined. The various options available are: • **Use First Value**: Integration Service will return the first matching record. • **Use Last Value**: Integration Service will return the last matching record. • **Use Any Value**: When you select this option, Integration Service returns the first matching value. • **Report Error**: When you select this option, Integration Service gives out an error in the session log. This indicates that your system has duplicate values.
Lookup condition	This is the lookup condition you defined in the **Condition** tab of the Lookup transformation.
Connection information	This property indicates the database connection used to extract data in the Lookup transformation.
Source type	This gives you information indicating that the Lookup transformation is looking up on flat file, a relational database, or a source qualifier.
Tracing level	This specifies the level of detail related to the Lookup transformation you wish to write.
Lookup cache directory name	This indicates the directory where cache files will be created. Integration Service also stores the persistent cache in this directory. The default is $PMCacheDir.
Lookup cache persistent	Check this option is you wish to make the cache persistent. If you choose to make the cache persistent, Integration Service stores the cache in the form of files in the $PMCacheDir location.
Lookup data cache size	This is the size of the data cache you wish to allocate to Integration Service in order to store the data. The default is Auto.
Lookup data index size	This is the size of the index cache you wish to allocate to Integration Service in order to store the index details such as the lookup condition. The default is Auto.
Dynamic lookup cache	Select this option if you wish to make the lookup cache dynamic.

Property	Description
Output old value on update	If you disable this option, Integration Service sends the old value from the output ports, so if the cache is to be updated with a new value, it first sends an old value to the output ports that are present in the cache. You can use this option if you enable dynamic caching.
Cache file name prefix	This indicates the name of the cache file to be created when you enable persistent caching.
Recache from lookup source	When you check this option, Integration Service rebuilds the cache from the lookup table when the lookup is called.
Insert else update	If you check this option, Integration Service inserts a new row into the cache and updates existing rows if the row is marked INSERT. This option is used when you enable dynamic caching.
Update else insert	If you check this option, Integration Service updates the existing row and inserts a new row if it is marked UPDATE. This option is used when you enable dynamic caching.
Date/time format	This property indicates the format of the date and time. The default is MM/DD/YYYY HH24:MI:SS.
Thousand separator	You can choose this separator to separate values. The default is no separator.
Decimal separator	You can choose this separator to separate the decimal values. The default is no period.
Case-sensitive string comparison	This property indicates the type of comparison to be made when comparing strings.
Null ordering	This specifies how the Integration Service orders the null values while processing data. The default is to sort the null value as high.
Sorted input	Check this option if you are passing sorted data to the Lookup transformation. Passing the sorted data enhances performance.
Lookup source is static	This indicates that the lookup source is not changing while processing the data.
Pre-build lookup cache	This indicates whether Integration Service builds the cache before the data enters the Lookup transformation. The default is **Auto**.
Subsection precision	This property indicates the subsection precision you wish to set for the date/time data.

We have now seen all the details of Lookup transformations.

The Update Strategy transformation

Update Strategy transformations are used to INSERT, UPDATE, DELETE, or REJECT records based on the defined condition in the mapping. An Update Strategy transformation is mostly used when you design mappings for slowly changing dimensions. When you implement SCD, you actually decide how you wish to maintain historical data with the current data. We have discussed SCDs in *Chapter 3, Implementing SCD – Using Designer Screen Wizards*. When you wish to maintain no history, complete history, or partial history, you can achieve this functionality by either using the property defined in the session task or using the Update Strategy transformation.

When you use the session task, you instruct Integration Service to treat all records in the same way, that is, either INSERT, UPDATE, or DELETE.

When you use the Update Strategy transformation in the mapping, the control is no longer with the session task. The Update Strategy transformation allows you to INSERT, UPDATE, DELETE, or REJECT records based on the requirement. When you use the Update Strategy transformation, the control is no longer with the session task. You need to define the following functions to perform the corresponding operations:

- DD_INSERT: This is used when you wish to insert records, which are also represented by the numeral 0
- DD_UPDATE: This is used when you wish to update the records, which are also represented by the numeral 1
- DD_DELETE: This is used when you wish to delete the records, which are also represented by the numeral 2
- DD_REJECT: This is used when you wish to reject the records, which are also represented by the numeral 3

Consider that we wish to implement a mapping using the Update Strategy transformation, which allows all employees with salaries higher than 10000 to reach the target and eliminates all other records. The following screenshot depicts the mapping for this scenario:

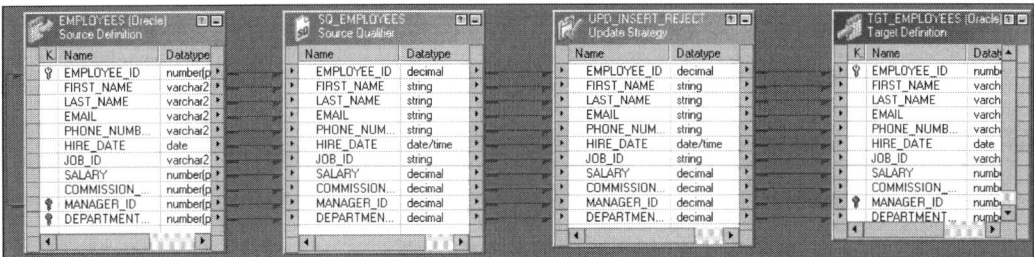

Double-click on the Update Strategy transformation and click on **Properties** to add the condition:

```
IIF(SALARY >= 10000, DD_INSERT, DD_REJECT)
```

The Update Strategy transformation accepts the records in a row-wise manner and checks each record for the condition defined. Based on this, it rejects or inserts the data into the target.

The Normalizer transformation

The Normalizer transformation is used in place of Source Qualifier transformations when you wish to read the data from the cobol copybook source. Also, a Normalizer transformation is used to convert column-wise data to row-wise data. This is similar to the transpose feature of MS Excel. You can use this feature if your source is a cobol copybook file or relational database table. The Normalizer transformation converts columns to rows and also generates an index for each converted row. A sample mapping using the Normalizer transformation is shown in the following screenshot:

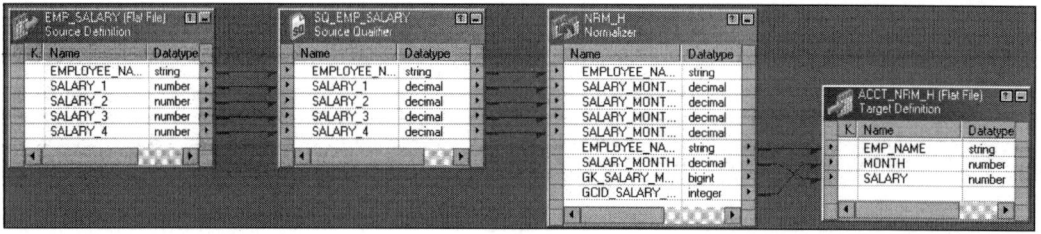

Consider the following example, which contains the salaries of three employees for four months:

```
STEVE 1000 2000 3000 4000
JAMES 2000 2500 3000 3500
ANDY 4000 4000 4000 4000
```

When you pass the data through the Normalizer transformation, it returns the data in a row-wise form along with the index, as follows:

```
STEVE 1000 1
STEVE 2000 2
STEVE 3000 3
STEVE 4000 4
JAMES 2000 1
JAMES 2500 2
JAMES 3000 3
JAMES 3500 4
```

```
ANDY 4000 1
ANDY 4000 2
ANDY 4000 3
ANDY 4000 4
```

As you can see, the index key is incremented for each value. It also initializes the index from 1 when processing data for a new row.

Configuring the Normalizer transformation – ports

Normalizer transformation ports are different from other transformations ports. You cannot edit the ports of Normalizer transformations. To define the ports, you need to configure the **Normalizer** tab of a Normalizer transformation. To add the multiple occurring ports to the Normalizer transformation, double-click on the Normalizer transformation and click on **Normalizer**. Add the columns to the **Normalizer** tab. You need to add the single and multiple occurring ports in the **Normalizer** tab. When you have multiple occurring columns, you need to define them under the **Occurs** option in the Normalizer transformation, as shown in the following screenshot:

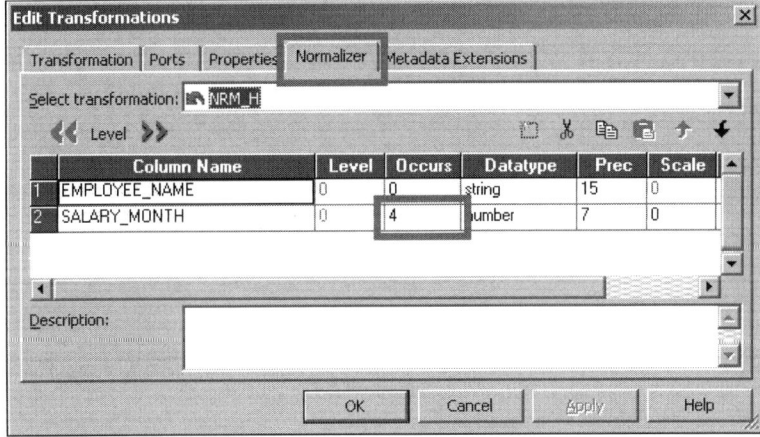

When you add the columns in the **Normalizer** tab, the columns get reflected in the **Ports** tab based on the options definitions. In our case, we define SALARY_MONTH under occurs 4 times in the Normalizer transformation. This creates the port four times in the ports tab.

The Normalizer transformation creates a new port called **generated column ID (GCID)** for every multi-occurring ports you define in the **Normalizer** tab. In our case, it is created for SALARY_MONTHLY. This port generates the index value to be assigned to new multi-occurring values. The GCID is incremented automatically each time it processes a new record, as shown in the following screenshot:

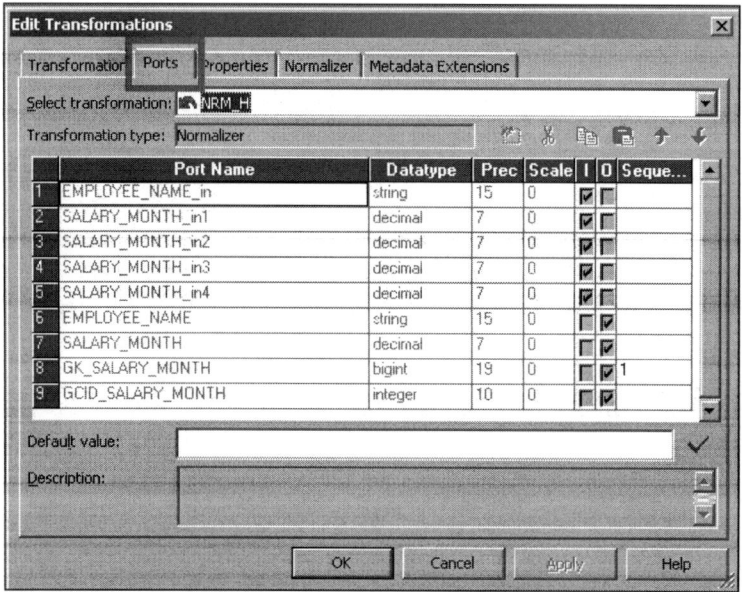

The attributes of the **Normalizer** tab are as follows:

Attribute	Description
Column name	This indicates the name of the column you wish to define.
Level	This defines the groups of columns in the data. It defines the hierarchy of the data. The group level column has a lower-level number, and it does not contain data.
Occurs	This indicates the number of times the column occurs in the data.
Datatype	This indicates the data type of the data.
Prec	This indicates the length of the column in the source data.
Scale	This indicates the number of decimal positions in the numeric data.

The Stored Procedure transformation

It stores procedure database components. Informatica uses the stored procedure in a manner that is similar to database tables. Stored procedures are sets of SQL instructions that require a certain set of input values, and in turn the stored procedure returns output values. This way, you either import or create database tables and import or create the stored procedure in the mapping. To use the stored procedure in mapping, the stored procedure should exist in the database.

Similar to Lookup transformations, stored procedures can also be connected or unconnected transformations in Informatica. When you use a connected stored procedure, you pass the value to stored procedures through links. When you use an unconnected stored procedure, you pass the value using the :SP function.

Importing Stored Procedure transformations

Importing the stored procedure is similar to importing the database tables in Informatica. Earlier, we saw the process of importing database tables. Before you import the stored procedure, make sure the stored procedure is created and tested at the database level. Also, make sure that you have valid credentials to connect to the database.

To import the stored procedure, open the mapping in Mapping Designer. Click on **Transformation** and select the **Import Stored Procedure...** option, as shown in the following screenshot:

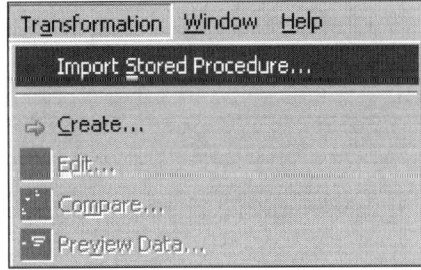

Connect to the database credentials, click on the required procedure, and click on **OK**.

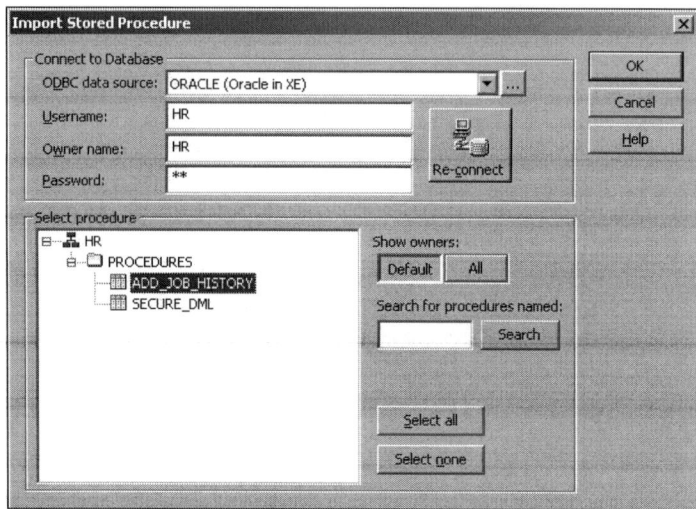

The stored procedure appears in the workspace. Connect the corresponding input and output ports to complete the mapping.

Creating Stored Procedure transformations

You can create Stored Procedure transformations instead of importing them. Usually, the best practice is to import the stored procedure, as it takes care of all the properties automatically. When you create the transformation, you need to take care of all the input, output, and return ports in the Stored Procedure transformation. Before you create the stored procedure, make sure the stored procedure is created in the database.

To create the Stored Procedure transformation, open the mapping in Mapping Designer. Navigate to **Transformation | Create**. Then, select the Stored Procedure transformation from the list of transformations and mention the name of the transformation, as shown in the following screenshot:

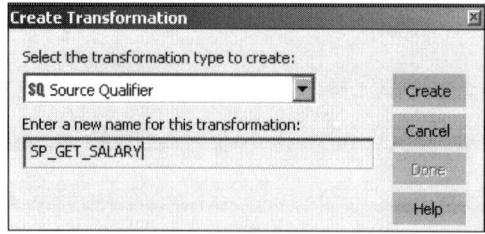

In the next window, click on **Skip**. A Stored Procedure transformation appears in Mapping Designer. Add the corresponding input, output, and variable ports. You need to be aware of the ports present in the stored procedure created in the database.

Using Stored Procedure transformations in the mapping

As mentioned, Stored Procedure transformations can be connected or unconnected. Similar to Lookup transformations, you can configure connected or unconnected Stored Procedure transformations.

Connected Stored Procedure transformations

A connected Stored Procedure transformation is connected in the mapping with the links. The connected Stored Procedure transformation receives data in the input port and sends the data out using output ports. A sample mapping showing the connected Stored Procedure transformation is shown in the following screenshot:

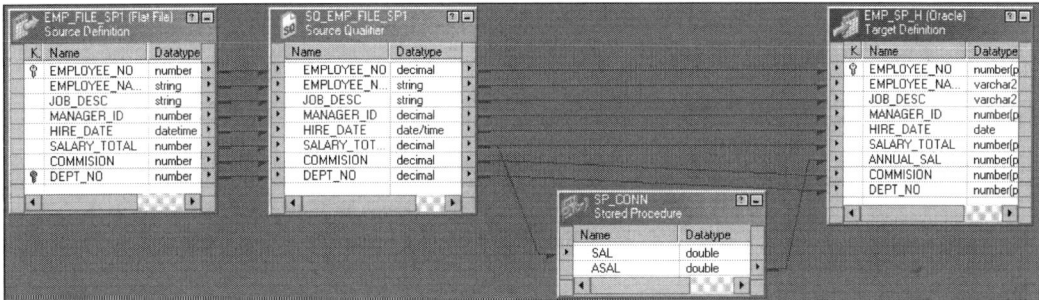

Unconnected Stored Procedure transformations

An unconnected Stored Procedure transformation is not connected to any other source, target, or transformation by links. The unconnected Stored Procedure transformation is called by another transformation using the :SP function. It works in a manner similar to an unconnected Lookup transformation, which is called using the :LKP function.

A sample mapping using the unconnected Stored Procedure transformation is shown in the following screenshot:

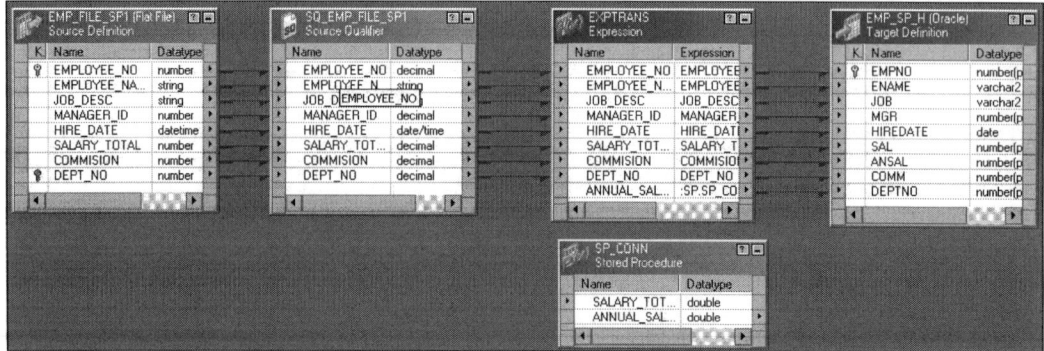

We have used Expression transformations to call the stored procedure. The function that is used to call the stored procedure is `SP.SP_CONN(SALARY_TOTAL,PROC_RESULT)`. Follow the steps similar to ones used for unconnected Lookup transformations in order to create the unconnected stored procedure mapping.

Transaction Control transformations

Transaction Control transformations allow you to commit or roll back individual records based on certain conditions. By default, Integration Service commits the data based on the properties you define at the session task level. Using the **Commit Interval** property, Integration Service commits or rolls backs the data into the target. Suppose you define **Commit Interval** as `10,000`, Integration Service will commit the data after every 10,000 records. When you use a Transaction Control transformation, you get the control at each record to commit or roll back.

When you use the Transaction Control transformation, you need to define the condition in the expression editor of the Transaction Control transformation. When you run the process, the data enters the Transaction Control transformation in a row-wise manner. The Transaction Control transformation evaluates each row, based on which it commits or rolls back the data.

A sample mapping using the Transaction Control transformation is shown in the following screenshot:

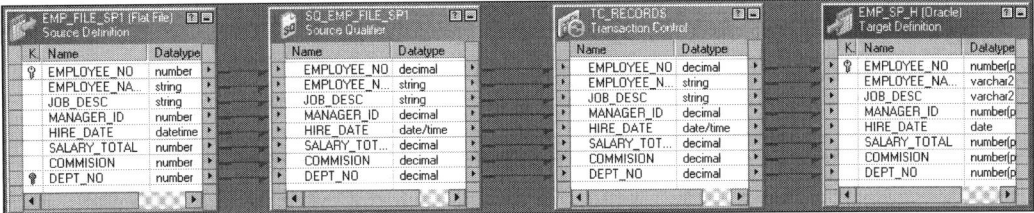

To use the Transaction Control transformation in the mapping, perform the following steps:

1. Open the mapping in Mapping Designer and create the Transaction Control transformation.

2. Drag the required columns from the Source Qualifier transformation to the Transaction Control transformation.

3. Connect the appropriate ports from the Transaction Control transformation to the target.

4. Double-click on the Transaction Control transformation and click on **Properties**. We need to define the condition in the Transaction Control transformation expression editor, as shown in the following screenshot:

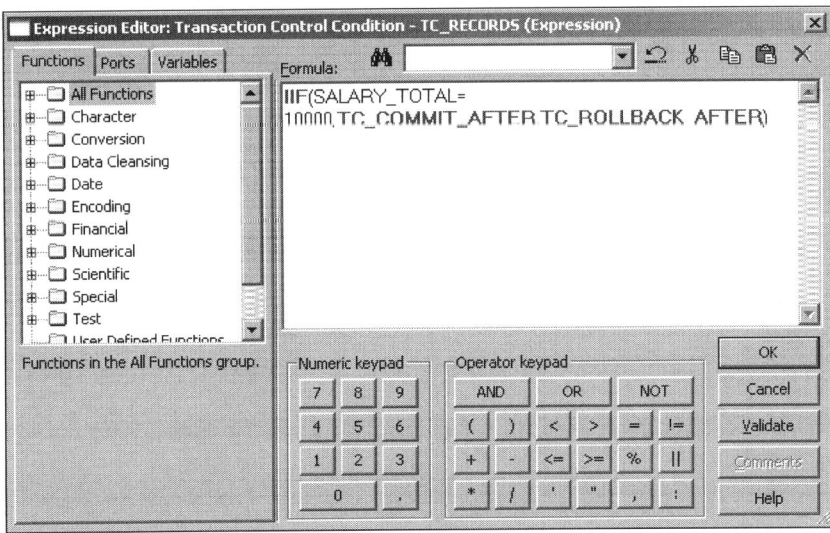

5. Finally, click on **OK**.

The mapping using the Transaction Control transformation is now complete.

The Transaction Control transformation supports the following built-in variables in the expression editor:

- TC_COMMIT_BEFORE: Integration Service commits the current record, starts processing a new record, and then writes the current row to the target.

- TC_COMMIT_AFTER: Integration Service commits and writes the current record to the target and then starts processing the new record.

- TC_ROLLBACK_BEFORE: Integration Service rolls back the current record, starts processing the new record, and then writes the current row to the target.

- TC_ROLLBACK_AFTER: Integration Service writes the current record to the target, rolls back the current record, and then starts processing the new record.

- TC_CONTINUE_TRANSACTION: This is the default value for the Transaction Control transformation. Integration Service does not perform any transaction operations for the record.

With this, we have seen the details related to Transaction Control transformations. It is not recommended that you use Transaction Control transformation in the mapping, as it hampers performance by checking each record for a commit or rollback. So the best way is to use the commit interval property in the session task.

Types of lookup cache

A cache is the temporary memory that is created when you execute the process. Caches are created automatically when the process starts and is deleted automatically once the process is complete. The amount of cache memory is decided based on the property you define at the transformation level or session level. You usually set the property as the default, so it can increase the size of the cache as required. If the size required to cache the data is more than the cache size defined, the process fails with an overflow error. There are different types of caches available.

Building the cache – sequential or concurrent

You can define the session property to create the cache either sequentially or concurrently.

Sequential cache

When you choose to create the cache sequentially, Integration Service caches the data in a row-wise manner as the records enter the Lookup transformation. When the first record enters the Lookup transformation, the lookup cache gets created and stores the matching record from the lookup table or file in the cache. This way, the cache stores only matching data. This helps save the cache space by not storing the unnecessary data.

Concurrent cache

When you choose to create caches concurrently, Integration Service does not wait for the data to flow from the source, but it first caches the complete data. Once the caching is complete, it allows the data to flow from the source. When you select concurrent cache, performance is better than sequential caches, as the scanning happens internally using the data stored in cache.

Persistent cache – the permanent one

You can configure caches to permanently save data. By default, caches are created as nonpersistent, that is, they will be deleted once the session run is complete. If the lookup table or file does not change across the session runs, you can use the existing persistent cache.

Suppose that you have a process that is scheduled to run every day and you are using a Lookup transformation to look up a reference table that is not supposed to change for 6 months. When you use a nonpersistent cache every day, the same data will be stored in cache. This will waste time and space every day. If you choose to create a persistent cache, Integration Service makes the cache permanent in the form of a file in the $PMCacheDir location, so you save the time required to create and delete the cache memory every day.

When the data in the lookup table changes, you need to rebuild the cache. You can define the condition in the session task to rebuild the cache by overwriting the existing cache. To rebuild the cache, you need to check the rebuild option in the session property, as discussed in the session properties in *Chapter 5, Using the Workflow Manager Screen – Advanced*.

Sharing cache – named or unnamed

You can enhance performance and save the cache memory by sharing the cache if there are multiple Lookup transformations used in a mapping. If you have the same structure for both the Lookup transformations, sharing the cache will help enhance performance by creating the cache only once. This way, we avoid creating the cache multiple times. You can share both named and unnamed caches.

Sharing unnamed cache

If you have multiple Lookup transformations used in a single mapping, you can share the unnamed cache. As the Lookup transformations are present in the same mapping, naming the cache is not mandatory. Integration Service creates the cache while processing the first record in the first Lookup transformation and shares the cache with other lookups in the mapping.

Sharing named cache

You can share the named cache with multiple Lookup transformations in the same mapping or in other mappings. As the cache is named, you can assign the same cache using the name in another mapping.

When you process the first mapping with a Lookup transformation, it saves the cache in the defined cache directory and with the defined cache filename. When you process the second mapping, it searches for the same location and cache file and uses the data. If Integration Service does not find the mentioned cache file, it creates the new cache.

If you simultaneously run multiple sessions that use the same cache file, Integration Service processes both the sessions successfully only if the Lookup transformation is configured for read-only from the cache. If there is a scenario where both the Lookup transformations are trying to update the cache file, or a scenario where one lookup is trying to read the cache file and the other is trying to update the cache, the session will fail as there is a conflict in the processing.

Sharing the cache helps enhance performance by utilizing the cache created. This way, we save the processing time and repository space by not storing the same data for Lookup transformations multiple times.

Modifying cache – static or dynamic

When you create a cache, you can configure it to be static or dynamic.

Static cache

A cache is said to be static if it does not change with the changes happening in the lookup table. A static cache is not synchronized with the lookup table.

By default, Integration Service creates a static cache. A lookup cache is created as soon as the first record enters the Lookup transformation. Integration Service does not update the cache while it is processing the data.

Dynamic cache

A cache is said to be dynamic if it changes with the changes happening in the lookup table. The dynamic cache is synchronized with the lookup table.

From the Lookup transformation properties, you can choose to make the cache dynamic. The lookup cache is created as soon as the first record enters the Lookup transformation. Integration Service keeps on updating the cache while it is processing the data. It marks the record INSERT for new rows inserted in dynamic cache. For the record that is updated, it marks the record as updated in the cache. For every record that doesn't change, Integration Service marks it as unchanged.

You use the dynamic cache while you process slowly changing dimension tables. For every record inserted into the target, the record will be inserted in the cache. For every record updated in the target, the record will be updated in the cache. A similar process happens for the deleted and rejected records.

Tracing levels

Tracing levels in Informatica define the amount of data you wish to write in the session log when you execute the workflow. The tracing level is a very important aspect of Informatica, as it helps in analyzing errors. It is also very helpful in finding the bugs in the process and you can define it in every transformation. The tracing level option is present in every transformation properties window. There are four types of tracing levels available:

- **Normal**: When you set the tracing level as **Normal**, Informatica stores the status information, information about errors, and information about skipped rows. You get detailed information but not at an individual row level.

- **Terse**: When you set the tracing level as **Terse**, Informatica stores the error information and the information of rejected records. **Terse** tracing level occupies less space than **Normal**.

- **Verbose Initialization**: When you set the tracing level as **Verbose Initialize**, it stores the process details related to the startup, details about index, data files created, and more details of the transformation process in addition to details stored in the normal tracing. This tracing level takes more space than **Normal** and **Terse**.

- **Verbose Data**: This is the most detailed level of tracing. It occupies more space and takes more time than the other three levels. It stores row-level data in the session log. It writes the truncation information whenever it truncates the data. It also writes the data to the error log if you enable row-error logging.

The default tracing level is **Normal**. You can change the tracing level to **Terse** in order to enhance performance. The tracing level can be defined at an individual transformation level, or you can override the tracing level by defining it at the session level.

Summary

We have discussed the most important aspect of the Informatica PowerCenter tool in this chapter. We also talked about most of the widely used transformations in this chapter. Other transformations that have intentionally not been discussed in this chapter are very rarely used. We have talked about the functions of various transformations. We learned about the usage of ports and expression editors in various transformations. We discussed the classification of the transformations: active/passive and connected/unconnected. We learned about the different types of caches and the different types of tracing levels available.

In the next chapter, we will discuss the fourth client screen, Repository Manager. We have seen the usage of other screens. We will see how the Repository Manager screen is used to deploy the code across the various environments in Informatica.

8
The Deployment Phase – Using Repository Manager

In the previous chapters, we discussed the different functionalities of the PowerCenter Designer, Workflow Manager, and the Workflow Monitor screen. At this stage, you know a lot about the various components of the Informatica PowerCenter tool. We are left with the last client tool, that is, PowerCenter Repository Manager. Repository Manager is not used for coding but is used for certain administration-related work and the deployment of PowerCenter components such as mapping, workflow, and so on. In this chapter, we will learn how to create and configure the domain and repository that we created in the Informatica Administrator console. We will also learn about the migration or deployment process that we follow to migrate the code in Informatica PowerCenter.

Using Repository Manager

The following screenshot shows you the Informatica PowerCenter Repository Manager screen:

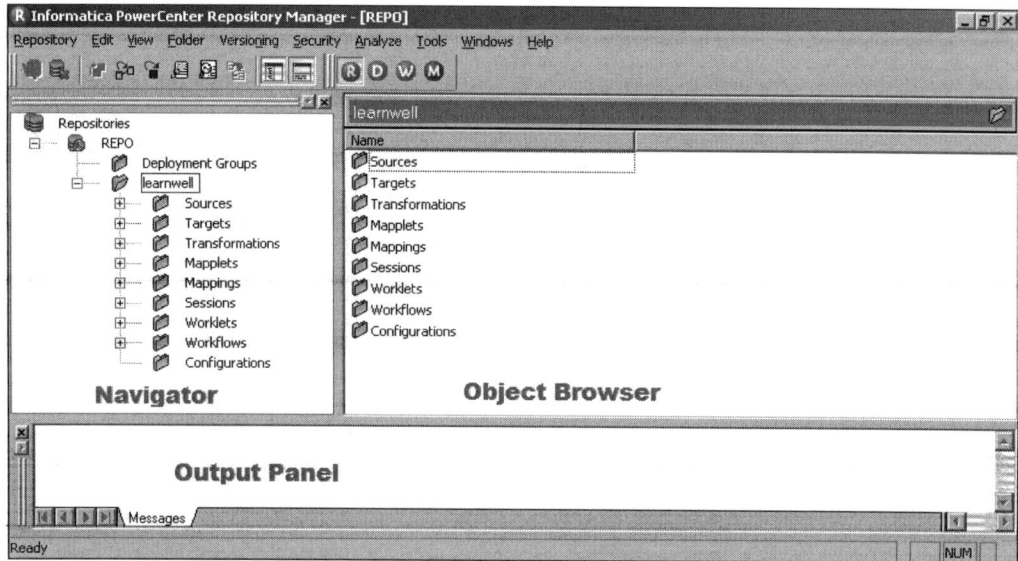

As you can see, the screen is divided into sections that we discussed when we talked about the Designer and Workflow Manager screen.

The navigator of Repository Manager consists of components such as sources, targets, mappings, workflows, and so on, as shown in the previous screenshot. It contains all the components of the designer and Workflow Manager.

As mentioned previously, Repository Manager serves two purposes: one is the client server configuration and the other is the deployment or migration.

Configuring the client tools

The Repository Manager screen is used to configure the client tools with the server of the Informatica PowerCenter tool. More about the configuration of the Informatica server is covered in *Appendix, Installing Informatica and Using Informatica Administration Console*. Once the configuration of the server is completed, we need to configure the server with the client tools so that the client can access the components and services from the server. To configure the client tools, we use Repository Manager. Perform the following steps for the configuration:

1. Open Repository Manager and navigate to **Repository | Configure Domains**, as shown in the following screenshot:

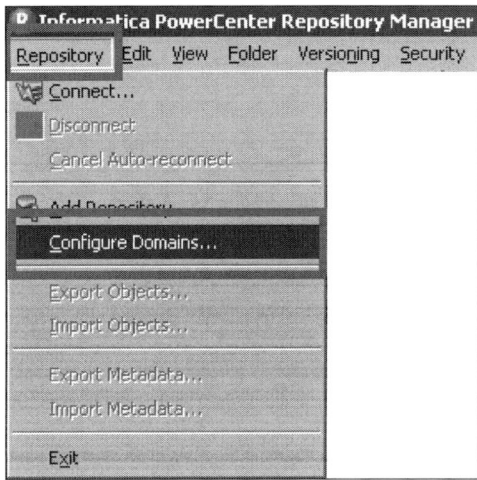

2. Click on the create a new domain icon as shown in the following screenshot:

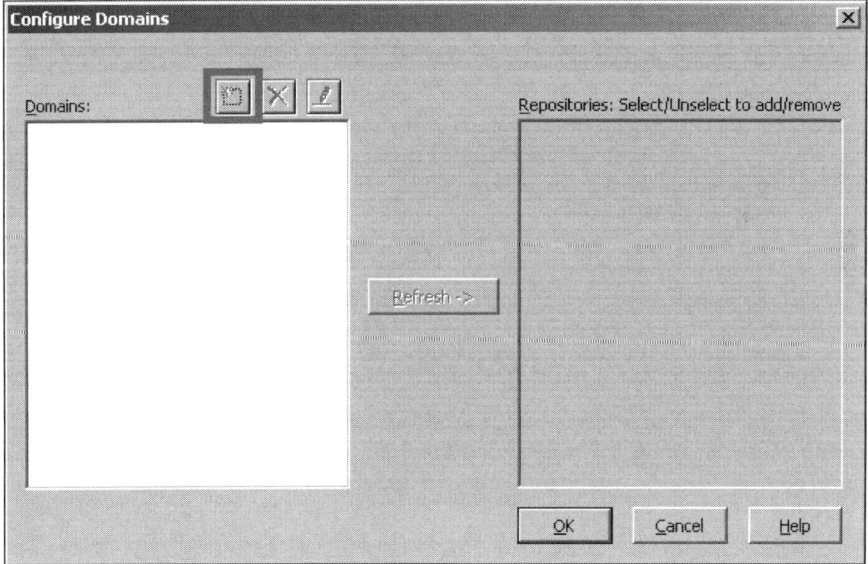

3. Specify the name of the domain, host, and port in the next window as follows:

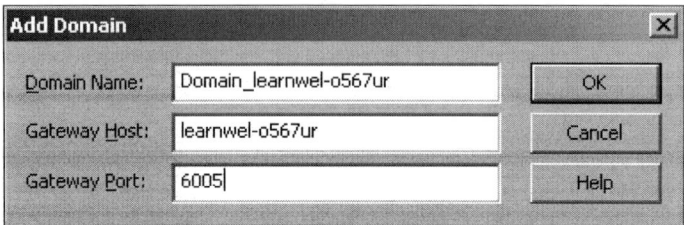

You will get these details from your administrator in your company. If you are doing this on your own, you can check the details in administrator console's home page.

4. Click on **OK**.

5. Check the name of the repository in the checkbox, as shown in the following screenshot, and click on **OK**:

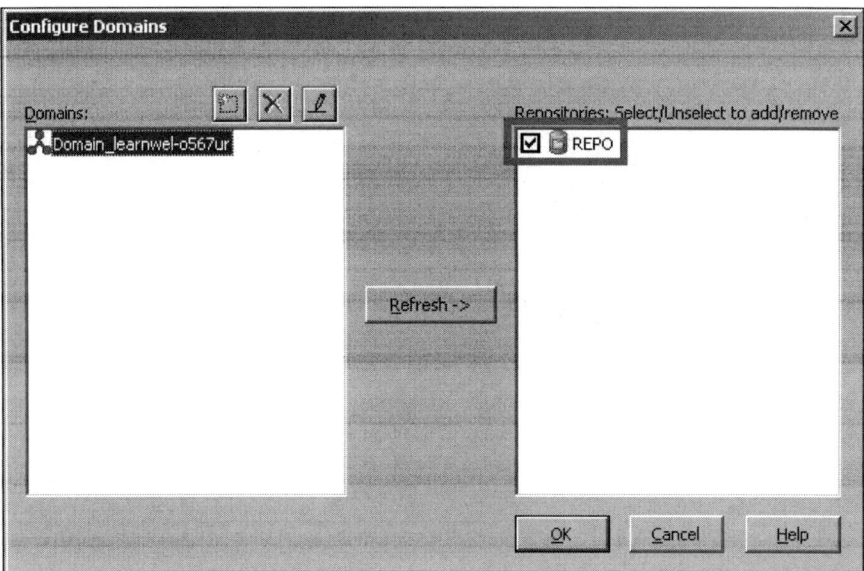

6. Once the domain configuration is complete, navigate to **Repository | Connect**, as shown in the following screenshot:

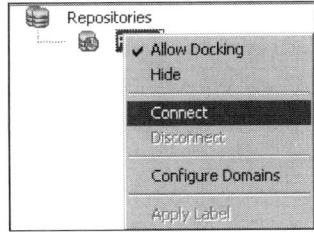

Specify **Username** and **Password** with the user you created in the server. We are using `learn` as the username and password, as indicated in the following screenshot:

7. Click on **Connect**. You will get connected to the repository as follows:

8. Navigate to **Folders | Create** in the toolbar, as shown here:

9. Specify the name of the folder you wish to create. Usually, this is the username you created earlier.

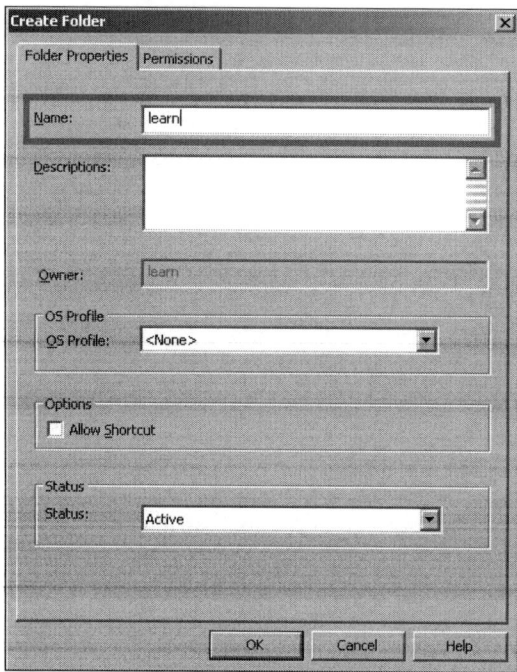

10. Click on **OK** to get your folder added under **Repository**, as shown in the following screenshot:

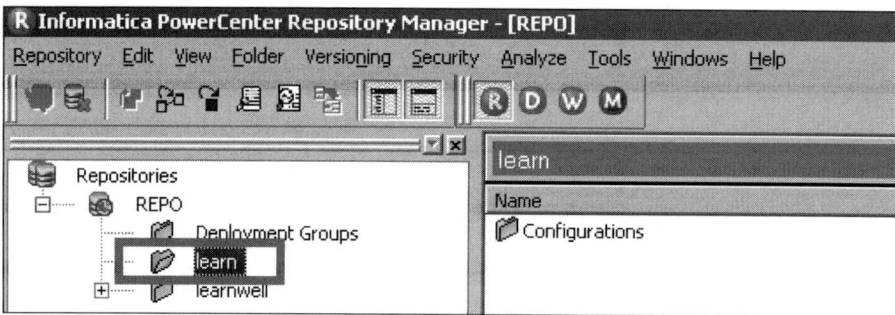

Note that `learnwell`, which was shown in the preceding screenshot, is another folder we created. We will be using the `learn` and `learnwell` folders to understand the migration activities. Note that the migration of components across repositories is similar to the migration of components across folders.

You are all set to work on the client tools.

This completes the configuration of Informatica client tools. In the next section, we will talk about another important aspect, that is, the migration of Informatica components.

Take me to next stage – deployment or migration

One of the most important phases of any software project is deployment or migration. Repository Manager provides a convenient way to migrate the code from one environment to another. As you are aware, we have three different environments for migration. Usually, we refer to them as DEV for the development environment, TEST for the testing environment, and PROD for production. DEV is the environment where you actually develop the code. You perform the unit testing, and then you migrate the code to the TEST environment, where the testing team performs the testing on the code to evaluate whether everything is running as per requirements. Once tested, the code is migrated to PROD, where it actually goes live. When we wish to migrate the code, we need to make sure that all the components along with their properties are migrated properly. We need to migrate all sources, targets, mappings, workflows, and session tasks used in the code. Transformations and tasks get migrated along with mappings and workflows. So, you need not migrate them separately. Also, if your code is using parameter files or Unix shell scripts, you need to migrate them though the parameter file and Unix scripts are migrated separately and not from the Informatica client tool.

To migrate the sources, targets, and mappings, you can use the PowerCenter Designer, and to migrate the session tasks and workflows, including other tasks, you can use PowerCenter Workflow Manager. Repository Manager can migrate all components in one go for you.

Informatica PowerCenter provides three ways to migrate the code from one environment to another, that is, **Export/Import**, **Copy/Paste**, and **Drag/Drop**.

Let's talk about all the options.

Export/Import

You can perform the **Export/Import** functionality from the PowerCenter Designer or the Workflow Manager screen. Whenever you export the components, Informatica creates the .XML file for those components. Similarly, you can import the components if they are available as .XML files. So, any export/import operation will happen in the .XML format.

You can view the file in the XML editor and, in fact, change the file before you import it. The code will be imported with the changes you made in the file. Ideally, you should not change the exported file to avoid consistency issues across different environments.

To complete the migration, you export the components from one repository and import in another repository. A similar approach can be used to migrate code from one folder to another folder in the same repository.

Migrating from the designer

Before we proceed, note that we can migrate only those components that are present on the the PowerCenter Designer screen. To migrate the components, perform the following steps:

1. Open the designer and from the navigator, select the component you wish to migrate and navigate to **Repository | Export Objects**. We selected a m_UNION mapping for our reference in this book, as shown in the following screenshot. When you export the mapping, corresponding sources, targets, and transformations get exported. Similarly, when you export the workflow from Workflow Manager, all the tasks present in the workflow gets exported. So, you need not export all components separately.

   We are exporting the components from the learnwell folder.

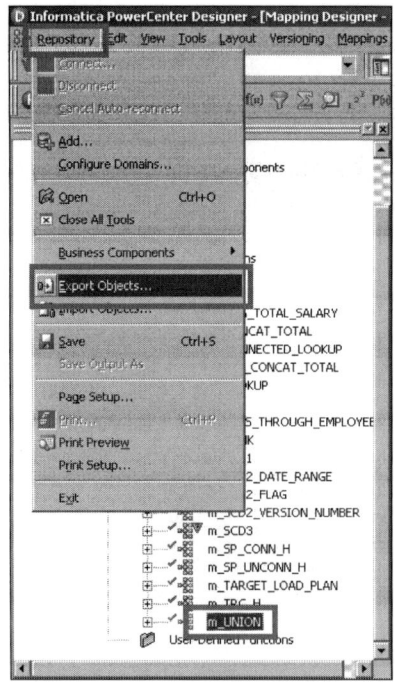

2. A new pop-up window will ask you to browse the location to save the `.xml` file. Specify the location and click on **OK**.

Informatica will start the export process, and once done, you will get the description of the process. It will show you the details of the components exported. Also, if it encountered an error, the error will be mentioned. Refer to the following screenshot:

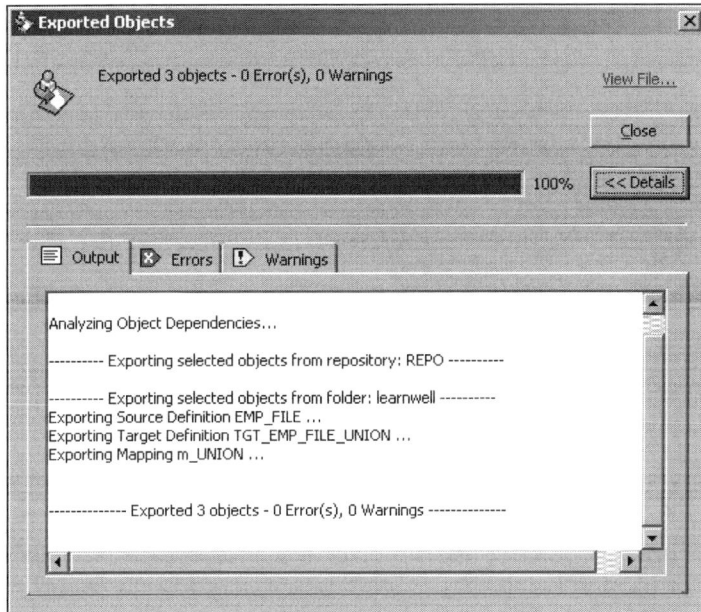

With this, the export process is complete and you will be able to see the components at the specified location.

Once you are done with the export process, you are all set to import the file to get the components in another repository or folder. We will be importing the mapping in the `learn` folder.

Perform the following steps to import mappings:

1. Open the designer and connect to the repository or folder that you wish to import the code to. Navigate to **Repository | Import Objects**, as shown in the following screenshot:

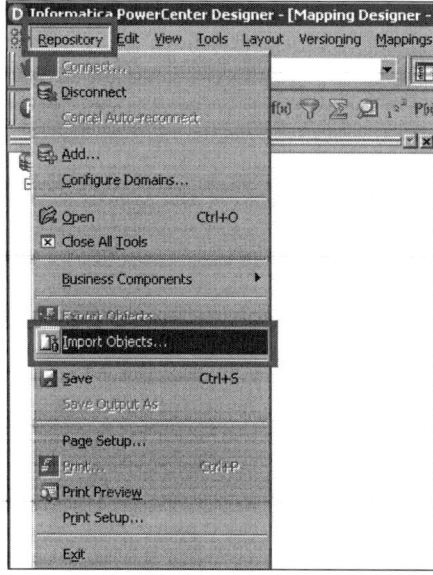

2. A new window will pop up asking you to browse the .xml file, which you saved while exporting the code. Select the location where you saved the file and click on **Next**.

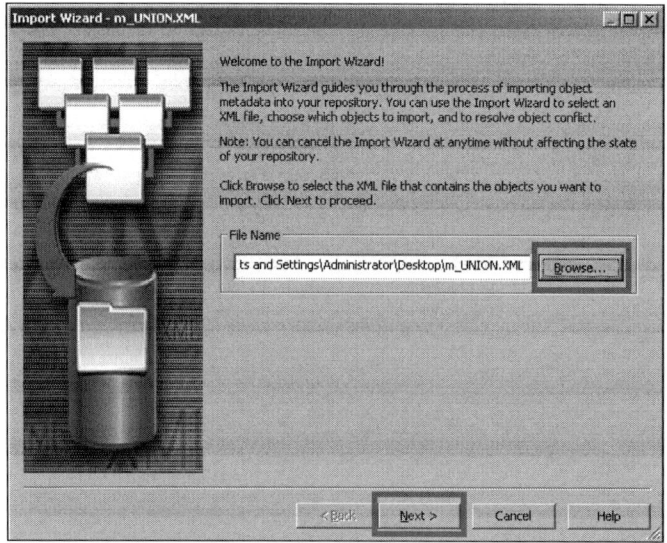

3. In the next step, you need to add the components to the new repository by clicking on **Add**, as shown in the following screenshot, and then clicking on **Next**.

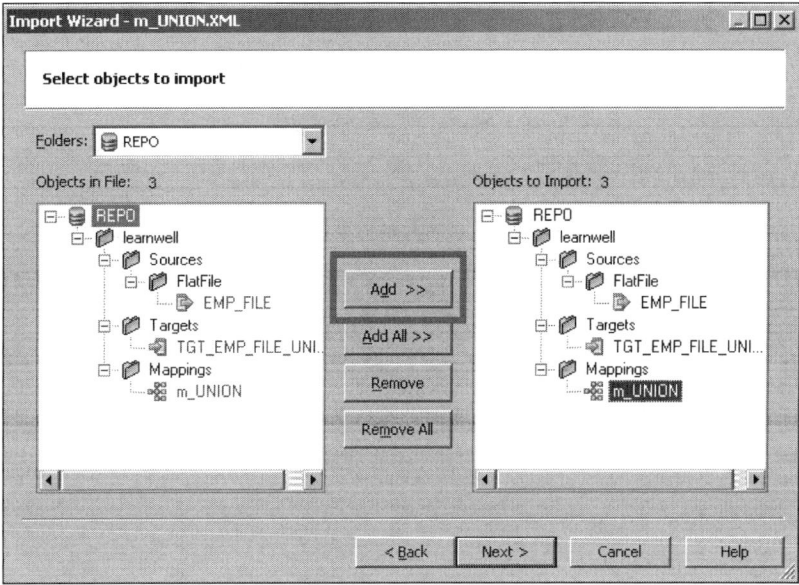

4. In the next window, you will be able to see whether there are any conflicts with the new code being migrated. If any conflicts are there, check the conflicts, else click on **Import** to allow the import process to finish.

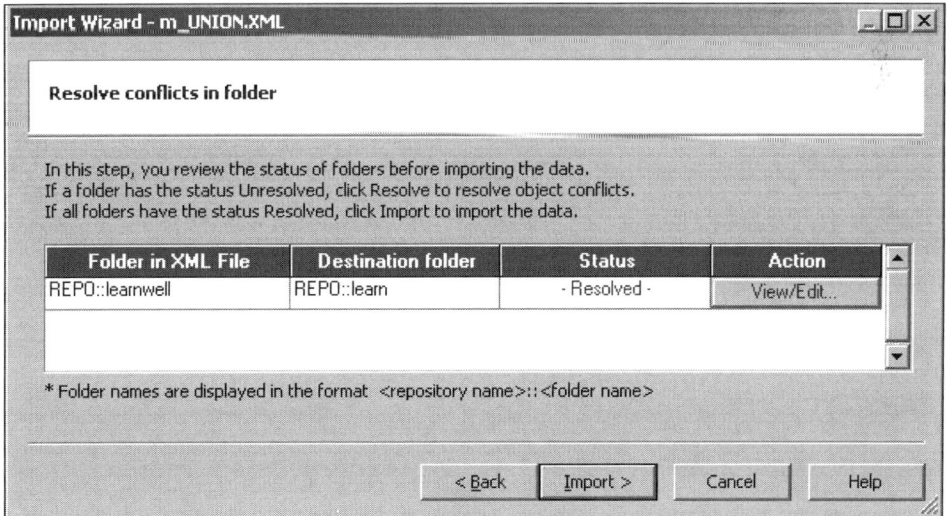

With this, the export and import process is complete for the designer components. Similar to this, perform the migration for Workflow Manager components. When you migrate components from the designer and Workflow Manager, you get two .xml files: one for the designer mapping and the other for the Workflow Manager workflow. You will need to import the XML file for mapping before you import the XML file for the workflow, as the mappings are associated in the session task. So, if your mapping is not available, importing the workflow with the session task will be invalid.

Migrating from Repository Manager

When you migrate the code from Repository Manger, you don't need to migrate the mapping and workflow separately. Repository Manager lets you migrate complete components at once. So, the advantage of migrating the code from Repository Manager is that it saves time and is an easier process. You get only one XML file instead of two files, as shown in the previous section. To export all the components from Repository Manager together, select the workflow related to your code in the navigator and navigate to **Repository | Export Objects**, as shown in the following screenshot. Selecting the workflow will allow all the components to be exported together.

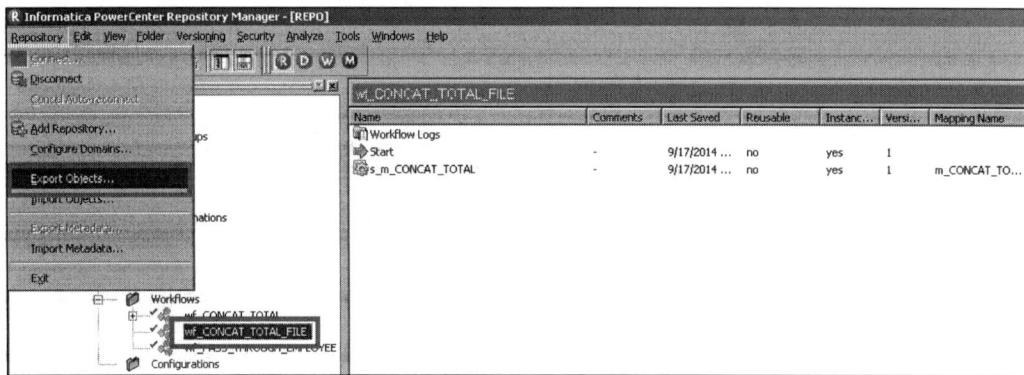

Follow the process in a manner similar to that mentioned in the preceding section to complete the migration. You will get a file at the specified location with all the code components migrated in one go.

Use the same file to import the component. When you import the file, Informatica puts the mapping-related components under the designer and workflow-related components under Workflow Manager.

The Copy/Paste feature

Another way to achieve the migration functionality is to **Copy** and **Paste** or drag-and-drop the components. This is another way in which you can achieve the migration.

To copy the code, select the required component in the navigator from the repository or folder and navigate to **Edit | Copy** in the toolbar—the components get copied. Open the repository or folder where you wish to paste the components and navigate to **Edit | Paste**. Informatica will paste the code, and this way, you can achieve the migration process.

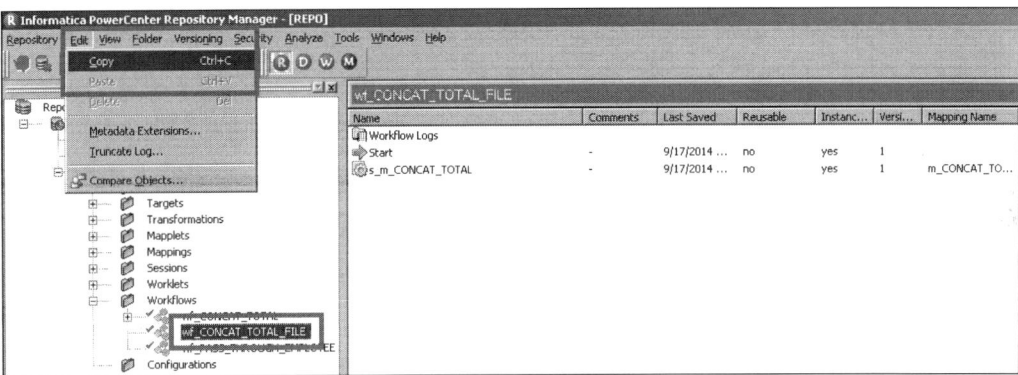

The drag-and-drop feature

Before we talk about this feature, let's take a look at the difference between **Connect** and **Open**. You must have noticed the **Connect** and **Open** option when you connected to your folder under **Repository** in the navigator, as shown in the upcoming screenshot.

The difference between **Connect** and **Open** is that **Connect** only connects you to the repository so that you can view the components present in the folder, but **Open** allows you to actually use those components in the workspace. When you click on **Connect**, you do not get the workspace. However, when you click on **Open**, Informatica performs the connect operation and also makes the workspace available to your folder, so any coding performed in workspace will now be performed inside the opened folder.

The folder that is open is shown in in the top-left corner of the screen, as shown in the following screenshot:

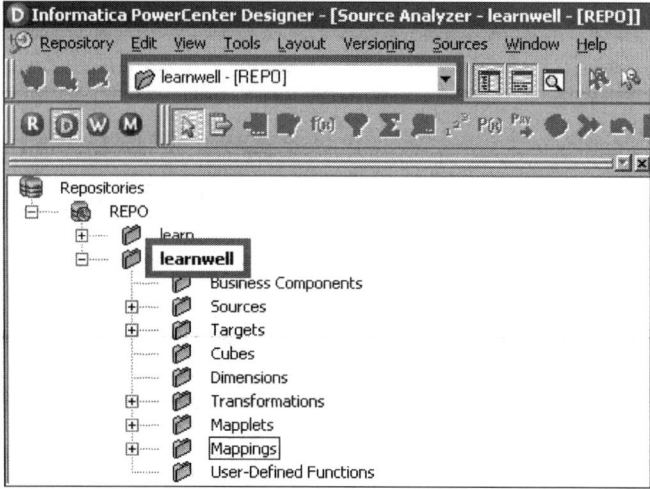

To migrate the code using the drag-and-drop features, perform the following steps:

1. Connect to the repository or folder from where you wish to migrate the code. We have connected to the `learnwell` folder.

2. Open the repository or folder where you wish to migrate the code. Click on **Open** to get the workspace assigned to the folder. We opened the `learn` folder.

3. Drag the required component from the connected folder to the opened folder. We are dragging components from the `learnwell` folder to `learn` folder.

4. A pop-up window will ask you to confirm whether you wish to copy the code, then click on **OK**.

With this simple method, your code will get copied from one folder to another. As mentioned previously, you can drag-and-drop the components across repositories as well. Now, we are done with the migration of the code. This simplicity in the processing is the beauty of the Informatica tool.

We have seen various options for migration, but the most recommended one is the export/import feature. When you use copy/paste or drag/drop feature, there are chances that some of the properties in the code might get missed. There are no known instances where the code missed the properties. Hence, it's always recommended that you use the export/import functionality using Repository Manager to complete the migration.

Summary

In this chapter, which was relatively small compared to other chapters, you learned about a very important aspect of Informatica, that is, migration. We saw various ways in which we can achieve migration. We also saw the configuration of client tools with the server components.

In the next chapter, we will discuss another very important aspect of Informatica tool, performance tuning.

Optimization – Performance Tuning

9

Having reached the last chapter, you must be very clear about all the components and features of the Informatica tool. As with any other technology related to data, we need to understand the performance tuning of Informatica. It is necessary to follow the best practices to achieve the best performance of your code. We execute performance tuning on Informatica similar to SQL tuning, which is done to enhance the performance of SQL queries. If you follow the best practices of Informatica, your code will be tuned automatically. There are various best practices that are recommended by Informatica, many of which we have already discussed in the previous chapters. We will be talking about these best practices in this chapter as well in order to understand how to use them to achieve better performance.

When we talk about performance tuning, you need to find out the issues in your code, which are called bottlenecks. The regular process is to first find out the bottlenecks and then eliminate them to enhance the performance.

We will discuss the various components that need to be tuned in order to enhance the process. In the next section, we will talk about how to identify the bottlenecks at various components, and we will also talk about how to eliminate them.

Bottlenecks

As mentioned, we can have bottlenecks at various stages of the Informatica PowerCenter code. Don't be in a rush to find all the bottlenecks and eliminate them together. Try to find the first bottleneck and resolve it, and then jump to the other bottlenecks.

Finding the target bottleneck

Always consider checking the bottlenecks at the target side first. There can be various reasons for bottlenecks in the target. First, we need to learn to find the target bottleneck.

Using thread statistics

Thread statistics are a part of the session log. When you run the workflow, the session log also generates the thread statistics that can provide you with information about the bottlenecks present in the source, target, or transformations. Thread statistics give you information about the total runtime, idle time, and busy percentage of the source, target, and transformations.

Thread statistics consist of the Reader thread, Writer thread, and Transformation thread. The Reader thread gives you information related to the total runtime, idle time, and busy percentage of the sources in the mapping. The Writer thread gives you information about the total runtime, idle time, and busy percentage of targets in the mapping. Similarly, the Transformation thread gives you information related to transformations in the mapping, as indicated in the following sample thread statistics:

```
***** RUN INFO FOR TGT LOAD ORDER GROUP [1] *****
Thread [ READER_1_1_1 ] created for [ the read stage ] of partition point
[ SQ_EMPLOYEES ] has completed.
    Total Run Time = [ 100.11 ] Secs
    Total Idle Time = [ 90.101 ] Secs
    Busy Percentage = [ 10.888141628 ]
Thread [ TRANSFORMATION_1_1_1 ] created for [ the transformation stage ]
of partition point [ SQ_EMPLOYEES ] has completed.
    Total Run Time = [ 123.11 ] Secs
    Total Idle Time = [ 100.23 ] Secs
    Busy Percentage = [ 18.585005278 ]
Thread [ WRITER_1_1_1 ] created for [ the target stage ] of partition
point [ TGT_EMPLOYEES ] has completed.
    Total Run Time = [ 130.11 ] Secs
    Total Idle Time = [ 1.23 ] Secs
    Busy Percentage = [ 99.054646069 ]
```

As seen in the preceding statistics, the Writer thread is busy for 99 percent of the time as compared to the Reader and Transformation threads. We can say that in this case, the target is the bottleneck. Similar to this, you can identify whether the Source or transformation have bottlenecks in other cases.

Configuring the sample target load

It is a simple thing to understand that loading the data into the target table will take more time as compared to loading the data into the target file. Consider that you are loading the data into the target table in your mapping, configuring a sample run, and trying to load the same data into a test target file. Check the difference between the runtime of both the processes. If there is a significant difference, you can easily say that the database target table has the bottleneck.

Eliminating the target bottleneck

There are various ways in which you can optimize the target loading.

Minimizing the target table deadlocks

There can be a scenario where Informatica is trying to load the data into a table that is already being used by another system. When Informatica encounters the deadlock, it hampers the processing by slowing down the loading process. To avoid this, make sure that the target table is not used by other processes at the same time.

Drop indexes and constraints

Loading the data into tables takes more time because multiple indexes and constraints are created on the table. Each time a new record is loaded into the table, it is checked for indexes and constraints before it gets loaded. This hampers the performance. To avoid this, you can use pre-SQL and post-SQL commands in the session task. Using pre-SQL commands, you can remove the indexes, and using post-SQL commands, you can apply the indexes. When you define pre-SQL and post-SQL, Informatica applies these commands before and after the data is loaded into the table.

Removing the indexes and constraints as described previously is not always recommended, but it definitely improves the performance. You can opt for this option if the data you are loading in the table is not very critical.

Increasing the checkpoint interval

When you run the workflow, the Integration Service keeps on creating checkpoints at a predefined interval. The checkpoints are used for recovery purposes. Reducing the checkpoint interval will help enhance the performance by storing less checkpoints and less data related to the checkpoint.

If you reduce the checkpoint interval, even though the performance will increase, it will hamper the recovery time if the system fails due to an error.

Using an external loader

Informatica PowerCenter supports the usage of multiple external loaders (IBM DB2, Oracle, Teradata, and Sybase IQ), which can help with faster loading into the target table. To add an external loader, open Workflow Manager and navigate to **Connection | External loader**, as shown in the following screenshot:

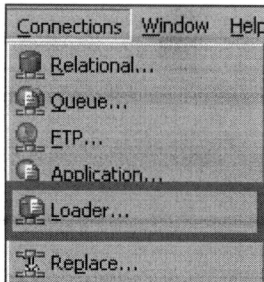

In the next screen, select the loader based on your requirement.

This will help in enhancing the performance by loading the data at a faster pace in the target.

Increasing the network packet size

Every table has a capacity, referred to as the network packet size, with which it can accept the data. If you increase the packet size, the table can accept a greater volume of data.

These properties can be enhanced by the database administrator. Consult your database admin team.

Using the bulk load

By configuring the session properties to use the bulk load, your performance can be significantly enhanced. When you use bulk loading, the database logs are not created, and in turn, it enhances the performance.

However, if you disable the database log, the recovery cannot be done as there is no log of the events in the database.

As you can see, performance can be achieved by compromising on some other factors. You need to decide and create a fine balance between all the factors.

These were the various ways in which you can find and eliminate the target bottleneck. In the next section, we will talk about the source bottleneck.

Finding the source bottleneck

Performance can also be impacted on the source side. Various factors can hamper the performance on the source side, just like we discussed for the target side.

Using thread statistics

As discussed in the *Finding the target bottleneck* section, use thread statistics to find the source bottleneck. Refer to this section to use thread statistics.

Test mapping

Using a pass-through mapping can help you identify whether the bottleneck is on the source side. Configure a test mapping to have only Source, Source Qualifier, and Target. Consider that you have a mapping with one source, one target, and 10 transformations, and the time taken to process the data through the mapping is 60 seconds. This means combining the source, target, and transformations is taking 60 seconds.

Create another mapping by eliminating all the transformations and run the process and check the time. Suppose the time taken to complete the process is now 50 seconds. As compared to the combined time of the target and transformation, which is 10 seconds, 50 seconds is relatively high, which can indicate that we have a source bottleneck.

Using a Filter transformation

You can use a Filter transformation to check whether the source has a bottleneck. Put a Filter transformation in front of the Source Qualifier and set the condition to **False,** that is, don't allow any record to pass through the filter in the mapping. Using this method, you can compare the runtime of the process with and without the filter condition. This way, you can identify whether the source has a bottleneck.

Checking the database query

This is another simple method to find the source bottleneck if you are extracting the data from the table. When you use the Source Qualifier to read the data from the database table, Integration Service writes a query to extract the data. Copy the query and run the same query at the database level in the SQL developer or a similar tool. Compare the time taken by the query to get executed at both places, which can give you an idea whether the source has a bottleneck.

Eliminating the source bottleneck

There are various ways in which you can optimize the source. They are discussed as follows.

Increasing the network packet size

As discussed in the *Eliminating the target bottleneck* section, increasing the network packet size of the table will allow a greater volume of data to pass through the network at a particular instance.

These properties can be enhanced by the database administrator. Consult your database admin team to increase the network packet size.

Optimizing the database query

When you read the data from the database table, Integration Service generates a query to extract the data from the table. You can fine-tune the query to extract only the required data. If you extract all the data and then add a Filter or other transformations, it will hamper the performance.

You can tune the query to extract only the required data, which will save time and help in performance enhancement. This is called a SQL override.

These were the various ways in which you can find and eliminate the source bottleneck. In the next section, we will talk about the mapping and transformation bottlenecks.

Finding the mapping bottleneck

If you don't have a source or target bottleneck, you might have a mapping or transformations bottleneck.

Using thread statistics

As discussed in the *Finding the target bottleneck* section, use thread statistics to find the transformation bottleneck. Refer to this section to use thread statistics.

Using a Filter transformation

You can use a Filter transformation to check whether the transformation in the mapping is causing a bottleneck. Put a Filter transformation before the target and set the condition to **False**, that is, don't allow any record to pass to the target. Using this method, you can compare the runtime of the process with and without the filter condition. This way, you can identify whether the transformations have a bottleneck.

Eliminating the mapping bottleneck

There are various ways in which you can optimize the transformations and mapping.

Using a single pass mapping

Consider a scenario where you have multiple targets to load from the same source; in such a scenario, avoid creating multiple mappings. You can save significant time by loading multiple targets in the same mapping. Use a single source and pass the data to different pipelines and then to multiple targets. This way, you can save the time of reading the same data multiple times in multiple mappings.

Avoiding data type conversions

Avoid changing the data types across the transformations in the mapping. When you change the data type, Integration Service takes time to perform the processing. It is always recommended that you do not change the data type wherever not required.

Unchecking unnecessary ports

Passing unnecessary data through the mapping will hamper performance. It is recommended that if you do not need certain data, disable the output port of the column so that you don't pass the data.

Processing the numeric data

Integration Service processes numeric data faster as compared to other data. Try to process as much numeric data as possible.

Using operators instead of functions

Integration Service processes operators faster as compared to functions. For example, consider using || (pipe) in place of the CONCAT function to concatenate the data.

Using decode in place of multiple IIF functions

If your logic contains multiple IIF functions, try replacing them using DECODE. The DECODE function is faster as compared to multiple IIF functions.

The tracing level

The tracing level defines how much detailed information you wish to write to the session log. When you run the process, Integration Service writes the information about the run in the session log. Setting a proper tracing level will help in improving the performance.

Using variable ports

If you are performing the same operation multiple times in a transformation, consider calculating the value in a variable port and use the variable port value multiple times in the transformation. Suppose you need to convert the first name and last name in uppercase, concatenate them, and also cut part of data. Instead of using the UPPER function every time, use the variable port to convert the data in uppercase and variable port to perform other operations. This way, you save the time of performing the save operation multiple times.

Optimizing Filter transformations

You can use Filter transformations as early as possible in the mapping to avoid processing unnecessary data. If you filter unwanted records early in the mapping, you can enhance performance.

Similarly, using the Router transformation instead of multiple Filter transformations will help save time.

Optimizing the Aggregator transformation

Always pass sorted data to the Aggregator transformation to enhance performance. When you pass sorted data, Integration Service needs to save less data in the cache, which helps in the enhancement of the performance.

You can also improve the performance of the Aggregator transformation by executing groups of numeric columns. For example, consider grouping the data in the department ID instead of the location. This is only possible as per your business requirement.

Use incremental aggregation whenever possible in the session properties to enhance the performance. When you use incremental aggregation, the performance is improved as the Aggregator transformation now needs to calculate fewer records.

Optimizing the Joiner transformation

It is recommended that you assign the table with a smaller number of records compared to the master while using the Joiner transformation. Also, the table with a smaller number of duplicates should be used as the master table.

It is also recommended that you perform the join in the Source Qualifier using the SQL override, as performing joins on the database is sometimes faster as compared to performing them in Informatica.

Also, pass the sorted data to the Joiner transformation to enhance performance, as this utilizes less disk space compared to unsorted data.

Optimizing Lookup transformations

Lookup transformations are one of the most complex transformations in Informatica PowerCenter. Optimizing Lookup transformations will significantly help in improving the performance.

When you use Lookup transformations in the mapping, use the concurrent cache. When you use the concurrent cache, Integration Service caches the lookup table data before it starts processing the data from the source; otherwise, the lookup performs caches on a row-wise basis, which takes up more time. So, it is recommended that you enable caching when you use lookups.

If your mapping contains multiple lookups with a lookup on the same lookup table, it is suggested that you share the cache in order to avoid performing the caching multiple times.

You can reduce the processing time if you use the lookup SQL override properly in the Lookup transformation. If you are using lookups to look up a database table, you can use the lookup SQL override to reduce the amount of data you look up. This also helps in saving the cache space.

If you are using more than one lookup condition in a Lookup transformation, it is recommended that you place the conditions in the optimized order, that is, place the equal to (=) condition first, then the less than (<), greater than (>), less than or equal to (<=), greater than or equal to (>=), and at last, not equal to (!=) condition. This enhances the performance.

These were the various ways in which you can find and eliminate mapping and transformations bottlenecks. In the next section, we will talk about the session bottleneck.

Eliminating the session bottleneck

If you do not have source, target, or mapping bottlenecks, you can make session properties check for bottlenecks.

Optimizing the commit interval

The commit interval is the number of records after which Integration Service commits the data into the target. Selecting an appropriate commit interval will help in enhancing the performance. If you select the commit interval as a low value, it will make Integration Service commit data more times, which will hamper the performance.

The buffer memory

When you run the workflow, Integration Service needs to allocate blocks of memory to hold the data at various stages of processing, including caches if required. Make sure that you have sufficient buffer memory available for the processing, else Integration Service fails the process because of lack of memory.

Performance data

Session properties allow you to store the performance-related details to the repository. If you select to save the performance details, Integration Service writes the log to the repository. This will consume processing time. Make sure that you are not checking the option if you do not need to save the performance details.

Eliminating the system bottleneck

The last step in performance enhancement that you can try is to find the bottlenecks in the system. Eliminating system bottlenecks might not be in your control; you can contact your admin team to improve the system capabilities in order to enhance the system's performance.

You can add multiple CPUs to make the process run faster or make the session run in parallel.

You can check with the admin team whether the network is working properly at the optimized speed to confirm whether the processing is optimized.

Contact your admin team to add extra memory if the buffer memory or cache memory is not sufficient. Adding extra space might save the processing time if your cache memory requirements are greater.

Using the previously mentioned performance rules, you can make your process optimized. After taking care of all these rules, if you feel your system is not utilized fully, you can make use of partitioning.

Working on partitioning

Before we learn about partitioning, note that partitioning is a high availability feature that you need to purchase separately from Informatica. If you enable the high availability feature, you can make use of the partitioning functionality.

By default, a mapping containing the source, target, and transformations has a single partition. A single partition means a single record can flow from the source to the target at a time. By adding multiple partitions, you logically divide the mapping into multiple sections, and each section can pass a record at a time. So, if you make three partitions in the mapping, three records can pass through the mapping, thus reducing your runtime by one-third. When you add a partition at any stage of the mapping, Integration Service adds partitions at other stages of the mapping. You need to make sure that you have sufficient memory space and system capacity to handle the processing of multiple records at a time.

If you have 1000 records to process, and you supposedly created four partitions, Integration Service will process four records at a time, and the total time required to process 1000 records will be reduced to a fourth.

To enable partitions, you need to set the partitioning properties in the session task.

Partitioning properties

To enable partitioning, you need to define the following attributes.

Partition points

You can define the partition points in a pipeline. By default, Integration Service sets the partition at various transformations. You can define the partition at any stage in the mapping.

The number of partitions

Based on your system capability, you can increase or decrease the partitions. When you add a partition at any stage of the pipeline, Integration Service adds the same number of partitions at other stages of the mapping. The number of partitions in a mapping should be equal to the number of database connections on the source and target side. When you create partitions, Integration Service processes the data concurrently. Suppose you created three partitions, then Integration Service reads three records from the source, passes three records to transformations, and concurrently loads three records to target.

Partition types

Informatica supports multiple types of partitions to distribute the data. The partition type controls how you wish to divide the data among the partitions you created in the mapping. If you have the high availability feature available, you can define the type of partition at different stages of the mapping. You can define the type of partitioning in session properties. The different types of partitions are mentioned as follows:

- **Pass-through**: In the pass-through type, Integration Service does not distribute the data among partitions. The data in the particular partition stays in the partition after passing through the partition point.

- **Round-robin**: In round-robin partitioning, Integration Service distributes the data evenly among the partitions. This makes an equal amount of data to pass through each partition.

- **Key range**: In key range partitioning, Integration Service distributes the data on the basis of ports, sets, or defined ports. You also define the range of values for each port. When the source and target are partitioned by the key range, select this type of partitioning.

- **Database partition**: This type of partitioning is possible with the Oracle or DB2 database. When you select database partitioning, Integration Service reads the partitioning information from the nodes in the database.

- **Hash auto-keys**: In hash auto-key partitioning, Integration Service divides the data based on the partition key using the hash function. All the grouped and sorted ports in transformations are used as partition keys. This type of partition can be used in Rank, Sorter, and Aggregator transformations.

- **Hash user keys**: Similar to hash auto-keys, Integration Service in this portioning uses the hash function to partition the data. You need to manually define the number of ports for the partition key.

Pushdown optimization

Pushdown optimization is a concept using which you can push the transformation logic on the source or target database side. When you have a source as the database table, you can make use of a SQL override to remove the logic written in the transformation. When you use the SQL override, the session performance is enhanced, as processing the data at a database level is faster compared to processing the data in Informatica. You cannot remove all the transformations from the mapping. The part of transformation logic that can be pushed at the source or target level is referred to as pushdown optimization.

Consider that you have a mapping with a sequence indicated as follows:

Source - Source Qualifier - Filter - Sorter - Aggregator - Expression - Lookup - Rank - Target.

In Filter transformations, we are filtering the data in a particular location. In Sorter transformations, the data is sorted in a particular department ID. In the Aggregator, we are grouping the data in the department ID. In Expression transformations, the unconnected Lookup transformation is called using the :LKP function, and finally, a Rank is used to get the top-salaried employee into the target.

We can remove the Filter transformation, Sorter transformation, and Aggregator transformation by adding the WHERE clause, the ORDER BY clause, and the GROUP BY clause, respectively, in the SQL override in the Source Qualifier transformation. We cannot remove the Expression transformation, as we cannot write the :LKP function in the SQL override.

So, our mapping becomes simple after using the SQL override, which is indicated as follows:

Source - Source Qualifier - Expression - Lookup - Rank - Target.

Using pushdown optimization will help in saving the processing time by extracting fewer number of records of data from the source and also fewer number of records in the transformations.

Summary

In this chapter, we talked about the various techniques using which you can enhance performance. To enhance performance, we talked about source, target, and transformation bottlenecks. Even after optimizing your source, target, and mapping, your performance was not up to date, so we took a look at your session and system bottlenecks. We also saw various ways of optimizing the components of the PowerCenter tool. Later in the chapter, we talked about partitioning and pushdown optimization, using which also you can enhance performance.

With this, we are done with learning all the concepts of the Informatica PowerCenter tool. In this book, you learned concepts that are useful for people with beginner and intermediate level experience in the Informatica tool. We also touched upon a lot of advanced level concepts in this book. With some more practice and theory exposure, you will be able to clear the first level in the Informatica PowerCenter certification.

Installing Informatica and Using Informatica Administration Console

As we initiate the installation of Informatica PowerCenter 9.5.1, we will need to understand the prerequisites. Informatica PowerCenter is a product that interferes with your filesystem, your database, and so on. So, before we start installation, we will need to check the machine requirements and components.

The Informatica architecture

PowerCenter has a service-oriented architecture that provides the ability to scale services and share resources across multiple machines. High availability functionality helps minimize service downtime due to unexpected failures or scheduled maintenance in the PowerCenter environment. To understand the architecture of Informatica PowerCenter, we will discuss various components that form the Informatica architecture.

The Informatica architecture is divided into two sections: server and client.

The server setup can be done on Windows or UNIX operating systems, while the client installation can only be done on Windows operating system. As best practice, we should always install the server first and then the client.

For a complete list of supporting operating systems, check the following link:

```
http://docs.oracle.com/cd/E14223_01/bia.796/e14221.pdf
```

Server is the basic administrative unit of Informatica, where we configure all the services, create users, and assign authentication. Client is the graphical interface provided to the users. Client includes Designer, Workflow Manager, Workflow Monitor, and Repository Manager.

The components of Informatica PowerCenter are explored in the following sections.

Domain

Domain is the first thing that gets created when you start the installation process. The following points describe a domain:

- It is a fundamental and primary administrative unit in PowerCenter.

- Domain is the first component that we install in Informatica. There will be only a single domain for each license that you purchase.

- Usually, the domain is installed over a common server, which is accessed by software-sharing software, such as Citrix.

- Domain configuration requires database connectivity. We will be using Oracle Database and a SYSTEM user for domain configuration.

- When you purchase the software, you install the server over a common server, which becomes your domain, and can be accessed via the client from multiple machines. The server is not installed on the personal system, which gives it flexibility to share resources across multiple machines. The domain takes the name of the common server computer.

Node

After the domain configuration, the node gets configured. The following points describe a node:

- It is a representation of a server running the PowerCenter Server software.

- It is a logical representation of a machine in a domain.

- The node takes the name of your machine.

- Only one node is possible per license.

- One node in the domain acts as a gateway to receive service requests from clients and route them to the appropriate service and node.

- Services and processes run on nodes in a domain.

- Later in the book, we will see that since we are installing server and client both on same machine, domain and node will have the same name. If we install the server and client on a different machine, they will pick different names.

Informatica services

Informatica services include various services that start the service manager on individual nodes.

The service manager

The service manager is the component that starts and runs the application services on the node in a domain.

Repository

Repository is the component that stores the metadata that is created when you work on client tools. The following points describe a repository:

- It is a centralized database of Informatica PowerCenter, which is used to store metadata.
- Repository is created in the database, which is used for installation purposes. In our case, the repository will be configured in Oracle Database under an HR Oracle user.
- Multiple repositories can be created under a domain with each repository representing a single environment. For example, the REPO_DEV repository represents the development environment, REPO_TEST represents the test environment, and REPO_PROD represents the production environment.

Repository services

In repository services, each service manages only one repository. All the communication with the repository (for example, from the designer or when running workflows) is managed by the repository service.

Integration Services

An Integration Service provides the connection required for the data flow. Integration Services have the following uses:

- It manages the running of workflows and sessions in the client screen.
- It provides the services required for flow of data from source to target through Informatica.

- Integration Services enables the extraction of data from source, transformations in Informatica, and loading into target. It makes the path for data flow from source to target.

- One Integration Service is sufficient to handle different types of sources and targets.

The following diagram shows the Informatica architecture:

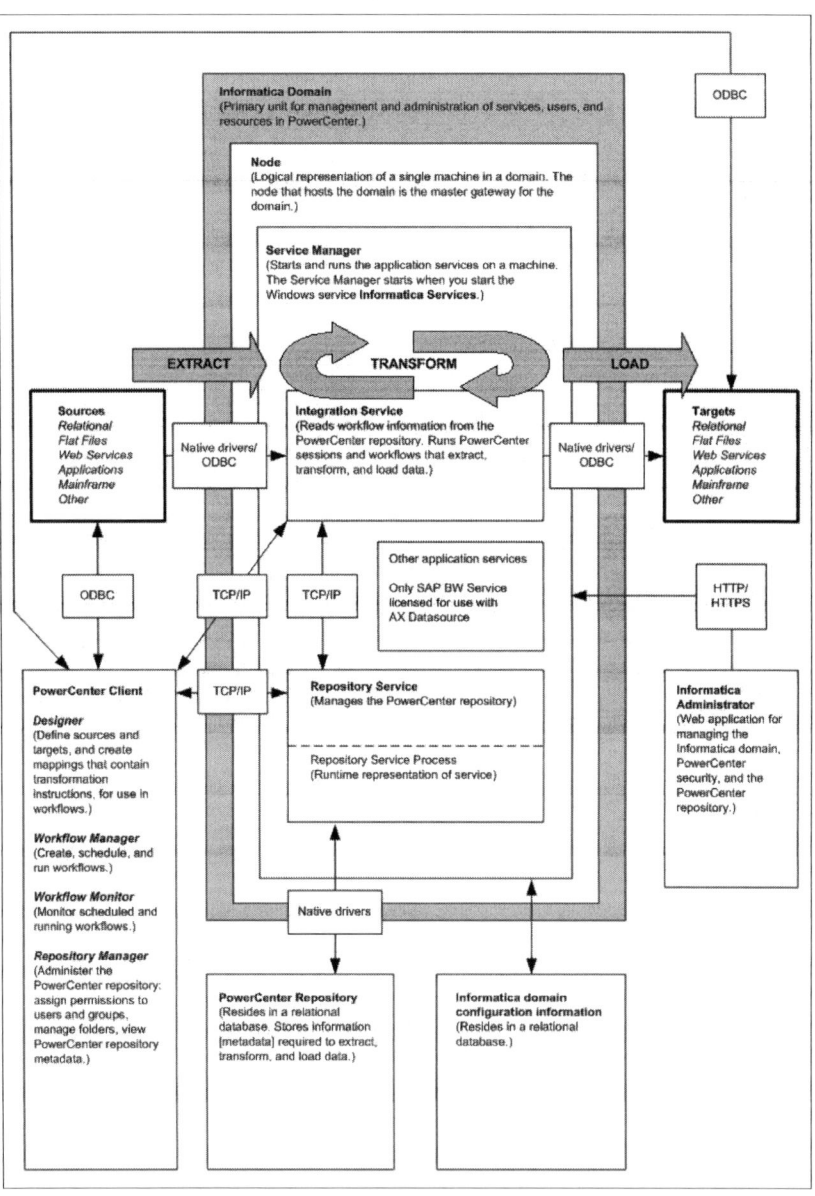

The preceding image reference is as follows:

```
http://docs.acl.com/ax/300/index.jsp?topic=/com.acl.ax.datasource.
help/AX_Datasource/c_informatica_powercenter_architecture.html
```

Informatica installation – the prerequisites

Please be careful while you are doing the installation, as any issues with the minimum system requirement might hamper the Informatica PowerCenter installation process and you might have to initiate the complete installation again.

The following points show some pre-checks that you need to do before initiating the installation:

- **Operating system**: Informatica PowerCenter can be installed on Windows-based operating systems or UNIX-based operating systems. Informatica releases different versions of software for different UNIX-based operating systems. For all Windows operating systems, we have a common installable. In this book, we will refer to the Windows operating system.

- **Database**: Informatica PowerCenter requires a database for configuration. Make sure you have installed a database (Oracle, Microsoft SQL Server, or DB2). In this book, we will refer to Oracle as a database.

  The installation process requires two different database users. Please make sure you create two database users with all the admin privileges. In this book, we are using SYSTEM as one user and HR as the other user.

- **System requirements**: We need to check the system capabilities before we proceed with the installation. Informatica recommends 4 GB of RAM for the installation, but practically even 1 GB of RAM works well. The difference shows up in the processing, but it won't hamper the installation process.

  Also, hard disk space of approximately 25 GB will be required.

  Before downloading the Informatica software, please check whether your machine is 32-bit or 64-bit. Also, make sure you install the correct database with 32-bit or 64-bit configuration to avoid any installation failure later.

Once you have checked the minimum system requirements, we are all set for the next step towards installation.

Downloading the Informatica PowerCenter software

As we proceed with the installation, let's make sure we have the correct copy of Informatica software available. The best place to download the Informatica software for training purposes is from the e-delivery website of Oracle. Please perform the following steps to download the latest version of the software:

1. Visit `https://edelivery.oracle.com`.

2. Sign in with valid credentials. If you do not have an account, register for free and create an account with Oracle. Once you log in with valid credentials, accept the terms and conditions of Oracle and click on **Continue**. This will take you to the next screen, as shown in the following screenshot. To download the Informatica PowerCenter software, select the following options:

   ° **Select a Product Pack: Oracle Business Intelligence**

   ° **Platform**: 64-bit

 Make sure you select a proper platform as per your system configuration. The Informatica software is available for both 32-bit and 64-bit systems.

After selecting the appropriate option, click on the **Go** button.

3. There are multiple products available apart from Informatica PowerCenter under the Oracle Business Intelligence product pack. Select the proper option, as shown in the following screenshot, to download the Informatica software:

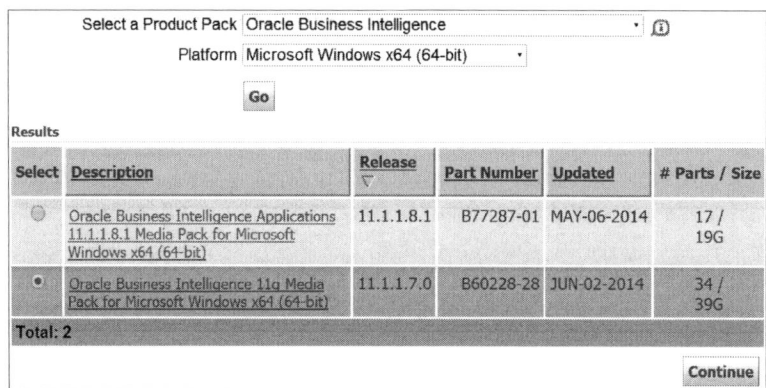

After selecting the appropriate option, click on **Continue**.

4. The next screen will display multiple options to download. Please download the files as indicated in the following screenshot:

Download	Oracle Business Intelligence Data Warehouse Administration Console 11g and Informatica PowerCenter and PowerConnect Adapters 9.5.1 for Windows x86 (64-bit) (Part 1 of 4)	V41973-01 Part 1 of 4	867M
Download	Oracle Business Intelligence Data Warehouse Administration Console 11g and Informatica PowerCenter and PowerConnect Adapters 9.5.1 for Windows x86 (64-bit) (Part 2 of 4)	V41973-01 Part 2 of 4	2.0G
Download	Oracle Business Intelligence Data Warehouse Administration Console 11g and Informatica PowerCenter and PowerConnect Adapters 9.5.1 for Windows x86 (64-bit) (Part 3 of 4)	V41973-01 Part 3 of 4	2.0G
Download	Oracle Business Intelligence Data Warehouse Administration Console 11g and Informatica PowerCenter and PowerConnect Adapters 9.5.1 for Windows x86 (64-bit) (Part 4 of 4)	V41973-01 Part 4 of 4	2.0G

 Oracle frequently changes the names of the files. Please make sure you read the description of the file properly before you download it if files with the same name, as indicated in the preceding screenshot, are not present.

With this download process completed, we now have valid software available for Informatica PowerCenter 9.5.1.

Extracting the package – opening the installable

Once the download process is over, you will have four ZIP files available for Informatica PowerCenter 9.5.1. Please make sure that you create a separate folder for the Informatica files. We are using C:\INFA9.5 for reference. Also, make sure you have sufficient space available (approximately 25 GB). The files will look as indicated in the following screenshot:

We will now start extracting the files. Extracting the files in the correct way is important for proper installation. It is recommended that you use the WinRAR software for extraction.

After you finish extracting the four ZIP files, you will see another file `dac_win_11g_infa_win_32bit_951` along with the other files. Extract the `dac_win_11g_infa_win_32bit_951` file in the same folder. You will get two ZIP files: `951HF2_Client_Installer_win32-x86` and `951HF2_Server_Installer_win32-x86`.

The last step is to extract the `951HF2_Client_Installer_win32-x86` and `951HF2_Server_Installer_win32-x86` files, which will give the final folder structure required for installation. Please make sure you have all the files available in the same folder, as shown in the following screenshot:

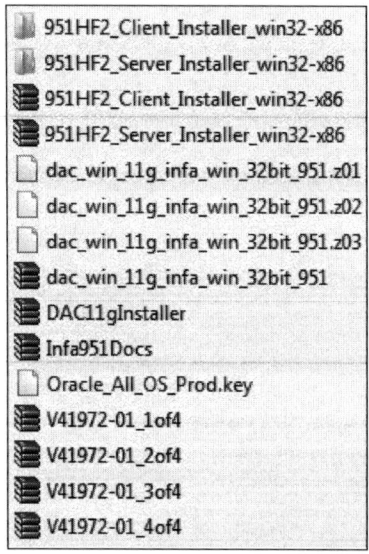

This completes the download and extraction process, and we can proceed with the installation process.

The license key, `oracle_All_OS_Prod.key`, required for installation is present in the extracted folder.

Starting the installation

The Informatica installation requires the installation of the server and the client separately. It is always recommended that you install the server first and then the client.

Installing the server

The installable file for the server can be located by navigating to **C:\INFA9.5 | 951HF2_Server_Installer_win64-x86 | Server | Install**.

Before you proceed, please make sure you have completed all the prerequisites for installation, as mentioned in the *Informatica installation – the prerequisites* section. We need to perform the following steps:

1. Please note, if you are using WIN7 or WIN8 for installation, it is advised to change the compatibility mode of the install file to XP. This is to make sure we don't have any problems later.

2. Right-click on the file and navigate to **Install | Properties | Compatibility**.

3. Change the compatibility mode to **Windows XP (Service Pack 3)**:

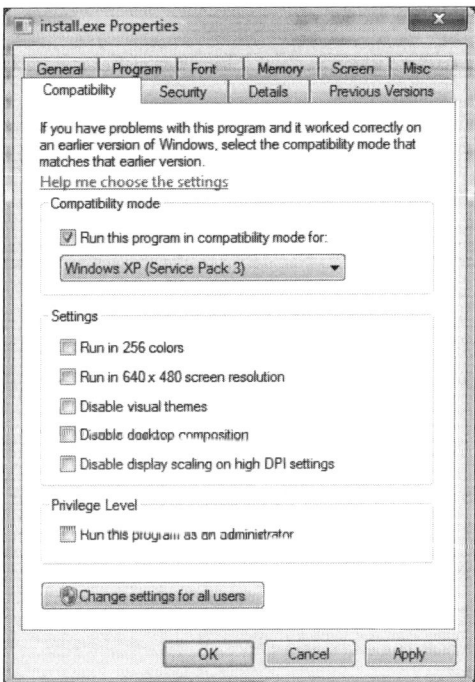

4. Double-click on **install** to start the installation. In some cases, the file can be present as install.exe. This will initiate the installation process for Informatica PowerCenter.

5. Choose the installation type. If you are installing the Informatica software for the first time, select **Install Informatica 9.5.1 HotFix 2**. To upgrade to the latest version from the previous versions, select **Upgrade to Informatica 9.5.1 HotFix 2**. Once you select the appropriate option, click on **Next**, as indicated in the following screenshot:

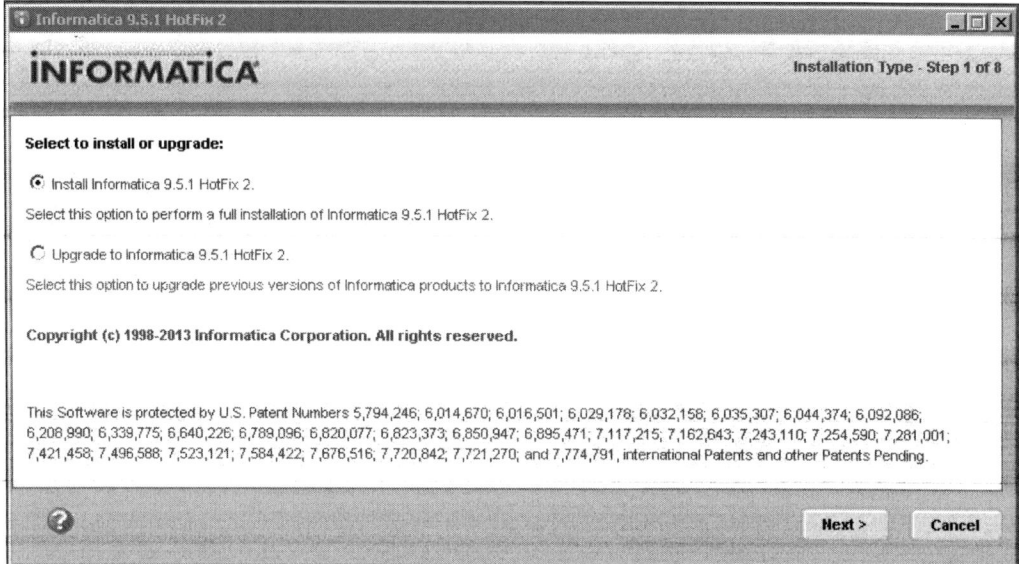

6. On the next screen, verify the prerequisites for installation. Please make sure you have satisfied all the prerequisites for installation. Click on **Next**.

7. The next step, as shown in the following screenshot, is to enter the license key. The license key can be located in the extraction folder C:\INFA9.5\ Oracle_All_OS_Prod.key. If you are not able to navigate to the path, then directly paste the path. Select the installation directory. Make sure you have sufficient space in the directory you specify. Click on **Next**:

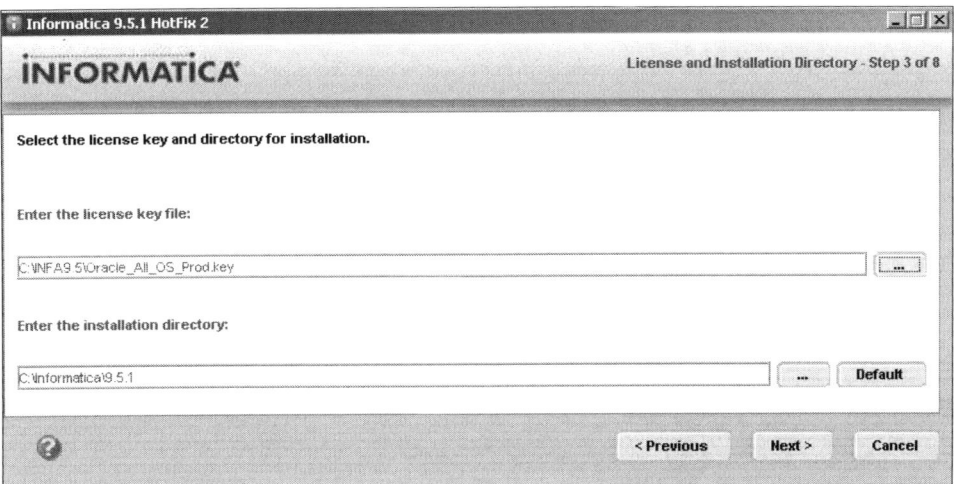

8. The next screen will show the preinstallation summary. Please check the details and click on **Install**.

The installation will begin. It will take a few minutes before your installation finishes. The installation time depends on your system configuration. Once the installation finishes, we will proceed to the next process of configuring the domain and node.

Configuring the domain and node

As explained previously in the architecture, domains and nodes are very important components of Informatica PowerCenter. In the following installation steps, we will create a domain and configure the domain with the database:

1. If you are doing a fresh installation, select **Create a domain**. This will initiate the process to create a new domain. If you are upgrading, you can select the option **Join a domain**.

2. Check the **Enable HTTPS for Informatica Administrator** option. Make sure the port 8443 is not utilized by any other process. In most of the cases, port 8443 will be used as default, so you need not worry about the port number.

3. Also, check the option **Use a keystore file generated by the installer**. Please refer to the following screenshot:

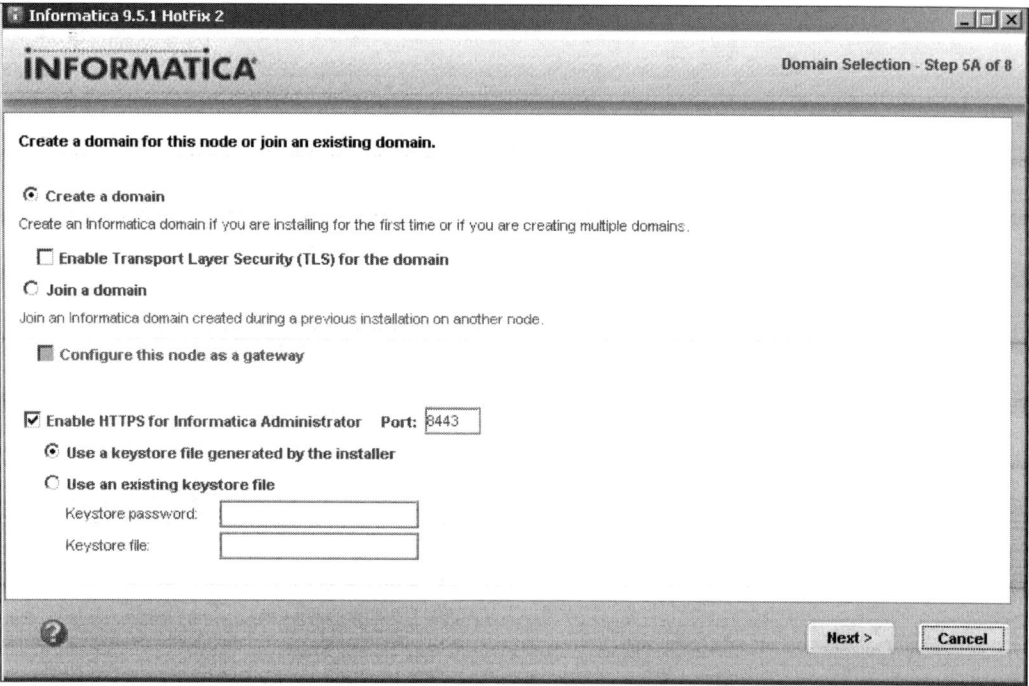

4. In this step, we will configure the domain with the database. Please select the appropriate option:

  ○ **Database type**: Depending on what database (Oracle, SQL, or DB2) you are using, please select the appropriate option. In this book, we are using Oracle as our database.

  ○ **Database user ID**: Mention the database user that you created for the domain configuration. In this book, we are using SYSTEM as the Oracle user.

- ○ **Password**: Specify the password for the database. We are using Oracle as our password for our reference in this book.

- ○ **Schema name**: Leave the schema name field blank. Informatica will take the default schema.

- ○ **Database address**: Mention the address for your database. The address consists of hostname and port number, that is, *hostname:port number*, where hostname is your computer name and port number is the default port number for the database you are using. Hostname can also be used as `localhost`. In this book, we are referring to the database address as `localhost:1521`, where `1521` is the default port number for Oracle 10*g*.

- ○ **Database service name**: Specify the service name for your database connection; in this book, we are using it as `XE`.

5. Leave the rest of the properties as they are.

6. Click on **Test Connection**. If all the properties that you mentioned are correct, the database connection will be successful, and we can proceed with the next step. If the connection fails, please recheck your database configuration details and test them again.

7. After the connection is successful, click on **Next**.

8. The next screen will give you the option to assign names to your domain and node. Informatica will assign the default name to your domain and node. You can leave those unchanged. If you wish to change the name, please mention the appropriate name. Specify the domain password and confirm the password.

[ Remember the database username and password for future reference.]

The following screenshot shows all the details filled:

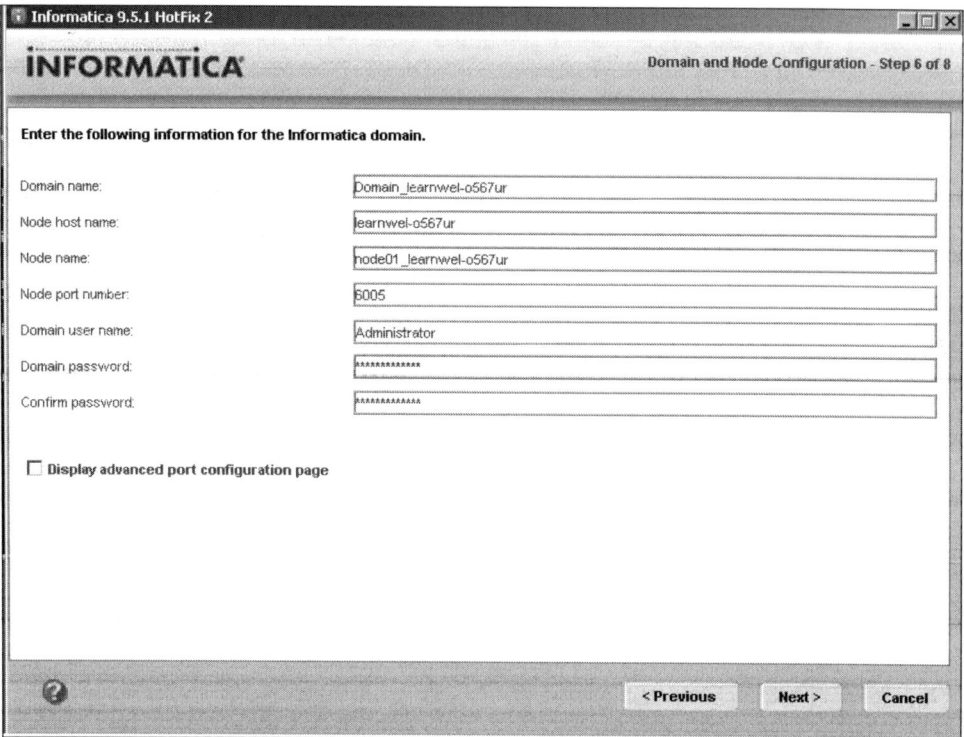

9. Click on the **Next** button.

10. On the next screen, uncheck the **Run Informatica under a different user account** option and click on **Next**.

11. The next screen indicates that the installation is complete. Please check the post-installation summary. You can keep those details for your future reference.

12. Click on **Done**.

With this, our server installation is complete, and you can see the program available in your **All Programs** section in the Windows start menu. We will now proceed with the client installation, which is simple and straightforward.

Client installation – the graphical interface tools

In this section, we will discuss the installation of the client tools.

You can locate the installable by navigating to **C:\INFA9.5 | 951HF2_Client_ Installer_win64-x86 | Client | Install**. In some cases, the filename can be `Install.exe`. Double-click on **Install** to initiate the client installation process.

Change the compatibility mode of the `Install` file, as shown in the server installation before proceeding with the client installation. We will perform the following steps:

1. Select the **Install or Upgrade Informatica** option. Click on **Start**.

2. Select the installation type **Install Informatica 9.5.1 HotFix 2 Clients** if you are doing a fresh installation; or, select **Upgrade to Informatica 9.5.1 HotFix 2 Clients**. Click on **Next**.

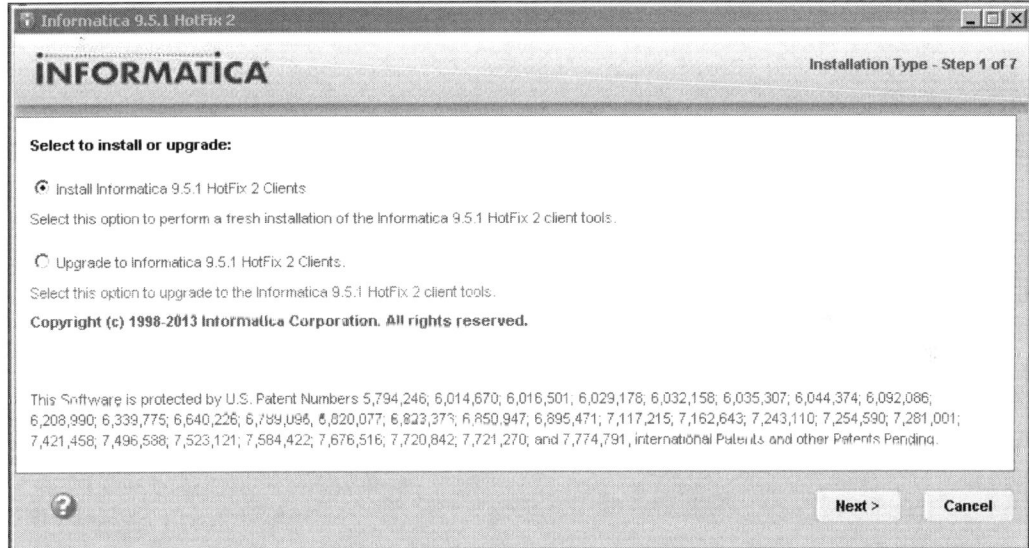

3. Please check the installation prerequisites for the PowerCenter client tool. Click on **Next**.

4. On the client tool selection screen, select **Informatica Developer** and **PowerCenter Client**. Click on **Next**:

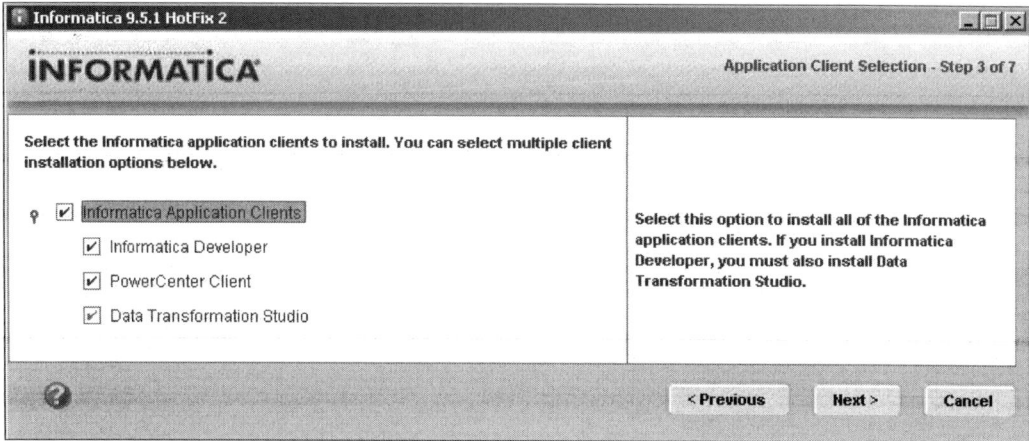

5. Enter the installation directory. You can select the same installation directory where you installed the server. Please make sure you have sufficient space in the directory. Click on **Next**:

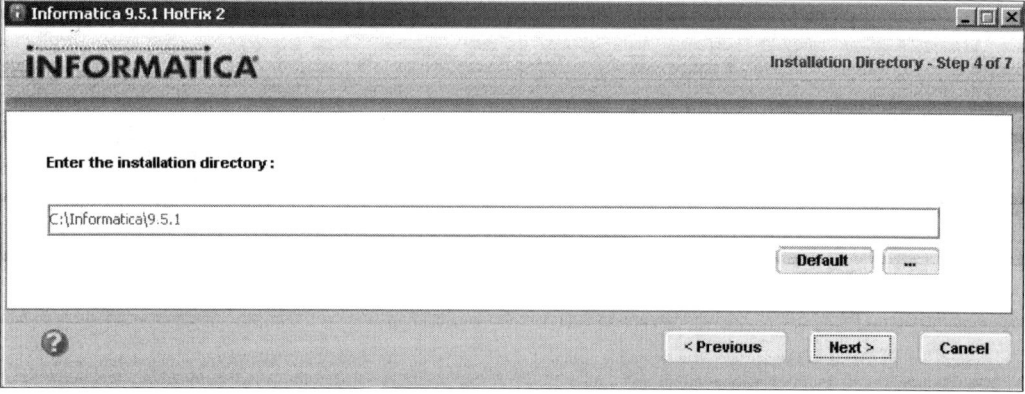

6. On the **Data Transformation Studio Configuration** screen, select the option **Install Data Transformation Studio and a standalone copy of Eclipse**. Click on **Next**:

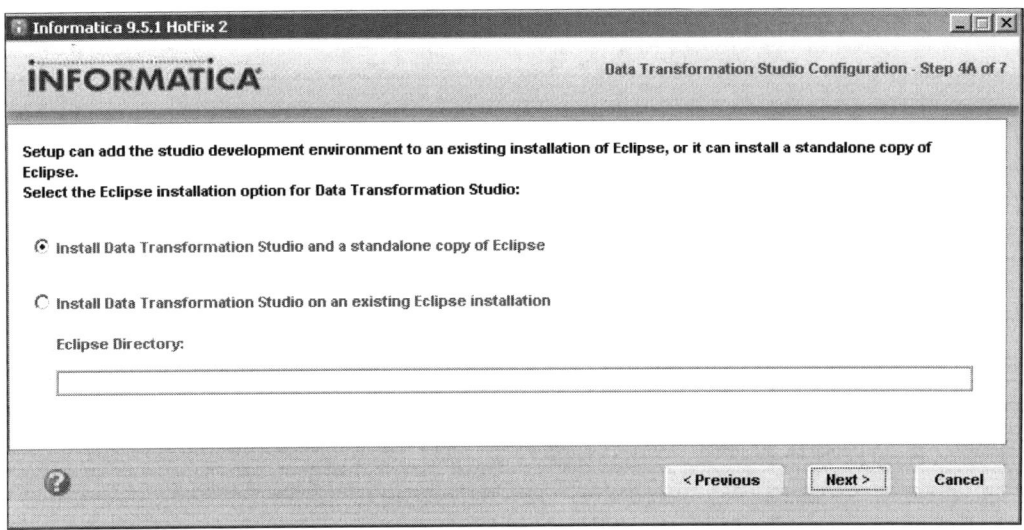

7. Check the preinstallation summary before you continue and click on **Install**. The installation of the client tool will start. It will take a few minutes to complete installation based on your system configuration.

8. Once the installation process is complete, you will get the **Post-Installation Summary** screen. Check the summary and click on **Done** to finish the client installation process:

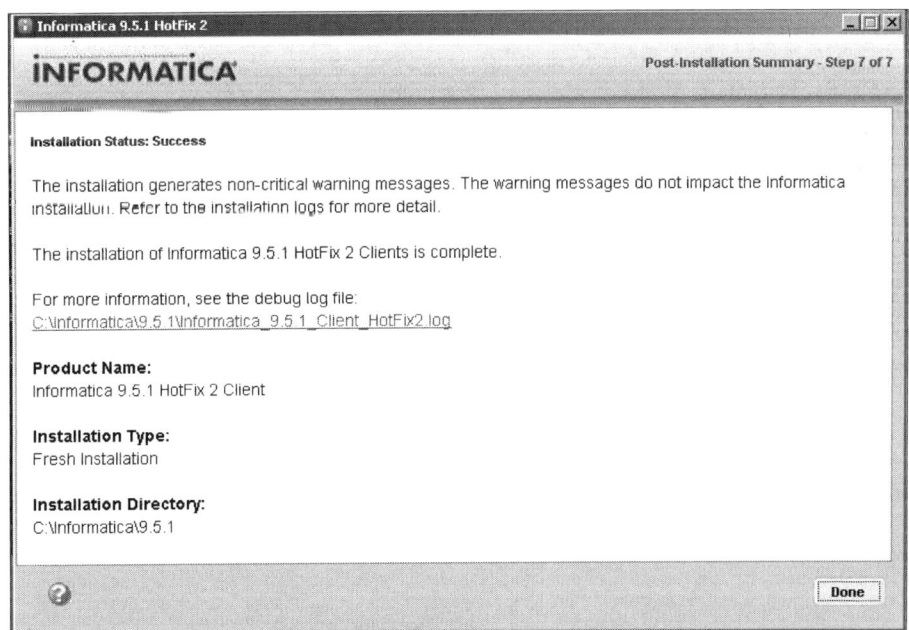

With this, the installation of the server and client is complete. You will be able to see the newly installed programs in your Start menu on Windows under **Informatica 9.5.1**:

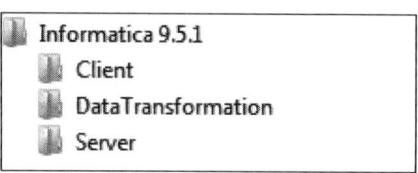

Now, we will configure the administrator console to add various services and components to the Informatica PowerCenter.

The administration console – configuration

The Informatica administration home page is the single place where all Informatica components can be created and configured. The administration console home page opens in the web browser. It does not require an Internet connection. You can use any browser to open the admin console. You might need to check the browser settings if the administrator home page is not opening. Based on your system configuration and settings, you might need to try using a different browser.

Perform the following steps to configure the complete Informatica components:

1. **Informatica Administrator Home Page** can be located under **All Programs** in your Start menu, as shown in the following screenshot.

2. Navigate to **Start | All Programs | Informatica 9.5.1 | Server | Informatica Administrator Home Page**:

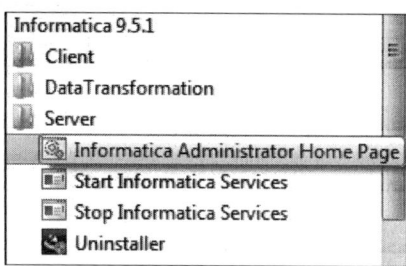

   This will open Informatica Administrator in your default web browser.

3. Log on to the Informatica Administrator using the username and password that you defined while creating the domain.

   In this book, we are using the default username Administrator and the password is Administrator.

4. Click on **Log In**.

5. Once you log in, you will see the following screen:

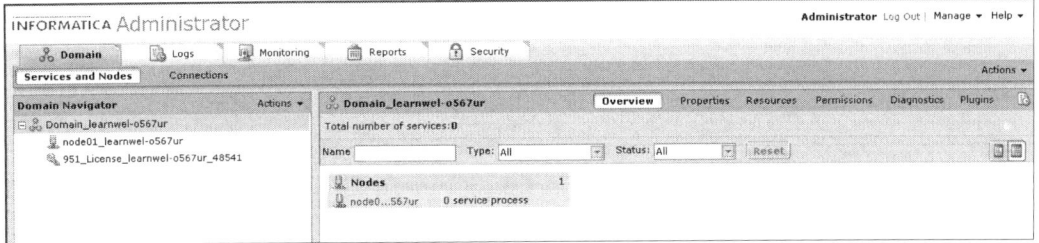

Please spare a few minutes to view all the options present on the screen.

6. You will see the domain name and node name on the left side of the screen, which we created in the earlier section.

Our next process is to create and configure the various PowerCenter components, which we discussed in the preceding section.

Repository creation – the first centralized database for Informatica

Our first step is to create a repository. As mentioned earlier in the book, the repository is the centralized database of Informatica that is used to store metadata generated in the client tools. To create the first repository, follow the process mentioned in the preceding section. Refer to the following screenshot:

Navigate to **Domain_learnwel_0567ur | New | PowerCenter Repository Service**:

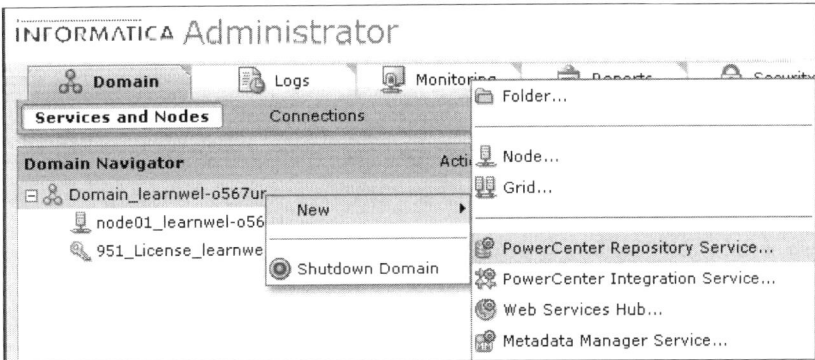

This will open a pop-up window that will allow you to provide details for creating the repository, as shown in the following points. Please insert the details.

- **Repository name**: Mention the name of the repository. You can specify any name as per your wish. We are using REPO for our reference in this book.

- **Description**: Write some description about the repository. This is an optional field.

- **Location**: Specify the domain name we created earlier. The domain name we created earlier will appear by default, as we have only one domain currently.

- **License**: Select the license key from the drop-down list. This is the default key as we have only one key.

- **Node**: Specify the node name from the drop-down list. This is the default key, as we have only one key.

The details are shown in the following screenshot:

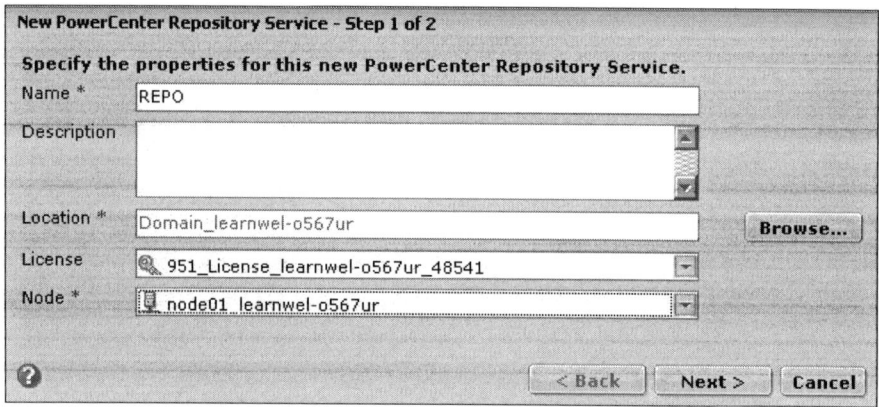

Click on **Next**.

A new screen will appear. Provide the repository database details as follows:

1. Select your repository database from the drop-down list. We are using **Oracle** as our user (Oracle/SQL Server).

2. Specify the repository database username that we created earlier to connect to the database. We are using HR as our database user.

3. Specify the repository database user password. We are using HR as our password.

4. Specify the database connection string. We are using XE as our connection string.

5. The code page is required to read the data in different formats. We will be using **MS Windows Latin 1 (ANSI)** as the default code page to read the data in English font. You can later specify multiple code pages to read the data in different fonts.

6. **Tablespace Name** is an optional field and can be left blank.

7. Choose **No content exists under specified connection string. Create new content.**

8. Check **Create as Global Repository (May not be reverted to local)**.

9. Check **Enable Version Control (A versioned repository cannot be unversioned)**:

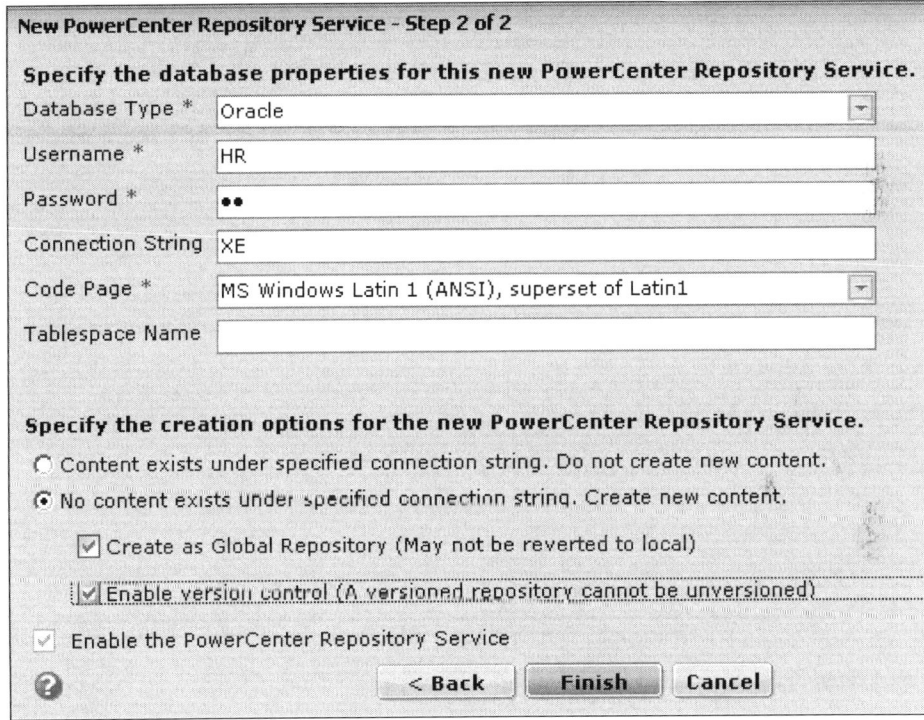

10. Click on **Finish**.

The process will take a few minutes to finish. Once done, you will see the REPO repository created under **Domain Navigator**.

As you can see, the repository service is running in **Exclusive** mode. We need to change to **Normal** before we proceed further. This can be done in the following way:

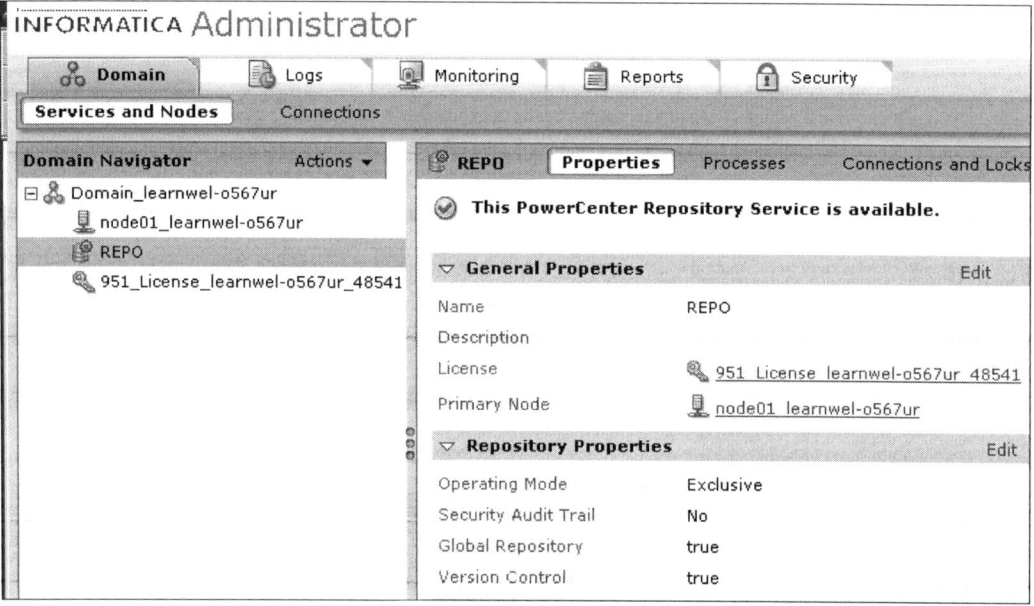

Click on the **Edit** option in **Repository Properties**. A pop-up window will appear, which will allow you to select the following properties:

- **Operating Mode**: Select **Normal** from the drop-down list
- **Security Audit Trail**: This should be set to **No** as default

Click on **OK**:

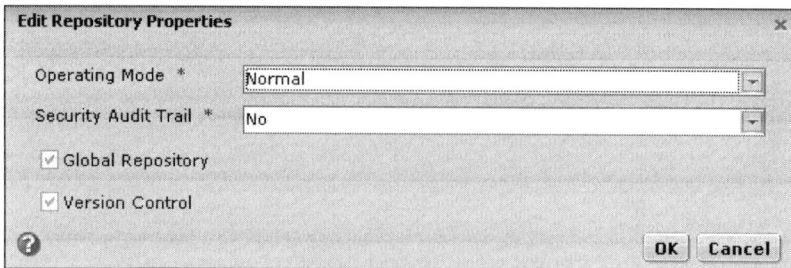

Click on **OK** when it asks to restart the service, which will restart the repository to change the **Repository Operating Mode** option to **Normal**.

The following screenshot shows your repository available and running in
Normal mode:

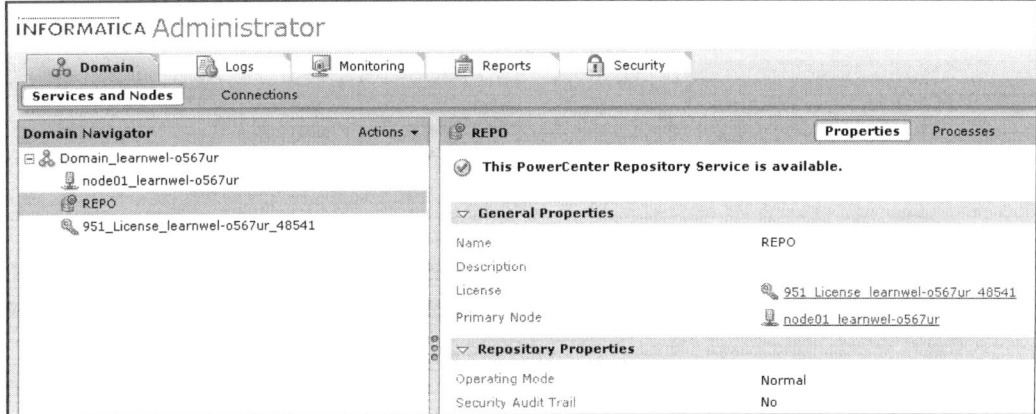

Creating the Integration Service – the path for data

Integration Service is required for flow of data from the source to the target through
Informatica. We have discussed the Integration Service in detail in the earlier section
in this book. Please perform the following process to configure Integration Service.

Navigate to **Domain_learnwel_0567ur** | **New** | **PowerCenter Integration Service**:

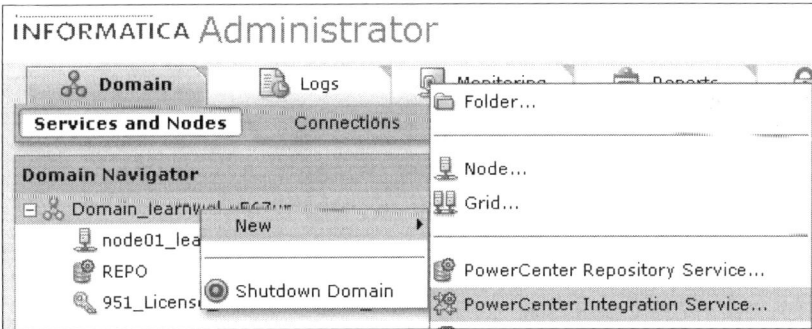

This will open a new screen, which will allow you to provide details for creating
Integration Services, as shown in the following screenshot. Please mention the
following details:

- **Name**: Please mention the name of the Integration Service. You can specify
  any name as per liking. We are using INTE for our reference in this book.

- **Description**: You can write some description about the Integration Service.
  This is an optional field.

- **Location**: Specify the domain name we created earlier. The domain name we created earlier will appear by default as we have only one domain currently.

- **License**: Select the license key from the drop-down list. This is the default key, as we have only one key.

- **Node**: Specify the node name from the drop-down list. This is the default node as we have only one node.

Click on **Next**:

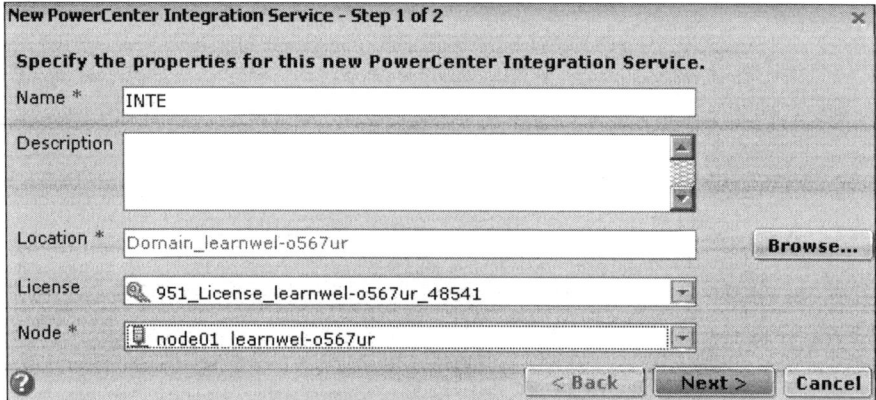

On the next screen, we need to configure the Integration Service with the repository we created in the previous step, as follows:

- **PowerCenter Repository Service**: Choose your repository service name from the drop-down list. Currently, we have only one repository present, that is REPO, which will come by default in the drop-down list.

- **Username**: Specify the Administrator username you assigned while creating the domain. We are using Administrator as an admin username for our reference in this book.

- **Password**: Specify the Administrator password you assigned while creating the domain. We are using Administrator as the admin password for our reference in this book.

- **Data Movement Mode**: Select **ASCII**.

Click on **Finish**:

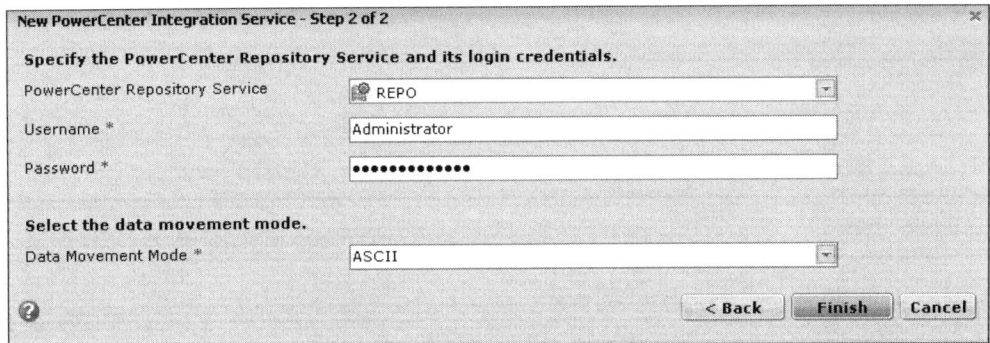

On the next screen, select the code page for configuration with the Integration Service. We will be using the default code page **MS Windows Latin 1 (ANSI)**:

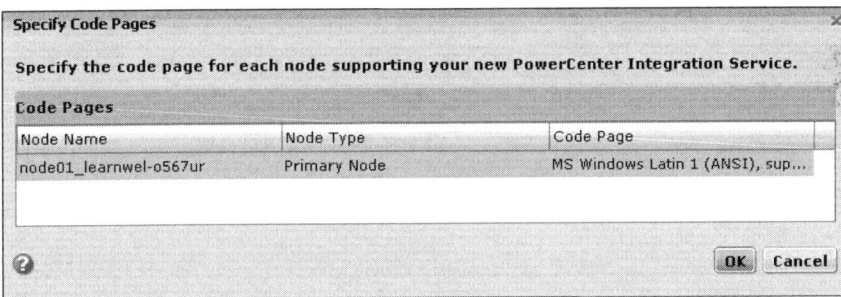

The next screen will indicate the creation of the Integration Service INTE under the domain in **Domain Navigator**. In some cases, the Integration Service might be in disabled mode, as shown in the following screenshot. We will need to enable the service.

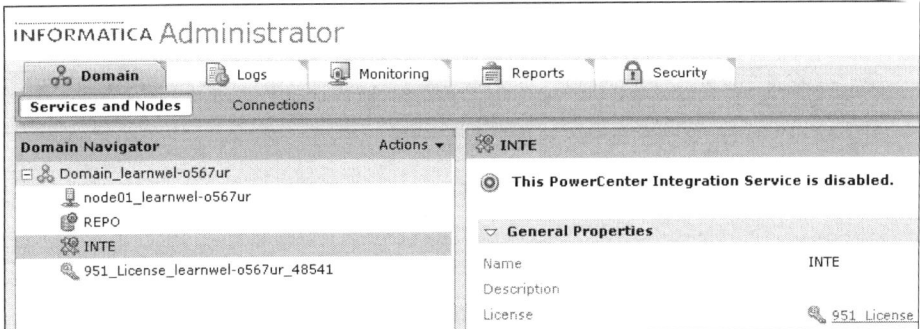

To enable the Integration Service, click on the **Enable** button in the extreme right corner of the screen, as shown in the following screenshot:

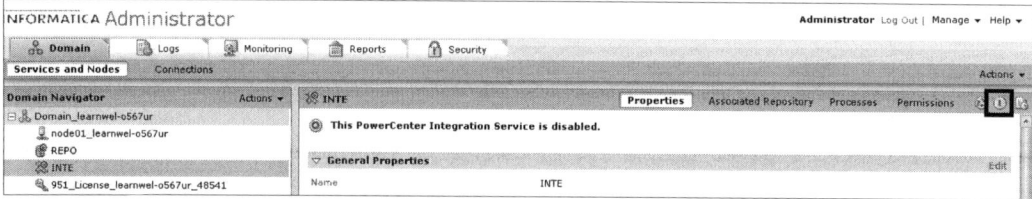

Once you are done with the process, the screen will indicate that Integration Service is available:

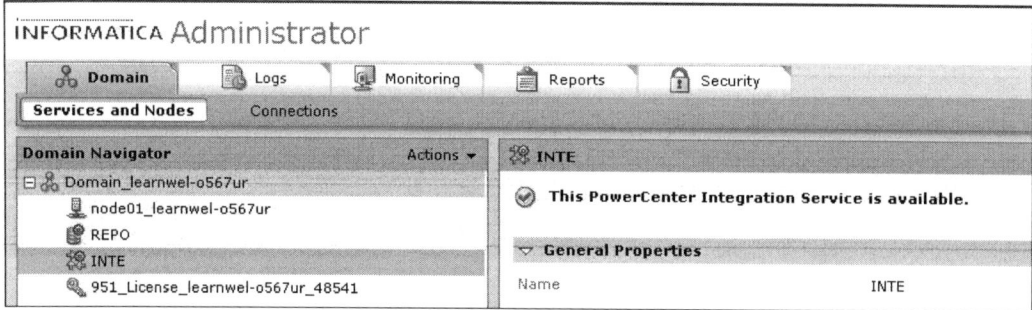

With this, we have completed the installation and configuration of Informatica PowerCenter components.

Informatica user and authentications

The next step is to create a new Informatica user and assign roles and privileges to the Informatica user. This user will be used for logging in to the Informatica client screens in the future. We need to perform the following steps:

1. Click on the **Security** tab on the administrator home page. This screen allows you to create Informatica users and assign roles and responsibilities to them:

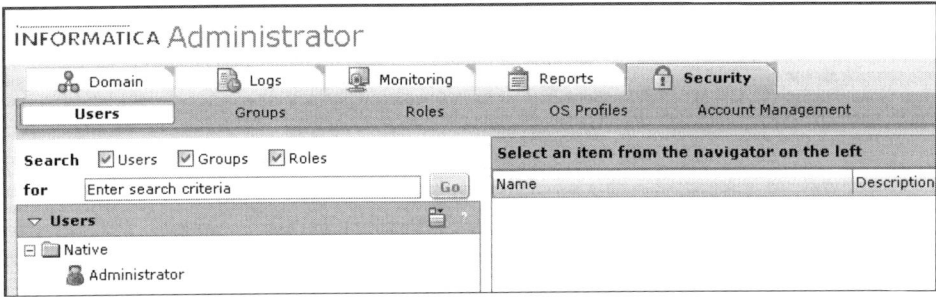

2. You will notice two default users available under the users box. To add a new user, click on **Actions** in the extreme right corner of the administrator home page.

3. Navigate to **Actions | Create User**:

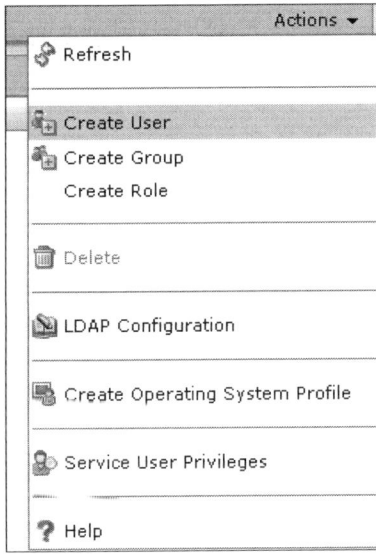

4. Specify the username and password you wish to create.

 It is very important to remember the username and password you define here, as this will be used for logging in to the client screens.

The screen is shown as follows:

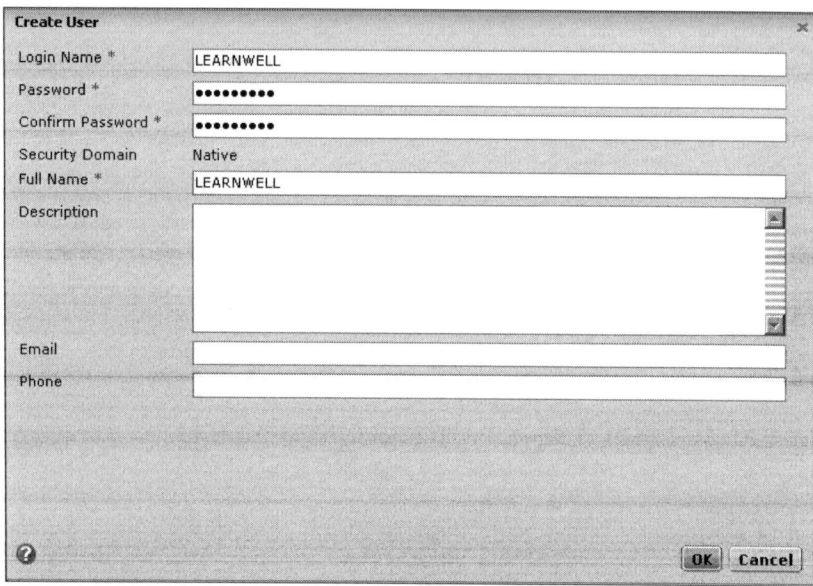

5. The next step is to assign roles and responsibilities to the user we created in the previous step:

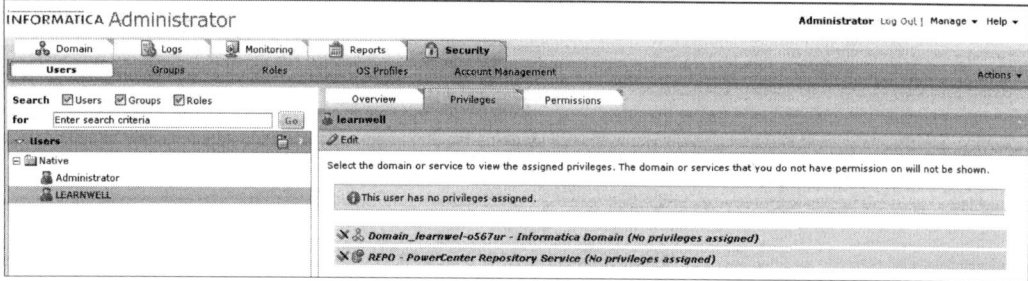

6. Click on the cross mark in front of the domain to view the screen where you can assign roles and responsibilities. Check both the boxes for **Domain** and **REPO** under **Roles**:

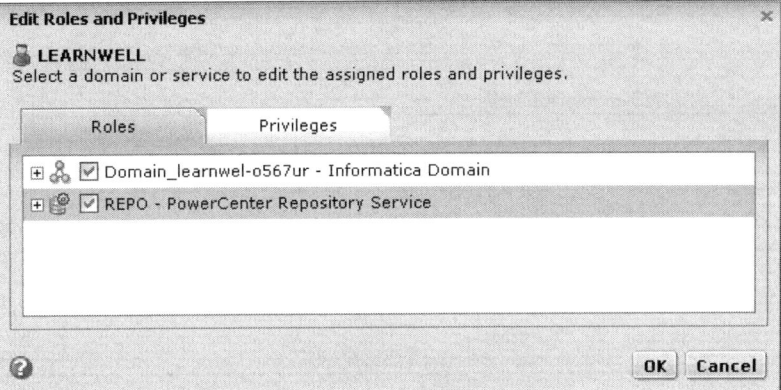

7. Check both the boxes for **Domain** and **REPO** under **Privileges**:

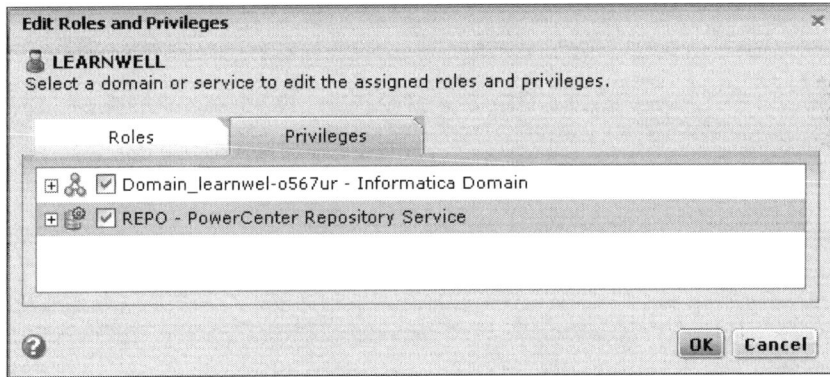

8. With this, we have assigned all the admin rights to the user we created:

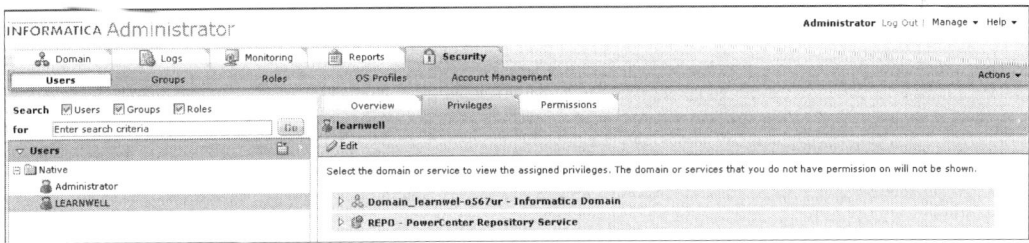

With this step, we have completed the server configuration. The final step in the installation process is to replicate the server configuration to the client screen.

Repository Manager – the client configuration

This is our first look at the client tools and before we can start working on them we need to configure the client tools with the server components:

1. To complete the configuration, open Repository Manager. To open the Repository Manager screen, follow this path: **Start | All Programs | Informatica 9.5.1 | Client | Power Center Client | Repository Manager**:

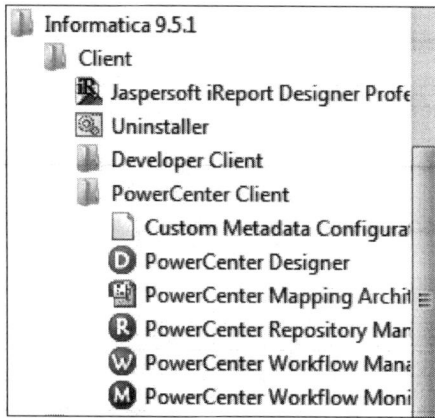

The Repository Manager screen will open, as shown in the following screenshot:

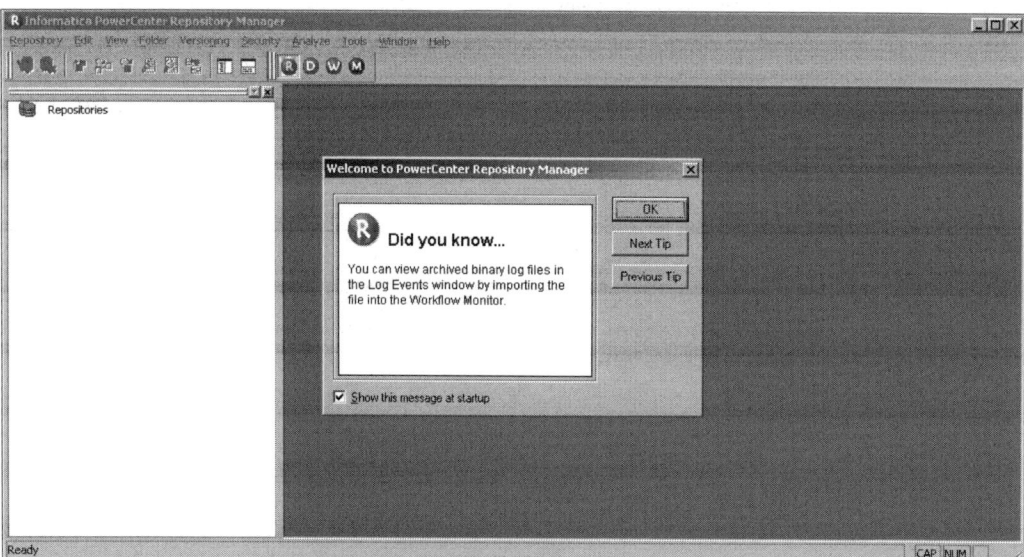

2. To configure the domain and repository with Repository Manager, navigate to **Repository | Configure Domains**:

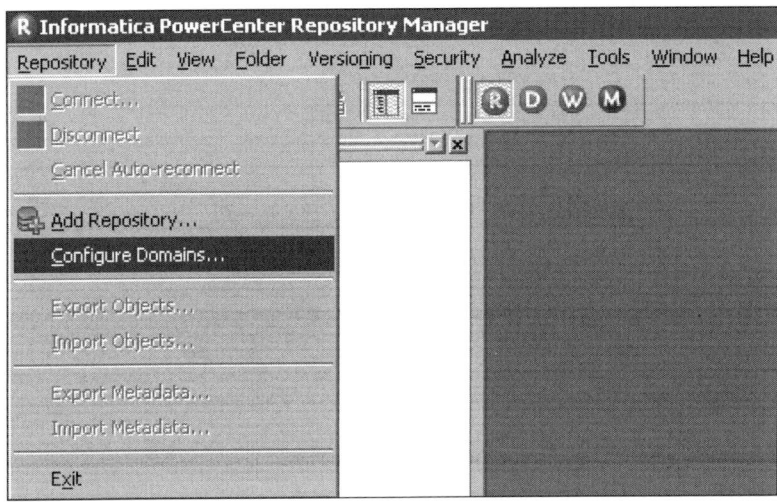

A pop-up window will appear on your screen. Click on **Add new Domain**, as shown in the following screenshot. This will open another pop-up window:

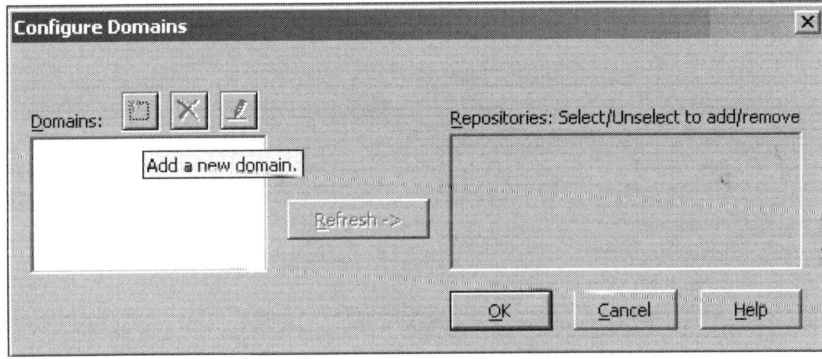

3. Click on **Add a new domain** and specify the following details:

   ° **Domain name:** Domain_learnwel-o567ur

   ° **Gateway Hostname:** learnwell-o567ur

   ° **Gateway Port number:** 6005

These are the domain details that we created earlier in the server installation process. Once you specify the details, a new domain and the REPO repository will appear in the box, as shown in the following screenshot:

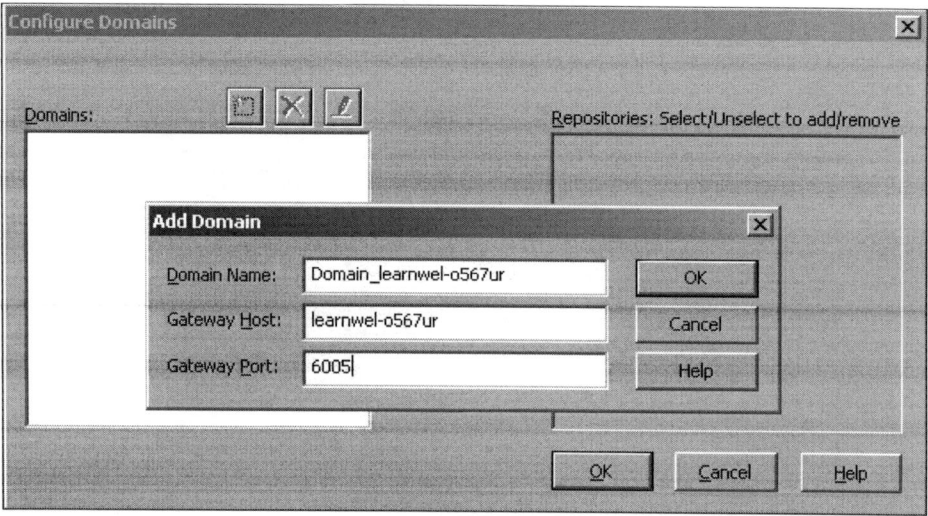

4. Click on **OK**.

5. This will configure your domain and repository REPO, which we created in the administrator console with the client tools:

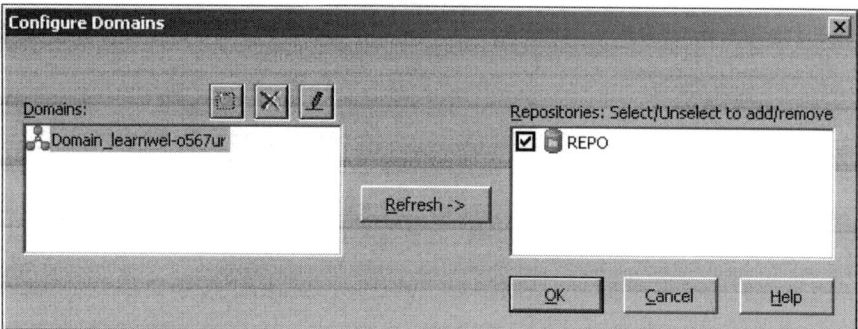

You will see **REPO** under **Repositories** on the screen.

6. We will now configure the user we created in the administrator console with the client. Navigate to **REPO | Connect**:

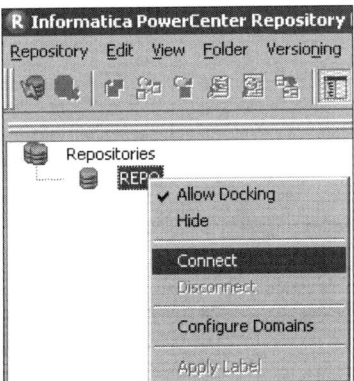

7. A new pop-up window will appear. Please specify the Informatica username and password that we created under the **Security** tab in the administrator console. We are using LEARNWELL as both username and password for our reference in this book:

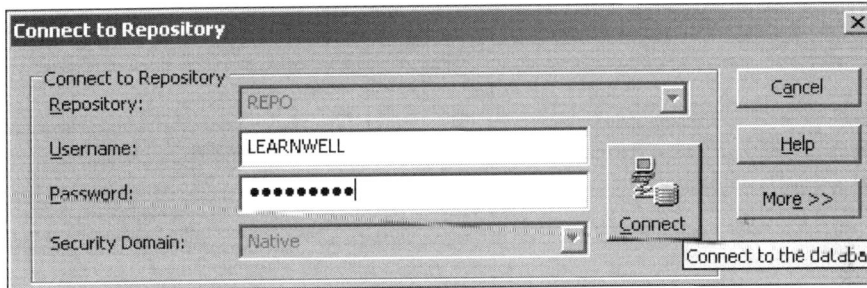

8. Click on **Connect**.

9. We are now connected to REPO using our username, as shown in the following screenshot:

10. We need to add a folder under REPO. A folder is created for every individual who will be working on Informatica in your enterprise. To add the folder, click on the **Folder** tab, as shown in the following screenshot:

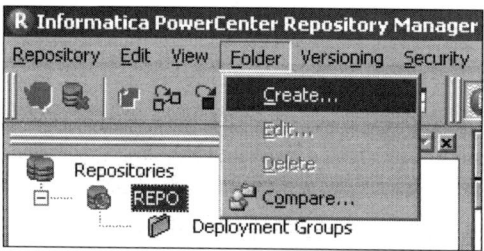

11. This will open a pop-up window. Specify the folder name. We are using LEARNWELL for our reference in this book. Mention the name and leave the rest of the properties unchanged, and click on **OK**:

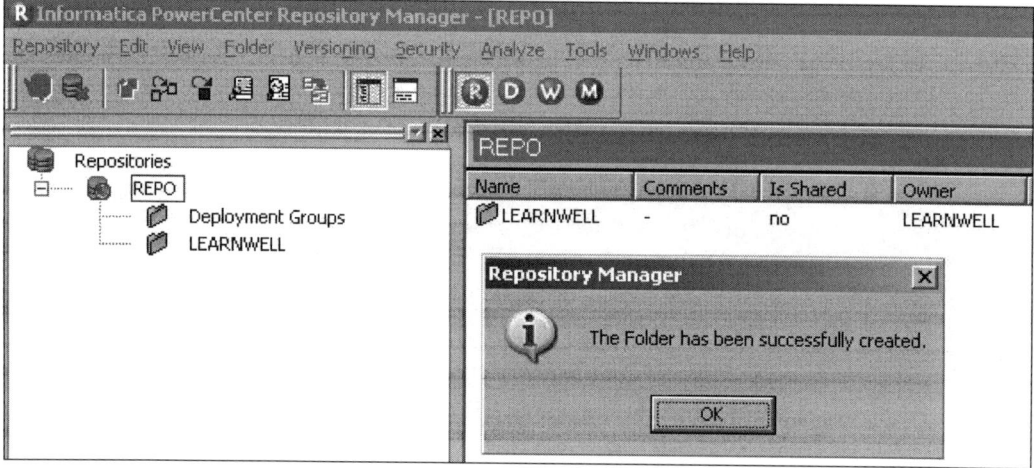

The newly created folder, LEARNWELL, is now present under REPO. We will be using this folder to create our code in Informatica.

With this, the installation and configuration of Informatica PowerCenter is done, and we are now ready to start with our first code.

Index

$Target connection value 140
Commit On End Of File 141
Commit Type 141
Enable Test Load 140
Java Classpath 142
Number of rows to test 140
Parameter Filename 140
Recovery Strategy 142
Rollback Transactions on Errors 141
Session Log File Directory 140
Session Log File Name 140
Treat source rows as 141
Write Backward Compatible Session Log
    File 140
generated column ID (GCID) 254
Group By option
  using, in Aggregator transformation 213

H

hash auto-key partitioning 293
hash user key partitioning 293

I

Import option 14, 29
incremental aggregation 176-178
indexes
  dropping 283
Informatica architecture 295
Informatica architecture, components
  domain 296
  Informatica services 297
  Integration Services 297-299
  node 296
  repository 297
  repository services 297
  service manager 297
Informatica components
  configuring 312, 313
Informatica installation
  administration console 312, 313
  client installation, graphical interface
      tools 309-312
  prerequisites 299
  server installation 303-305
  starting 302

Informatica installation, pre-checks
  database 299
  operating systems 299
  system requirements 299
Informatica PowerCenter
  components 296
  software, downloading 300, 301
Informatica PowerCenter, events
  predefined events 166
  user-defined events 166
Informatica services 297
Informatica user
  authentications, assigning to 320-323
  creating 320-323
Integration Service
  about 297-299
  assigning, to workflow 125, 126
  creating 317-320
  Data Movement Mode 318
  Description 317
  License 318
  Location 318
  Name 317
  Node 318
  Password 318
  PowerCenter Repository Service 318
  Username 318

J

join condition, Joiner
        transformation 229, 230
Joiner transformation
  about 228
  detail pipeline 228, 229
  join condition 229, 230
  join type 230
  master pipeline 228, 229
  optimizing 289
join type, Joiner transformation
  about 230
  detail outer join 232
  full join 232
  master outer join 232
  normal join 231

N

named cache
  sharing 262
naming conventions, PowerCenter tool
  URL 107
navigator 8
Navigator section, Workflow Monitor
    screen 188
network packet size
  increasing 285, 286
node 296
Normalizer transformation
  about 252
  configuring 253
normal join
  defining 231
number of partitions, partitioning 292
numeric data
  processing 288

O

objects
  comparing 60-62
ODBC data source
  adding 11-14
operating systems, Informatica
    installation 299
options, control task properties
  Abort Parent 163
  Abort Top-Level Workflow 164
  Fail Me 163
  Fail Parent 163
  Fail Top-Level Workflow 163
  Stop Parent 163
  Stop Top-Level Workflow 164
options, domain configuration
  database address 307
  database service name 307
  database type 306
  database user ID 306
  password 307
options, schedule screen
  Customized Repeat 174
  End after 174
  End On 174
  Forever 174

Run continuously 174
Run Every 174
Run once 174
Run on demand 174
Run on Integration Service
    initialization 174
Start Date/Start Time 174
options, Source/Target statistics of Session
    run properties
Affected Rows 200
Applied Rows 200
Bytes 200
End Time 201
Last Error Code 200
Last Error Message 201
Node 200
Rejected Rows 200
Start Time 201
Throughput(Bytes/Sec) 200
Throughput(Rows/Sec) 200
Transformation Name 200
options, Task Details of Session
    run properties
Deleted 199
End Time 199
Instance Name 199
Integration Service Name 199
Mapping Name 199
Node(s) 199
Recovery Time(s) 199
Source Failed Rows 199
Source Success Rows 199
Start Time 199
Status 199
Status Message 199
Target Failed Rows 199
Target Success Rows 199
Task Type 199
Total Transformation Errors 199
Version Number 199
output/control panel 8
output panel, debugger
  instance 48
  notification 48
  target instance 48
Output section, Workflow
    Monitor screen 188

P

package
  extracting 301, 302
parameter file
  creating 182, 183
  example 178
  mentioning, at session level 184, 185
  mentioning, at workflow level 184
parameters
  about 178
  using, on PowerCenter Designer
    screen 58-60
partitioning
  about 291
  number of partitions 292
  partition points 292
  partition types 292
  properties 292
Partitioning Options property,
    Config Object tab of session task
  Dynamic Partitioning 150
  Number of Partitions 150
partition points 292
partition types
  database partition 292
  hash auto-key partitioning 293
  hash user key partitioning 293
  key range partitioning 292
  pass-through partitioning 292
  round-robin partitioning 292
passive transformation 240, 241
pass-through partitioning 292
password 307
performance data 290
Performance properties, Properties tab of
    session task
  Allow Pushdown for User Incompatible
    Connections 144
  Allow Temporary Sequence for
    Pushdown 144
  Allow Temporary View for Pushdown 143
  Collect performance data 143
  DTM buffer size 143
  Enable high precision 143
  Incremental Aggregation 143
  Reinitialize aggregate cache 143

Session retry on deadlock 143
  Session Sort Order 144
  Write performance data to repository 143
persistent cache 261
ports, in transformation 206-208
ports, Lookup transformation
  about 244
  Input Ports (I) 244
  Lookup Port (L) 245
  Output Port (O) 245
  Return Port (R) 245
PowerCenter Designer
  about 7
  screen components 8, 9
  tools 9
PowerCenter Designer screen
  parameters, using on 58-60
  variables, using on 58-60
predefined events 166
properties, Lookup transformation
  Cache file name prefix 250
  Case-sensitive string comparison 250
  Connection information 249
  Date/time format 250
  Decimal separator 250
  Dynamic lookup cache 249
  Insert else update 250
  Lookup cache directory name 249
  Lookup cache enabled 248
  Lookup cache persistent 249
  Lookup condition 249
  Lookup data cache size 249
  Lookup data index size 249
  Lookup policy on multiple match 249
  Lookup source filter 248
  Lookup source is static 250
  Lookup SQL override 248
  Lookup table name 248
  Null ordering 250
  Output old value on update 250
  Pre-build lookup cache 250
  Recache from lookup source 250
  Sorted input 250
  Source type 249
  Subsection precision 250
  Thousand separator 250

Tracing level 249
Update else insert 250
properties, Sequence Generator
        transformation
  about 224
  Current Value 225
  Cycle 225
  End Value 225
  Increment By 225
  Number of Cached Values 225
  Reset 226
  Start Value 225
  Tracing Level 226
pushdown optimization 293

Q

queries, Lookup transformation 245
queue connection 131

R

Rank transformation
  about 219, 220
  group by ranking functionality 221
  rank index column 222
relational database connection object
  configuring 132-134
relational database tables
  working with 14, 15
relational data source
  data, previewing in 35, 36
relation connection 131
repository
  about 297
  creating 313-317
  database 314
  description 314
  license 314
  location 314
  node 314
  repository name 314
Repository Manager
  migrating from 276
  using 266
repository services 297

reusable task
  adding, to workflow 117
reusable transformation
  about 51
  creating 51
round-robin partitioning 292
Router transformation 217-219

S

sample target load
  configuring 283
SCD
  about 63
  example 64-67
SCD1
  implementing, wizard used 68-72
SCD2 (date range)
  implementing 90-94
SCD2 (flag)
  implementing 82-87
SCD2 (version number)
  implementing, wizard used 75-80
SCD3
  implementing, wizard used 97-101
SCD, types
  Type 1 Dimension mapping (SCD1) 63
  Type 2 Dimension/Flag mapping 64
  Type 2 Dimension/Version Number
        mapping (SCD2) 63
  Type 3 Dimension mapping 64
schedule
  creating 172, 173
schedulers 172
scheduling 172
screen components, PowerCenter Designer
  about 8
  navigator 8
  output/control panel 8
  status bar 8
  toolbar 8
  workspace 8
Sequence Generator transformation
  about 222
  properties 224, 225
  usage 226

Thank you for buying
Learning Informatica PowerCenter 9.x

About Packt Publishing

Packt, pronounced 'packed', published its first book, *Mastering phpMyAdmin for Effective MySQL Management*, in April 2004, and subsequently continued to specialize in publishing highly focused books on specific technologies and solutions.

Our books and publications share the experiences of your fellow IT professionals in adapting and customizing today's systems, applications, and frameworks. Our solution-based books give you the knowledge and power to customize the software and technologies you're using to get the job done. Packt books are more specific and less general than the IT books you have seen in the past. Our unique business model allows us to bring you more focused information, giving you more of what you need to know, and less of what you don't.

Packt is a modern yet unique publishing company that focuses on producing quality, cutting-edge books for communities of developers, administrators, and newbies alike. For more information, please visit our website at www.packtpub.com.

About Packt Enterprise

In 2010, Packt launched two new brands, Packt Enterprise and Packt Open Source, in order to continue its focus on specialization. This book is part of the Packt Enterprise brand, home to books published on enterprise software – software created by major vendors, including (but not limited to) IBM, Microsoft, and Oracle, often for use in other corporations. Its titles will offer information relevant to a range of users of this software, including administrators, developers, architects, and end users.

Writing for Packt

We welcome all inquiries from people who are interested in authoring. Book proposals should be sent to author@packtpub.com. If your book idea is still at an early stage and you would like to discuss it first before writing a formal book proposal, then please contact us; one of our commissioning editors will get in touch with you.

We're not just looking for published authors; if you have strong technical skills but no writing experience, our experienced editors can help you develop a writing career, or simply get some additional reward for your expertise.

Getting Started with Oracle Data Integrator 11*g*: A Hands-On Tutorial

ISBN: 978-1-84968-068-4   Paperback: 384 pages

Combine high volume data movement, complex transformations, and real-time data integration with the robust capabilities of ODI in this practical guide

1. Discover the comprehensive and sophisticated orchestration of data integration tasks made possible with ODI, including monitoring and error management.

2. Get to grips with the product architecture and building data integration processes with technologies, including Oracle, Microsoft SQL Server, and XML files.

3. A comprehensive tutorial packed with tips, images, and best practices.

Data Visualization: a successful design process

ISBN: 978-1-84969-346-2   Paperback: 206 pages

A structured design approach to equip you with the knowledge of how to successfully accomplish any data visualization challenge efficiently and effectively

1. A portable, versatile, and flexible data visualization design approach that will help you navigate the complex path towards success.

2. Explains the many different reasons for creating visualizations and identifies the key parameters that lead to very different design options.

3. Thorough explanation of the many visual variables and visualization taxonomy to provide you with a menu of creative options.

Please check **www.PacktPub.com** for information on our titles

Practical Data Analysis

ISBN: 978-1-78328-099-5   Paperback: 360 pages

Transform, model, and visualize your data through hands-on projects developed in open source tools

1. Explore how to analyze your data in various innovative ways and turn them into insights.

2. Learn to use the D3.js visualization tool for exploratory data analysis.

3. Understand how to work with graphs and social data analysis.

4. Discover how to perform advanced query techniques and run MapReduce on MongoDB.

Oracle Data Integrator Essentials [Video]

ISBN: 978-1-78217-048-8   Duration: 02:08 hours

Develop, deploy, and maintain your own data integration projects with a clear view of Oracle Data Integrator essentials and best practices

1. Develop the necessary skills for effectively carrying out data integration and transformations in ODI interfaces.

2. Understand the use of ODI development objects with methods and concepts illustrated from real projects.

3. Master the key concepts of ODI's physical and logical architecture and the use of Knowledge Modules and data models.

Please check **www.PacktPub.com** for information on our titles

Made in the USA
Middletown, DE
01 September 2015